# BUILD YOUR OWN SOLID-FUEL BURNING STOVE

## BY ROBERT C. & LENORE ROSER

**TAB** **TAB BOOKS Inc.**
BLUE RIDGE SUMMIT, PA. 17214

FIRST EDITION

FIRST PRINTING

Copyright © 1982 by TAB BOOKS Inc.

Printed in the United States of America

Library of Congress Cataloging in Publication Data

Roser, Robert C.
    Build your own solid-fuel burning stove.

    Includes index.
    1. Stoves, Wood.   2. Stoves, Coal.
I. Roser, Lenore.   II. Title.
TH7438.R65      683'.88      82.5682
ISBN 0-8306-0392-1          AACR2
ISBN 0-8306-1392-7 (pbk.)

# Contents

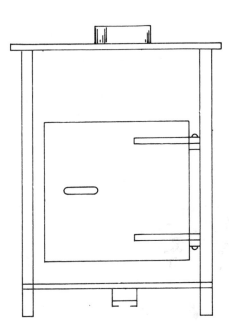

DEDICATED TO JOHN 3:16

# Acknowledgments

To Sandy and Robbie: for all the family activities that were put aside. We love you.

To Sue: for the time and dedication, but most of all for the sincere concern to make this book a success.

To Tom: for just being my friend, and for always making himself available for my needs.

To Andy and Bob: for caring enough that we never gave up and this book became a reality.

To my customers: for those of you who allowed me to take photographs of your units, in use, and for all the others who gave me the incentive to share my knowledge.

# Preface

Several years ago my wife and I, like many other couples, saw our dream come true. We purchased our first home. Four years later, our dream turned into a nightmare when I found myself laid-off and unable to find a job. My prime concerns became not only how to feed my family, but, also, how to heat my home for the winter—only weeks away.

Having a "totally electric" home, I received a number of notices from the electric company. Their patience was wearing thin over the nonpayment of my bill. Necessity is the mother of invention, and I decided to build my own wood stove. Knowing nothing about the working principles of wood stoves, I visited a number of libraries and bookstores looking for information on how to build a wood stove. I was surprised to find very little information on the subject, although there was a great deal of information on burning wood.

After much trial and error, I did sucessfully, design and build my own stove. This eventually led to my own business: Shaker Stove Works, Inc. For four years, I designed and manufactured wood stoves and boilers. During that time, I was approached by many people who wanted to build their own unit but did not know how to go about it. After I helped a number of these people, they were surprised to find how easily and inexpensively a wood stove can be fabricated.

Although previous welding and burning experience is needed to fabricate a boiler unit, only a familiarity with the equipment is required to construct other models. In other words, no professional experience is required to fabricate the easier "box-style" stoves.

# Introduction

Anyone can build a wood stove. All that is needed is a feeling of self-confidence and a basic understanding of the simple fabrication procedures described in this book. *Build Your Own Solid-Fuel Burning Stove* is a practical and uncomplicated introduction to the design and manufacture of wood stoves or coal stoves, and their operation. It is also a study in the use of alternate sources of fuel.

The main purpose of this book is to provide the average energy consumer with designs, material lists, blueprints, and instructions. With a little effort, the average homeowner can build a stove at approximately half the price of a retail unit.

With the aid of this book, you can develop your own ideas and designs for a stove or boiler. This feature has been included to reach the adventurous do-it-yourselfer. The illustrations and designs in this book make fabricating a stove easy, but the more advanced welder will be challenged into designing and fabricating his own idea for a stove.

Those who pursue the challenge of building a unit of their own design will find joy and satisfaction in taking an idea and developing it into a detailed drawing, and then developing the drawing into a working model. Much satisfaction can be obtained by watching an idea perform as predicted.

# Part 1
# Before
# Building Your
# Solid-Fuel Unit

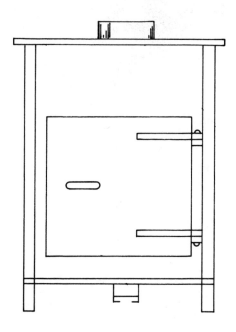

# Chapter 1

# The Solid-Fuel Burner

**B**EFORE YOU BEGIN BUILDING your wood stove or coal stove, you should have an understanding of what it is and how it works. A wood- or coal-burning stove is actually a *solid-fuel burner*. It is a container that holds solid fuel, burns the fuel safely, and emits heat. *Solid fuel* is defined as solid material that burns. Radiant stoves and heat exchangers are two types of solid-fuel burners. A *radiant stove* radiates heat to the area near the stove. Such units are usually made of cast iron or steel. They also are usually lined with firebrick and they are most often baffled. Radiant stoves can burn either coal or wood. A *heat exchanger* is a unit that directs heat to a designated place—not an open area. A hot-air furnace is a heat exchanger. In a hot-air furnace, the radiant heat of the firebox is directed into an exterior box or tubing. Hot air is then sent through heating ducts to various parts of the house.

## WOOD-BURNING AND COAL-BURNING UNITS

There are intrinsic differences in wood-burning units and coal-burning units. It is simply not possible to burn wood and coal in the same unit with the same amount of efficiency.

The most important difference between wood-burning units and coal-burning units is the control of air. In a wood-burner, especially if it is an industrial model, the air controls are usually mounted on the doors. This is not the most efficient system. It is preferable to use a slide air-control system. Either system is good for a wood-burning unit because it brings the air to the fire at a direct level. This creates turbulence in the stove and helps the baffling system to work efficiently.

In a coal-burning unit, however, the air should be induced into the firebox at the lowest level possible. A coal fire, unlike a wood fire, burns not only from the center out, but also from the bottom up. Therefore, air must be induced from underneath the coal. Figure 1-1 illustrates how a coal fire burns and how the air is induced to create combustion.

Wood, on the other hand, burns inside and outside the wood pile (see Fig. 1-2). The illustra-

3

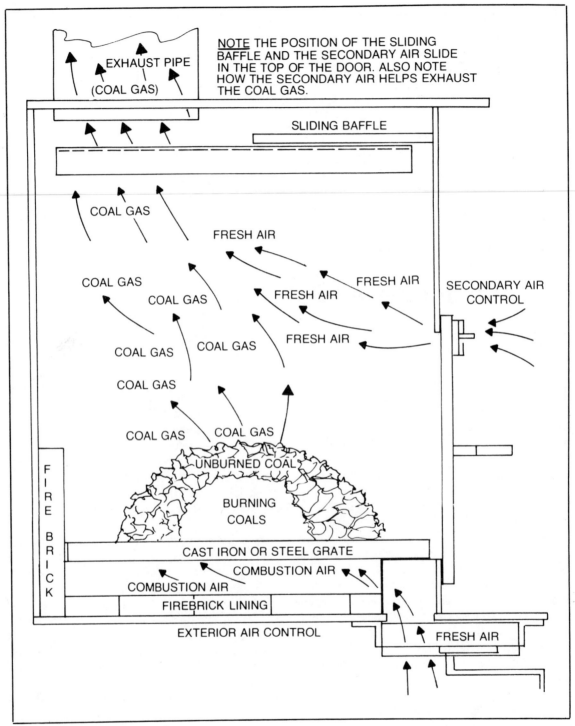

Fig. 1-1. Air turbulence in a coal fire.

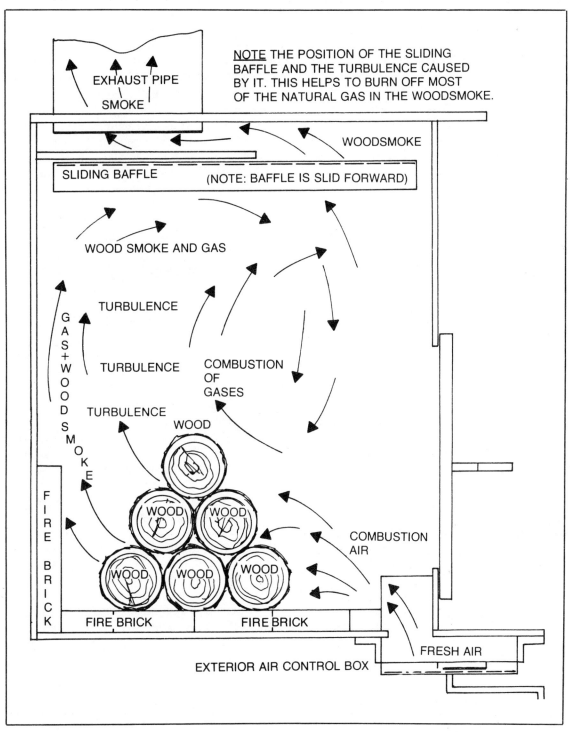

Fig. 1-2. Air turbulence in a wood fire.

tions in this chapter should help you understand the differences between the combustion of wood and the combustion of coal.

By using the air control system, you can accomplish a number of things. The air is brought into the firebox at the lowest level possible (just above the floor brick). This allows you to fit a coal grate into the unit and to fit a fair amount of coal into that grate.

By bringing the air in at such a low level, when burning wood, a larger turbulence is created in the firebox. When the air bounces off the back wall and off of the baffle plate, a larger circular motion will take place. The air, being drawn in from under the stove, will be preheated and cause more complete combustion.

The air controls, being under the stove instead of on the doors, enhance the beauty of the stoves that are detailed in this book.

A by-product of burning coal is commonly referred to as *coal gas*. Coal gas, being detrimental to one's health, is a large concern to most people when burning coal. This problem can be resolved with a secondary air system.

A secondary air system, which is usually a slide system, induces air at a high level into the firebox. This, in turn, helps create a larger draw on the chimney to help send coal gases up the chimney rather than forcing them out into the room. Figure 1-1 shows how a secondary air system works in the firebox of a radiant stove.

It is futile to have a stationary baffling system (that is one that is permanent) in a stove when you plan on burning both wood and coal. You do not want to hinder the gas. Instead you will want to vent the gases as fast as possible. If you do decide that you want to burn wood and coal in a radiant stove, bear in mind two things. A sliding baffle, rather than a permanent baffle, should be placed in the stove. A sliding baffle can be made by following the drawings in the section in this book on baffling systems. Also, a secondary air system will be needed when burning coal.

## A WOOD- AND COAL-BURNING BOILER

Notice that the wood and coal burning boiler in Figs. 1-1 and 1-2 has two completely independent types of air systems mounted on the boiler: one is for coal and one is for wood. Also notice that there is a sliding baffle. This is the only way, especially with boilers, that wood and coal can be burned with any amount of efficiency in the same solid fuel burner.

The three lower slides are to allow air in for coal burning under the grate. The top air control allows air in (the secondary air system) to help vent coal gas. When wood is burned the three lower air controls are closed and the air slide for wood is used. The sliding baffle can be easily slid into place for burning wood and slid out of the way for burning coal. When wood is burned on a grate, small pieces of charcoal—that would normally burn on brick—will fall through the grate and lay unburned in the ashpan.

## HEAT EXCHANGER

A hot water boiler is a type of heat exchanger. In a hot water boiler, the heat is transferred to a water jacket or a series of coils. The water stores heat. Therefore, the heat can be stored in a reserve tank and can be used at a later time. The boiler can be tied into your own furnace in such a way that, if the wood runs out, your furnace will automatically turn on without any interruption of heat.

A domestic coil can be installed, during fabrication of the hot water boiler, to also heat your domestic hot water. Think of the savings involved. The filling and heating of a hot water tank can be a substantial part of your utility bill. Isn't it a fantastic thought to be able to wipe away such a huge cost of two energy sources with just one convenient unit?

Heat exchange boxes or coils are designed to be used with a radiant stove to heat a home. They can also be used to heat hot water or to collect the hot air and direct it to a certain part of the house through a duct system or tubing.

A box is mounted onto the sides of the stove or on the back during fabrication. Once the stove is heated, the radiant heat—from the side that it is mounted on—is collected into that box and then dispersed through the house, or to a certain part of the house, through the use of a duct and duct fan.

Hot water can be collected in a heat exchange box or coil. Coils are usually made of copper because it is a good conductor of heat. Hot water heat

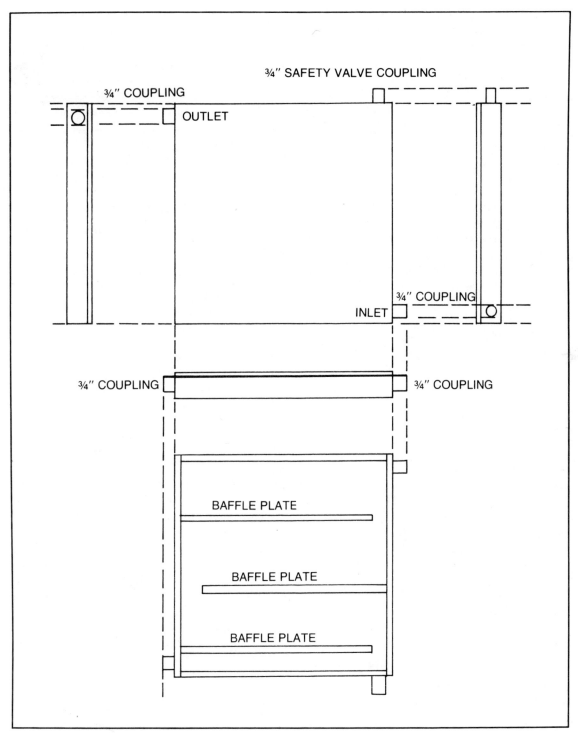

Fig. 1-3. Heat exchange coils.

exchange boxes and coils are usually mounted on the sides or the back of the stove for the purposes of heating domestic hot water (tapwater). This is another way of bringing down your heating bill. At the same time, you will probably get even more hot water from you system.

The user of heat exchange boxes or coils will see a larger creosote buildup on the interior wall of the side that these heat exchangers are mounted on. This is because these type of heat exchangers are used for drawing heat away from the firebox to where they are mounted. Remember that once the temperature drops below 200° F there will be a buildup of creosote. The solution is to burn your stove hotter for a longer period of time in order to burn the creosote off. See Fig. 1-3 for sketches of heat exchange boxes or coils that can be made for the stoves in this book.

## BAFFLES

A proper baffling system can be a most important factor as to just how well your solid-fuel burner operates. A baffle is a smoke deflecting plate, placed in the stove, to retard the wood smoke and radiate additional heat to the stove. It also creates turbulence to guide the smoke back into the fire to burn the natural gases. A proper baffle system can burn 2000 to 2100 cubic feet of natural gas by burning one cord of wood.

A baffle is not recommended for burning coal. The sliding baffle is recommended for any unit burning both coal and wood. This type of baffle can be slid into position for burning wood and slid out of the way for burning coal.

For those of you who are going to design your own stove the importance of a well-designed baffle system cannot be overstressed. You must put in enough of a baffling system to make the stove efficient, but not enough to cause effects such as backdrafting, backpuffing, or smoking.

## STEEL VERSUS CAST IRON

All of the solid-fuel burners illustrated in this book require steel plate. Steel is denser than cast iron. Cast iron has the quality of being hard but brittle. Cast iron has little elasticity and it has little capacity to expand and contract. This is why a cast-iron stove can crack. Steel is malleable and it has a greater amount of elasticity. This is why cast-iron stoves are bolted together and not welded. Due to the tremendous heat of welding, the cast iron would crack in production. Steel can be welded. This gives a more airtight seal at the joints and it also will help prevent warpage of the floor plate and sides.

## FIREBRICKING

Due to expansion and contraction, crackage, and warpage, it is understandable why a stove must be lined with firebrick. Cast-iron stoves are lined with firebrick so that the bricks hold heat. This prevents rapid contraction that causes cracking. Steel stoves are lined with firebrick to prevent warpage of the immediate area of the coals in the firebox. Therefore, being able to retain most of the heat in the firebox and being away from the floor of the stove, the stove floor will not warp. Any airtight stove that is built and used, not having been lined with firebrick, will eventually crack or warp.

## AIRTIGHTNESS

Airtightness is a crucial factor in box stoves. The burn rate of wood in nonairtight stoves can only be controlled by the amount of wood put into them. An airtight stove, on the other hand, is controlled by the air allowed into the combustion chamber of the stove. This in turn controls the combustion and the burn rate of the stove. This also controls the heat emitted or radiated from the surface area of the stove. Proper fit of the doors can determine the airtightness of a stove. Also remember that welded joints are much more airtight than bolted joints. Gaskets on doors are recommended.

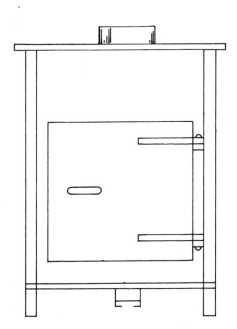

# Chapter 2

# Deciding Which Solid-Fuel Burner to Build

HOW MUCH OF YOUR HOUSE do you want to heat? If all you want to do is heat two or three small rooms, then a stove about the size and weight of the Pilgrim stove is all that you will need (see Chapter 14). It can be something as simple as a plain box stove similar to the design of the rectangular or square stove (see Chapter 13). All you need to put together is four sides, a top, and a bottom. Make sure that the surface area and the weight is about the same.

Most people would prefer to heat an entire house. The difference in the cost of building a small stove, as compared to one that is sufficient to heat their entire home, is surprisingly little. Why just heat two or three rooms when you can heat an entire house comfortably and save even more money?

## FIGURING SQUARE FOOTAGE

After deciding what portion of the house you want to heat, you will have to figure the square footage involved. This can be easily determined by taking the length of your area to be heated and multiplying it by the width of the area to be heated. This is a very simple procedure. For a single-story house, you multiply the length by the width. If you are going to heat a two-story dwelling, then you must multiply this number by two because it is twice the area. Radiant units illustrated in this book can heat up to 3000 square feet. The smaller of the two water-jacketed boilers will heat up to 3000 square feet. The larger water-jacketed wood and coal combination boiler heats up to 5000 square feet.

Take the insulation of your home into account. If your home is well insulated, you can expect the unit of your choice to adequately heat the square footage it has been designed to heat. If your home is not well insulated, you should select the next larger unit.

## WHAT FUEL TO BURN?

What fuel you are going to burn is important because of the size of the unit. There are differences in size between a good coal-burning unit and a good wood-burning unit. A good wood-burning unit is usually massive. It has to have a large surface area in order to radiate the heat and hold a large amount of wood. A coal unit has better operating capabilities if it is smaller. This way the coal can come into contact with the sides of the unit. See the diagram of a coal fire in Fig. 1-1. Due to the smaller surface area, you are going to lose a little of the heating capabilities that you would have with a wood stove.

You might have noticed that most older coal stoves are loaded from the top. This allows the operator to shovel the coal in from the top of the stove and the coal will contact the sides of the unit. Today's coal units, however, are designed airtight to produce more efficient combustion and a more efficient burn.

In making your decision on which fuel to burn, you must consider the availability and storage of the fuel. Trees grow faster than coal, oil, or natural gas. Wood can usually be obtained by a homeowner. This is a crucial factor in determining which fuel to burn. Most families will enjoy the aesthetic value of a wood fire. And you can keep the wood stored with much less of a mess than with coal.

## LOCATION OF THE UNIT

The location of the stove is a crucial factor in heating your home. If a house is a single-story dwelling, a radiant stove would operate at top capacity if placed in the middle of the house. If this cannot be done, place the stove at one end of the house and mount wall fans or registers in the top of the ceilings to circulate the heat properly to other parts of the house. An existing flue might influence the location of the stove. Bear in mind, however, that proper circulation of the heat can make an important difference in heating comfort. See Chapter 23.

Regarding the location of the solid-fuel burner, it is important to take general rules of safety into consideration. Make sure that you investigate the safety codes for your town, county, and state. Check into the clauses of your homeowner's insurance policy. The protection these rules provide will be worth while. All solid-fuel burners should be placed at least 12 to 14 inches from a noncombusti-

ble surface and at least 3 feet from a combustible surface.

## SELECTING A UNIT

You must decide which type of solid-fuel heater will best suit your needs. A radiant stove can be appreciated and enjoyed by the whole family.

A hot-air furnace or a water-jacketed boiler require an existing heating system. They both can be installed in the basement, and away from the living area. A hot-air furnace must be installed near the existing system. The heat of a hot-air furnace is carried through the house through ducts. The advantage of this type of system is that individual rooms can be heated.

A water-jacketed boiler requires a furnace and baseboard heat. It can be installed away from the family area, and it does not necessarily have to be installed close to the furnace. Water retains heat longer than heated air from a furnace. As shown in Chapter 1, a coil can be attached to heat domestic hot water.

You must weigh the amount of time that you are willing to invest and your welding and burning skills (or the skills of whomever is going to do the fabrication of the unit) in deciding whether to go with a radiant stove or a heat exchanger. General information on the time required to build each unit is given in Part 2 of this book. You will have to compare your own welding and burning experience against those of professionals to determine how long it will take you to build your unit.

Welding and burning proficiency is of utmost importance in the fabrication of water-jacketed boiler units. Once these units are put together and welded, the interior box cannot be reached. Bear it in mind that these designs (the water-jacketed boilers) are included in this book for those people who are accustomed to welding and burning. It can be more costly and time-consuming to put together one of these units, but if you are proficient enough to do so the advantages of this unit will be more than worth your endeavors and financial investment.

# Chapter 3

# Heating with Wood

I AM SURE THAT BEFORE YOU begin building your own solid-fuel unit you will have thoroughly researched the economics of heating with wood or coal. For generating heat, about 200 gallons of fuel oil are approximately equal to one cord of wood. Heating bills can be cut to a minimum even if you have to purchase the wood. There is considerable effort involved in gathering your own wood, but you must decide the worth of heating with wood and the means by which you intend to obtain it.

### HARVESTING WOOD

Harvesting wood should be of utmost concern. It is only through selfishness and laziness that our forests could be lost. Indiscriminate cutting can destroy the beauty of our woodlands and result in land erosions. This is totally unnecessary. A rule of thumb that can easily be applied is that one cord of wood can be cut per acre of land a year. You would only be removing the amount of wood that the land would turn over naturally. This does not hurt the ecology of the area.

Ironically, it is only during the last half century that wood began to lose it's important role as a heating source. Previously, wood was not only harvested for heating needs, but for a far greater number of uses. Periodic harvest can be done without great disturbance to the environment.

Contact a local forest ranger. Chances are that he will be able to advise you on which trees will make the best firewood, and on planting new seedlings. He also will be able to advise you on the best way to manage your land for environment control.

Prepare a plan to serve as a guide for possibly the next decade. The plan should include which stands, species, and the amounts, and the sizes of the timber to be scheduled for cutting for some time to come. Your plan should indicate where planting is necessary. Determine the number and species of trees and what area needs improvement. You could also schedule the dates to take care of the needs. A good management plan will include a fire protection system and it will also include provisions for the control of insects and disease.

## MANAGING WOODLAND

Wood is indeed a renewable source. Managing a woodland actually cooperates with nature. It can improve the beauty and the health of trees by giving the reforested area better fertilization, drainage, and irrigation. New seedlings, of a faster growing species, could convert partially forested areas to a woodland that could be quickly used as a source of fuel. This also shortens the period of rotation and allows the growth of improved variations of species. Thinning the forest is doing nothing more than helping nature take it's course. An overgrown forest can easily be lost through fire, insects, and disease.

Cutting practices have, in the past, been atrocious. We need to establish good habits. Our forests have been overcut and neglected. We have woodlands full of trees that are crooked and diseased. Trees do need thinning. If they are to grow at their maximum rate, they cannot compete for water, sun-light, and nutrients. Stands of young trees start with 4000 to 6000 stems per acre. Most young trees will die before they ever reach maturity or even before they become large enough to be harvested as saw logs. A mature tree will measure 20 inches in diameter. Needing the room for this growth, it boils down to survival of the fittest. Approximately 100 trees per acre will survive.

If you thin hardwood stands while the trees are still young, it will permit the more desirable trees to complete their growth at a hastened rate. A greater volume of wood will be produced per acre. When the woodlands are properly cut, the growth potential of the forests can be transferred from a low timber value to that of a much higher value.

When a forest contains predominantly over-mature trees, it can be said that nature is out of balance. The only thing that will stimulate the growth of such a woodland is a natural catastrophe. The skillful forester is far more gentle in the

## HARVESTING FIREWOOD

This section has been paraphrased, in part, from the U.S. Department of Energy publication *Heating With Wood*, and from *HEATING WITH WOOD* by the Editors of "The Family Handyman" magazine, © 1978 by Butterick Publishing. By permission of New Century Publishers, Inc., Piscataway, New Jersey.

The crop tree selection method is considered to be the best way to thin a young pole stand of the better crop trees. This simple method for thinning stands works to the greater advantage of the best trees in the stand. The competing trees should be cut for firewood.

Trees selected for harvest should stand straight and tall, contain relatively small branches, and show signs of self-pruning. *Self-pruning* means that the lower 10 to 16 feet of the tree should have few or no branches. If a few small branches are dead on this section of the tree, it is a good indication that the tree is developing into a quality tree. Trees that have swollen stems, broken or seamed bark, mechanical wounds, and poorly healed branch stubs should be removed for firewood.

A good crop tree should have a crown of three to four feet of open space on at least two sides. The trees touching the sides of your selected crop trees are competitors. It would be a good idea to remove these for firewood. If you remove competing trees, you will allow the crop tree needed space to grow to a fuller and healthier maturity. Do not hesitate to remove competing trees.

The best field procedure for selecting crop trees is to start approximately 10 to 20 feet into the stand, or from where the property line begins. After you select a tree valued as a crop tree, mark it at eye level with a spot of paint or tie it with a ribbon. Use a pace of approximately 20 feet parallel to the edge of the starting point. A 5- to 7-foot radius of trees should be marked. If there are no trees within this 5- to 7-foot circle, then choose what you would consider to be the next best trees and mark those.

maintenance of the woodlands than an indiscriminate act of nature. We need our forests for wild life, recreational parks, and water supplies.

Before you begin the management of your stand, learn the value of the trees you are thinning. Your local forest ranger can give you advice of this nature. You might want to note that white birches, yellow birches, ash, and sugar maple will probably not be of more value than aspen, a species of poplar, oaks, and hickorys.

If you are to gain maximum benefit from the thinning process, it should begin at an early stage of woodland development. When the trees in a stand average 4½ feet above the ground with a diameter of between 4 and 10 inches, you should begin to thin a hardwood stand. This is the point where the survival of the fittest will begin.

The saplings that are between 1 inch and 4 inches will be the easiest to weed out. Your woodpile will not quickly grow with this type of harvest. It will take approximately 100 of these saplings to produce 1 cord of wood. These sticks will probably be of no more worth than kindling.

Harvesting stands of trees with diameters of 4 to 10 inches is more rewarding. Stands containing these size trees are referred to as *pole stands* because the wood is commonly used for pulpwood and fence posts in addition to fuel wood. The thinning process will promote what would otherwise be slow diameter growth because of a stagnant period.

Stands of larger trees, with an average diameter of 10 to 12 inches, can be thinned. These hardwood stands are approaching the stage when they can be sold as timber for saw logs. Obtain professional assistance before you begin this procedure. A professional will best be able to advise you on which trees should be left for more complete growth.

## WHERE TO GATHER WOOD

Not everyone owns property with readily available wood. But you might have friends or relatives who

If there are no trees worth considering for crop trees, keep pacing out approximately 5 additional feet, to a maximum of 7 feet, and mark those trees. Skip a section, if necessary, and go on to an area approximately 20 feet away to choose crop trees. Continue until you have reached the far edge of your stand or property line. At this time, pace approximately 20 feet at a right angle to the first line. Mark the crop trees also to guide you as you proceed.

It would be most ideal to be able to pick a crop tree every 20 feet and free it's crown by harvesting competing trees. This suggested procedure can only be used as a guide. Do not hesitate to choose what you consider to be good crop trees even if they are growing within 15 feet of the last one. Do try to choose a crop tree within every 25 feet.

Remember to remove the trees that touch or are very close to the crown of the crop trees. They will be direct competitors so it is best to use these competing trees for your present firewood needs. You might have to remove highly valuable trees in order to environmentally control an area. If these trees are not removed, they will not live to maturity. They will be shaded out and die as a result.

You might find an abundance of "under-story trees." These are trees that are much smaller than the valuable crop trees. Their crowns will be lower than those of the crop trees. They are being deprived of the much-needed sunlight. This is one of nature's ways of taking care of it's own. If these trees are large enough to be used as fuel for your fire, harvest them. Under-story trees will have next to no effect on the growth and maturity of your crop trees, but they will be valuable firewood.

Next, concern yourself with any dead, dying, and deformed trees that could hinder the growth and health of trees in the area. Remember also that planting new seedlings, of a faster growing nature, does not necessarily mean production of only softwoods. Black locusts seem to grow as fast as any weed. Shagbark hickory trees are one of the best producers of wood heat in America.

are more than willing to allow you to take out any unnecessary wood. Dead and fallen wood alone might keep you in fuel for many years to come. It will also clear up any unsightly litter at the same time.

You can check dumps and landfills for fallen trees felled during ice and wind storms. You may be even more than welcome to take whatever wood you may want. This wood might even be in small sizes.

Private landowners and state forests, sometimes only charge a small fee for you to cut on their land. They sometimes even mark trees that have to come down. This is a very inexpensive way to obtain your fuel.

Construction sites frequently have some scrap lumber. Ask for permission. You might be able to pick up bits of fir and pine, or even enough kindling to keep you going for a long while to come.

## AIR POLLUTION

Pollutants that result from burning of wood can be considered natural. They actually occur within nature's process; it cannot be assumed that they would be harmful to the environment. The pollutants from a wood fire are comparable to the decay of wood that takes place in the forest. The carbon dioxide released during woodburning cannot be compared with air pollution such as sulphur dioxide. Some pollutants are created naturally, and they should not be compared with those of a man-made variety. Burning wood for heat will not interfere with the natural growth of plants or animals.

## WHY CHOOSE WOOD HEAT?

I cannot tell you that heating with wood is easy. Aside from cutting and hauling the wood, there is continuous work involved. Your attitude toward this undertaking will determine how you go about performing these tasks. Obtaining wood can be very self-satisfying. It is almost like mastering a sport. You are in complete control of necessary function of life—keeping your family warm.

Yes, wood is heavy and bulky. Stacking wood can be a strenuous activity, and you will need a great deal of space for storage. There is also the chance that your wood might carry insects.

You must plan ahead to provide your wood sufficient time to season. As much as nine months time for seasoning should be considered. Your wood needs protection from the elements. There is no question that you will have to use all the rules of safety. Your fire will need to be tended to and radiant heat is sometimes difficult to control (until you get the knack of it).

Wood is comparatively inexpensive. Even paying top dollar, wood is still almost half the price of fuel oil in most areas. In some areas, wood prices seem totally outrageous, but on the other hand, you might be able to have wood hauled in bulk for approximately half the going price of a cord of wood. This is definitely worth considering.

### Wood Heat can be most Enjoyable

The aesthetic value of a wood fire is difficult to over-emphasize. Our stove is a family project. Both of our children, Sandy and Robbie, who are now considerably older than when our wood stove was first brought into our home, learned how to tend the wood fire immediately. Of course this was done under supervision. It has been their job to maintain the wood pile in our family room full at all times. This has given them an important responsibility, and they have experienced the pleasure and warmth in participating in a home project that is totally family oriented. They probably have more knowledge of wood burning than the average homeowner—including all safety rules!

The radiant stove we use in our home was previously displayed and operated in the showroom of our manufacturing business; it is the Liberty Model. This particular model has a large surface area that is great for cooking. It can make fun out of what sometimes can be a monotonous chore.

When our son, Robbie, accompanied me to work on Saturday mornings, we cooked eggs on top of the stove with a cast-iron skillet. We have kept a slow simmer for sauces, soups, and stews. With the aid of a *trivet,* which can be purchased in most hardware departments, you can keep your cooking temperatures at a true simmer. Our daughter,

Sandy, who is now 12, enjoys the responsibility of supervising the cooking of beans, on the surface area, and roasting hot dogs and marshmallows on an open fire. This method of preparing a dinner has become a neighborhood favorite. The children enjoy inviting their friends in to share in this event.

### Wood Heat can be a Tension Fighter

Another of the advantages of heating with wood is the great relaxing powers it produces. For a person in good health, the physical labor, from bucking and stacking to hauling the wood, is a great tension reliever.

No one can deny the trance-like powers a wood fire can have on spectators. Just close your eyes and imagine a screen-guarded stove with a roaring wood fire, and the snow falling to form drifts outside your windows. You might even learn to look forward to those cold winter nights you previously dreaded.

### Wood Heating Knowledge

If you decide to undertake the adventure of burning wood in your solid-fuel unit, it will take a little more knowledge than learning how to ignite a log. I once had to go out to the home of a customer who insisted that his stove, that I had built for him, did not work. The match would not set the log on fire. I had to teach him the proper way to lay a fire, and, the basics of burning wood. Even the most experienced of woodburners will run into a problem every now and then. To understand wood burning, you must first understand the combustion process.

### GREEN WOOD

Everyone knows that the safest burning wood is dry wood, right? Green wood is not only dangerous because it can build creosote, but it is simply wasteful of heat and it is often very difficult to ignite. By the time green wood burns off it's moisture and allows the evaporated moisture to flow up the chimney, you have lost a great deal of the valuable heating capacity that should be used for radiant heat. Green wood provides as much as over 40 percent *less* heating capacity.

If you must use green wood, and you are going to take every safety precaution involved in the use of this unseasoned wood, then use it in addition to very dry wood. A mixed load would be the only advisable way to use it. Green wood can slow down the combustion process to produce a fire that will burn slower. I do not recommend this. Once you learn to operate your solid-fuel unit with the aid of the air controls and simple tricks described in this book, you will not have to waste valuable wood. In essence, that is all you are doing by burning green wood.

### THE COMBUSTION PROCESS

Even the driest of wood contains a small percentage of moisture. About 20 percent moisture content is average for dry wood. Green wood will contain much more moisture. Dry wood will burn much faster than green wood and give the maximum amount of heat. The moisture that burns off wood is not heat that radiates well. During the first few minutes a seasoned piece of wood burns, it's moisture content is consumed.

Before the combustion process can even take place, oxygen and high temperature must be present. If both temperature and air supply are not maintained throughout the burning process, the fire will die out.

The next phase of the combustion process is when the wood begins to catch fire. This phase can only begin when the wood reaches 212° F; that is the boiling point of water. At this point wood breaks down into volatiles and will, eventually, turn into charcoal.

The wood begins to fire up when it reaches a temperature of approximately, 600° F. An efficient solid-fuel burner will use these volatiles to it's maximum efficiency. The longer that you are able to reuse the gases, without causing a creosote build up, the more warmth you will be able to get out of your wood supply.

Completing the combustion of these volatiles is not necessarily an automatic process. All the advice given in this book—pertaining to proper installation, a sound chimney, constructing your solid-fuel unit with all the care that it deserves, and checking out your baffling and air control systems—is an absolute must. The efficiency of a solid-fuel unit can be evaluated by the completeness of the burning process. You can see volatiles burn off in the form of gases.

The volatiles begin to chemically break down at approximately 300° F to 400° F, but this is not complete until your wood fire reaches approximately 1000° F. This is the point when the formation of charcoal begins. The gases would not be able to reach these temperatures if they were not restricted and given a flame path to follow. In a very hot fire, you are able to see the gases burn off in the formation of charcoal. You will learn to appreciate the invention of a baffling system when you realize that the volatiles have natural tendencies to rise out of the firebox and up the chimney. By retaining the volatiles, and using them at maximum efficiency, you obtain the most heat possible.

The first wood stoves did not even come close to the design of the modern-day, solid-fuel unit. Study the flame path shown in Fig. 1-2 to better understand the complete consumption of the volatiles. Variables such as the air controls, the type and dryness of the wood, the outside temperature, and the draft outside are all factors affecting the efficiency of the burn.

## COMBUSTION AND WOOD-HEAT EFFICIENCY

Benjamin Franklin, who was associated with the invention of the first free-standing fireplace, observed that most of the flame was lost up the chimney along with much potential radiating warmth. Although the stove was a great deal less than airtight, thus making it inefficient in terms of temperature control and wood use, Franklin did attempt to use the complete combustion process to provide more radiant heat.

He attempted to design his unit to contain the flame and smoke within the firebox for as long as practical. He devised a false back in the firebox, similar to a hollow wall, halfway back into the stove. He exhausted this into what would otherwise have been a bricked-up fireplace. This hollow plate acted as a baffle. The flame and smoke were retarded because it had to pass up and around it. This allowed the wood to burn more thoroughly.

This version of the "Pennsylvania Fireplace" contained channels within, the stove itself, that admitted outside air, circulated it, and radiated additional heat into the room. His second stove invention, the "down drafter," employed the volatiles and smoke even more efficiently by pushing the draft down through the fire.

## THE CHARCOAL STAGE OF COMBUSTION

Charcoal plays it's role in a good wood fire by maintaining the temperature of the fire for an efficient wood burn in the firebox. You will usually find that the charcoal remains after an overnight burn. You will also find a white-powdered ash. This is further proof of an efficient burn.

Stove owners should allow some of that white ash to remain within the firebox because it continues to insulate the fire for a longer burn period. It will also help protect the firebox by providing a good base for a new fire. With luck, you will only have to start a new fire at the beginning of each woodburning season. One dealer used to advertise my units as only needing one match a year. Once you become proficient, in fire tending, this could very well become the case.

Do not allow your fire to remain in the charcoal stage for any prolonged period of time. It should not be in the charcoal stage any longer than the few early morning hours, after it has burned down to the low stage, before you reload it in the morning. A good airtight stove *could* burn beyond 24 hours, even up to 36 hours, at the charcoal stage, but a low, consistent burn creates creosote buildup. Obviously creosote buildup will result from the cooled gases given off by the charcoal.

## WOOD HEAT VERSUS OTHER HEATING SYSTEMS

Many types of wood are good for use in a wood fire. What you want is wood that will combust at the greatest performance. Hardwood can deliver the equal of more than 250 gallons of fuel oil. Softwood might only produce the equivalent to just over 120 gallons of fuel oil.

If you become proficient at identifying the various types of wood, mixed loads can be desirable. In this way, you can coordinate burning your wood according to the temperatures outside. When it is 40 degrees you obviously do not want a roaring fire that would blast you out of the house. But on zero-degree night, this type of fire would be perfectly agreeable.

If you purchase your wood, rather than cut it yourself, you will be paying premium prices for hardwood such as white birch. A mixed load should be less expensive. If you convey a knowledge of wood to your dealer, you should be able to get a better deal on a mixed load. The following is a list of the types of wood commonly used for burning. The list is in the approximate order of the greatest heating equivalent to the lowest heating equivalent. For example, shagbark hickory is considered to burn at the highest rate of heating capacity and American beech heats at approximately the equivalent to just over 230 gallons of fuel oil.

Equivalent to over 230 gallons of fuel oil:
    Hickory, shagbark
    Locust, black
    Ironwood (hardhack)
    Apple
    Elm, rock
    Hickory, bitternut
    Oak, white
    Beech, American

Equivalent to over 190 gallons of fuel oil:
    Birch, yellow
    Maple, sugar
    Oak, red
    Ash, white
    Walnut, black
    Birch, white
    Cherry, black

Equivalent to over 175 gallons of fuel oil:
    Tamarack, (Eastern larch)
    Maple, red
    Ash, green
    Pine, pitch
    Sycamore, American
    Ash, black
    Elm, American
    Maple, silver

Equivalent to over 120 gallons of fuel oil:
    Spruce, red
    Hemlock
    Willow, black
    Butternut
    Aspen, (poplar)
    Pine, white
    Basswood
    Fir, balsam

## THE IMPORTANCE OF DRY WOOD

How important is dry wood? For safety and burning efficiency, it is most important. The driest of wood will still contain approximately, 20 percent moisture. This is considered about the best that you can expect from seasoning your wood under normal conditions and proper protection from the elements. Because wood is a moisture absorbing substance, storing wood so that it is protected from the elements clearly makes sense. Although six months aging time is adequate under some circumstances, nine months is recommended.

Plan your cutting season or buying season (for better prices) for the late winter or early spring. This will allow drying over the summer months and immediate readiness for the cold-weather season. If you are buying wood, the peak season is usually around January.

A wood dealer's best prices will be at the time of the year when he is cutting and storing (around spring). Think of this as doing the dealer a favor; this should be repaid by a good financial deal. You will be allowing the green wood to dry at your house and not in his storage space. If you must burn green wood, (this is not recommended) woods such as white ash, beech, sumac, and some birches might give you the best burn

Remember that green wood burns at up to over 40 percent less heating capacity than dried out wood. It doesn't make much sense to lose all that heat up the chimney, take the chance of a tremendous creosote buildup, and create the elements needed for a creosote fire. Taking apart your stove chimney, once a week to check for creosote build-up, is not too often when burning green wood.

## WOOD-DRYING PROCESS

Drying out wood is a very uncomplicated process. All that is necessary during the summer months is perhaps a piece of plastic. Condensation will form on the inside of the wood pile. The plastic should be turned on occasion. The plastic will retain hotter temperatures and speed up the drying process. Keeping the wood covered also helps keep insects out.

Green wood should be stacked to allow for circulation. If you want to create the most desirable of drying circumstances, stacking the wood, alternately, at right angles to the preceding layer will ensure the greatest air circulation. About three months of drying time would be required for this procedure. Then you can stack it in normal fashion for the remainder of the drying time.

When trees are felled during the months they retain leaves, more moisture will be present than if the leaves are not present. Remember, too, that wood drys much faster through the ends and sides of the wood. Logs cut to size and split will dry out faster due to more exposure. The drying time can be cut to six months in most cases.

All wood, whether green or dry, should be stored on a waterproof foundation such as a concrete patio. If the foundation is a few inches above ground level, you will have less chance of the wood becoming filled with added moisture. Once the wood is thoroughly dried out, it can be stacked close together. During the winter months, thorough protection from the elements is needed; a roof would best protect the wood.

Even if a corner of a wood-stack covering comes loose, the entire wood stack can become frozen together. Tie the covering down and anchor it securely. If you are storing green wood in the winter season, allow for air circulation. In our home, we keep the wood pile stacked, inside our house, for approximately two weeks before it will have to be used. Do not, however, stack wood too close to the walls or close to the solid-fuel burner due to safety precautions.

---

### THE CHAIN SAW

This section has been paraphrased, in part, from *HEATING WITH WOOD* by the Editors of "The Family Handyman" magazine, © 1978 by Butterick Publishing. By permission of New Century Publishers, Inc., Piscataway, New Jersey.

If you will be cutting your own wood, the most important piece of equipment you will need is a chain saw. A heavy-duty model—more than likely expensive—will be the best investment. Do not be fooled by advertisements for chain saws that will do no more than prune garden bushes. Buy a chain saw that is specifically made for use by professional loggers. Automatic features are unnecessary. You'll spend more time attempting to automatically oil your chain or automatically sharpen your saw then it would take by hand. If these gadgets break, it could retard the use of the equipment.

Chain saws with a bar length of 12 to 20 inches are probably the best for cutting firewood. Length capacities of 25 inches are too large and could prove awkward for the homeowner who is cutting wood for heating needs. Select a chain saw that has the significant safety innovations. These would include antivibration systems and provisions for quick-stop brakes. To reduce possible operator fatigue from vibration, shock-absorber mounts go a long way. The quick-stop brakes will stop the chain if problems arise. Some chain saws have designs that will reduce kickback. *Kickback* is a common problem that occurs when a saw hits an immovable object and kicks back at the operator. This is blamed for at least one-third of all chain saw accidents. Optional safety devices are offered in the form of a wraparound chain brake and hand guard. This not only reduces kickback, but it will protect the user when the saw is being used in a horizontal position to fell trees. It might even be advisable to check into the models with heated handles that protect the user's hands from becoming stiff in colder weather.

## HOW TO PURCHASE WOOD

If you are going to purchase your wood, estimate the amount of wood that you will need, by the consumption of fuel for the previous few winter seasons. Overestimate rather than underestimate. Most stove owners will use less than 5 cords of wood during any winter season. Some of the many variables that must be taken into consideration are the size of the area that is going to be heated, the insulation of the area, the length of the season and what you consider to be a comfortable room temperature.

Know exactly what you are buying. Be knowledgeable when you are talking to a wood dealer. Ask how the wood has been stored and if it is to be considered dry. Dry wood has more cracks than green wood and the cracks will usually radiate from the center out. Although there is no sure way to tell how dry a piece of wood is, you can try knocking two pieces of wood together.

A piece of wood would be considered fairly dry if the sound resembles that of a baseball bat hitting a hardball. If the thud is dull, assume that the wood has not been dried out enough. You might be able to derive some bargaining power.

Mixed loads of wood are not always less expensive than full loads of hardwoods, but they can be. Ask the right questions. Find out what varieties of wood are contained in the load. After speaking to enough dealers, you will learn, approximately, how to estimate what to pay for what you are getting.

You should not pay the same price for a mixture of aspen, maple, and red oak as you would for a mixture of apple, black cherry, and red maple.

Aside from the heating capacities involved, hardwood is hard wood. It is much heavier in terms of lugging and stacking. The most desirable way to divide your wood load would be to have it stacked and separated according to heating capacity. You could more easily be able to vary the stove temperature and begin to acquaint yourself with the identification of wood types.

Before using your chain saw for the first time, have someone accompany you who is familiar with it's use. A chain saw is a dangerous piece of equipment in the wrong hands. Follow all the manufacturer's instructions. All chain saws do not use the same fuel mixture. Be sure to take the advice of the manufacturer or dealer about what fuel would work best.

Transport and carry the chain saw with care. Leave the guard in place until you are ready to begin using the chain saw. Shut off the engine when it is not in use. Wear steel-toed shoes, a hard hat, gloves, and safety goggles. When the saw is in use, always grip it tightly. Brace your body against the engine handle. Never push on the cutting bar.

When your saw is not in use shut the engine off. If your saw is not cutting up to par, or perhaps smoking, your chain might be in need of adjustment or it just may require sharpening. Your saw should not require any more pressure than a gentle rocking motion. Tree sap can build up on the top backside of the teeth.

You can block out the potentially dangerous chain saw sounds by using fiberglass stuffing. Professional loggers put it in their ears to block out painful noises. Such fiberglass stuffing is often sold by chain saw dealers. Cotton will be of little help. In the cooler weather, earmuffs can also be of use.

Keeping your chain saw in good working order is of the utmost importance. Keep your saw from overheating. Brushing away the sawdust before it clogs the cooling fans on the cylinder will help you avoid repairs. Make sure that you completely clean the saw before storing the unit for the next wood-cutting season. High-pressure air or water will clean out the fins.

You can coat the inside of the motor with oil by removing the spark plug and putting a few drops of light engine oil in the cylinder. If you give the starting rope a pull or two, your oiling will be complete. Oil the chain. Before you put it away, do any tuning work that is necessary. Polish it. Make sure that you have emptied the gas tank completely.

Wood is not always sold in the standard cord size. Beware. A *standard cord* should stack up 4 feet in width and 8 feet in length. Technically, this adds up to 128 cubic feet, 80 feet of which is solid wood, but the remainder would be made up of the space in between the logs.

Many wood dealers advertise their wood sold "by the cord"; this is actually a *face cord*. The problem with the use of the term face cord, which is also sometimes referred to as a *run* or a *rick*, is that it does not have an absolute standard of measurement. A face cord can measure 8 feet long, 4 feet high, but less than 4 feet wide, and usually 2 feet wide. This type of face cord would equal half a standard cord and probably cost more than half a standard cord. Face cords are also sold only 16 inches wide; this represents one-third of a standard cord. The price of this type of face cord would again be higher than the cost of a standard cord of wood.

As with most products on the market, buying in bulk is much less expensive. In the case of a wood dealer, the smaller logs have been chopped and more work has been involved. On the other hand, there is also a loss in space that could equal up to 25 percent of the original cord if the logs are cut small enough.

When ordering your wood, specify the lengths that you want. The designs for each of the stove models in this book, list the log size that is best used for that particular unit. Make sure that you and the wood dealer come to terms on exactly what size cord you are ordering.

If you order your wood split, it will be more costly. If you are able to split your own wood, the wood will be less expensive and more easily identified by 4-foot lengths.

Wood is sometimes advertised as being sold by the truckload. This is usually done for practicality. The average pickup truck cannot hold a 2-ton full cord of wood. The problem with this standard of measurement is judging it's relationship to the standardized cord. The only way you would be able to determine it's exact measurement is if you haul the wood in a truck with a known capacity. Do not allow the wood to be unloaded from the truck until you have at least checked it's measurements by

eye. A full cord requires a truck the size of a dump truck. You must bear in mind that delivered wood is additionally expensive and the quoted price will not necessarily include stacking.

## BE PREPARED FOR LOGGING

How you are going to log your wood is a very important consideration. If you are able to bring your truck close to the site of the cutting, good, but if not a wheelbarrow might do the trick. If you are going to be driving your pickup truck over a rough logging road, your truck should have heavy suspension and cooling, and it definitely should be a four-wheel-drive vehicle.

If you decide to buck on the site of the felled tree, you will have to have other equipment such as a handsaw, a hacksaw, an extra blade for the hacksaw (or at least a sharpener), a sharpened axe, a sledge or splitting maul, and wedges.

When you begin your harvest of wood, it might even pay to have a professional accompany you on your first few expeditions. Never go out alone. You will need to know techniques that only someone skilled in this field can teach you.

Your harvest should begin with wood that is already downed. When this valuable debris is cleared, felling of other previously dead trees should begin. Felling a tree is a task not to be taken lightly. It requires both knowledge and skill, and most of all it requires safety.

Practice felling techniques, with professional guidance, on trees in pole stands. These trees will not provide the actual felling dangers of mature trees, but the process will serve to exhibit some of the dangers that are present in felling trees. Check the direction of the wind to establish whether it will coincide with the direction you determine your tree should be felled. The stiller the wind the better; it can spell trouble when it is too strong.

## FELLING A TREE

Know where the tree is going to fall. When it does, make sure that you are no where near it. If the tree is to fall in an eastward direction, plan to be northwest or southwest. To determine which way the tree is leaning, use a pencil dangling straight down, the eraser end being up, and compare it with the tree trunk to see which way the trunk is leaning.

The sites at three points should be checked. Stand a good arm's length away. To see which side is the most heavy with growth, put the pencil point at mid point of the base and walk around the tree. Compare the lean with the weight distribution. Make this judgment as if your life depended on it. As you become more experienced, do not allow yourself to be careless and lazy.

You will not want the downed tree to be hung up in the branches of another tree. You will want the tree to fall into a cleared area.

Check the immediate area for any trees that have died, but are still standing. The impact produced by a tree hitting the ground could knock over one of these "dead heads." Dead trees should have been the first to be harvested. If you find enough firewood from the dead trees, you will not have to fell the more potentially dangerous ones.

Before making the felling cut, make sure that you know exactly where you are going to be before the tree begins to lean. In other words plan your retreat. Trees should be cut to fall down the hill.

Cut off any limb that may seem to weigh the tree in the wrong direction. The trunk condition and the location of the limbs contribute to the balance of a tree. Make a cut, partially through the bottom of the limb, close to the trunk. Proceed to cut from the top down through to the bottom. The method of first cutting the bottom will prevent a hang up on a hinge or a healthy strip of bark as it goes.

To begin felling a tree, a notch must be cut in the fall side of the tree. This cut should go about one-third above the horizontal cut, as compared to the thickness of the tree. When this is completed, kick out the notch. The tree will begin to fall. The uncut portion acts like a hinge and it will guide the tree down as you want it.

If you feel that there is a risk that the tree will not fall right, or there is a chance of binding up the saw, do not complete the back cut. Use wedges to further open the cut and tilt the tree in the proper direction. The tree will begin to fall, slowly at first, but once that notch pops, it will move fast. Timber!

You have about five seconds to get to safety. Perhaps the tree will fall exactly the way you want it to, but it simply doesn't always happen. That is why, ideally, a professional should be at the site.

**Limbing.** Thoroughly check the felled tree before you begin to limb it. Limbing might seem like a fairly easy operation, but there are underlying dangers. There could be a great deal of compressed energy from the limbs that the tree is resting on; the limbs will be sprung. If you cut a limb that is full of this type of pressure, it could cause a serious accident.

It is a good idea to begin cutting the limbs, from the top, in pieces ranging from approximately 12 to 14 inches. This wood is lightest in weight. It is best to start with the limbs flush with the trunk. An axe will probably be adequate for the start of this job. Remove the branches that are not supporting the trunk from the base of the trunk on up. These are the free branches. Make your cuts as flush to the trunk as possible. This will avoid protruding stumps.

For safety sake, it is best to stand on the opposite side to the branch that you are cutting. Make sure that you keep the limb between you and the piece of equipment that is used for the cutting. Cut these limbs from the base side to the crotch.

After you have removed the free branches, you can begin to work on the supporting branches. You will have removed some pressure by removing the free branches first, but you will still have branches bent under pressure from the trunk weight. It would be best to cut these branches on the outside curve of the bend. If you do cut on the inside curve, you would be wise to have an axe or another saw available to put an additional cut in the trunk in case a tool is bound up.

You must work very quickly when cutting supporting branches. There is always a chance of a branch whipping out or the tree dropping or shifting. If you are working on an incline, it is best to work on the uphill side of the trunk. This will avoid the chance of the tree rolling on top of you, after you have freed all of the supporting branches.

**Bucking.** Bucking large pieces of wood is most easily done with a chain saw. First score each length. Work from the tip of the trunk to the base. Cut the trunk into lengths previously scored off. Cut the supporting branches as you come to them. If a section is free, that is not supported directly by a branch, the method of bucking differs. Make an undercut one-third the thickness of the section and finish it from the top side. This will allow the section to drop straight down. If you cut completely through the section from the topside, it could cause the outer end to drop prematurely.

Reverse the procedure when a section is supported by a branch. In such a case, the cut should be made from the top, approximately one-third through the thickness, and finished with an undercut. If you cut a supported piece completely through the top, it could cause buckling inward; this could bind the saw.

It is easiest if the trunk rests on the ground. You can then make all the cuts halfway through the thickness of the tree. After rolling the trunk over, you can finish making the cuts from the other side. If necessary, large sections of the wood can be lifted onto a sawbuck to complete bucking.

**Splitting.** Green wood splits more easily than dried wood. Splitting should take place soon after bucking. Pieces cut 6 inches in diameter are the speediest to dry. Use an anchored chopping block when splitting. It can be a stump that is larger in diameter than the largest piece of wood to be split. It is not a good idea to split wood directly on the ground. The dirt will not only dull your axe, but the ground absorbs much of the energy of the swing. Small pieces will require an average-size axe. Larger pieces can be easily split with a maul. A *maul* is a variety of an axe that has a heavy, blunt, thick-edged head. You might need a wedge or a sledge hammer for the larger pieces. You could make the first cut with a maul, insert the wedges, and then use the sledge hammer. The tools required will depend on the type of wood, the grain pattern, and the moisture content. It is best to chop the extremely bulky logs at the logging site and save the rest for homework.

When using splitting equipment, it is best to use a direct blow rather than an angular blow. Make your swing perpendicular to the piece of wood that you are splitting. If you center your body in front of the target and swing down directly in front of you, you will achieve better accuracy. Do not swing to one side. To make a clean split, it might help to rotate or twirl the handle of the axe, ever so slightly, when contact is made with the wood. It won't take much to get the hang of it.

## WOOD-CUTTING EQUIPMENT

If you are serious about woodcutting becoming a part of your life, it might pay to invest in log-splitting equipment. You can purchase log-splitting equipment that ranges from the simple to the elaborate. Unless you are cutting wood for yourself and for others, or if you will be selling some of your harvest, the elaborate equipment is not necessary.

## LAYING A FIRE

Last, but not at all least, is the laying of the fire itself, and it's management when heating with wood. Before starting a fire, you should be aware of the dangers involving the instant heat producers such as paper and kindling. You do not want to allow your fire to get out of control. Always make sure that there is proper ventilation within the room. Improper ventilation could result in slower airflow to the fire and smoke penetrating out into the room. The flue should be in excellent working order, and it could be checked by a professional before you commence the use of your solid-fuel unit.

The first step to building a good fire is to lay a bed of ash directly on the firebrick lining of the firebox. An inch or two of ash is best because more would be in conflict with good air flow. When cleaning your solid-fuel burner, consider saving the ashes in a bucket for laying a new fire and for covering burning logs with ash for the preservation of a longer fire life. Do not allow the ash to clog the air control system.

Make sure that you have a permanently opened damper. A closed damper would allow smoke to be emitted into the room (it would have no other place to go).

Start your fire with crumpled paper around very dry kindling. Use ½-inch to 1-inch diameter

## TOOLS AND EQUIPMENT

This section has been paraphrased, in part, from *HEATING WITH WOOD* by the Editors of "The Family Handyman" magazine,© 1978 by Butterick Publishing. By permission of New Century Publishers, Inc., Piscataway, New Jersey.

Be totally prepared with all the tools necessary for the variety of jobs, from felling to splitting, with the equipment necessary for the different types of wood. A large bow saw is worthwhile to have for it's many uses. Smaller saws are recommended for limbing. It might be difficult to find circular cutoff saws, timbersaws, and backsaws, but they are available through manufacturers or through mail order houses. They will be expensive, but worth the cost.

The circular cutoff saw is considered by specialists on the subject to be the fastest piece of equipment for reducing pole stand logs into firewood. This type of saw is often powered by tractor, but a small saw—that is in good working order—can be hooked up to an electric motor. This is a handy system and it runs fairly quietly for the cutting of saplings and branches.

Caution is always advisable when using any type of saw. There is always a hazard involved. If saws are not properly maintained, you might have to transform an inoperable saw into working order. Bear in mind that fitting a saw involves a process that is more than just sharpening the saw. Any wood-cutting saw—whether it is one-man, two-man, straight, or circular—can have crosscut or rip-cutting teeth.

Choose an axe that is a good weight (2½ pounds to 3½ pounds is preferable) so as not to induce fatigue. You will want to be able to take advantage of the axe's momentum. A single-bit axe can be used to drive felling wedges and for other household uses. An axe of a heavier weight discourages many of the safety rules that one should always maintain. The axe could easily bounce off it's target when a glancing blow is applied. You would be unable to take hold of small trees or brush while holding the axe and swinging with the other hand.

The size of the axe handle can be crucial. Most cutters are comfortable with a 30-inch axe handle (or what would be considered crotch high). Check the suitability of the axe handle material. Fast-growing hardwood handles are good choices. If you want to check the suitability of a handle by ring growth, it should show 16 or fewer growth rings per inch. The rings should run parallel with the cutting edge of the axe. Painted handles could cover up defects of the handle. This is especially true if the grain does not run the entire length of the handle. Make sure that the axe has been matched properly with the handle. The handle should line up with the bit upon sighting along it.

To complete your preparation of tools for woodcutting, it is best to include both a double-bit axe, a single-bit axe, splitting mauls (of 6 to 10 pounds in weight), and various sizes of splitting wedges.

soft woods such as lumber scraps for kindling. Lay the kindling in a crisscross fashion. This allows air to pass through, but it is close enough together to encourage the fire to spread. Arrange two to four logs in a sort of horizontal pyramid. Allow space between the logs for the air to circulate.

Use a progressive layer for the logs from small to large. It wouldn't hurt to add a little more kin-dling. This arrangement of the lobs, paper, and kindling will produce the type of fire that is slow in formation and performs combustion at it's greatest performance. Remember that the combustion process cannot take place without oxygen and high temperatures, and it must continue to take place throughout the burning process. Fire materials that are packed too tightly is probably the most common error that leads to a failure in building a good fire.

To make a good draw, first heat the chimney by holding a lighted piece of newspaper up to the chimney. Then light the pyramid arrangement by lighting the crumpled paper and allowing the fire to spread or place newspaper on the top of the pile. If the chimney has not been heated enough, expect some smoke to be emitted into the room. It will not last long.

Add logs gently. It is best to lay the new logs toward the rear of the solid-fuel burner on top of the burning fire. This way the additional logs will best be able to reflect heat off the back of the stove and into the room.

You can move the logs closer together once you have a good fire going. The heat that is reflected, between the logs, will keep the fire burning longer by providing the necessary temperatures for combustion.

Maintain the fire by the regular adjustment of the logs; push the ends of the logs into the flame. You can add more kindling if the fire needs to be revived. The coals might begin to die out if a slow burn is maintained. If a revival isn't necessary, then by all means add new logs in the fashion previously mentioned.

You should always rake the coals to the front of the firebox, but never past the front of the logs that are burning. Continue to let the ashes accumulate to a depth of 2 inches. This will allow a bed for the glowing coals to form, heat will be concentrated and drafts will be directed up through the base of the fire for more efficiency.

Bank the fire for an overnight burn. This is a good time to cover the burning logs with the saved ash to add to the burn time. In addition, adjust the air control to a slower rate for more complete efficiency.

If you need to rekindle a fire, just sift the ashes to the back of the firebox and add more kindling and some newspaper, if necessary, on top of the charcoal. If you know how to manage your fire, you will still have enough burn time to allow the night to pass without having to feed the fire.

☐ Never burn materials such as poison ivy twigs, plastics, or any material that is chemically treated, such as poles and railroad ties, that could produce noxious gases. Bear in mind that fumes can leave deposits on the wall of the flue that could be potentially dangerous, or even add sticky deposits to the ashes.

☐ Do not operate your solid-fuel burner without completely closed doors or a screen cover. A fire could get out of control in the time it takes you to answer the telephone. It does not make sense to take a chance.

☐ Do not use fire starters such as the liquids that are commonly used for barbequeing. A properly built fire will light just as fast.

☐ Keep a fire extinguisher handy at all times.

☐ Never operate your solid-fuel unit without a safe and properly operating chimney.

# Chapter 4

# Heating with Coal

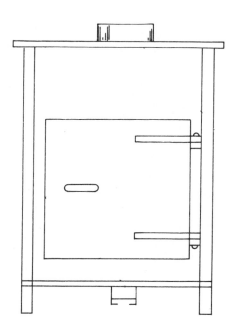

THERE IS A VERY STRONG argument for heating with wood, but coal is a heating source that can be an equally economic fuel. Methods for burning coal have changed since the time coal was used as this country's primary source of heat. Safe mining methods have been developed along with new burning techniques that are considered environmentally safe.

Wood was our primary source of heat until approximately the middle of the nineteenth century. At the time, petroleum products were first being developed, coal began replacing wood as our primary heating source.

Woodburning and coalburning were in no way as efficient in those times as it would be now. Pot-bellied stoves, being used then, were made of cast iron and the doors were somewhat less than airtight. The firebox and the flue were ill-fitted. A home's warmth could not reach anything close to it's fullest potential.

## ADVANTAGES AND DISADVANTAGES

Most people think that burning coal produces soot and dinginess. This is certainly understandable because coal is black, smudgy, and dirty. There are many problems associated with mining coal, and coal gases are potentially dangerous. In addition, coal is not easily ignited. Coal burning is not always an easy process. You will have a much better chance of using coal successfully if you take the time to learn about it. I suggest that you read *HOME HEATING WITH COAL* by Steve Sherman, published by Stackpole Books. This author has thoroughly researched the subject of coal.

Many people do not feel that it is worth their time to cut down enough trees to equal 5 or 6 cords of wood. Because the woodlands have been previously mismanaged, wood is not always as readily available in some parts of our country. This increases the price of the wood per cord to exorbitant levels. This situation would obviously not justify a switch from your existing heating system to wood as fuel. There is also the consideration of the space needed for seasoning the wood, the increased need for chimney cleaning, and the time required for seasoning green wood. When these factors are weighted, the use of coal as a heating fuel might be your best choice.

Coal producers have developed an excellent method of production and distribution. Railroad carloads of coal are delivered to coal dealers in areas where coal is in demand. Coal can be used immediately upon delivery.

A ton of coal is the approximate heating equivalent of a cord of hardwood, and takes up only 50 cubic feet as compared to the 128 cubic feet that a cord of hardwood would take up. Rain and snow have little effect on coal. Even if snow is allowed to melt and refreeze on a coal pile, it will not soak in. A tarp or a piece of heavy plastic is all that is required to cover a coal pile that is kept out of doors.

It is difficult to compare the cost of wood and coal because prices vary a great deal throughout the country. In other words the gap between the prices of wood and coal do not have the same relationship in all parts of the United States. Just as wood is in short supply in some parts of the country so is coal. If a dealer has to go to great lengths to obtain the type of coal you choose, there will be a cost increase reflected.

In most cases, a ton of anthracite coal is approximately equal to 170 gallons of fuel oil and it is equal to 1 full cord of a very hard wood or 1½ cords of a medium-hard wood. If a ton of coal costs $100, which is a fair conjecture, then the obvious savings of fuel oil use would be at least $70. If your coal stove is set up properly, coal can burn with 90 percent efficiency. That figure injects optimism; it would be best to use 70 percent efficiency as a base for comparison.

We have barely touched our coal resources. This country has approximately 30 percent of all the coal beds that are recoverable in the world. We are not going to run into long-range shortages. Coal provides for less than 20 percent of the energy demands in this country, and that is mostly consumed by industry and public utilities. On a national basis, residential use of coal is negligible.

*Acid rain* is a result of the coal-burning process. Sulfur and nitrogen oxides are emitted from the smokestacks of utility companies and factories. With the wind in action, these oxides can be mixed with the water in the atmosphere and come back to Earth. Restraints and standards have been recently enacted. We will need more of the same such rulings for the future.

There are now strict federal pollution standards for new coal-fired plants. Industry is being forced into developing methods necessary to begin the elimination of many of the harmful elements of burning coal. Right now there is work being done on the upgrade of *fluidized bed combustion*. This means combining a bed of hot coal and limestone granules. The limestone allows the coal to burn at a lower temperature, and this prevents pollutants such as nitrogen oxides from being formed. Further, the sulfur that would be released in the burning of bituminous coal combines with the calcium in the limestone. The sulfur is actually trapped in the limestone and the ashes are unable to escape.

Consumers can improve their coal-burning standards. This is not particularly difficult. Use low-sulfur coal in your solid-fuel unit. Efficiently maintain flues and chimneys, and use the better methods of burning coal developed by modern technology.

The use of anthracite coal is a good choice for, efficient burning and as a more environmentally, safe fuel. This country has a more plentiful supply of bituminous coal but anthracite coal has a considerably, lower percentage of sulfur, fewer volatiles to be burned off, and a higher percentage of fixed carbons. The chief value of anthracite coal lies in the way that it burns. It provides a red-hot glow at a steady rate. Warmth is provided more immediately and you do not have to wait for the flames to burn off the gases.

**Ash.** Nonburnable elements form ash; this is inorganic substances. More than three times the amount of ash will form in an anthracite coal fire than forms in a wood fire. This ash will interfere with the efficiency of the coal fire. Coal ash forms into chunks, referred to as *clinkers,* that must be removed. Coal ash cannot be recycled as easily as the ash formed from a wood fire. Wood ash has high potassium levels and coal ash can have heavy metals present. Do not use coal ash as a fertilizer. Nevertheless, coal ash can be used to melt an icy walkway and it can also make an excellent cinder.

**Creosote.** Creosote is a potential danger that results from burning wood. This is especially true when you are burning unseasoned wood. Creosote, being dark, flaky, and sticky, can adhere to the sides of the flue. If thick amounts of creosote are allowed to accumulate, being a very volatile property, it can easily combust and cause a fire.

Coal creates no creosote. It does, however, produce a substance in the chimney called *fly ash*. Fly ash does not ignite. The chimney will just need to be freed of it, on a seasonal basis, to keep it from clogging.

**Coal Gases.** Although both wood and coal produce gases such as carbon dioxide, carbon monoxide, hydrogen, nitrogen, and sulfur, they do so at different proportions. The efficiency of the solid-fuel unit—in the way in which it uses up these gases—will be determined by the completeness of the burning during combustion (changing carbon monoxide into carbon dioxide). Some bituminous coals contain as much as 2 percent sulfur. Anthracite coal contains only traces more sulfur than is contained in wood.

As in the combustion of wood, ignition of the gases cannot happen unless temperatures of over 1000 degrees Fahrenheit are present along with oxygen. For the units described in this book, air for combustion is brought into the firebox at the lowest level possible. This allows the fire to burn from the center out and from the bottom up.

## HOW TO BUY COAL

Before you go out to buy coal, it is important that you have an understanding of what it is that you are buying. There are many grades and classifications of coal. Do not be fooled into buying a "poor man's coal" or a coal that does not have the components that will make it an efficient alternate source of heating. Lack of knowledge can cause you to give up on burning coal. If you know what you are doing, you will have a much better chance of attaining success.

Thoroughly investigate the market in your area to see if the grade of coal you want to burn will be readily available to you in not just one season, but also in the next few seasons to come. You must

determine what prices to expect. There is no sense to even building a unit that uses a particular solid fuel if you are not going to be able to obtain the quality or quanity of fuel that you need.

What exactly is coal? It is sometimes debated whether coal should be considered organic material or inorganic material. *Coal* is defined as a black combustible mineral substance that has resulted from the partial decomposition of vegetable debris, away from air and under various degrees of increased temperature and pressure, over a period of perhaps a million years.

A *mineral* is described as an *inorganic* substance that has occurred naturally in the earth's surface, and has components that can be expressed by a chemical formula. This can be applied to a substance of *organic* origin, such as coal. Organic is defined as being composed of living organisms.

Classifications of coal are ranked by the degree of density caused by the geological pressure under which the material was transformed. The three classifications of coal are *lignite*, the softest coal, *bituminous*, a soft coal found in tremendous reserves, and *anthracite*, a hard coal that has the best-burning qualities. The components of each grade of coal vary. In other words, it is possible to have bituminous coal that contains the proper components for better burning efficiency, and anthracite coal that contains components that would not make it of the best burning quality.

The first thing that should be determined is the amount of fixed carbon that the coal contains. The carbon content is the determinent of the firepower of coal and the ignition temperature. Although a high percentage of fixed carbon very often does mean a high burning temperature—combined with other factors such as it's relation to volatile matter and ash content—it does not necessarily contribute to a super-hot fire all of the time.

The proper relationship of fixed carbons can contribute to an efficient, even burn. In anthracite coal, when a high fixed carbon rate is present, there is a need on the stove for a precision air feed inlet, or lower air control system, to introduce the air directly to the coal fire. If there are areas within the firebox where air can pass, without reaching the fire, the coal will be extremely difficult to ignite. Just bear in mind that you do want a high percentage rate of fixed carbons in your coal. A good rate would be considered over 80 percent and under 90 percent.

Volatile gases are an important concern. If a high percentage of volatile gases are present, especially in a lower grade of coal, it will produce a long flame that might produce smoke and could leave a fused ash.

A high percentage of volatile matter in the coal can release excessive hydrocarbons during the burning process. A quality air control system is of utmost importance in burning these gases. If the air control system is unable to complete the burning of these gases, the gases can condense in the flue pipes and chimneys and create blockage. The noxious products of the combustion process will be emitted into the living area of the house. This could take place within a two-week period or take a much longer time for the blockage to be created.

You can learn to appreciate the value of the secondary air control system when you realize that, by burning a coal high in volatile matter in a solid-fuel unit that has not been designed to deal with these gases, a back flashing explosion could be created above the combustion zone due to the buildup of hot volatile gases. There have been cases when the loading doors have been blown open or even off of furnaces and stoves.

The efficiency of the solid-fuel unit will be significantly reduced due to a loss of energy from the volatiles released. You stand the chance of a black odorous smoke escaping into the atmosphere and sullying the environment.

Low volatile gases will cause the coal to burn with a short flame or, possibly, no flame at all. When a high grade coal contains low volatile matter, it will take a longer time to ignite; this is not a bad sign. Anthracite coal can contain less than 11 percent of the volatile gases; 5 percent would be considered ideal.

Ash content should be low. Obviously, the higher the ash content the more ash that is formed. Some anthracite coal that is being sold has a 15 percent ash content. Anthracite coal should have less than a 12 percent ash content. Although 7 percent ash content is normal, coal with a lower percentage is to your advantage.

Ash interferes with the efficiency of a coal fire. The clinkers formed by ash are a nuisance. They must be removed or they will stop a fire. Ash should fall through the grate to the ash pan. That is not a real problem other than the ash pan has to be emptied on a continual basis. The problem with ash content is that it is a nonburnable substance. The higher percentage of ash in the coal the less burnable substance will remain.

Check the sulfur content of the coal. Sulfur burns odorous gases. This is certainly not desirable. This pollution is often associated with the burning of coal. Sulfur also is the element— especially when mixed with a high ash content— that is a leading cause of clinkers. Sulfur content should always be under 2 percent and preferably it should be under 1 percent.

Moisture content can be crucial to an efficient burn. Moisture must be burned off at the first stage of combustion. This effects the amount of a radiant heat that is expelled from the product. If there is a high moisture content, there will not be as much solid fuel for heat output. For maximum efficiency, coal should contain less than 5 percent moisture.

Coal should be high in fixed carbons, for burning temperature, low in volatile gases for better flame control, low in ash content, and low in sulfur content. If a coal dealer is unwilling to give you statistics, then you cannot be sure of what you are getting. A telephone conversation with a coal dealer should take less than five minutes. A coal dealer with a good product should have no reason to be reluctant to give you the information that you request. If you do not know what you are burning and what to look for, you should not be using an alternate source of heat.

By understanding the components of coal, you will generally know what to expect and you will be better able to use this energy source more than just adequately and without too many surprises. You will need to experiment, at the beginning, to get the best results. You will be better able to understand what to expect if you know about factors such as the ash fusion temperature, the percentage of organic and inorganic materials, and the tendency of the coal to agglomerate. For a complete combustion efficiency analysis, check the percentages of carbon, hydrogen, nitrogen, and oxygen.

The following text contains, basically, the kinds of coal that you will encounter on the market. Weigh your particular needs against the prices of your present heating system and alternate sources of heat. Some coals can be mechanically compressed to obtain better characteristics.

**Peat.** Peat is coal in it's young stage. It is being used overseas with the aid of mechanical compression and a drying-out process. The radiant heat that can normally be expected would be comparatively low. This coal is also used in commercial ventures.

**Lignite.** Lignite is the softest of the more mature coals. It is sometimes referred to as *brown coal.* It's hardness has been produced by natural geological means, but during the mining process it has a tendency to fragment. It easily smudges. As it is high in volatile gases, special precautions have to be taken to prevent spontaneous combustion even when it is being used industrially. It has little value for the home consumer.

**Black Lignite.** In between bituminous coal and lignite, there is a coal that is referred to as black lignite. It's characteristics are no more desirable for the home consumer than the brown lignite variety. It also smudges and it has a tendency to crumble. It is black and its components have relatively little quality.

**Bituminous Coal.** Bituminous coal, a soft coal, is the most available coal in this country. Although bituminous coal is not usually the most efficient burning coal, this type of coal has been used by homeowners for decades. It is dense and it usually breaks into uniform-size pieces. This, in addition, to the varieties of lower volatile gases (about 30 percent) contributes to a more even heating quality.

It can be burned in solid-fuel units with some efficiency. The bituminous coals are further subdivided into varieties. The color can vary from a greyish color to very black. It easy soils. *Cannel coal,* a popular variety of the bituminous coals,

burns with a candle-like glow. It does contain a high percentage of volatile matter.

**Anthracite.** Anthracite coal is a hard coal. It is the most compact of the coals. The various subdivisions of anthracite coal are all usually shiny. Smudging is not usually, a characteristic. The volatile gases are usually low in relationship to it's usual high fixed carbon rate. It will burn with short flames (if any visible flames) and emit an even heat. Anthracite coal takes a fairly long period of time to reach high ignition temperatures—which would be approximately 660 degrees Fahrenheit—but, then it will burn for a much longer time and with a consistent burn rate.

Most coal is sold in five or six sizes. Stove-size coal is the largest; it is about fist size. Rice-size coal is penny size. For the solid-fuel units, described in this book, nut-size coal is highly recommended. It is just a little smaller than the stove-size coal. The grate designs for these units will not tolerate any of the smaller-size varieties. This size coal, of the better character anthracite varieties, will produce a good heat value.

Anthracite coal requires a precise air feed inlet because it contains less volatile matter. The designs described in this book have fully focused drafts, as provided in the lower air controls, allowing the required air intake to ignite anthracite coal. Bituminous coal, on the other hand, does not require as much oxygen to burn to it's full capacity.

In other stove models, where a precise air feed inlet is not provided, bituminous coal would be a better choice because it would still be able to burn to it's full potential. Anthracite coal would not be able to do so. Pea-size coal will not be able to burn on the grate designs provided in this book.

Coal dealers, usually the larger ones, might be able to offer you coal that has been previously coated with an oil, at the preparation plant, before being shipped to the dealer. This oil, which might be a banana oil, is used to aid in the reduction of the dust usually associated with coal. This is certainly worth considering because it will eliminate the dirt that could rub off on your hands, clothes, and storage areas. This convenience will make the coal seem almost dustless.

You should be aware of the various types of manufactured forms of coal. The pressed shapes, that are to be burned in the fireplace as a substitute for log burning, are usually made of a bituminous or even a lignite coal. If you read the package carefully, the candle-like glow, that many of these forms of coal present, is the burning characteristic of cannel coal. Although the sulfur content has, in most cases, been measurable reduced to eliminating most of the odor it is still not a good substitute for natural coal.

These "fireplace coals" are not recommended for use in anything other than a fireplace, definitely do *not* use this product in a coal stove. It usually will contain a substantial amount of volatile materials that have a tendency to expand when heated. If it is burned in a confined area, the fire could become too big and too hot. It will not be readily controlled, and a small explosion of this volatile material could occur. Their expense is not condusive to saving energy costs. They have been designed to create a friendly fire, in the fireplace, where their energy is simply wasted up the chimney. The average fireplace is rarely evaluated at more than 10 percent efficient. The coal stove can be used with 90 percent efficiency.

Upon embarking on a new coal-burning experience, you might want to experiment with the burning of the various sizes and classifications of coal. Do not begin by buying your solid fuel in bulk. Although it might seem much more expensive, in some cases, to buy by the bag rather than by the ton, it will be beneficial to you not to have already bought a large quantity of coal that has unsatisfactory burning qualities.

Once you have decided upon the coal that burns best for you, in the combination of burning characteristics and economy, then buy by the ton or even by the truckload if that is feasible. Buying coal by the ton is common. You might be able to have it discounted by buying over 5 tons or via the truckload system. If you are in a mining region, you might very well be able to obtain quite a savings by purchasing your coal directly from a wholesaler. In such a case, you will probably have to pick up the coal yourself. If you buy your coal from a dealer, transportation costs might be tacked on as an additional expense.

Here's how a coal-dealing operation works. When your order is being handled, the coal truck travels to the storage area, usually a large silo of coal, that is located near the railroad tracks for convenience of the delivery from the mines or wholesalers. The coal will then be chuted into the truck.

Weighing takes place when the truck is driven over the scale. The scale that the truck is driven over is very much the same as the scales that are used for weighing cargo trucks at state inspection stations. The scale will be a certified state inspected scale and it will imprint a receipt of the transaction. The truck weight, having been predetermined, will be subtracted from the total weight to give you an accurate calculation of the coal weight. The coal can now be delivered to your home.

You must decide how the coal will be dropped off at your home and stored. A coal bin is not a necessity, because the elements have so little effect upon the burning qualities. Nevertheless, it will make the storage of your coal much more convenient. It will make access to the coal an easier procedure.

Coal should be stored in a cool area, below 75° F. Coal can be stored in an excavation, but that would involve stepping into the hole and hauling it out. If necessary, the coal could be left in a pile with nothing more than a tarp for covering. It would be a good idea to weigh this tarp down with rocks or pipes to keep snow and ice out.

You will need a 4-foot by 4-foot storage bin to accommodate about 2 tons of coal. Note that nut coal weighs in the vicinity of 58 pounds per cubic foot. You can purchase an inexpensive plywood bin for your purpose. Some coal users prefer a more elaborate container, to blend in with their garage or house.

Galvanized trash barrels can be used to great advantages. Bear in mind, that whatever your storage container consists of, it must be accessible to coal delivery truck. The driver is going to chute the load into the storage area. The area must be free of elements and debris that would prevent the coal truck from being driven to the chute.

If you are going to have your coal chuted

through a basement window, into a bin or whatever, the window should be one that will not be inaccessible at the time of delivery. If you do decide to build a permanent storage area for your coal, allow enough room for the possibility of an automatic stoker, to work in conjunction with an add-on boiler. It would be advisable to completely enclose the area, from the floor to the ceiling, to prevent the dust from flying. It would also keep the coal from view. The storage area will become a separate compartment in the room.

## BURNING COAL

To understand the benefits of the stove designs in this book you should have an understanding of how to lay a coal fire, how it burns, and what to expect. Do not even begin to use your solid-fuel unit until you have checked to be sure that your installation has been done safely and legally according to the building codes in your area. A homeowner's insurance policy could be easily voided if you have not followed all the codes that the policy requires.

Check the chimney to make sure that there is no debris blocking the chimney opening. Make sure that you check the exhaust pipe to be sure that the stove pipe dampers are open. If you are using an add-on boiler system, check your piping system (the inlet and outlet pipes to your heating system, and if you have installed a domestic coil, those inlet and outlet lines) to be sure all check valves are completely open. You have to be sure that the aquastate, which controls your minicirculator, is set high enough to prevent the circulator from coming on until the water reaches the desired temperature. Manually lift 30-pound safety valve to be sure that it is in good operating order and free of any scale that would prevent it from opening in the event of an emergency.

Proceed by moving the sliding baffle plate toward the front of the solid-fuel burner, fully exposing the exhaust pipe. All of the slides should be open (those used for both wood burning and coal burning). This will aid in starting a fast fire.

An understanding of the working principles of the secondary air control on the units described in this book is a must. For a coal fire, the reason for using the secondary air control is solely to aid the venting of coal gases created by the coal fire. This is done by allowing fresh air into the top of the firebox through the secondary air slide. This air, while not effecting the coal fire itself, does effect the draw in the chimney.

Giving the chimney another source to draw air speeds up the draw in the chimney. Therefore, coal gases are vented at a faster rate. With a wood fire, the baffle plate is slid back in front of the exhaust pipe. The secondary air slide provides fresh air to the natural gas (which is trapped by the baffle) produced in wood burning. The air and gas combined causes ignition. In either case, the secondary air slide should only be used for 1 to 15 minutes after loading your coal. This will be the time when most of the coal gases are created. In wood burning, the secondary air is only used when a really hot fire is desired.

For the designs in this book, the secondary air system is always located at the highest point possible in the firebox. This is to protect the secondary air from coming in contact with the coal fire. If the secondary air is located too low, it will have a tendency to dampen down (or slow down) the burning process of the coal. This is because air coming in from such a low level will restrict the air coming in under the grate—an absolute necessity for coal burning.

This would not allow the air to be pushed up or passed through the coal, and it will therefore slow down the coal-burning process. Bear in mind that the secondary air controls will act in *no way* to regulate your fire. To regulate the temperature, you must use the main air controls, underneath the grate, that supplies the actual feed air.

Before you actually begin to build a fire, become familiar with the basic characteristics of a coal fire. Coal is very, very dense. This particular solid fuel requires a higher ignition temperature (about 660° F) than wood. Coal builds heat very slowly. It works at a constant pace. The only one way to speed up this process is to force air in (at a high rate of speed), under the grate with the use of a blower fan (squirrel cage blower).

This is not recommended because, once the fire is running properly, the blower will no longer be needed and it must be removed. In addition, the opening must be closed off to prevent air from uncontrollably entering. Remember too that each variety of coal will burn differently. Some burn with high flames, some burn with low flames, some burn with a crackling sound, others burn with an odor. You will have to aquaint yourself with the standard characterizations of the coal that you use.

**Starting a Fire.** To start a fire, oxygen, solid fuel, and a hot enough, ignition temperature—for the solid fuel that is being burned—is necessary. The more completely that a solid fuel burns the more efficient the solid-fuel burner will operate.

To start a coal fire, begin by placing crumpled newspaper on the grate. The more newspaper that you use, the faster the chimney will be able to heat up and start the chimney drawing. Place kindling wood on the crumpled newspaper. Lighting the kindling wood will create the temperatures necessary for the ignition of larger wood (regular fire wood), and then the coal. If you leave a layer of ash, about 1 or 2 inches thick, it will help to insulate the grate from overheating and it might prevent some of the coal from falling through the grate.

The third ingredient, oxygen, is needed for complete combustion. It is being supplied by the air that has been induced through the lower air controls. Air is pushed up through the coal at a controlled rate of speed and it is continually pushed up the flue pipe and out of the chimney. Understanding a simple law, that heat rises and smoke is lighter than air, you can visualize how a chimney pulls the hot rising air, grown lighter from the fire, into a continuous drawing action. This continuous drawing action will draw the air from the main air controls (for coal burning), through the coals and up and out of the chimney. A draft is created.

To light the newspaper, do not use any type of charcoal lighter, kerosene, or paint thinner. You are starting a fire in a confined space (the firebox), and fumes could build up in the top of the firebox and cause an explosion when a match is lit. The fumes, being lighter than air, will rise to the top of the top of the firebox and build a layer of ignitable gases. When a match is lit, if those ignitable gases are low enough or once the paper catches fire and the flame reaches those gases, there is a chance of ignition and an explosion. This can happen because the gases ignite into flame when the draw of the chimney is not working properly. Due to the lack of having the chimney heated, there is no place for the flame to go but out of the mouth of the door.

**Regulating a Fire.** Once the kindling has started you can add larger wood until you have a large wood fire going. Make sure to allow for space between the wood pieces for the proper circulation of air. Place three scoop fulls of coal in the fire. After you have added the coal (for the wood and coal boiler *only*), close the wood-air control, located in the firebox door. From this point on, use only the air controls, located under the grate, and the secondary air control that is located at the top of the firebox door.

For the radiant stoves described in this book, the air control will act as your air control for both the wood and coal. When burning coal in your radiant stove, make sure—in addition to using your air control and air-feed inlet—to use your secondary air slides located in the top of the door or doors.

Leave the lower air controls open enough to provide a good amount of oxygen. You might have to adjust them according to the classification and characteristics of the coal that you are burning. You will learn, in time, what will work best in your particular case. Once that you have added coal, you must keep the main door and ash door *closed*. The more that you open the door, the longer that it will take to ignite the coal. Opening the door effects the burning process of the coal, by interrupting the stove draw.

Wait about 40 to 50 minutes and then you can open the door and add more coal. You do not want to add too much coal at a time. You are now building your coal bed. Keep your ignited coal in a pile. Continue to repeat this process. You should be able to build a good bed of coal. You will want your fire bed to build up to approximately 8 inches deep. Most likely you will have better efficiency, when burning coal, if you keep the coal in a deep bed. Remember, coal does need a lot of oxygen to circulate and create the needed heat. Follow the methods recommended, when adding new coal to old coal, for the particular characteristics of coal that you are burning.

You will build up some ash, and possibly clinkers, as the fire begins to build. It is not usually necessary to shake down the fire until new fuel is required unless the accumulation of ash is excessive. Once or twice a day will be generally sufficient. When you do shakedown your coal, use a few short strokes. Stop when you notice the first red coals appear. You do not want to overshake the coal nor undershake it. *Undershaking* might keep the proper amount of oxygen from reaching the fire, but *overshaking* could cause the fire to die.

If you want to recover coal that has not fully burned, you can screen the ashes through a piece of ¼-inch to ⅜-inch. When it is necessary to refuel the fire, rake the coals forward. Allow the ashes to shake down and get rid of any of the fused ash that could interfere with the burning process.

Although clinkers can be caused by coals with a low-ash fusion temperature, it is difficult to determine the ash fusion temperature because there are any number of conditions that will relate to the mineral content of the ash.

Leave an area of approximately 10 inches in diameter exposed. This is especially important if you are using anthracite coal. Never totally cover a bed of glowing coals with new ignited coals. Leaving an area exposed allows the new coals to quickly burn off their gases soon after ignition. Although the secondary air system will continue to do it's job well, the hotter area will pull these gases up and out. This will eliminate any chance of accumulation and sudden ignition.

**The Draft.** Draft is the turbulence, or the speed of the air, that passes from the room into the solid-fuel unit. It provides the much-needed oxygen for the feed air from the lower air controls. This is never a problem in homes that are not well insulated. The newer homes, being constructed with good insulation in mind, are sometimes too airtight. If an adequate amount of oxygen does not reach the fire, there is a possibility that not all of the gases from the coal will ignite and burn off. The completeness of the burning process cannot be accomplished. The carbon monoxide is not transformed and it could build up in the room.

Cracking open a window will create the necessary draft. The chimney will draw the air through the fire, and the fire will burn with more efficiency.

**Banking the Fire.** Banking the fire at night will call for a fire with lower temperatures. This is a good time to empty the ash pan. Shake the grate down enough to allow for a sufficient amount of coal to remain for an all-night burn. Do not forget to rake the coals forward, leaving a space exposed, to allow for the gases to burn off.

A coal fire should never be poled or broken up. This will do nothing more than defeat your purpose by bringing ash to the surface of the bed. There it could fuse and create lumps or clinkers that would obviously interfere with the complete burning process.

Pile the coal higher toward the back of the firebox, sloping it to the fuel door. Reduce the temperature if you are using an add-on boiler. Do not attempt to slow down the fire too much. Your fire could die or the household temperature could be reduced during the course of the night.

**Special Instructions.** Burning bituminous coal is similar to burning anthracite coal, but once the coal fire has been established it will require tending of a little different nature. When adding coal to an existing fire, add it to the center of the firebox to form a cone shape. If possible, the larger pieces should be placed to the outside of the pile. This will allow more of the primary air to flow through to create a hot fire to surround the coal. This heat will aid in driving off the volatile gases. The turbulence that is created will increase the efficiency of the solid-fuel unit.

The air controls should be adjusted about the same as you would if you were burning anthracite coal. An exception is that more secondary air might be necessary to burn the additional volatile gases that usually accompany bituminous coal. When banking the fire at night, you will have to check for a caking, crust-like layer. If this is the case, carefully poke at it. Make sure that you do not mix up the coal because this increases the possible formation of clinkers. Break up the cone shape, just a little, and add the fresh coal to the center of the pile. Bear in mind that the burning of bituminous coal will involve more maintenance, and probably more dirt and soot.

## THE GRATE

The design for shaker grate in this book can be greatly improved. It does have the necessities. There is only one moving part for the shaker grate. Moving parts in solid-fuel units can warp due to heat or they can burn out (whether it is cast iron or steel). The *cradle grate* has been specifically designed for the wood and coal combination boiler. Both sides of the cradle go up on an angle in the form of a V. To shake it down, you rock it back and forth. The only moving part is the grate itself.

Another type of shaker grate is the lever-type grate. These types of grates must be purchased from a foundry or from a dealer of coal stoves as additional parts. It will be difficult to fit the grate into the models that are designed in this book or any solid-fuel unit that it was not specifically designed for. These are sections of grate, usually 4 or 5 inches wide, that taper down to a point and resemble a triangle. The bottoms of these pieces are tied into a rod that pivots. As you push down and pull up on the lever, outside of the stove, sections of grate rotate around in a circle. The mechanical action of this type of shaker grate is fine, but over a period of time armatures and rotating connecting parts will warp. Once they do, it will automatically prevent the shaker from rotating.

Another type of shaker grate that you may be able to purchase is the circular type. This is actually a square grate with a circular grate in the middle of it. These both sit on the same level. You stick a bar into the circular part and rotate it back and forth. This action is what shakes the ashes down. This type of system has very few moving parts that can freeze, warp, or burn out.

The do-it-yourselfer should stay with the cradle grate for the models of stoves and boilers described in this book. It is easily constructed and it has only one moving part. The only problem that this grate has is a tendancy to warp. This is because steel expands when it is heated. The grate is welded together and the steel has no room for expansion. Therefore, the steel buckles or warps.

Cast iron almost never warps (it has little capability to expand and contract). The reason the grates described in this book are made of steel,

rather than cast iron, is that steel, while it may warp, will not burn out. It will take a tremendous amount of heat and it will last a very long time. As a true "do-it-yourselfer," you can always construct a new grate in the event that it becomes necessary. This will not be the case for a long time to come, and especially if you burn coal that does not have to heat up to high temperatures to radiate a sufficient amount of heat.

The ash content of the coal that you burn has a significant effect on the life of any coal grate. If you continuously burn a grade of coal that is low in ash content (below 6 percent), it will take longer for the ashes to build up over the exposed parts of the grate. This will result in rapid oxidation and possible warping of the grate. Of course, a high ash content, contained in coal, will require the frequent shaking down of the ashes. This will increase the period of time within each of the burning cycles that hot coal is exposed to the grate. This too will possibly result in oxidized and warped grates.

## THE ASH PAN

The ash pan should be made out of sheet metal. This is basically because a very large ash pan is required for the wood and coal combination boiler. It would be too heavy and expensive if it were made of steel. It is really much more convenient and economical to present the ash pan design to a sheet-metal shop and have it made for you.

## OPTIONAL EQUIPMENT

There are a number of options that can be bought to help your coal stove or boiler reach maximum efficiency. The solid-fuel burners described in this book operate by manual control. You will have to weigh the worth of optional controls for your particular situation.

**Thermostats.** Automatically controlled thermostats are sometimes recommended for a coal fire, but I really feel that their purpose is defeated in a wood fire. Because moving parts near the heat output of a wood fire are not recommended use manual control.

A bimetal thermostat, which is used to automatically control the draft intake, is actually a heat-sensing spring. It works on the same principle as an automatic choke of a car. With the bimetal thermostat, the operating principle is the same. When the spring is closed, a rod or a chain holds the air control open. This allows air to enter the firebox, and the fire is enlarged. As the fire gets hotter, the spring begins to expand—turning or pushing a shaft or chain—closing the air control. This is how the bimetal thermostat controls the fire.

If you want to use this particular thermostat, it can be hooked into the sliding air control system. It would, however, operate by going back and forth instead of around. A bimetal thermostat is futile in a wood fire, but because a coal fire burns differently it can have value. The heat sensing spring is attached to the stove. This automatically opens and closes the damper pedal, therefore, it can pick up the radiant heat from the sides of the stove and will adjust according to that temperature and not the room temperature.

Another type of control is the mercury control. This is perhaps the most precise system. Nevertheless, this type of system is usually electrically operated. In the event of a breaker switch being thrown or an electric blackout, the system would give inaccurate control of the fire. It functions like a liquid thermostat, and it is attached to the primary feed intake air controls. It is a very small tube that is balanced on wires. The mercury causes the thermostat to tilt back and forth. This gives the maximum amount of control over fuel.

**Barometric Damper.** A barometric damper can be referred to as a secondary air system for fuel oil furnaces or natural gas furnaces. It supplies the extra air to the chimney to help vent exhaust fumes in oil and gas furnaces.

Most barometric dampers operate on a counterweight principle. A counterweight is set in a shaft and connected to the bottom of a damper plate. The damper plate is set vertically into the exhaust pipe with a tee.

By adjusting the weight, you also adjust the vertical balance of the damper. The damper can then easily open on it's own due to the suction effect of the draw in the chimney. Once the oil furnace or gas furnace, is turned off, the draw ceases in the chimney. The barometric damper closes due to the weight of the counterweight.

Before hooking up a solid-fuel burner, check local and state building codes. Some states require that, when a coal-burning radiant unit or a boiler unit is hooked up, a barometric damper be installed inside the exhaust pipe. This supposedly will help vent the coal gases up the chimney.

While understanding and appreciating the concern of state and local officials trying to deal with the problem of coal gases, it is difficult to see the necessity of a barometric damper being installed onto a coal-exhaust chimney. Unlike oil or gas furnaces, a coal furnace or radiant stove burns continuously. This causes a continuous draw in the chimney; in turn this will cause the barometric damper to always be open.

Bearing in mind the principles of chimney draw, this would make the starting of a wood fire difficult and the starting of a coal fire almost impossible. The chimney can draw air from an alternate source. Therefore, it would cease to draw air from the firebox. In a short period of time this would cause your coal fire to go out because no air would be drawn through the coal unless the draft of the chimney is negative. A *negative draft* occurs when an excess of air is allowed to be drawn up the chimney.

If your building codes demand such an installation, or if you feel it would be an aid to your coal burning capabilities, it would be wise to contact a serviceman to measure your draft. It would certainly have a purpose in a chimney that provides a negative draft. The barometric damper is set up in such a way that if a strong wind blown across the chimney—drawing up the draft from the hotter air in the firebox any faster than you want it regulated—it can provide a steady pressure of the draw from the air intake, through the solid fuel, and up and out of the chimney. This will result in a more efficient burn rate.

**Automatic Stokers.** An automatic stoker can make your add-on coal boiler operate with the same ease as just setting your thermostat. An automatic stoker is designed to automatically draw the coal from a bin and feed it to the add-on boiler unit. This will eliminate the manual action of feeding the coal, maintaining the fire, and shaking down the ashes. Your only responsibility is to keep the coal bin full and empty the ash barrel on occasion.

There are many varieties of these stokers on the market. The price range of some might seem out of sight, but a good automatic stoker will pay for itself in the long run when you consider the efficiency of it's operation and the reduction of your labor. Automatic stokers function in many different ways. You might find one that operates through a tube that is enclosed and inserted in a downward angle into the coal bin. The attached thermostat will indicate changes in temperature. This will activate the motor, and draw the coal, by way of the tube, into the boiler. A fan will turn on and create the proper draft by forcing the air through the firebed. The weight of the firebed automatically activates the shaker grate to shake the ashes from the grate.

The coal will burn at a preregulated rate and the heat that it provides will continue to keep the water transferred at a proper ratio. The water can be flowed to where it is needed in the house within five minutes. Perhaps 150 gallons of water can be stored for future use. The automatic stoker and add-on boiler can be installed in such a way that a steady temperature of 140° F can be maintained through a valve. Fly ash is whirled through a heat absorber and collected in a container or automatically removed from flue gases by gravity.

Other stokers can boast of the same features, but they simply operate in a different manner. A room thermostat can be regulated to activate a combustion air blower to draw coal out of the bin and into the boiler. Parts can be purchased to rotate and help prevent the formation of clinkers. There are attachments available for almost any convenience from a water preheater to automatic air conditioning.

**Van Wert Models.** It would be most advisable to install an automatic stoker only after you have become familiar with the burning characteristics of coal. You can then appreciate the many convenience. Impressive automatic stokers are manufactured by the Van Wert Manufacturing Company, Inc., 739 River Street, Peckville, Pennsylvania 18452. The Van Wert models contain very few moving parts. Their advertisement states that the automatic action is clean, because there is absolutely no shoveling of coal or shaking of grates. Coal is fed automatically from the bin or hopper to the fire. Ashes are dropped in a steel basket, placed in the dust-tight base, out of the way and out of sight.

The Van Wert models can be economical because they burn anthracite coal (buckwheat size) that should cost several dollars less per ton than the larger sizes. Fire beds of live coals, under constant thermostatic control, prevents the needless waste of overfiring. It burns this inexpensive fuel with scientific efficiency. The unit is fed from the *bottom* of the fire bed. This permits the gases to be fully consumed and converted into heat as they pass upward. With ordinary hand firing, you might find that about 40 percent of the fuel is wasted up the chimney in the form of unburned coal. With the Van Wert boiler unit stoker, your fuel goes further and you get more heat out of each dollar.

Healthful conditions are created by the uniformity of the temperatures. There are no chilly or overheated rooms. It automatically controls every function of heating with a minimum amount of attention. Fire is automatically increased or checked to conform immediately to the indoor temperature.

The operation is safe, odorless and smudgeless. Just the right amount of air is constantly provided for complete combustion. Everything in the coal—that will burn— is converted into heat.

The following are 10 points of mechanical excellence built into Model B, Van Wert conversion stoker.

☐ The coal worm is fabricated of corrosion proof stainless steel.

☐ The genuine Oilite self-lubrication bearings eliminate the necessity of constant greasing.

☐ It features a ball-bearing ash sweeper ring.

☐ The gear reduction unit is equipped with genuine ball and roller-bearing for low power consumption and long life.

☐ It is fabricated with gray iron construction throughout.

☐ The firepot, which is designed with special

heat-resisting alloy, allows for expansion and contraction for a long life.

☐ The solid, cast-aluminum blower wheel is designed for quiet, efficient operation.

☐ It has a specially designed breather device to prevent all back-gassing.

☐ It features a manual air adjustment gate.

☐ It is designed with a floor line binfeed that increases coal bin capacity.

The ash sweeper ring is standard equipment of a full ball bearing type. A stainless steel binfeed worm is available at an additional cost. The transmission is constructed with a double-reduction work and gear, right angle type for compact construction sealed in oil, a vee belt, a silent chain drive, and a full ball bearing. The firepot is of the ring-type constuction; it is self-cleaning.

To get a complete idea of how trouble-free coal burning can be with an automatic stoker, read the following instructions that should be followed with all of the models made by the Van Wert Manufacturing Co., Inc.

With a Van Wert Automatic Stoker, you will not have to start the coal fire by first starting a wood fire. It is recommended that you keep a supply of *Kindle Pacs* on hand for the purpose of getting a fire going. After thoroughly inspecting the boiler unit, and making sure that everything is intact as it should be, remove all ash from the retort or firepot. Keep the automatic stoker switch off. Then you can start the stoker and allow enough coal to cover end of feed worm in bottom of firepot.

Ignite the Kindle Pac outside of the boiler. Impregnated paper keeps combustion low. This enables you to ignite it safely in your hands. Deposit the ignited Kindle Pac in the retort with the *ignited end down*. Once ignited, the Kindle Pac will not blaze until the stoker switch has been turned on. Cover the Kindle Pac with a layer of coal. Preferably this should be enough to bring the level of coal even with top ring. Turn the stoker on. The Kindle Pac will now begin to blaze. It will hold it's own flame until the coal has been ignited.

The coal feed has been properly set before leaving the factory to what is considered correct for normal operating conditions. The coal feed, when operating, is considered to be properly adjusted when—with the proper air setting—a 1-inch or 1½-inch dead ash ring forms around edge of retort pot. A proper fire bed should always be level or slightly heaped. Curly blue flame tips are evidence of the proper combustion of gases. The presence of clinkers in the fire bed might be due to the quality of the coal, excessive air, or unsatisfactory draft conditions. Be sure to provide adequate air for combustion and ventilation.

Improper air adjustment can result in less than satisfactory efficiency in coal burning. Excessive unburned coal indicates a shortage of air. Air can be increased by gradually opening the air adjustment slide until the proper combustion is attained. Do not try to burn all tracks of black in ash. Remember, a stoker makes a soft cinder ash entirely different in character from that obtained by hand firing.

To obtain a resonably accurate draft setting, the adjustable weight on the barometric draft control should be adjusted so that the flame of a lighted match held to the firing door, while slightly cracked open, shows a slight inward pull.

All models of the Van Wert Automatic Stokers are equipped with Oilite self-lubricating bearings in the main stoker body. This eliminates necessity of oiling. Occasional oiling, however, is recommended after several years of operation. Do *not* apply any grease to the three cast-iron gears (teeth) located on the coal transfer.

Maintenance is very easy. The gear box of the transmission need only be checked twice a year. The roller chain need only be lubricated twice a year. The chain should never be allowed to become dry. The motor bearings should also be lubricated only twice a year.

On the models with steam and water units and the warm air units, soft brass shear pins have been installed in two different locations for protection against breakage of stoker parts. This is in case any foreign materials jam the feed work (from the hopper or storage bin) or pusher worm (from the coal transfer retort or fire pot). One pin is located in the binfeed worm bevel gear. The other shear pin is located in the sprocket on the coal feed worm or pusher worm (which carries the coal into the firepot). Generally, this pin will shear when trouble occurs. On other models of the Van Wert Automatic Stoker, two shear pins are located on each end of the transmission output shaft. One pin controls coal feed and the other controls ash sweeper drive.

Failure of the stoker to operate might be due to the following reasons. Make sure that the power is off before you attempt any servicing.

☐ Check fuses and replace them if necessary.

☐ Check the water level of boiler on a steam installation. The water level should be maintained about 1 inch above the center of the glass gauge.

☐ Check to see if an obstruction in the coal feed work has caused a pin to shear. Obstructions must be removed before you restart the stoker.

For the maximum amount of proficiency, with your Van Wert Automatic Stoker, take into consideration the general advice that is given in the operation instructions.

☐ Use a well-prepared Pennsylvania anthracite coal that is uniform in size and free from dirt.

☐ The best performance will be attained with medium free-burning Buckwheat-size coal.

☐ Rice-size coal may be used where capacity is not taxed. More frequent cleanings will be required with this size of coal because more fly ash will accumulate due to a smaller size.

☐ Be sure that the coal feed worm is kept covered with an adequate supply of coal at all times.

☐ To ensure a cleaner and more efficient fire, the hopper or coal bin should be cleaned once a year, and particularly around area at the end of the feed worm.

☐ If an oil drum is used as a hopper, it should be placed on 2-inch cinder blocks and five or six ¾-inch holes should be drilled in the bottom of the drum. This will allow excessive water or moisture to drain out and it will give added life to the bin feed pipe and hopper.

Annual maintenance consists of removing the smoke pipe, and brushing and cleaning it. Inside boiler surfaces should also be brushed and cleaned. The motor should be lubricated and the transmission oil level should be checked. If poor burnout of coal is being experienced, after years of operation,

a competent serviceman should be called to check the stoker unit thoroughly.

*Don't* allow the boiler to remain idle for longer than one week without boiler being filled with water and rust preventative added.

*Don't* alter the air adjustments unless you are really experienced.

*Don't* ever start the fire with wood.

*Don't* throw refuse, garbage, sweepings, or any foreign material into your coal bin, hopper, or stoker retort. This can cause damage and result in costly repairs.

*Don't* attempt to start the stoker, after it has stopped, without first determining the cause of the failure. Correct the problem.

If an automatic stoker is going to be used, your boiler unit should be installed, with this in mind. The following installation instructions are the type that are given with the Van Wert steam and hot water models and with the warm air unit. You will have to check the instructions given by manufacturer of the automatic stoker. The boiler unit should be located in a predetermined position best suited for the proper lineup with the coal bin, and as close to the chimney as possible so that a minimum length of flue pipe has to be used. You must allow at least a 32-inch clearance from the rear base of the boiler to the wall. Where units are installed in a confined space, adequate air for combustion and ventilation should be provided. The boiler must be level and plumb. It is recommended that the boiler be installed on a level concrete base that should be smoothly finished. The assembly is not difficult.

On some of the Van Wert Models, it is necessary to remove the rear ash deflector plate to allow for the installation of the stoker unit. You will have to get specific instructions on how to best install your automatic stoker. For example, the clinker arms might have to be removed from the stoker before it is installed in the boiler.

Caulk the edge of the stoker unit opening on the boiler with wet asbestos cement and mount the stoker unit in place. Evenly tighten the ½-inch fastening nuts until all are snug. Do *not* apply excessive pressure on the wrench because fastening nuts are made of brass.

Smooth off excess asbestos from around the edge of the unit. This forms a tight seal and it is very important in eliminating any possibility of dust.

If necessary, reinstall the ash deflector plate in some of the Van Wert Models or the clinkers arms, it will have previously had been removed for the installation.

Connect all main lines.

Throw a good shovel-full of cement (actually a thin mixture of sand and cement) into the ash pit area. Force the cement under the boiler base flange, from inside out, until you're sure there is a tight seal. Trowel smooth the entire floor area. This includes a very thin layer over the boiler flange. Be sure that this is as level as possible. You will now have a dust-tight seal in the ash pit compartment. Do not allow the cementing procedure to interfere with proper alignment of jacket.

Spot tappings in the boiler that will be used for accessories, piping, and controls. Square head plugs should be installed in openings not being used.

Install tankless heater connections. It is recommended that two 6-inch copper nipples be installed for water connections.

Install the left side panel of the jacket and complete the piping return lines to the boiler. The installation of the jacket, the dog house, the ash door, and the fire door can be completed at this time. (See jacket instruction sheet that will be enclosed.) A package of sheet metal screws is provided with each jacket. Do *not* allow cement to come in contact with jacket at base of the boiler; this would interfere with proper alignment.

Fasten the ash door to the boiler with a door hinge. Necessary nuts and bolts are furnished in a bag attached to the ash door.

Remove the dummy shaft from the binfeed bevel gear by first removing the shear pin spring and the retaining clip ring. Then tap out the shear pin. The dummy shaft can be disposed because it is used only for shipping purposes.

Loosen the three ⅜-inch set screws on the coal transfer housing to allow for proper adjustment of the angle of coal tube. Insert the binfeed worm loosely into steel binfeed pipe. Slide the shaft of the worm into the coal transfer, through Oilite bearing of the housing cap, and then install the binfeed bevel gear. Replace the shear pin and the holding spring clip ring.

Install the steel binfeed pipe by first daubing the end of pipe with cup grease for easier insertion of tube into the coal transfer. The grease will also act as a permanent seal against any dust discharge and will allow for easier removal if it becomes necessary to replace it.

Secure the binfeed pipe by firmly tightening the two square-head screws in the housing. Set the steel coal tube at the proper angle with the end of feed worm 6 inches above the floor of the coal bin.

Retighten the three ⅜-inch set screws on the coal transfer housing. Note: The binfeed worm and pipe must always angle toward the floor. The coal feed worm should protrude no more than 6 inches beyond the end of the steel pipe. More than 6 inches of exposed feed worm can cause crushing of coal with a resultant dirty fire. Less than 6 inches of exposed feed worm can cause improper coal feed with resultant decrease in efficiency.

Fill the gear box with SAE-90 oil, by removing cover of the gear box and filling it to the level of the plug or just cover the top of bottom shaft. Replace the cover with vent plug over the slow-speed shaft (the stoker drive sprocket shaft). Transmissions for certain models of the Van Wert Automatic Stoker are filled at the factory and only require inspection.

Now you can run the flue pipe to the chimney. Install the barometric damper as near to the boiler as is possible. Seal the flue pipe connection to the chimney with wet asbestos cement. Note: In situations where Simplex Fuel Savers are used, this should be installed between boiler and barometric damper.

Install accessories, controls, and wiring in accordance with good engineering practice.

The boiler unit should, now, be ready for firing. Make sure that you follow all of the operating instructions. The instructions for the installation of your add-on boiler and automatic stoker will have to be adapted to each other.

Before installing your add-on boiler—if you are considering the eventual use of an automatic stoker—decide on your choice and install your boiler unit so that an automatic stoker can easily be installed when you are ready.

## CHECK THE CHIMNEY

A chimney should be inspected by a professional chimney sweep before a solid-fuel unit is connected to it. If you have been previously burning wood in a stove or boiler, it is still necessary to have it inspected before you begin to burn coal. There is always the chance of some creosote build-up if you have been burning wood in an airtight solid-fuel unit.

For the best rate of efficiency, wood is burned at a slow consistant rate. The chimney temperature will be cool from a lower stack temperature. This is the primary cause of condensation of *pyroligneous acid*, which is creosote. Creosote has been the cause of many a chimney fire.

Coal does not produce creosote. Nevertheless, if you have as little as a ¼-inch thick residue of creosote, from woodburning, it can ignite from the heat that is produced from burning coal.

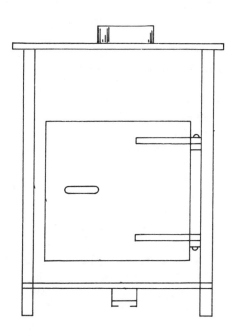

# Chapter 5

# Reading and Sketching Blueprints

T HIS CHAPTER EXPLAINS HOW to read the drawings in this book and how to draw your own sketches. Never undertake the building of a project without first drawing it out to scale. This gives you an idea of what the project will look like and it also saves you time and material costs.

## WHY DO SKETCHES?

A sketch or drawing is a map of your project. A sketch is a necessary aid to the instructions on fabrication of the stoves described in this book. Sketches give you a visual idea of how the stove will look. You will be able to anticipate problems, that may arise in the fabrication of the unit. In addition, it is much less expensive to make a mistake on paper than with steel.

It is essential for the do-it-yourself designer to do a detailed sketch of what it is he wants to build—before he builds it. It will greatly aid him in gaining a perspective on the size and shape of the unit that he wants to build. It addition make a material list to give the steel supplier. It is reassuring to know that, when you are ready to fabricate your project, you'll have something to refer to if your memory needs refreshing.

## MATERIALS NEEDED FOR SKETCHING

A number of materials will be needed to do your drawings. A drawing board of some sort will be needed to draw on. A piece of 24-inch-by-24-inch plywood will do. When it is cut be sure that all four sides are kept square. The sides will be used as a guide for drawing straight lines.

Other materials that will be needed are an inexpensive T square, a 12-inch ruler, pencils, cellophane tape, and drawing paper. I would recommend a lightweight sketching pad containing paper that measures 18 inches by 24 inches. If this cannot be obtained, use bond typing paper. I find that the larger the paper the larger you can make the scale of your drawing.

## PREPARING TO SKETCH

Once all the materials have been gathered, you are ready to start sketching. Tape the drawing paper to your drawing board. Keep the paper at the lower

lower left-hand edge of the board. Line up the edges of the paper to the edges of the drawing board. Once they're in the line with each other, tape the paper to the board. Tape the top of the paper and the center right side of the paper to the board; use two small pieces of the tape.

Using your ruler, divide the width and length of your paper in half. Using your T square, and the edge of your board as a guide, lightly draw a line down the center and across the center of your paper. This will pinpoint the center and, at the same time, divide your paper into four equal parts. From now on, all measurements will have to be broken down to scale.

To break your measurements down to scale is relatively easy. I think that using a scale, of ¼″ equals 1″ or—better yet, if the size of your paper allows—a scale of ½″ equals 1″ will suffice for the size of the project you will be doing. This means that ¼″ or ½″, on your drawing, will equal 1″ of the actual object you want to build. For example, if the front of your stove measures 25″ long in actual size, then the drawing of the front of your stove, will measure 6¼″ (using a scale of ¼″ equals 1″; in this case the 25″ is divided by ¼). If you were to use a scale of ½″ equals 1″, then on the drawing the front of your stove will measure 12½″ (there are 25 one-half inch marks in 12½″).

If your measurement includes a fraction, you will have to scale it down in the same manner. For example, using ¼″ equals 1″ scale, ¾″ actual size equals 3/16″ scale size; ½″ actual size equals ⅛″ scale size; ¼″ actual size equals 1/16″ scale size. Using the scale of ½″ equals 1″, ¾″ actual size equals ⅜″ scale size; ½″ actual size equals ¼″ scale size; ¼″ actual size equals ⅛″ scale size.

Select the view that you want to show in your drawing. There are five basic views that should be shown in your drawings. The *front* (or face) *view* of the unit is the view that you would see if you were standing in front of the stove looking straight at it. The *back view* of the unit is the view that you would see if you were standing behind the stove looking at it's back. The *side view* of the unit is the view that you would see if you were standing along side of the stove looking straight at it. The *overhead view* of the

unit is the view that you would see if you were above your stove looking straight down. The *bottom view* is the view that you would see if you were laying under the stove looking straight up.

I have just described what is called *orthographic projection*. This is one of the simplest forms of mechanical drawing. An orthographic projection can either show one view or all views on one drawing. As an example of how all views can be shown on one drawing see Fig. 5-7. The drawings shown in this book have been broken down into individual diagrams. For examples, see Fig. 5-1 through 5-7.

Using the example stove as a guide, you can now begin to draw your stove.

### SKETCHING YOUR STOVE

☐ First draw a front view to see if your stove will have an appealing look. Match the drawing with the mental image you have for your stove. Use an appropriate scale.

☐ Taking your scale measurement, of the stove's width, dividing it in half on the left side of your vertical center line (already on your paper) and half on the right side of the vertical line. Mark each of these measurements with a dot. Using your T square and the bottom edge of your drawing board as a guide, line up the T square, to the left dot, and draw a light vertical line down the paper. Do the same, to the measurement on the right-side dot. This will become the sides of the front view. See Fig. 5-8.

☐ Take your scale measurement of the height of your stove, divide it in half, and place one half above the horizontal center line, on your paper, and mark it with a dot. Repeat this procedure below the horizontal center line. Use your T square, and the left side of your drawing board as a guide to draw your top and bottom lines, lightly, with a pencil. Once this is done, you should have a box drawn in the center of the paper. Using your pencil and T square, darken the lines of the box to make it stand out. See Fig. 5-8.

☐ Using your scale measurements, locate the door(s) and draw them in. Use the original center marks of the paper as points to work from. This will always keep everything exactly where it is sup-

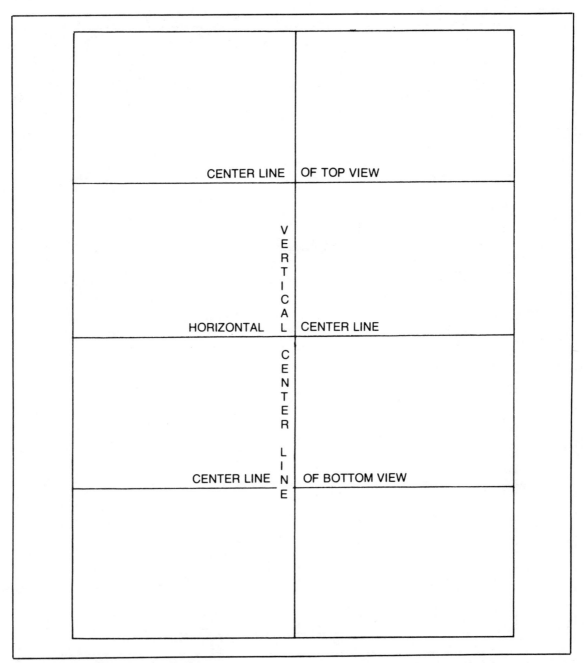

CENTER LINE | OF TOP VIEW

VERTICAL

HORIZONTAL | CENTER LINE

CENTER LINE

CENTER LINE | OF BOTTOM VIEW

Fig. 5-1. Centering a drawing on drawing paper.

posed to be (centered on the stove). Draw them in lightly at first to limit the length and width of the piece being drawn. Then darken the lines to make the piece stand out. Once the doors are drawn in, draw in the door handles, hinges, legs, and exhaust pipe. Keep in mind, at all times, to work from the center lines of the paper. See Figs. 5-9 through 5-11.

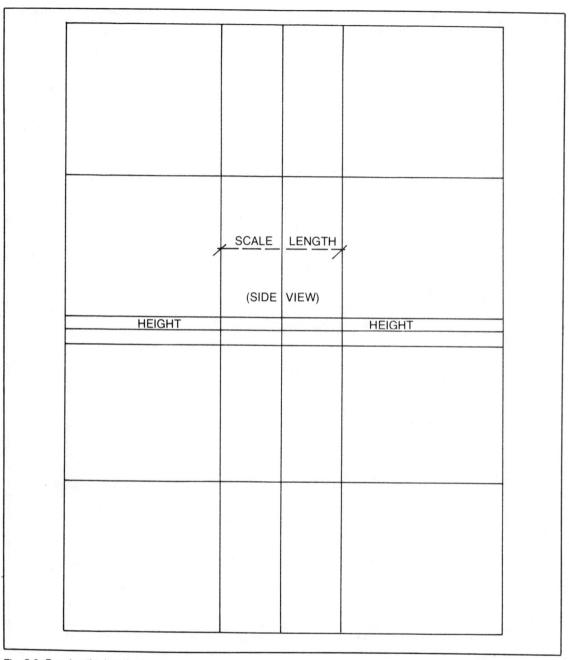

Fig. 5-2. Drawing the length of a view.

☐ This step is not essential, but it is recommended, to give your drawing a realistic look and a finished look. Take another piece of paper and lay it over your drawing. Tape it to your drawing board. Using a black ball-point pen and your T square, trace your darkened lines onto the second piece of

44

paper. When completed, this gives you a clear, accurate sketch of what your stove will look like. You will, probably, do a number of sketches, using a number of ideas, until you find one that you are happy with. See Fig. 5-12.

The next steps will deal with the detailed views of the stove. These drawings show side, back, overhead, and bottom views of the stove. They also show the measurements of each piece of steel and measurements to pinpoint their location.

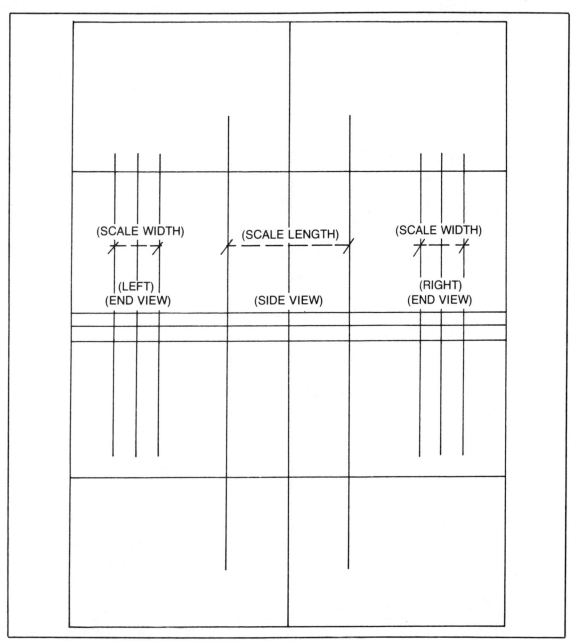

(SCALE WIDTH)

(SCALE LENGTH)

(SCALE WIDTH)

(LEFT)
(END VIEW)

(SIDE VIEW)

(RIGHT)
(END VIEW)

Fig. 5-3. Beginning the end view or side view.

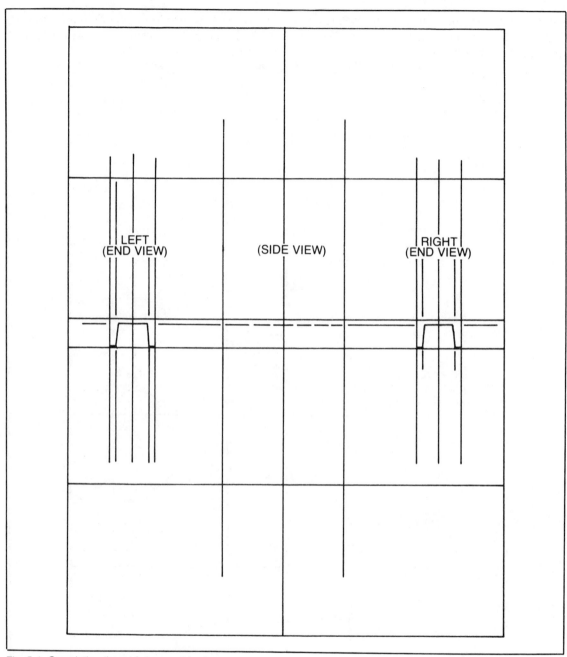

Fig. 5-4. Completing the end view or side view.

Remember when you are drawing these views to draw only the things that your eyes would see if you were standing there looking directly at what you are drawing. You should do your drawings in the same order as the steps you are going to use in actually fabricating your stove. For example, you would start by attaching your back plate to your floor plate. That should be your first detailed sketch. Next, you would attach your side plates to your floor plate and back plate; that should be your second sketch. And so on until your stove is completed. As you complete a drawing, a number or letter should be placed on it so that they can be kept in order.

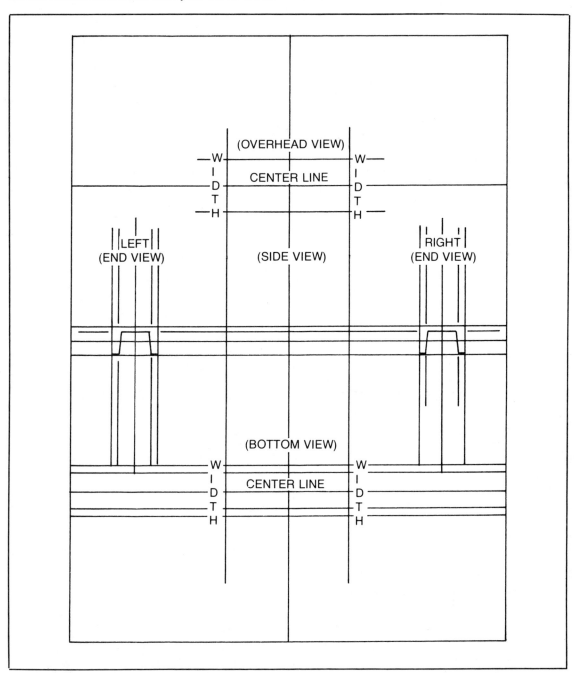

Fig. 5-5. Adding the bottom and overhead view.

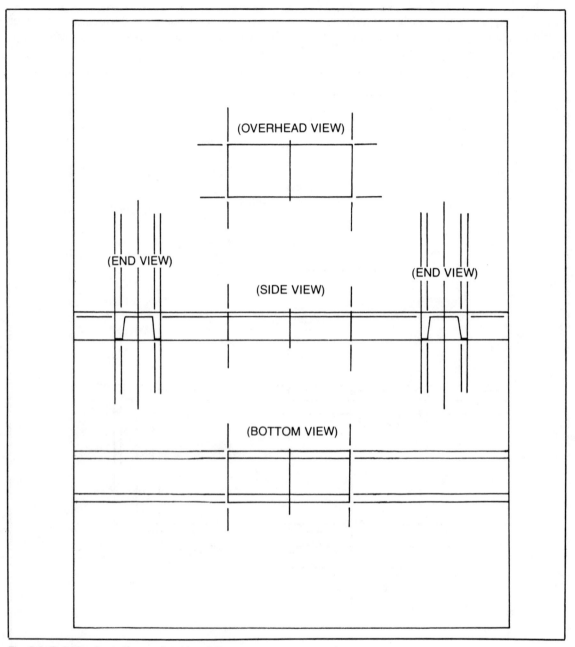

Fig. 5-6. Finishing the bottom and overhead view.

By doing your drawings in order, you should be able to pickup any errors that you might have made in the measurements of your plates. These errors (if any) will probably be found in the connection of your *plate edges* or what is commonly referred to as the joints.

A problem that usually arises here is which plate at the joint will overlap and which plate will butt. This has to be taken into consideration because the plate that is designed to overlap will have to be made longer to be able to do this. Usually what has to be added is the thickness of the plate that you will be overlapping.

As you are doing your sketches, you'll want to add measurements to your drawings to clarify the size of the plates that you will be using, and to locate the miscellaneous parts on the stove such as the door handles, hinges, etc.

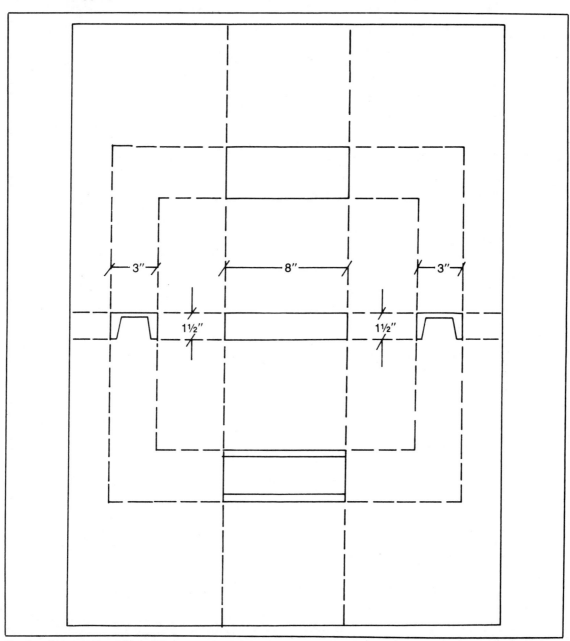

Fig. 5-7. Orthographic projection (5 views in 1 drawing).

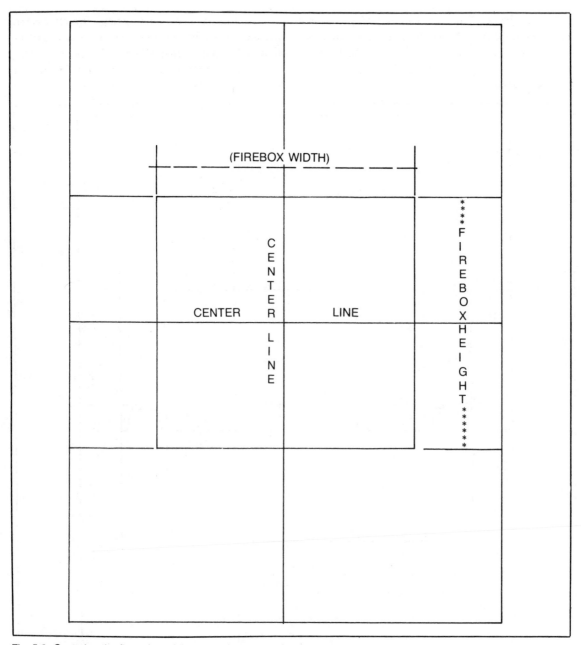

Fig. 5-8. Centering the front view of the stove drawing on drawing paper.

To do this, use what is referred to as *extension lines*. These are lines made up of a series of dashes (to show invisibility) to show where a measurement starts and ends. In the drawings, the measurements are near the sketch lines. This is done to keep the view of the drawing as clear as possible. It also makes the measurement stand out, instead, of being lost in the view.

The following are the main points you should keep in mind when doing drawings of your stove.

☐ Try to keep your drawing as simple as possible. Don't overload the drawing with nonessential measurements.

☐ Always use center marks. For example, when you are sketching door handles, draw a center line in the middle of the door and a line indicating where the handle will begin in relation to the door edge. Using these lines as center lines, draw your

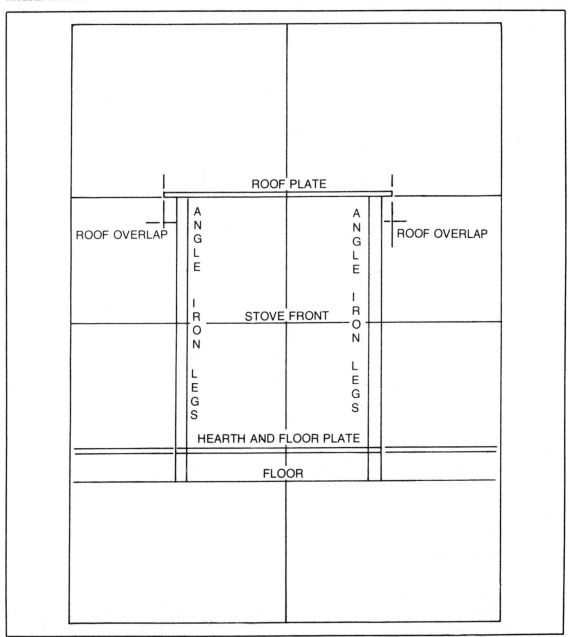

Fig. 5-9. Front view of Example stove.

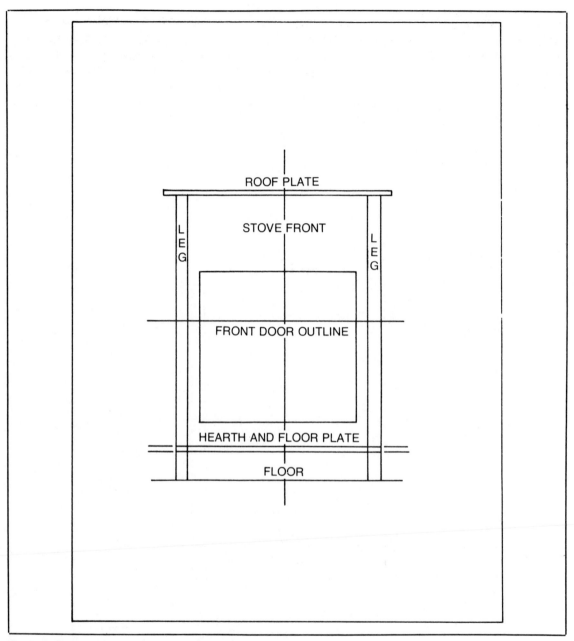

Fig. 5-10. Progression of front view of Example stove.

handle—making the center of the handle—the same as the center of the door. This will give balance to your drawing, and balance to the stove.

☐ Take as much time and care doing your drawings as you would doing your stove. The draw-

ings should be considered a dress rehearsal of the fabrication of your stove. If the drawings are poorly done, then the stove will come out poorly done. Take your time and do it right.

☐ In doing your drawings and fabricating your

stove, you will eventually run into problems. You might even feel that you will be unable to overcome them. At such a point, stop and take a break. Let your mind clear. Then return to the problem and resolve it.

## READING BLUEPRINTS

The drawings and sketches in this book are based on the simplest form of blueprinting: orthographic projection. Each of the five views—front, back, side, bottom and overhead—show exactly what the

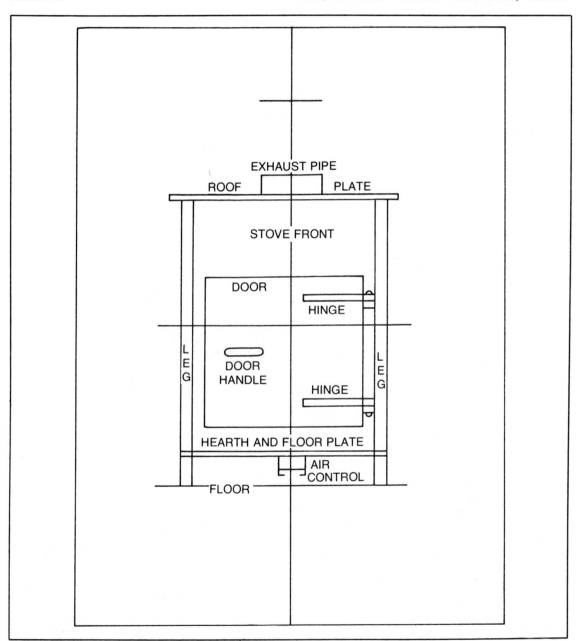

Fig. 5-11. Continued progression of front view of Example stove.

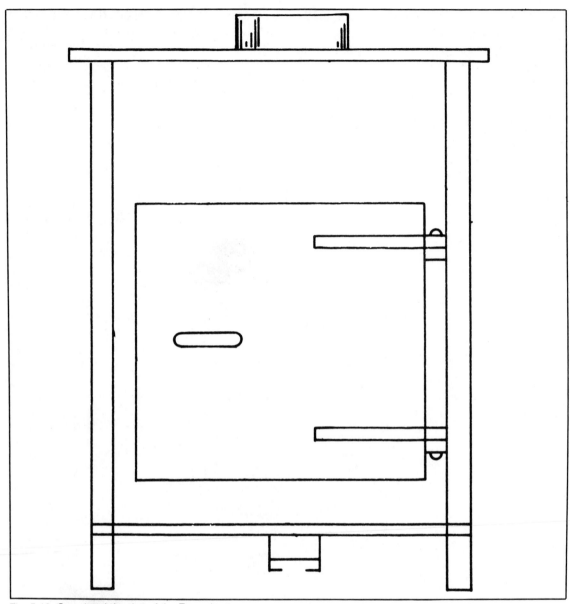

Fig. 5-12. Completed drawing of the Example stove.

eye would see if you were standing in that position and looking directly at the object in the fabrication of your solid-fuel burner.

As you come to each stove model described in this book, the first drawing you will see is the front view of the completed stove. This will give you an idea of what the stove will look like when it is completed. If you are going to build a radiant stove you will probably install it in the living room of your house. Family members will definitely want to know what that "thing" looks like.

Material lists are provided for the stoves. The lists give the different sizes of each steel plate that will be needed along with the amount of required plate, of each size, the location of each plate, and the weight of each plate.

The Pilgrim model, the Liberty model, and the Lowboy model, have illustrations of *cut sheets*. On these models, there are plates with edges that must be cut on an angle. The cut sheet illustration tells the steel distributor which plates need extra cuts and at what angles they are to be cut. When ordering your steel *don't* forget to give them a copy of your cut sheet illustration. If you do forget, they will cut all the edges straight and the plates will *not* fit.

The fabrication instructions for the stove models are numbered. This is the order in which the stove should be fabricated. The instructions begin with directions for the fabrication of the "miscellaneous" parts. Once the miscellaneous parts are made, full attention can be paid to the fabrication of the main units of the stove.

Strict adherence must be paid to how you fit the plates together. Some of the plates will butt and some of the plates will overlap. You will avoid problems if you follow the instructions in order.

Supplementing the instructions are diagrams of the fabrication stages. These are provided as a visual aid to the written instructions. They will be of great value when you begin fabricating your stove.

## READING SKETCHES

In reading sketches, as in reading your instructions, there is a set order pertaining to when and what to look for. Listed below is the order that should be used when you are reading the sketches in this book.

**Find the View.** To understand the sketch you must first know what view it's drawn in. Look at the center of the drawing. This is where the view— front, back, side, top, or bottom—is labeled.

**Plate Names or Letters.** Names of plates are labeled along side the plate or on the plate itself. They will be labeled, for example, side plate (D) or front plate (C).

**Find the Type of Joint.** In fabricating your stove, you'll be using two types of joints—the *butt joint* and the *lap joint*. The butt joint is when a plate

butts against or is placed flush to the side of another plate. As an example, in radiant stoves all side plates butt the front and back plates. The lap joint is when a plate (that it is being butted to) overlaps the butt. As an example, in radiant stoves the side plates butt the front and back plates; then the front and back plates must overlap the side plates. In other words, where the plates come together the front and back plates overlap the ends of the side plates.

**Each Plate is Set into Position.** To find how each plate is set into position, look at the drawing and you'll notice that—coming up from or going out from—each plate there is a series of short dashes. These are known as extension lines. The purpose of these lines is to show where something starts and where it ends or—depending on what is represented in the sketch—the progression of fabrication.

If you follow these extension lines away from the view, a series of dashes will connect the extension lines. On this line, you'll see a measurement. That is the actual distance (not scale distance) from one extension line to another.

Measurements are labeled in this manner to keep the view as clear and uncluttered as possible. When setting plates, check your extension lines to see what side of the plate is placed where. Extension lines are used to indicate measurements for the location of such items as air controls, exhaust openings, and door openings.

**Watch for Notes.** As you read each drawing, you will notice places labeled *cutout* or *note*. The term cutout means to take your cutting torch and cut out the steel that is indicated by those dimensions. This work must be done with a torch. A shear used by the steel distributor to cut plate can make cuts on the edges of a plate, but not inside it.

Pay particular attention to something, areas of drawings labeled *note*. These will help you to better understand the project and particularily a section of the view. Notes are used to make a particular item stand out.

The drawings in this book have been made as simple and as clear as possible. As long as you take your time and read the drawings carefully, you should have little trouble fabricating your unit.

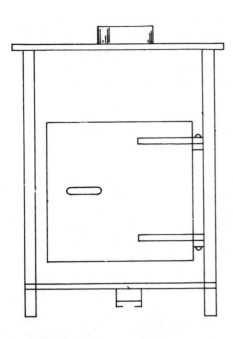

# Chapter 6

# Designing Your Own Stove

THIS CHAPTER IS FOR MORE adventurous readers. Such a reader might want a stove that is larger than any that are illustrated in this book or have some special design in mind. If you decide to take the plunge and build a stove of your own design, don't make a mistake on your material list. Whatever you have on your material list will be exactly what you get. If you make a mathematical error on your part, a measurement on your material list will be wrong. Be prepared to absorb the cost for that mistake. If an error is made on the part of the steel shop, the cost should be absorbed by the supplier.

Before you turn in your material list to a steel shop, be sure that all your calculations are correct. It is well worth the extra 10 minutes it will take you. Remember, the idea is to save money. Don't allow your project to become more costly because of errors on your material list.

The following is a description of how a stove is designed. First decide on the size of the box. As an example, suppose that the stove has a firebox that is 30″ long, 24″ deep, and 30″ high.

**The Floor Plate.** The floor plate is the most important plate of the stove. Everything else is built around it. To determine the length of the floor plate, you must take into account that the interior sides of the stove are going to be lined with brick. The split brick is 1¼″ thick. By adding 1¼″ to the right side, to include the floor brick, and 1¼″ to the left side, to include the floor brick, you get a total of 32½″.

To obtain the depth of the floor, you must include the size of the hearth. The *hearth* is a plate that protrudes past the door to catch any ash, hot coals, or wood that might fall out of the door. The width of the floor plate is determined by taking the depth of the stove and adding the width of the hearth. In this example, the hearth will be 6″. The total width of the floor plate will be 30″.

| | |
|---|---|
| 30″ | (stove length) |
| +2½″ | (firebrick) |
| 32½″ | (floor plate length) |
| 24″ | (stove width) |
| +6″ | (hearth) |
| 30″ | (floor plate width) |

The floor plate will measure 32½" × 30".

**The Back Plate.** To determine the size of the back plate, you must decide which ends of the back plate will make a butt joint and which ends will make a lap joint. To better understand the difference between lap joints and butt joints, see Fig. 6-1.

In this example, the back plate will *overlap* the floor and side plates. For the back plate to overlap the side plates, the thickness of each side plate, which is ¼", must be added to the length of the floor plate—for a total of 33". In determining the height of the back plate, you must add the thickness of the floor plate, which is ¼", for a total of 30¼".

| | |
|---|---|
| 32½" | (floor plate length) |
| + ½" | (¼" each side wall, × 2) |
| 33" | (back plate length) |
| 30" | (stove height) |
| + ¼" | (floor plate) |
| 30¼" | (back plate height) |

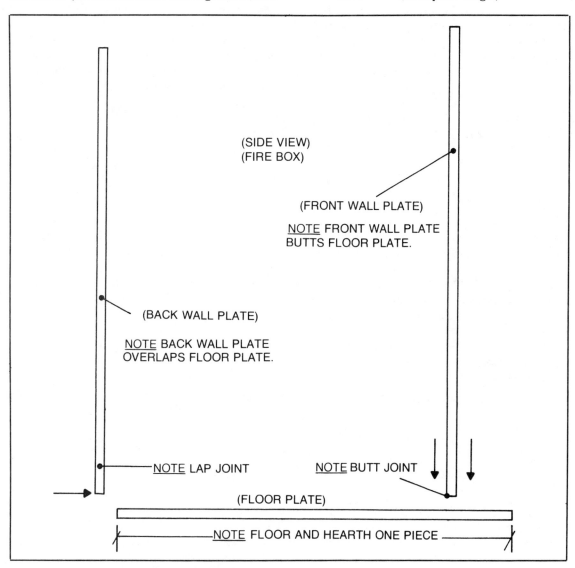

Fig. 6-1. Visual explanation of lap and butt joints.

The back plate will measure 33″ × 30¼″.

**The Front Plate.** You must determine where your front plate will make a butt joint and where it will make a lap joint. In this example, the front plate will lap the sides, to be consistent with the back plate, and *butt* the floor plate because the floor plate extends beyond the firebox to include the hearth.

For the front plate to overlap the side plates, ¼″ must be added to the length of the example stove's floor plate for the thickness of each side wall. The total will be 33″ for the length of the example stove's front plate length. The height of the front plate, which is 30″, remains the same as the example stove's height because there is no added thickness to include.

| | |
|---|---|
| 32½″ | (floor plate length) |
| + ½″ | (¼″ each side wall, × 2) |
| 33″ | (front plate length) |
| 30″ | (stove height) |
| + 0″ | (no added thickness) |
| 30″ | (front plate height) |

The front plate will measure 33″ × 30″.

**The Side Plates.** To determine the size of the side plates, you must be aware of what the side plates will butt and lap against. In this example, the side plates must butt the front and back plates because the front and back plates will overlap the side plates. The side plates' width will remain the same as the depth of this example stove (24″) because there is no added thickness. The side plates' height must include the thickness of the floor plate (¼″) for a total of 30¼″.

| | |
|---|---|
| 30″ | (stove height) |
| + ¼″ | (floor plate thickness) |
| 30¼″ | (side plate height) |

| | |
|---|---|
| 24″ | (stove depth) |
| + 0″ | (no added thickness) |
| 24″ | (side plates' width) |

The side plates will measure 30¼″ × 24″.

**The Roof Plate.** In this example, and in most cases, the roof plate will overlap all sides of the stove's box by 1″. The overlap covers the welds and gives the stove a finished look. It also makes the welding of the roof easier. With a 1″ overlap on all sides, the stove can be rolled over and the roof can easily be welded from the outside.

To determine the size of the roof plate, you must calculate the outside measurements of the completed box. Adding the depth of the stove, which is 24″ (the width of the side plates), plus the ¼″ thickness of both the front and back plates, plus a 1″ overlap for each side, gives you a measurement of 26½″ for the example stove's roof plate width. The stove's length of the front and back plates, which is 33″, plus a 1″ overlap, results in a roof length of 35″ for the example stove.

| | |
|---|---|
| 24″ | (stove depth) |
| ½″ | (¼″ thickness of front and back plates) |
| + 2″ | (1″ overlap for each side) |
| 26½″ | (roof width) |
| 33″ | (stove length) |
| 2″ | (1″ overlap for each side) |
| 35″ | (roof length) |

The measurement for the roof plate will be 26½″ × 35″.

Remember to add the additional dimensions to the roof plate if you decide to extend your roof plate over the stove more than 1″.

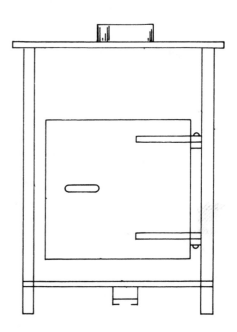

# Chapter 7

# Welding and Burning

THIS CHAPTER DESCRIBES THE skills that are necessary to fabricate a stove. To be able to construct any of the units shown in this book, you should have a knowledge of are welding, know how to use a welding machine, and know how to cut (burn) with a cutting (burning) torch. Learning to weld and burn proficiently often takes a number of years. Nevertheless, the instructions given here explain enough about welding and burning for you to be able to put your stove together. For additional information on welding, see *The Welder's Bible* (TAB Book No. 1244) or *Do Your Own Professional Welding* (TAB Book No. 1384). Other books on welding can be consulted at your local library.

## GENERAL WELDING PROCEDURES

*Stick welding* is the fusion of two pieces of metal with the use of a stick (or welding rod). The rod is used to melt the edges of the metal you want to weld. At the same time, the rod is melted and joins the two edges with the molten metal from the rod. To summarize this explanation, you melt, flow, and join both edges using the welding rod. The welding machine is your source of energy.

To begin, imagine, a steel floor, a wall, and a ceiling.

The first position the apprentice welder should learn is the *flat position*. This is the position where you would weld two sections of a floor or you would weld the floor to the wall.

The second position is the *horizontal position*. Using this position, you would be able to weld two sections of a wall that would come together horizontally. You would start halfway up the wall and weld either left to right or right to left.

The third position is the *vertical position*. This is the position that is used to weld two walls.

The fourth position is the *overhead position*. This is the position used to weld the ceiling to the walls.

Of the four positions just described, the welding position that you will be mostly concerned with is the flat position. The other position you will occasionally use is the vertical position. The only time the vertical welding position will be required is when you are tacking your stove together.

In order to completely weld your stove in the flat position, it is necessary to turn your stove over a number of times. This will keep all of the seams flat. Even though it will seem like a time-consuming task to do this, you will save time in the long run. The flat position is the easiest position to learn. It is also the fastest position in which to weld. To weld in the flat position, a *drag rod* called Jet rod (⅛″ diameter) is recommended.

Jet rod is a type of welding rod used by most steel shops for the welding of steel plate. Jet rod is recommended because anyone can learn to use it in a short period of time. All that you have to do is lay (or strike) it on the metal you want to weld and drag it across the seam, keeping it in touch with metal. Another reason that Jet rod is used by steel shops is that it's much faster than conventional welding rod.

As a perfect example of how easy Jet rod (7024) is to use, our son, Robbie (who was 5 at the time), learned to strike an arc and lay a bead of weld (on a steel plate) in about an hour. He did have trouble keeping the weld on the seam, but children at that age are not yet always well coordinated enough to keep something on a line. The average homeowner will have little trouble welding a stove together with Jet rod (7024).

For *tacking* your stove use a mild steel rod known as 6013. The only problem that might occur is with the rod sticking. This would be due to trying to weld (the 6013) at too low a temperature or keeping the rod too close to the metal. The rod (6013) should be kept at a distance from the metal, of about 1/16″ to 1/8″. Any further away could cause you to loose your arc.

If you find that your rod is sticking too often, try turning the temperature up on your welding machine. When someone is learning to weld with 6013, the temperature can be turned up, a little hotter than normal in order to prevent sticking. After you learn how to keep the proper distance, the machine can be turned down to the normal range recommended by the manufacturer.

## SAFETY APPAREL AND EQUIPMENT

Safety procedures must be followed before you begin to weld. Certain safety apparel must be worn while you are welding. Wear a welding helmet. This protects your face and eyes from sparks and ultraviolet light. Wear a pair of welding gloves to protect your hands from the heat generated by the welding. Gloves will also protect your hands from sparks, hot metal, and electrical shocks. After you have completed your stove, the gloves can be worn while working around or loading your stove.

You should wear a welding jacket. They are expensive, but it will be worth every nickel you pay for it. If you cannot afford a welding jacket, at least wear a long-sleeve shirt. Any shirt that does not contain polyester, such as a shirt of 100 percent cotton, will do. Polyester shirts are extremely combustible and dangerous when they come in contact with welding or burning. If they catch fire, they are hard to put out. With cotton, a hot spark will usually burn a tiny hole about the size of the tip of a ball point pen. For other safety tips, see Chapter 8.

## INSTRUCTIONS FOR WELDING

☐ Turn on your welder and set the temperature indicator at about 130 amperes (for the welding machines designed for home use) or about 110 amperes (for the large industrial welding machines). It is simple to identify which you are using. If your welder is on a 100 or 200 amperes service, then, you have a welder designed for home use. If your welder is hooked up to a 440 line, you have an industrial machine. If you have a gas-driven welder, it is also an industrial machine.

☐ Next, take your ground clamp and connect it to the material you're going to weld.

☐ With your welding helmet and your gloves on, place a Jet rod into your rod holder.

☐ Grasping the holder, position the end of your welding rod over the seam or joint that you are going to weld. Keep the rod on a slight angle. If you are welding a flat seam (such as two plates butting together), and you are welding right to left, lean your rod on a right angle (about 70°) toward the direction you're heading.

If you are welding a flat seam, and welding left to right, lean your rod on a left angle (about 70°) toward the direction you are heading. Whether you will weld left to right or right to left will depend upon which you are more comfortable doing and what you are welding.

If you are welding a corner, you will also have to keep the welding rod pointed (at a 45° angle) to the corner. Once the welding rod is positioned, lower your helmet and scratch the end of the welding rod against the steel.

Do not *hit* the rod to the steel, but do *scratch* it. Hitting the rod to the steel will cause it to stick. Scratching the steel will cause an arc almost instantaneously.

Once you have an arc, slowly drag the rod while keeping, a slight downward pressure on the rod (remember the rod is constantly becoming shorter). Be sure to keep the rod in contact with the metal.

Make sure that you keep the rod over the seam or joint. Speed will be the important factor here. The faster you go the smaller the weld. The slower you go the wider the weld. Every welder has their own speed. You will invariably have to try different speeds until you find the most comfortable rate for you that ensures the best results.

When your rod has melted down to where it's about 1″ to 1½″ long, pull your hand toward you and break the arc. You have layed your first weld.

☐ Eject the remaining part of the rod from your holder. While wearing a pair of safety glasses use a chipping hammer to chip your weld. If you have holes in your weld, it will be due to working too fast or because your material is too dirty. If holes are found, chip and clean them thoroughly. Place another rod in your holder, strike your arc, behind your hole, and slowly go over the hole and fill it in.

☐ To pick up where you left off, strike your arc, on your weld, just behind where you stopped. This is called *overlapping*. All apprentice welders should learn to continue welds in this manner. When you become proficient, you will be able to begin your weld at the point where you left off.

Practice. Welding is like learning to drive a car; the more you do it the better you get at it. If you run into a problem, consult books on welding procedures.

## TACK WELDING

When assembling your stove, you'll be tack welding the parts to hold them in place. A *tack weld*, is exactly what the name implies. It is a small weld (no longer than about ⅛″) that temporarily holds something together until a permanent weld can be applied.

Tack welding is done with No. 6013 rod (⅛″) diameter). Although No. 7024 Jet rod is faster and easier, it is meant only for flat welding. It cannot be used for all four positions of welding. Tack welding rod also comes in handy when you want to take two walls together or tack a roof to a stove without having to turn the stove upside down. After your stove is completed, No. 6013 makes a fantastic general-purpose welding rod for at-home repairs.

To tack weld, execute the following list of instructions.

☐ Turn on your welding machine and adjust your temperature range indicator to (about) 100° (for home-use welding machines) or (about) 90° (for industrial machines).

☐ Take your ground connection and connect it to the metal you are working on.

☐ To make a vertical tack, point the end of your welding rod at about a 60° angle from the floor. Using the face of a clock as an example, angle place your rod at 10 o'clock. Strike your rod against the steel using a downward, scratching motion. Once your arc is struck, wait a moment for the rod to begin to form a puddle of molten metal that adheres to both pieces you are trying to tack.

As soon as this occurs, move the end of the rod up and away from the puddle; give the puddle a second to cool. Then, once again, bring your rod back down to your cooled puddle and form another puddle on top of the puddle that has cooled. Once this puddle has formed, pull the rod up and away. Repeat this procedure about four or five times and you will have a vertical tack. The puddle might fall to the floor. This can happen when you wait too long before pulling up and the puddle gets too hot. Or you possibly didn't wait long enough before pulling up. As you'll find, it's all a matter of timing.

☐ Pulling your welding rod away from your material, stop welding. Wearing a pair of safety glasses to protect your eyes, chip the weld and visually check to make sure your tack has adhered to both pieces of metal. A minivertical weld has been completed.

An *overhead tack* is basically done in the same manner except that you move the rod forward and backward instead of up and down. This position will be an aid to you in tacking on your roof.

To do a *flat tack* drag the rod the same as you would if you were using your Jet rod.

Learning to tack weld, using all four positions, is a little more difficult than running Jet rod. But with a little practice, you'll have little trouble. Remember, it's all in the timing of your wrist action.

## USING A CUTTING TORCH

A *cutting torch,* also referred to as a *burning torch,* will be needed to cut the door opening and exhaust opening in your stove or boiler. The cutting torch will also come in handy in cutting other materials such as angle iron and flat stock. Another useful purpose for this tool is in heating and bending material for door handles and slide handles.

The use of a cutting torch necessitates the wearing of certain safety apparel. Wear a welding jacket (if possible) or a 100 percent cotton shirt, a pair of welding gloves, and a pair of cutting glasses or goggles to protect your eyes from the bright light and sparks. Do not be confused by the difference between welding lenses and cutting lenses. A *welding lense* is much darker and cannot be worn for cutting. You will be unable to see through them to do anything other than welding. Don't be mislead into thinking that a welding lense or cutting glasses will serve a dual purpose. Listed below are the procedures for cutting with a cutting torch.

☐ After connecting your tank gauges and before turning on your oxygen and acetylene tanks, turn your pressure adjustment screw, on both gauges, counterclockwise until loose. Note: the oxygen bottle should be green and the acetylene bottle should be black. If they are not, call your supplier and check with him. There have been some instances where hospital oxygen or pure oxygen has been accidentally used. Pure oxygen is extremely combustible and therefore dangerous.

☐ Once your adjustment screws are loose, turn your bottles on and check for leaks at the tank connection. This can be easily accomplished by smelling around the connections. Oxygen has no odor, but you will feel the air leaking out. Acetylene, definitely has an odor. If a leak is found, retighten the connections and check again.

☐ Once your bottles are on, begin to turn your adjustment screw clockwise. Watch the gauges. Soon you'll see one of the gauges begin to move (that is your hose gauge). This gauge indicates the amount of pressure in your hose. Continue to turn the gauge (turning the oxygen adjustment screw) until you have about 40 pounds of pressure in the hose and—turning the acetylene adjustment screw—until you have about 6 or 7 pounds of pressure in the hose. Do not take your acetylene hose pressure over 15 pounds. When it is above 15 pounds, acetylene becomes unstable to the oxygen in the atmosphere.

☐ Once your hose pressures are set, check your hose connections and torch for leaks. If a leak is found, retighten the connection. If a leak is found in the hose it can be patched with duct tape. If the leak cannot be patched, the bad section, on both sides, must be cut out and a splice fitting (with hose clamps) must be installed.

☐ Once the hoses are pressurized, take a *striker* (*not* a match or a lighter) in hand. Slightly cracking open the acetylene valve on your torch (the valve the red hose is attached to), light the end of your torch. Slowly continue to increase acetylene until you have a bright yellowish flame and the black smoke has disappeared.

☐ Crack open the oxygen valve on the torch. The flame will turn blue or the yellow flame will pop out (leaving no flame at all). If the yellow flame pops out, turn off both valves on the torch and begin again. This time open the oxygen valve slower. A blue flame is what you need.

☐ Once you have a blue flame, slowly continue to increase the oxygen until the little blue flames, at the end of the torch, become visually clear and sharp. Once the flames are adjusted, press the trigger (or hand lever) on the torch. You should hear air coming out the end of the torch. That is the cutting air. You should also see a clear space form in the middle of the flames.

☐ If in the event you press the lever and the torch goes out, that means you have opened the air valve too much or that you have not opened your acetylene valve enough. If the torch does go out, turn the valves off and begin again. (The idea, is to have a clear, blue set of flames at the end of the torch before and during the time you have the cutting air lever depressed. Once this is accomplished, move on to the next step.

☐ With the torch adjusted, place the torch over the material you want to cut. Keep the tips of the blue flames just barely touching the material. Keeping the head of the torch completely vertical, heat the place where you want to start cutting.

☐ When you begin to see small sparks coming from the material, the steel is heated enough to cut. When the steel is ready, fully depress the air lever. This will blow a hole through the steel. If it doesn't take, it means that the steel wasn't ready and it needs more heating. If this should happen, release the lever and reheat the material.

☐ Once the hole is cut, begin to move the end of the torch (following the cut line) while leaving the air lever depressed. If while moving the torch you should loose the cut, it means that you were moving too fast. If this happens, back up the torch, release the lever, and heat the material where you lost the cut. Once heated, depress the lever and move on. When you want to turn off the torch, turn off the acetylene valve, and then turn off the oxygen valve.

### HINTS FOR GOOD BURNING

When you are moving the torch (while cutting). Keep the movement as smooth as possible. A steady hand shows in your cut line. You could use a straightedge. A straightedge is often a piece of 2″ × ½″ flat stock, about 24″ long, with a handle on it. It is used to rest the side of a torch tip against during the cutting of a line. It keeps the torch from shaking; and it helps you to cut a straight, clean line.

Keep the torch tip clean. Use tip cleaners. They are small, different-sized wires used to clear the holes in the ends of your torches.

Always be aware of where sparks are going. Don't start a fire.

Once you've learned to follow the preceding instructions, all that will be needed is some practice. The more you practice the more accomplished you will become. Remember, this chapter is only a basic course on welding. If you feel it is necessary, get further instructions before you build your unit.

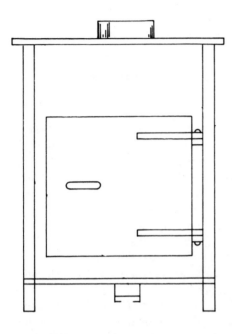

# Chapter 8

# Preparations

**T**HE MOST IMPORTANT THING to consider in preparing to build your solid-fuel burner is safety. There is no way that this factor can be overemphasized. Very definite safety procedures have to be followed when you are using the equipment needed to build a solid-fuel unit. This is especially true for welding and burning equipment. When welding, the two most important things you have to concern yourself with are eye protection and skin protection.

### SAFETY IS NO ACCIDENT

You must consider your own eye protection and the eye protection of anyone that might be in your work area. The flashing light produced by welding contains ultraviolet light. This is the same kind of light produced by sunlamps. Even indirect contact, such as when ultraviolet bounces off a light-colored wall, can cause temporary eye damage. When ultraviolet rays come in contact with the eye, the coating of the eye is burned. The result is a painful irritation of the eye. This irritation usually only lasts just three or

four hours and does not cause permanent damage. This is referred to by welders as a *flash*. The most typical ways to inflict or receive a flash are as follows:

☐ Bystanders without eye protection watching you weld.

☐ Accidently touching the welding rod to the material you are working on, causing an arc, while your welding helmet is up.

☐ A cracked welding helmet or welding lense.

A cracked welding helmet is easy to see, but a cracked welding lense, at times, is impossible to see. Once a day, the welding lense should be taken out and checked for cracks.

In 15 years of welding, I have probably been flashed 50 to 100 times. This was mostly due to my own carelessness and sometimes because of the carelessness of others. I still have not done permanent damage to my eyes. If you take the proper precautions from the start, you can avoid problems with flash.

When welding or cutting with a torch, you must protect your skin. This is relatively easy: a long-sleeved shirt, preferably cotton, is sufficient. Do not wear a polyester shirt. When ultraviolet light comes in contact with skin a *flashburn* results. This burn is similar to sunburn. Due to the intensity of the ultraviolet light, the pain is more intense and it usually lasts from three to five days. A long-sleeved shirt is necessary when you are burning with a cutting torch. The shirt will prevent sparks from burning your skin.

When burning or cutting with a cutting torch, gloves should be worn to prevent sparks from burning your hands. When you are welding, gloves should be worn to avoid electric shocks. Welding machines melt steel with electricity. While these machines are set to run at very high amperages, they are usually set for low voltage. It is very annoying to receive a shock from a welding machine. Proper ventilation is absolutely crucial in building a solid-fuel unit. Welding and burning create many fumes and much smoke. Adequate ventilation in the work area is essential. One of the precautions you can take is to mount a fan in an open window to exhaust the fumes.

Before using any equipment, check the handbooks about rules of safety that should come with it. If no such material accompanies the equipment, check your local library for books on burning and welding procedures. Know exactly how to operate the equipment before beginning it's use! You cannot be too careful in operating any equipment.

## SHOULD YOU RENT OR BUY EQUIPMENT?

Before you begin to gather your equipment to build a solid-fuel unit, consider whether you should buy or rent your tools. The two major pieces of equipment that will be needed to fabricate a stove are a welding machine and a burning outfit. Such equipment can be bought or rented. With the rise of home heating fuels, one or more of your neighbors or friends might also be interested in building their own solid-fuel unit. This can be advantageous in a number of ways. You will have someone with whom to share the cost of the equipment. Once the units are completed the equipment could be sold. By

ordering your steel together, you will probably obtain a better price for a volume buy. When you are building a solid-fuel unit, it will be nice to work with someone. Neighbors can get together and go out to cut wood together. This brings neighbors together and gives them a common bond, that they otherwise might not have shared. It is definitely worthwhile thinking about.

Welding machines vary in price from $50 to $1000. The type of welder needed for this kind of home project is a single-phase welder with a range from 30 to 200 amperes. These machines need 100- to 200-amp service for power and they can be hooked up to a 50-amp breaker. The cost for one of these machines should range from approximately $150 to $180.

Burning equipment, torches, gauges, and hose can be purchased for approximately $160.

Try the "articles for sale" column in local newspapers, visit flea markets, read the telephone book listings under welding distributors, and try various store catalogs and hardware stores. The machines that I used in my business cost $135. I have found them to be durable and dependable.

Renting equipment can be arranged by looking in your telephone directory under rentals or welding supplies. Sometimes welding suppliers do rent their equipment. It is more advantageous to own your own equipment, but this decision has to be weighted by you. Most rental agencies usually rent equipment for 24-hour periods. A plug-in welder or a gas-driven welder can be rented from many agencies. The only difference in them is that one is driven by a gas engine and the other is powered by household current.

Another piece of equipment that you might need is a disc grinder. This equipment should be rented. Disc grinders are used for finishing cuts made by a cutting torch. This is not necessary for a solid-fuel unit, but it may come in handy.

The factors in determining whether to buy or rent equipment are how much of a financial investment the builder is willing to invest, how many others will join in building the unit and units for themselves, and the cost of renting equipment.

When you are making this decision, bear in mind just how handy owning your own equipment can be in your neighborhood. There are many other projects—such as railings and go-carts—for which this equipment can be used. It will be possible to sell your equipment to someone else upon the completion of your solid-fuel unit. Perhaps another do-it-yourselfer will use it to build another solid-fuel unit. A basic course on welding and burning is included in Chapter 7. Once you have mastered those skills, almost any project will seem possible.

### MISCELLANEOUS TOOLS

Some small, hand tools will also be needed for your project. You will need a tape measure, a combination square, a 2-foot square, a hammer, two C-clamps, and a chipping hammer for chipping the welds.

### THE MATERIAL LIST

To build a radiant stove or heat exchanger; you must first prepare a material list. This will be one of the most important things that you do. If you are designing your own unit, refer to Chapter 6 on designing your own stove. Chapter 6 explains how to calculate the size of the plates you will need according to the dimensions of your design. You will also find out how to prepare a material list according to those dimensions.

If you are going to use one of the designs in this book, the material list will be found in the chapter on the design of your choice. Make sure that you understand the material list before you begin to order your steel. Chapter 6, on designing your own stove, will be most helpful in explaining the cuts of the steel plate and how a stove goes together.

### ORDERING THE STEEL

When ordering your steel, the most important thing to express or convey is a feeling of self-confidence. If you know exactly what you want, and exactly what you are doing, this feeling will speak for itself. This can be done by using the right terminology by requesting a price-per-pound quote, and by having a neatly prepared and accurate material list for the use of the shop personnel.

If they want to use your material list, in contrast to preparing their own from the cuts that you have requested, make sure that you have a duplicate copy. In the event of a mistake in a cut, it can be more easily proven where the mistake lies. If you are responsible for an inaccurate measurement on the material list, you will have to absorb the cost. If the manufacturer or supplier makes a mistake, the correction should be at their expense.

Do not make an error in preparing your material list. The idea of building your own solid-fuel unit is to save money by reducing home heating costs and, by building your own unit. In doing so, you are eliminating a manufacturer's labor costs and profit, a distributor's or representative's commission, and a dealer's overhead, commission, and delivery charge. Do not allow your project to become any more costly than necessary. If you take an additional 10 minutes to check your material list, before turning it in to the steel distributor, it will be well worth your while in the long run.

Steel shops are generally cordial and fair. Remember, however, that they are in business to make money. They will charge as much for the steel as necessary for them to make a profit. This is another instance where it pays to shop. Your local telephone book will list steel suppliers. You can call and request a price per pound of both ¼″ and ⅜″ steel plate. They might not want to talk business over the phone, but you can try. It will take just a few minutes, and, it could save another valuable energy source—the fuel consumed by your automobile.

You will want to take into consideration—when you are making the decision about which steel supplier to choose—whether the supplier cuts his steel with a torch or a shear. Steel plate, cut with a torch, can warp from cutting and might not leave an accurate straight edge. Cutting with a shear produces a clean straight edge. This is important because you will be the one fitting this steel together. It will pay to work with nice flat material, that has a straight, clean edge.

If you are in a business that makes it possible for you to be able to cut your own steel plate, here is a recommendation. Obtain an accurate and straight cut on each piece of steel plate. First make a cut line to the exact measurement. Then measure ⅛″ out toward the scrap side of the plate and draw another line.

Use a straightedge to guide the torch along the cut line to make a nice clean straight edge. A long straightedge can be the 2″-×-⅜″ flat, used for the hinges, a piece of scrap iron, or just something that is about ½″ thick. Light the torch, prepare for burning, and then lay the torch beside the straightedge and rub the side of the straightedge with the torch tip. This gives you a guideline. If you are simply going to buy the steel from a steel supplier, you are better off paying for the cutting by a shear.

Prepare the material list. Be sure that all your measurements are correct. Keep all your measurements in inches. This will help the steel shop personnel. Use a copy of the appropriate material list in the book that accompanies each model or use the formula given in Chapter 6 on designing your own stove.

Make sure that each plate is marked with a letter. This will help the steel shop personnel cutting your steel, and it will make fabricating your stove or boiler a much easier task. Do not forget to include the miscellaneous material listed with each stove or heat exchanger and the material that you will need for any extra trim, the baffle of your choice, the air controls necessary for the burning of the solid fuel of your choice, and the steel plate for the door(s).

Don't forget to include sanding and painting material. Most of your hand tools can be purchased in any hardware store. You will want soap stone (chalk) for drawing your lines on the steel. Keep a wire brush on hand for cleaning your welds.

Welding equipment needed includes a box of 7024 Jet rod, about 51 pounds of 6013 straight rod, a bottle of oxygen, and a bottle of acetylene. (Oxygen and acetylene can be rented from a welding supply store.)

# Part 2
# Building Your
# Solid-Fuel Unit

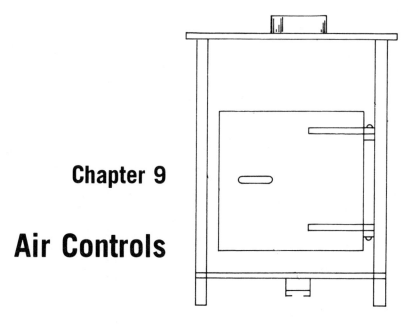

# Chapter 9

# Air Controls

THERE ARE TWO BASIC TYPES of air controls used to supply air to the firebox. The first is the screw type. This type of air control is usually mounted in the door(s). When more air is needed for burning, the control is screwed out to allow more air to flow to the firebox. When too much air is being fed to the firebox, the control is screwed in to reduce the flow of air to the firebox. While there is nothing wrong with this type of system, it might be a little too difficult for the average homeowner to fabricate.

The second type of air control used is the slide air-control system. A slot is cut into either the door or the underside of the stove, and a plate is mounted on tracks. Sliding the plate back allows more air to enter the firebox. This is what controls the rate of burning of the fire in the stove.

The slide air-control system is the best type to use for the projects described in this book. For the average homeowner who wants to burn wood and coal in the same stove, it would be difficult to obtain an airtight fit with the screw-type control.

Chapter 1 explains in detail the advantages to the slide air-control system. Also, see chapters on heating with coal, or heating with wood, and maximum efficiency, to learn how the feed air can be, and should be, controlled through the air control system.

### FABRICATION OF AIR CONTROLS

☐ Make sure that all parts to the air control are properly cut.

☐ Take angle iron (1½″ × 1½″ and 3″) and butt to each end of the channel (C3 × 5.0 pounds, 7″ long). When angles are in place, tack weld together. Once tack welded, turn over and weld the joints inside. See Fig. 9-1.

☐ Turn the iron right side up and cut an opening in the channel. See Fig. 9-2.

☐ While the channel is cooling, take the ½″ flat iron (13″ long), measure in an inch from each end and draw a line. Then take your cutting torch and heat the lines. Once the steel is red hot, bend it to a 90° angle. See Fig. 9-2.

71

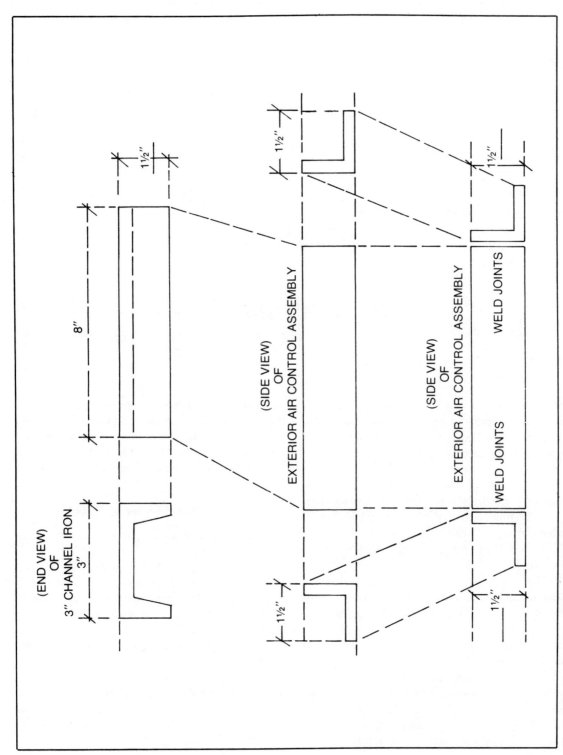

Fig. 9-1. Progressive view of exterior air control.

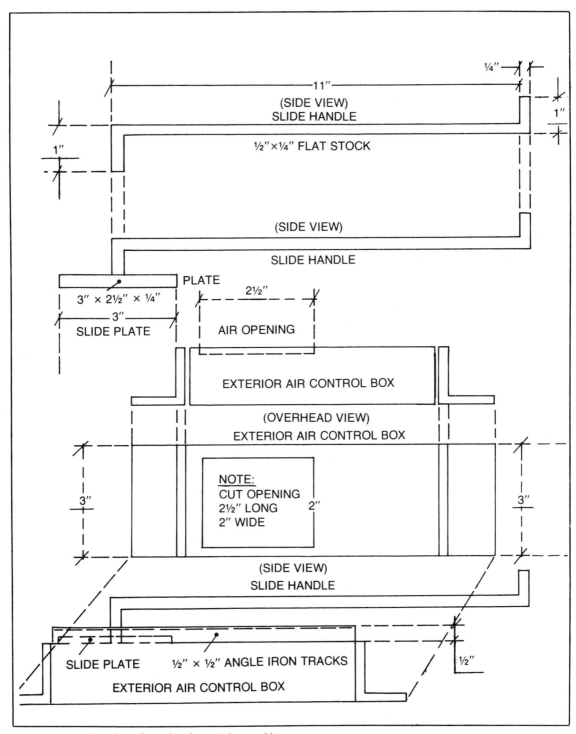

Fig. 9-2. Progressive view of exterior air control assembly.

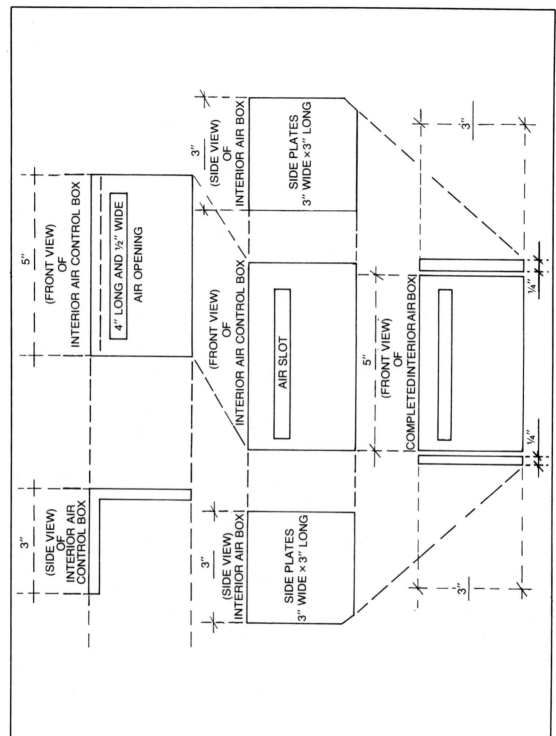

Fig. 9-3. Progressive view of interior air control assembly.

74

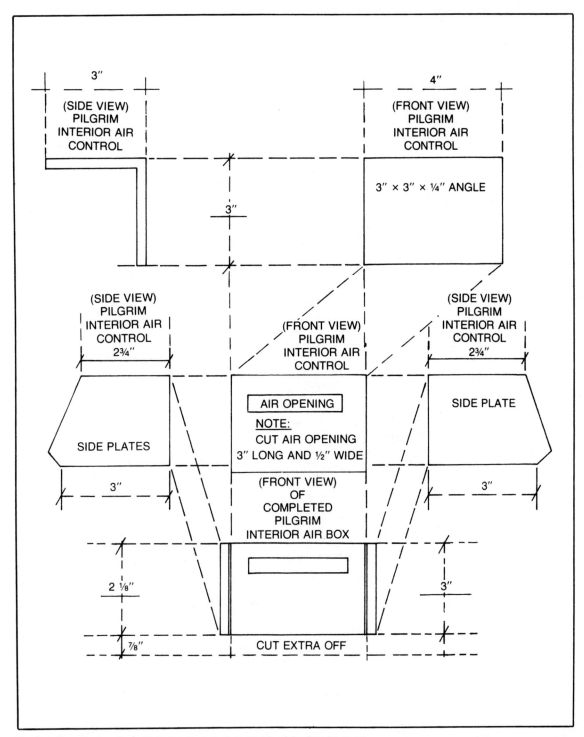

Fig. 9-4. Progressive view of interior air control assembly of the Pilgrim stove.

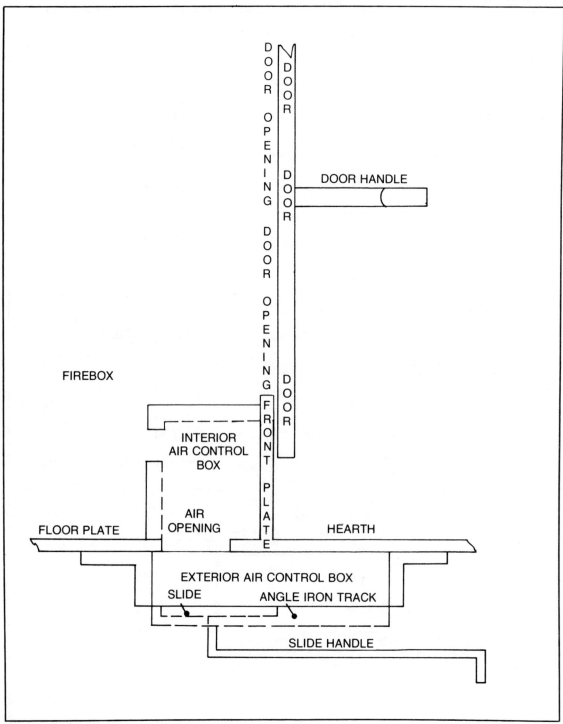

Fig. 9-5. Side view of installed air control.

76

**Table 9-1. Air Control Material List.**

| amount | material description | | | | | use |
|:---:|:---|:---|:---|:---|:---|:---|
| 1 | Length 7″ | C3 | × | 5.0 | lbs. | exterior air control box |
| 2 | Length 3″ | 1½″ | × 1½″ × | ¼″ | angle iron | exterior air control ends |
| 2 | Length 2½″ | 3″ | × | ¼″ | flat stock | exterior air control slide |
| 1 | Length 5″ | 3″ | × 3″ × | ¼″ | angle iron | interior air control box |
| 2 | Length 3″ | 3″ | × | ¼″ | flat stock | interior air control ends |
| 1 | Length 3′ | 2″ | × | ¼″ | flat stock | door slide plates |
| 1 | Length 3′ | ½″ | × ½″ × | ⅛″ | angle iron | slide tracks for all air slides |
| 1 | Length 3′ | ½″ | × | ¼″ | flat stock | slide handles for all air controls |

☐ Take the slide plate (3″ × 2½″) and center the handle end on it and weld it to the plate. See Fig. 9-2.

☐ Once the handle has been attached to the slide plate, take the slide and mount it onto the channel with ½″ × ½″ angle iron tracks. See Fig. 9-2.

☐ Now that the exterior air control is completed, do the interior air control. First, take the piece of 3″-×-3″ angle iron (5″ long) and cut a slot in it 4″ long and ½″ wide. See Fig. 9-3.

☐ Take the end plates (3″ × 3″) and fit them to ends of the interior air control. Once the plates are in place, tack weld them. After tack welding, turn it over and weld the interior joints. See Fig. 9-3 and 9-4. Figure 9-5 shows the installation of the interior and exterior air controls.

## FABRICATION MATERIALS

To fabricate interior and exterior air controls, in addition to the air controls to be mounted on the doors, you will need materials not listed in the stove material lists.

Due to the large variety of sizes needed for air controls on the doors, there is, in most cases, more material than will be needed. This is to assure you of enough material to fabricate the door of your choice and the interior and exterior air controls.

Table 9-1 lists material you will need to fabricate your interior, exterior, and door air controls. Remember, if you finish fabricating your air controls and have material left over, it's because there is more material than necessary in the material list.

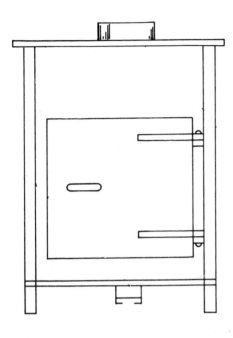

# Chapter 10

# Door Fabrication

THE INFORMATION IN THIS CHAPTER is for those readers who want to design their own stove or door(s).

The airtightness of a solid-fuel unit depends mainly on how well the doors or door fits. The airtightness of the radiant stoves that I manufactured were ultrasonically tested. The double-door models were rated at about 89 percent airtight and the single-door models ranged about 93 percent airtight. The space that must be allowed between the doors of the double-door units accounts for the difference. This is about the maximum amount of airtightness that can be expected, and still allow for a certain amount of expansion when the stove is really hot. Otherwise, the door(s) could stick. The small amount of air that would be allowed in, with a high percentage rating of airtightness, will have virtually no affect on the combustion rate of the fire.

If the door(s) are not fitted airtight, there is no way that the burn rate of the unit can be regulated. You would not be able to account for the amount of air allowed in through the leaks. For maximum heat

and burning efficiency, you will want to be in complete regulatory control of the amount of oxygen that reaches the fire.

Gasket material will seal the door(s) tightly, when closed, and allow for a precise fit. Measure, fabricate, and follow all of the instructions very carefully and you will be assured of a much easier time when you mount the door(s) onto your unit.

## SINGLE DOOR OR DOUBLE DOORS

You will have to make the decision whether to fabricate your unit with a single door or double doors. A single-door unit will give you the best airtightness. You will, however, have to allow for a very wide swing, upon opening the door, when sitting the unit. The double doors do allow for more aesthetic value.

For an attractive and personalized affect on the radiant units, you can mount trivets on the doors. The trivet is a handy little device that has been designed to hold a pot near a fire or for cooking on the stove. Trivets (metal stands) are sold in many

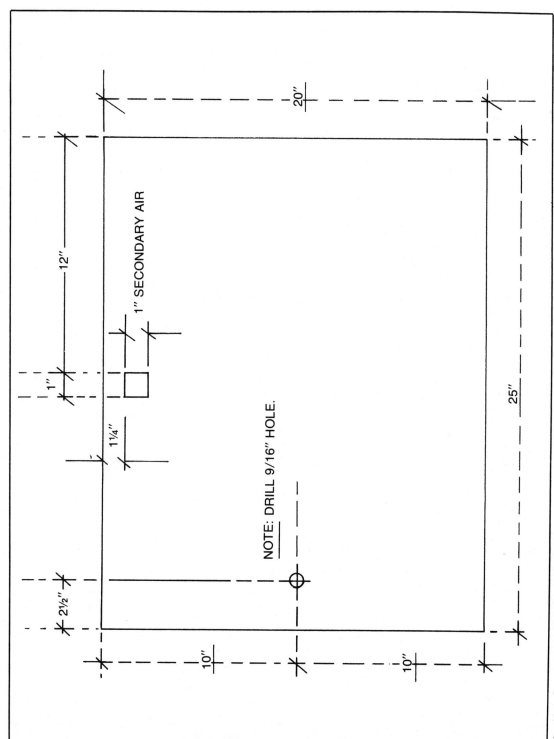

Fig. 10-1. Door plate of the Example stove.

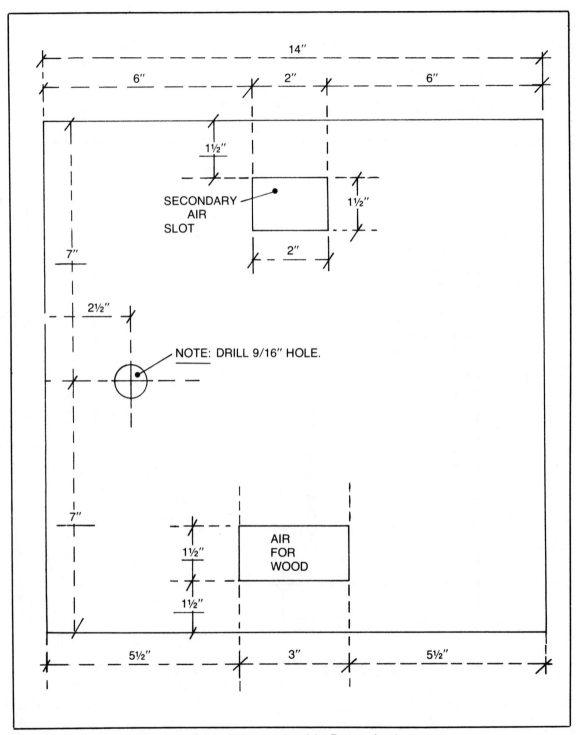

Fig. 10-2. Front view of the door layout for the Square stove and the Rectangular stove.

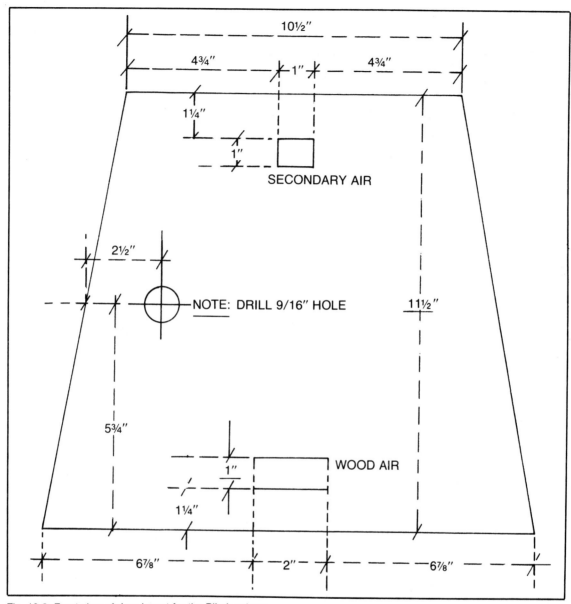

Fig. 10-3. Front view of door layout for the Pilgrim stove.

hardware stores and department stores, and they come in various designs. This little decoration can make a great deal of difference in the appeal of the stove. You can use your imagination on choosing a color, but make sure that the paint is for high-heat use. Gold and black painted trivets are common. Paint it the color of your choice, drill holes in the trivet and the middle of the door, and screw in the trivet.

## DOOR FABRICATION INSTRUCTIONS

☐ Inspect the door plate and check to see that all four sides are square. This can be done with a 2-foot carpenters' square.

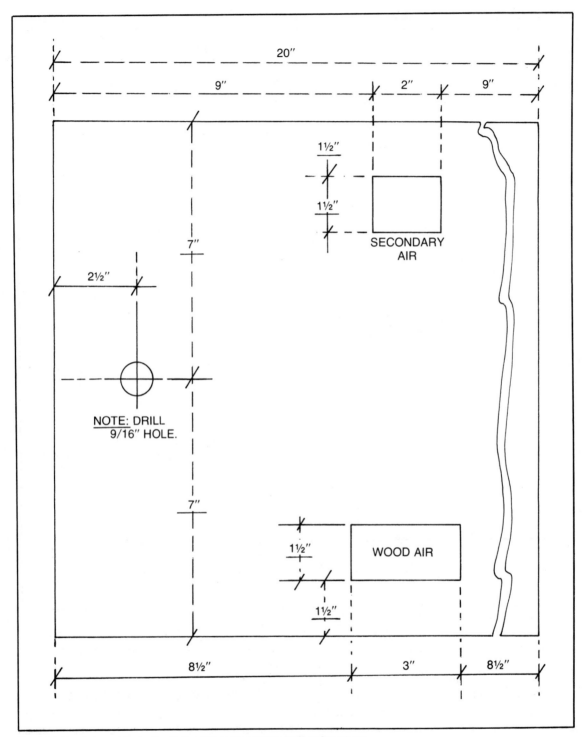

Fig. 10-4. Front view of single door layout of the Liberty stove and Lowboy stove.

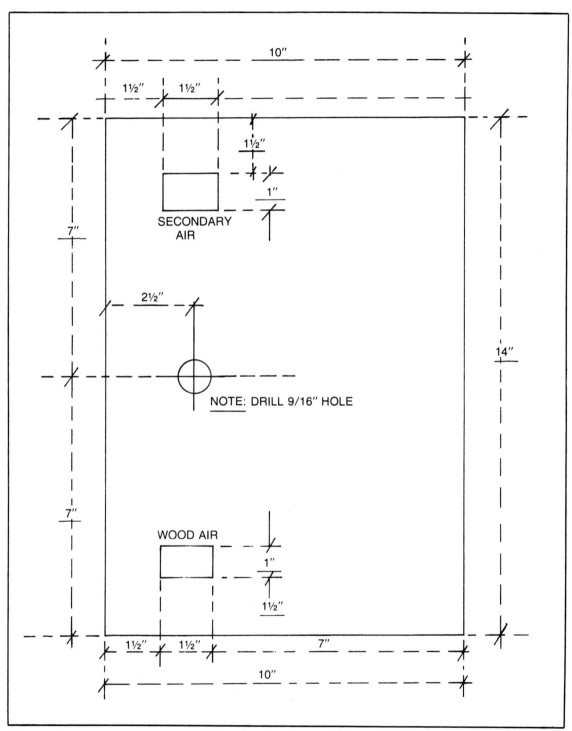

Fig. 10-5. Front view for double doors, and right door layout for the Liberty and Lowboy stoves.

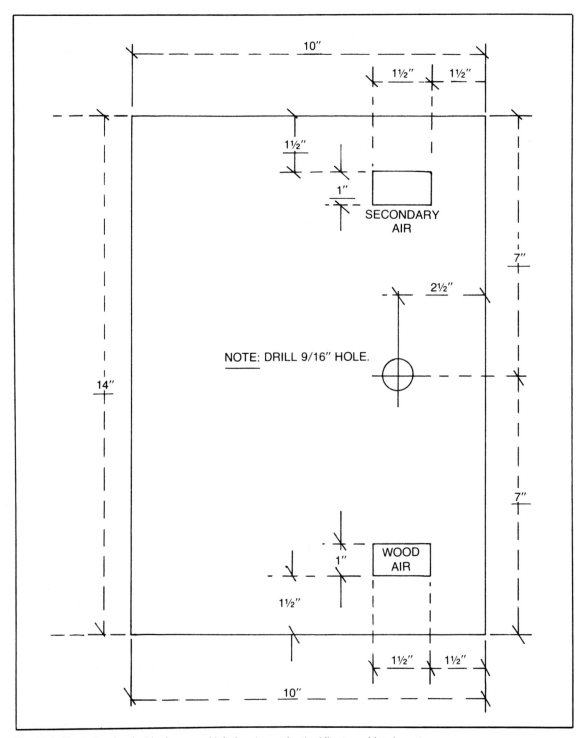

Fig. 10-6. Front view for double doors, and left door layout for the Liberty and Lowboy stoves.

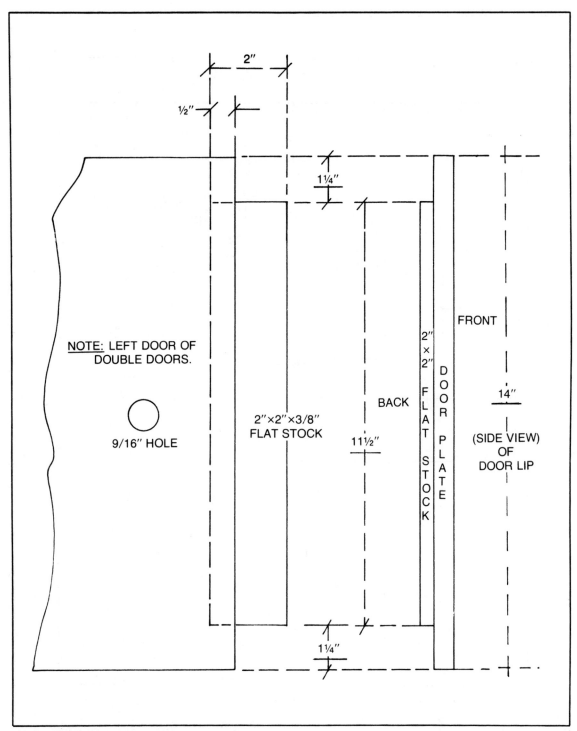

Fig. 10-7. Front view of double doors, and left door lip.

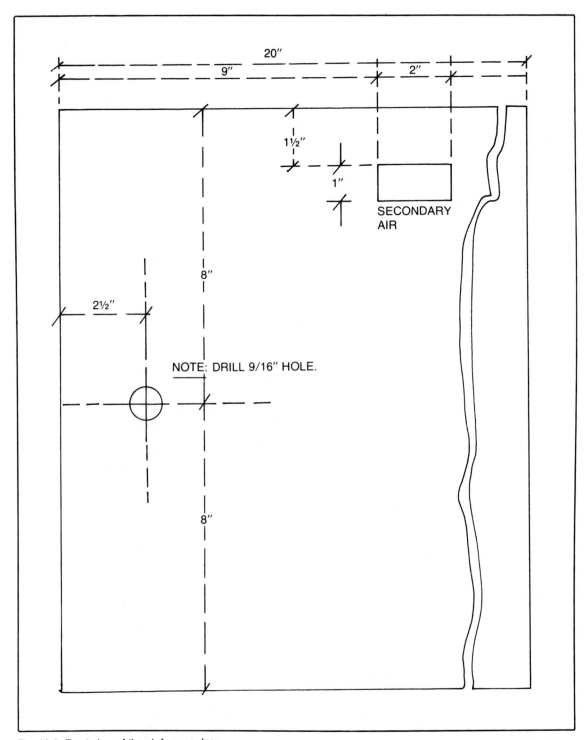

Fig. 10-8. Front view of the air furnace door.

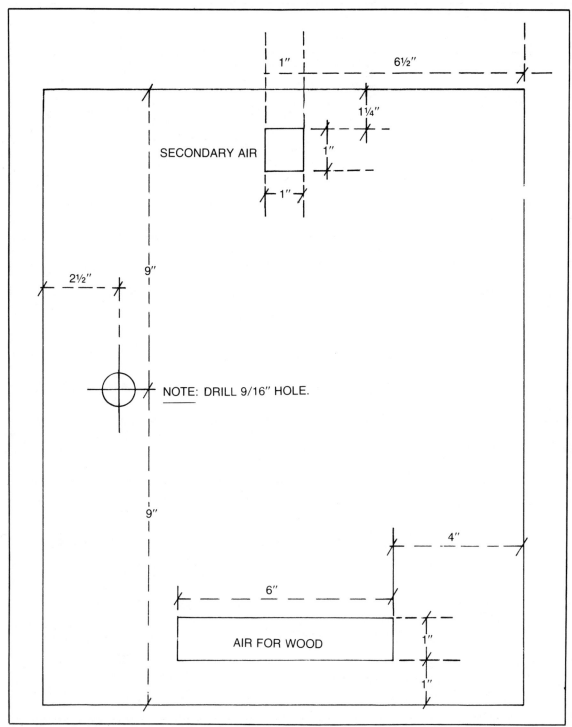

Fig. 10-9. Front view of the door layout for a wood boiler door.

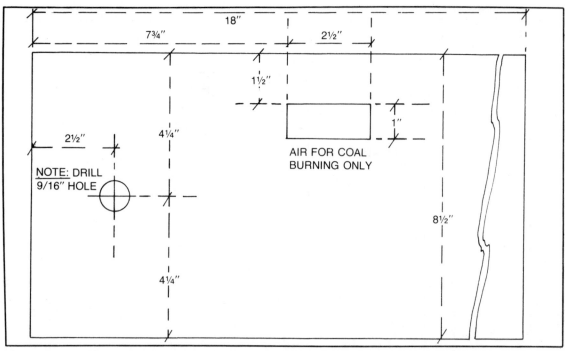

Fig. 10-10. Front view of ash door for the coal and wood boiler.

☐ Turn to the detailed drawing of the door that you're doing. See Figs. 10-1 through 10-11. With soapstone, draw the cut and drill lines.

☐ Once all the cut lines have been drawn, take a hand drill with a small bit and drill a hole in the corner of the slots to be cut. Note: when you start your cut, start in the hole; this prevents trouble going through the door.

☐ While the door is cooling, take the round stock for the handle and lay out bend lines. See Fig. 10-12 if your unit has a single door. See Fig. 10-14 if your unit has a double door.

☐ Once the round stock is layed out, C-clamp the round stock to a bench, C-clamp one of the stove plates to the bench, and then C-clamp the round stock to the plate. Make sure, when clamping the round stock to the plate, that the bend line is lined up to the edge of the plate. Using your torch, heat the round stock until it turns red and bends as shown in Fig. 10-12.

☐ Repeat the direction in the preceding para-

graph if you are building a double-door stove. See Fig. 10-14.

☐ When the handles are cool, use 9/16″ washers to attach handles to the door plates. See Figs. 10-13 through 10-15.

☐ If you are building a double door, attach the center plate to left door of double doors. See Fig. 10-7. If you are building a single door, skip this instruction.

☐ Take the pieces of ½″ flat stock—used for slide handles—heat and bend. See Fig. 10-16.

☐ Attach to the slides as shown in Fig. 10-16.

☐ Take your ½″-×-½″ angle iron tracks and attach them to doors as shown in Figs. 10-17, 10-18, and 10-19.

☐ Now that the door is fabricated, take water-glass glue or furnace cement and border the inside edge of the door(s) with gasket material. This gives you an airtight seal. An alternative to glue the gasket to the door openings' edge.

☐ The door(s) are ready to mount. See Fig. 10-20.

☐ Fabricate the stove.

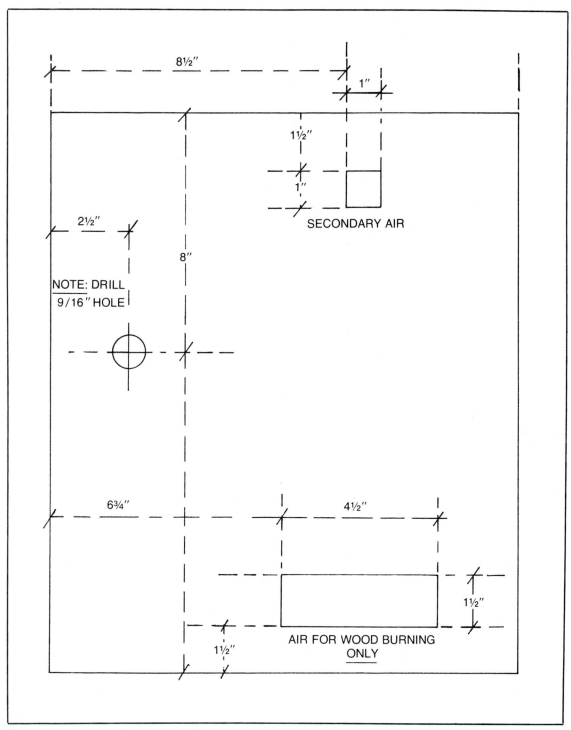

Fig. 10-11. Front view of the door layout for the coal and wood boiler.

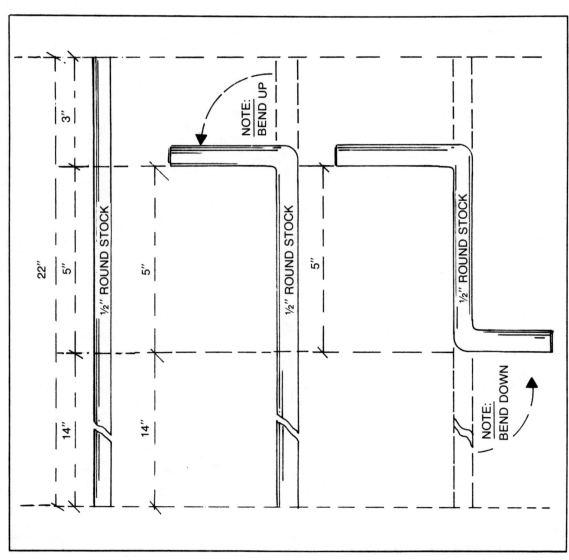

Fig. 10-12. Side view of the handle fabrication, and right door handle.

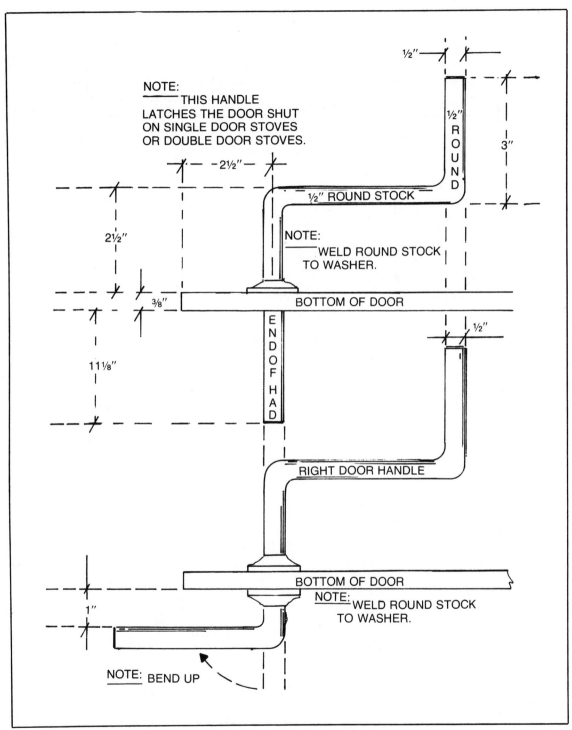

Fig. 10-13. End view of the right door handle (double or single door stove).

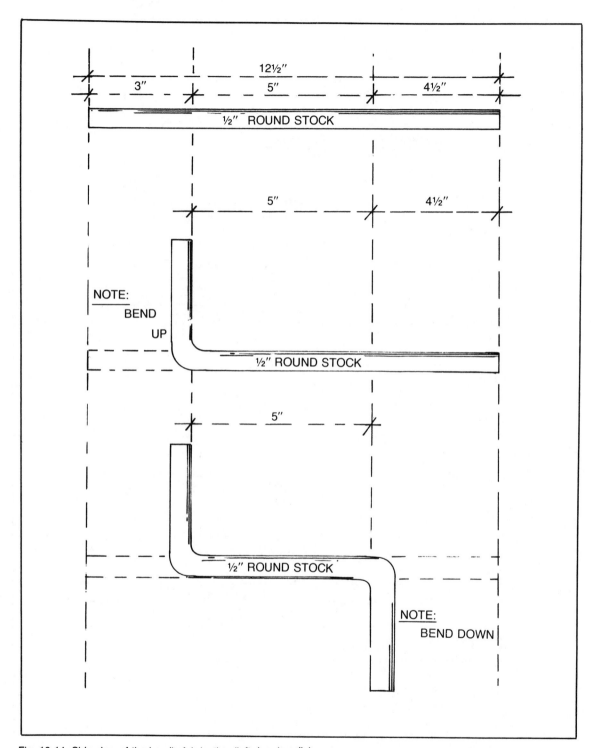

Fig. 10-14. Side view of the handle fabrication (left door handle).

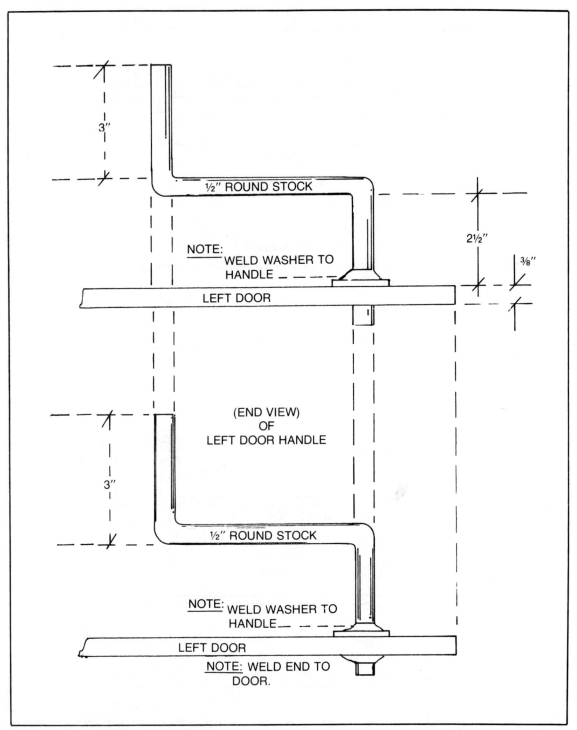

Fig. 10-15. End view of the left door handle.

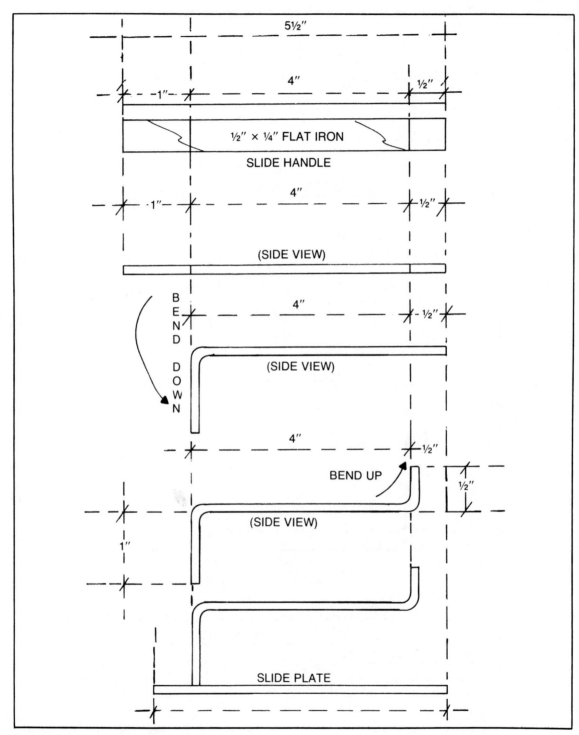

Fig. 10-16. Side view of completed slide handle.

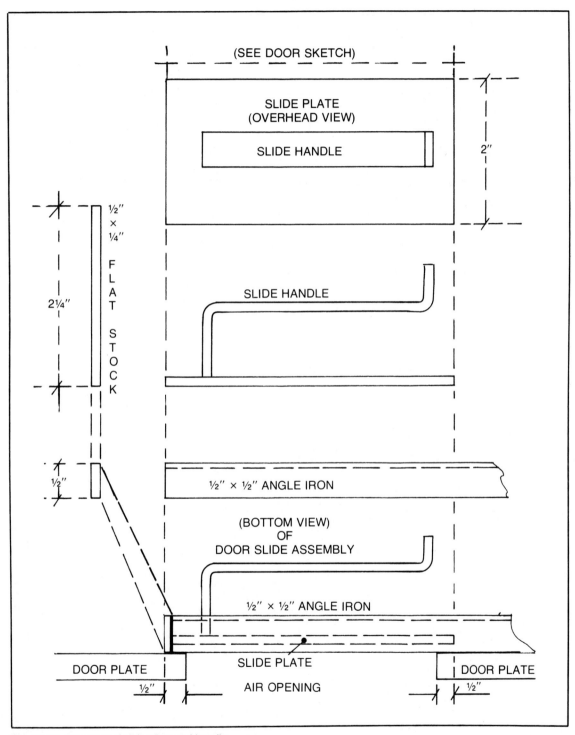

(SEE DOOR SKETCH)

SLIDE PLATE
(OVERHEAD VIEW)

SLIDE HANDLE

2″

½″ × ¼″ FLAT STOCK

2¼″

SLIDE HANDLE

½″

½″ × ½″ ANGLE IRON

(BOTTOM VIEW)
OF
DOOR SLIDE ASSEMBLY

½″ × ½″ ANGLE IRON

DOOR PLATE

SLIDE PLATE

AIR OPENING

DOOR PLATE

½″

½″

Fig. 10-17. Side view of slide plate and handle.

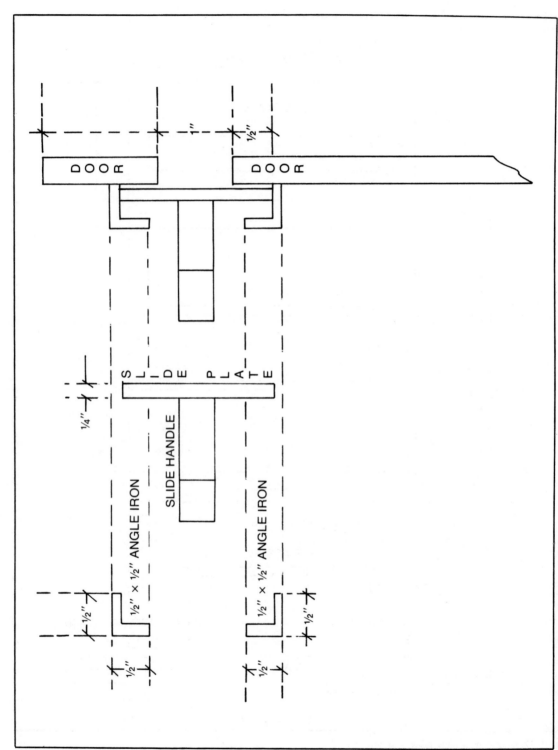

Fig. 10-18. Side view of the air slide assembly.

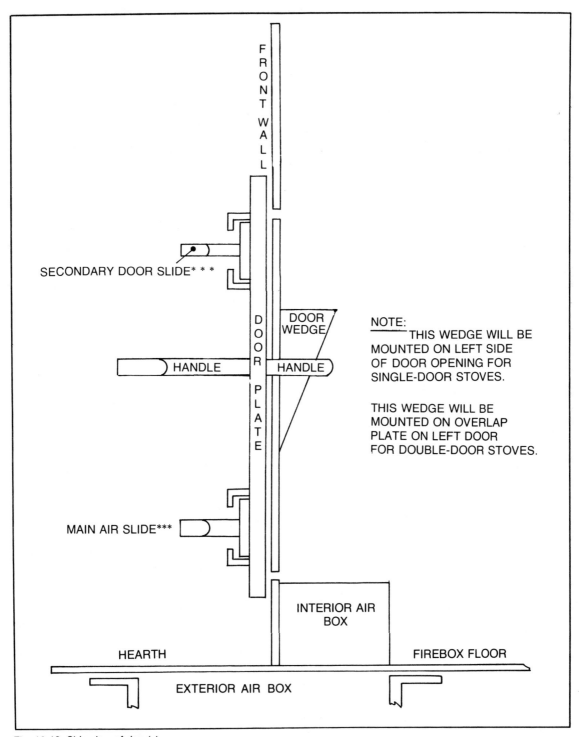

Fig. 10-19. Side view of door(s).

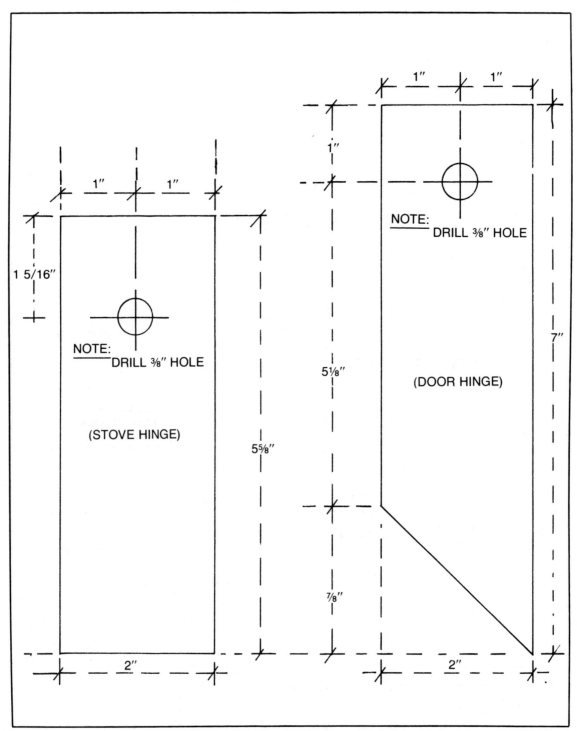

Fig. 10-20. Front view of the standard door hinges.

# Chapter 11

# Baffling Systems

VARIOUS FACTORS SUCH AS the length, width, and depth of the stove determine the type of baffle that should be installed. Another factor is the size of the exhaust that is to be mounted on your stove. If you are designing your own stove, install an 8″ exhaust pipe. You can always reduce the exhaust, with stove pipe reducers, but you can never enlarge it at a later time. Refer to the section on stovepipe in Chapter 24.

If you are planning to burn only coal, you should completely omit a baffling system. If you will be burning wood and coal, a sliding baffle system is best. The sliding baffle should only be used in a top exhaust stove. Nevertheless, if you build a stove with sufficient height, it can be installed in a back-exhaust stove.

If you will be burning only wood, you can choose between the nortic baffle (Fig. 11-1) and the extended baffle (Fig. 11-2). Both designs are efficient. The sliding baffle is shown in Fig. 11-3. If you are designing your own baffling system, you must take into account two very important factors. First, the distance from the roof of your stove (total number of square inches) should equal the total number of square inches of space of the exhaust. Second, do not extend the baffle plate too far.

Too long a smoke path, due to too much baffling, can be identified by the following.

☐ The fire refuses to burn hot.

☐ When the doors are left open, smoke escapes out the door opening.

☐ A large buildup of creosote in the stovepipe or chimney is found within one or two days of using the stove.

In addition to checking your baffling system, you must also check the entire exhaust and chimney systems and use the process of elimination to determine the cause of problems. Similar symptoms, as those associated with a baffle plate that has been extended too far, can occur. You can experience the same symptoms with the use of single-wall pipe, air drawn through the stove because of the chimney

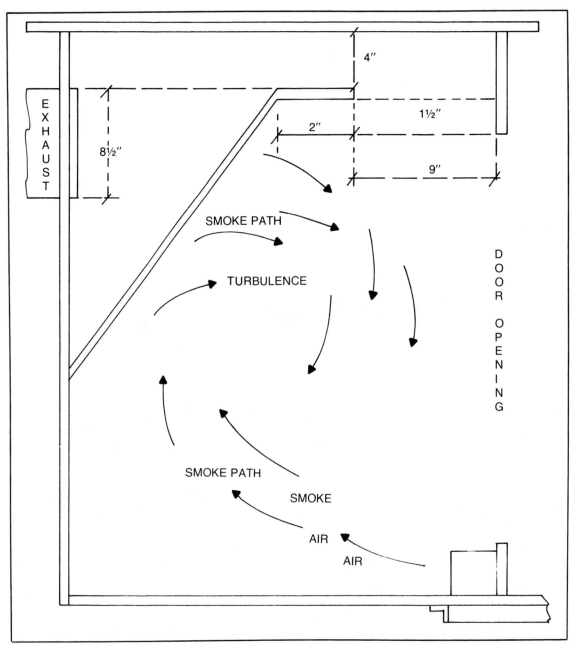

Fig. 11-1. Side view of the smoke path, nortic baffle system.

clean-out door being left open or the use of an old chimney with rotten mortar, burning green wood, or too short a chimney.

Make sure that you read Chapter 24 on instal-lations and Chapter 23 dealing with operating your solid-fuel unit at maximum efficiency. Potential problems that can cause you a great deal of aggrava-tion can be eliminated from the start.

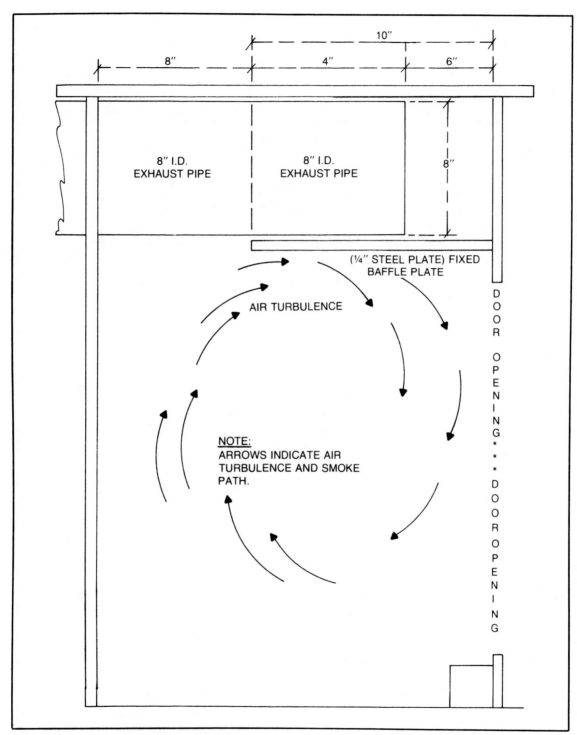

Fig. 11-2. Side view of the extended baffle system.

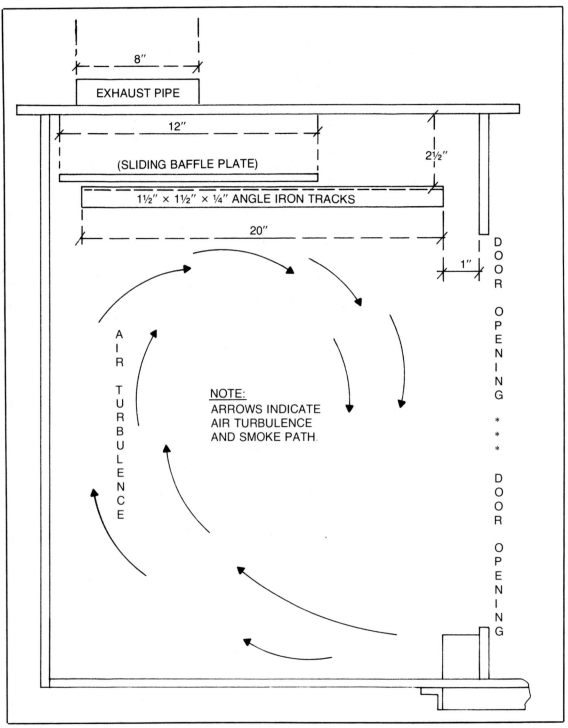

Fig. 11-3. Side view of the sliding baffle system.

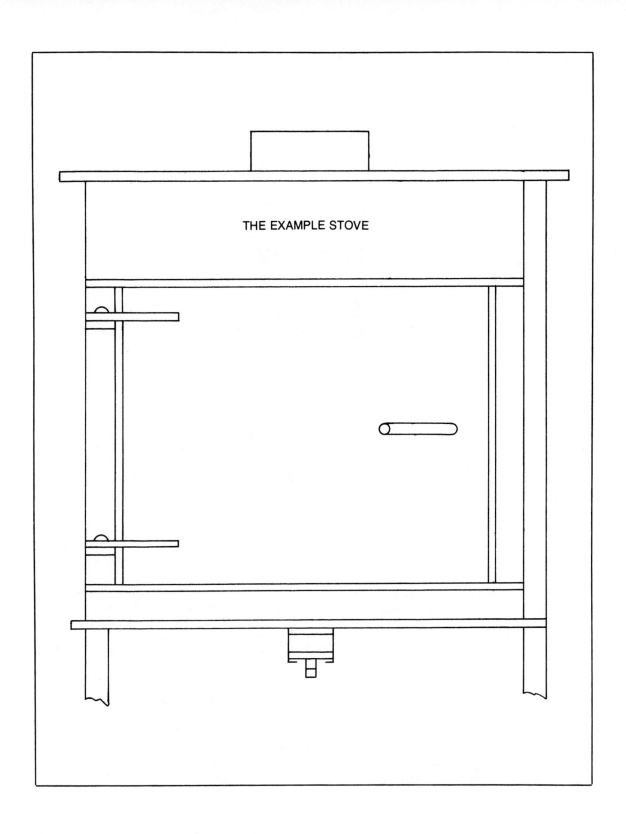

THE EXAMPLE STOVE

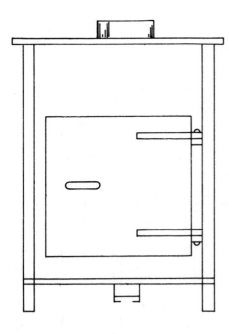

# Chapter 12

# Example Stove

**T**HE EXAMPLE STOVE IS INCLUDED in this book as a model to follow for those of you who would like to design your own stove. To do so, you must understand how to determine the size of the plates according to predetermined dimensions of the stove. How to make this determination is included in Chapter 6. See Chapter 5 for how to draw sketches, hints on reading sketches, and drawing your own sketches.

## FABRICATION OF MISCELLANEOUS PARTS

To start this project, start with the miscellaneous fabrication (see Tables 12-1 and 12-2). This section is the hardest to explain and the most time-consuming part of the stove. You should previously have decided on the following:

☐ The type of exhaust (top or back).
☐ The type of baffle that you are going to use.
☐ The type of solid fuel that you are going to burn.

You are now ready to follow the fabrication instructions for your stove. Remember that a wood-burning unit requires an air slide in the bottom of the door. A wood-and-coal-burning unit, however, requires an air control system as shown in Figs. 10-2 through 10-6 and Figs. 10-8 through 10-11.

Turn to Chapter 9, the section of the book on air controls, and gather together the parts shown in Figs. 9-1 and 9-2. Fabricate the illustrated interior air control. Instructions are given in Chapter 9 on how to do this.

Fabricate the exterior air control. Refer to Fig. 9-3 and 9-4.

Referring to the diagram of your stove, and depicting the mounting of the door (on your stove), you will see trim pieces around the door. Using this drawing, cut the door trim pieces according to the size shown on the sketch (See Fig. 12-15).

Once the trim pieces are cut, refer to the door diagram (Fig. 10-1) and find the door that corresponds with your stove. Lay out the door according to Fig. 10-1. Using Figs. 10-12 through 10-20, fabricate the parts that will be mounted on the door. Drill the door handle hole and cut the openings.

Table 12-1. Example Stove Data.

Firebox height: 30″
Firebox depth: 24″
Firebox width: 30″
Heating Capacity: 1800 square feet (approximately)
Fuel: wood or coal depending on your air-control system and if you build a grate
Burn time: 10 to 12 hours (approximately)
Fabrication time: 15 to 18 hours (at home)
Exhaust pipe: 8″ Inside Diameter (ID) recommended directions are given in the fabrication instructions
Plate weight: 474.49 pounds
Log size: 27″

Once the door is prepared, mount the slides and handles to the door.

Refer to Fig. 10-20 showing standard hinges. Fabricate the hinges using the sketch as a visual aid. Figure 10-20 shows one set of hinges. If you are using a single door on your stove, you will need two sets of hinges. If you are building a double-door stove, four sets of hinges will be needed.

If you decide you want to trim the edges of the roof plate, now is the time to do it. Take the roof plate and measure it's width and length. Add the two measurements and multiply the answer by two. The answer gives you the length of the trim you'll need. Add 2 inches to that measurement for waste.

**Table 12-2. Example Stove Material List.**

| amount | size | | | | letter mark | location | weight |
|--------|------|---|---|---|-------------|----------|--------|
| 1 | 32½″ | × | 30″ | × ¼″ | A | floor | 69.12 lbs. |
| 1 | 33″ | × | 30¼″ | × ¼″ | B | back | 70.78 lbs. |
| 1 | 33″ | × | 30″ | × ¼″ | C | front | 70.19 lbs. |
| 2 | 30¼″ | × | 24″ | × ¼″ | D | sides | 102.95 lbs. |
| 1 | 35″ | × | 26½″ | × ¼″ | E | roof | 65.76 lbs. |
| 1 | 25″ | × | 20″ | × ⅜″ | F | door | 53.15 lbs. |
| 1 | 20″ | × | 30″ | × ¼″ | G | baffle | 42.54 lbs. |
| | | | | | | Total plate weight: | 474.49 lbs. |

**Steel List**

| amount | length | description | use |
|--------|--------|-------------|-----|
| 1 | 20′ | 1½″ × 1½″ × ¼″ angle iron | legs and brick stays |
| 1 | 20′ | ½″ × ¼″ flat iron | roof hearth and door trim |
| 1 | 12′ | 2″ × ⅜″ flat iron | hinges, top door trim, baffle end |
| 1 | 14″ | ½″ round stock | door handle |
| 1 | 5″ | 8″ inside diameter pipe | exhaust for stove |

Material needed for air controls is listed in Table 9-1.

**General Material**

| amount | description | use |
|--------|-------------|-----|
| 30 | split firebrick | firebox and side lining |
| 60 | asbestos or spun-glass gasket | door gasket |
| 2 | ⅜″ rivets | hinge pins |
| 1 | small can of furnace cement | door gasket glue |
| 2 | 9/16″ flat washers | door handle stays |
| 3 | spray cans (or 2 quarts) of high-heat stove paint | surface paint |

Using the ½″-×-¼″ flat stock as the trim material, cut a piece that measures the sum of the four sides (plus 2″). Using a flat surface, lay the roof plate upside down and, starting in a back corner, stand the ½″ flat stock on edge (the ½″ side vertical to the roof). Place it against the edge of the roof. Once the trim is in place, tack it to the roof (tacking every 6″) making sure that you are keeping the trim straight. When you reach a corner stop tacking.

Using your cutting torch, heat the trim at the corner. When the trim is red hot, slowly bend the trim around the corner. Once you have made the turn, begin tacking again until you reach the next corner. Then repeat the same procedure until you're back where you started. When you have reached that point, and the last tack is made, cut off the extra trim.

Using the 1½″-×-1½″-×-¼″ angle iron, cut leg angles. Their length will be determined by the height of the firebox plus the height that you want the stove to be from the floor. To figure the length of the front stove legs (when partially sitting on a hearth), determine the height of the hearth and add 2 inches (for clearance) and take into account the height of the firebox. The length, (or height) of the back legs can be determined by the height of the firebox plus 2 inches (the clearance that was allowed in the front).

While cutting the leg angles, you might as well cut the brick stay angles. The length of these can be determined by the interior depth of the firebox and by the length of the back wall.

## FIREBOX PREPARATION

Now that you have completed the miscellaneous pieces, you can prepare to build your firebox. Before starting the actual fabrication of the stove, the plates should be layed out on the floor in order of the fabrication. This can be done very simply by:

☐ Sweeping down the area where you are going to be working.

☐ Laying your floor plate down in the middle of the floor.

☐ Laying your back plate on floor just behind the floor plate.

☐ Laying the side plates along side of the floor plate in their respective places.

☐ Laying the front plate just in front of the floor plate.

The roof plate, the door, and miscellaneous steel parts should be layed out to the side of the work area in order to be close at hand when it is needed. Make sure that all rules of safety apply before going any further.

## STOVE FABRICATION INSTRUCTIONS

With the plate in position, take the back plate B and place it against the back of floor plate A. Leave a ¼″ overlap hanging past the floor plate on each side. When plate B is in place, tack weld it to floor plate A. Keep a 90° angle. See Figs. 12-1 and 12-2.

Once plate B is tacked, take side plate D and place it against the side of floor plate A. Butt plate D to back plate B. When side plate D is in position, tack weld it to floor plate A and back plate B. See Figs. 12-3 and 12-4.

Repeat the direction, given in the preceding paragraph, on the opposite side. See Figs. 12-3 and 12-4.

Take front plate C, stand it on top of floor plate A, and lean it against (or butt it against) both plates (D). When in position, tack weld to the floor plate and side plates. Pay attention to the alignment of the edges. See Figs. 12-5 and 12-6.

Using Jet rod, weld the floor of the stove to the walls. Once the floor is welded, lay the stove on it's side and weld the side plate to the front and back plates. Upon completion of this, lay the stove on it's opposite side and weld the other side plate to the front and back wall plates.

When welding your sides, you can also, as you finish welding each side, tack weld the brick stay angles into position. This can be done quite easily by taking a split firebrick and laying it into position. With the stove upright, the brick would be standing with the 9″ side vertical. Take the angle, (one leg touching the wall, the other leg overlapping the brick by about ½″) and tack the angle to the wall (using 2″ long tacks). When tacking, the angle will lean away from the brick. This is preferred. It leaves room so that you can put in, or take out, the brick. See Fig. 12-15. With the brick stays in, the next thing to install is the baffle system. Refer to

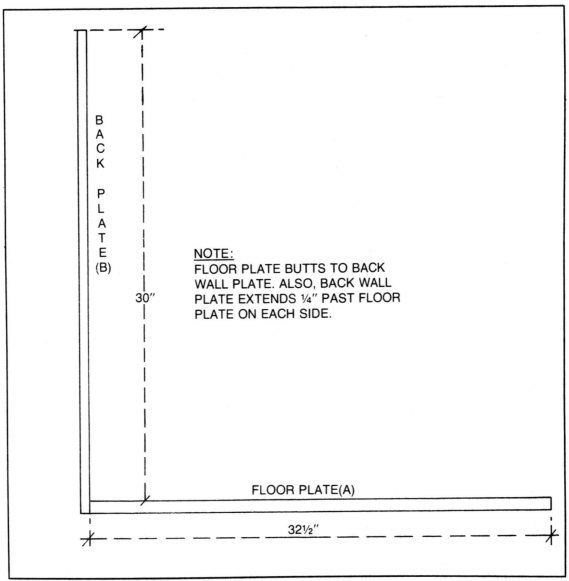

B
A
C
K

P
L
A
T
E
(B)

30″

NOTE:
FLOOR PLATE BUTTS TO BACK
WALL PLATE. ALSO, BACK WALL
PLATE EXTENDS ¼″ PAST FLOOR
PLATE ON EACH SIDE.

FLOOR PLATE(A)

32½″

Fig. 12-1. Side view of the back wall assembly.

Fig. 11-3 and Figs. 12-7 through 12-9 that show baffling systems. Install the baffle.

Install the roof plate. To do this, take the roof plate and lay it on the floor, upside down. Take the firebox, turn it upside down, and place it on the roof. Pay strict attention to the following:

☐ That the firebox is square to the roof.
☐ That the firebox is centered to the roof.

Make sure that the distance from the box to the edge of the roof is equal on all four sides. Once the box is in position, tack weld the four sides. After the four sides are tack welded, weld all four sides solid. See Fig. 12-8.

After the roof plate is in place, install the exhaust pipe. When positioning the exhaust pipe, always keep the pipe centered and in 1″ from the

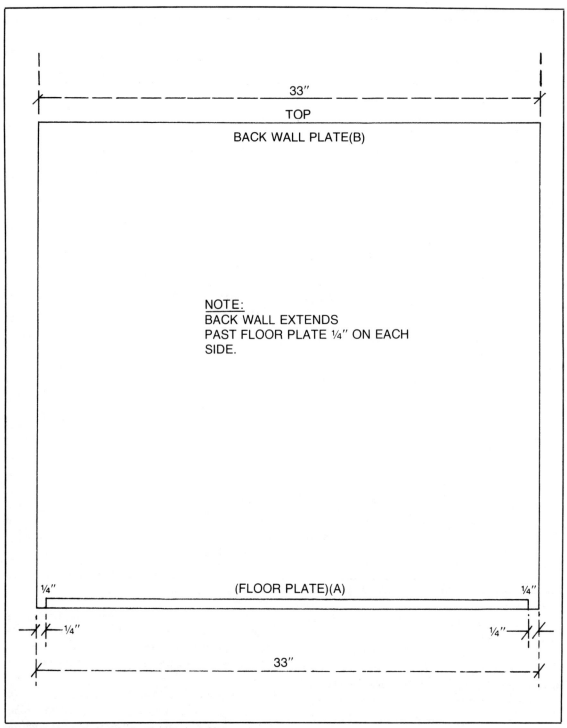

Fig. 12-2. Front view of the back wall assembly.

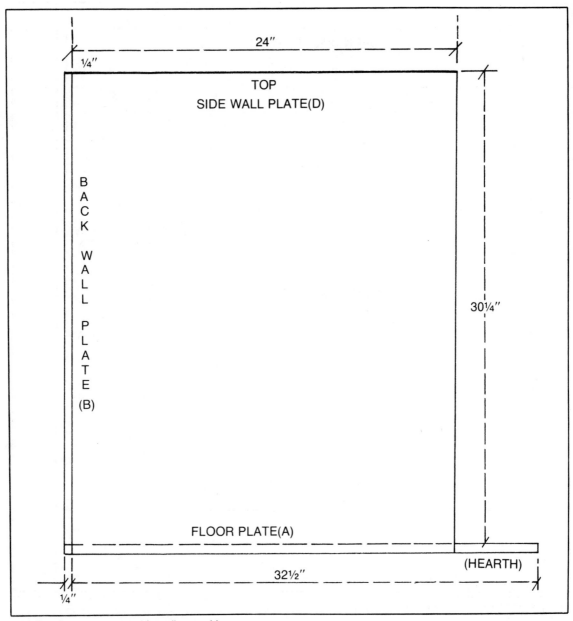

24"

¼"

TOP
SIDE WALL PLATE(D)

B
A
C
K

W
A
L
L

P
L
A
T
E

(B)

30¼"

FLOOR PLATE(A)

(HEARTH)

32½"

¼"

Fig. 12-3. Side view of the side wall assembly.

back wall plate, if top exhaust, or down 1″ from the roof plate if the stove is a back exhaust.

To install the exhaust pipe, measure the length of the roof plate (or back plate) and draw a center line. Using the 1″ line as the one side of the box (you're about to draw), draw a square box with a length and width that equals the exhaust pipe's *outside diameter* (OD). In this example, it will be 8½″. The box will measure 8½″ × 8½″.

Once the box is drawn, place the exhaust pipe in it and draw a circle around the inside of the pipe, using the pipe as a guide. Remove the pipe, and cut

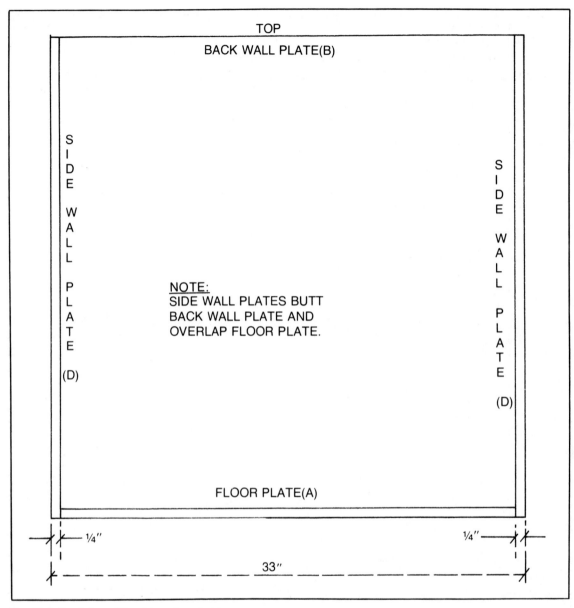

Fig. 12-4. Front view of the side wall assembly.

the circle out, with your cutting torch. After cutting the circle out, place your exhaust pipe back into position on the plate. Tack, in at least two places, and then weld it solid with Jet rod. See Fig. 12-9.

The legs and the exterior air control are the next to be installed. To do this, measure in 15" from each side of the stove and draw a straight line.

Measure back, from the front edge of the floor plate, 6½" and draw a line. Measure back, from the line you've just drawn, another 2" and draw another line. You should now have a 2"-×-2½" box that is 6½" in from the front of your floor plate.

You can now draw the leg slots as shown in Fig. 12-10. Using a paint can as a guide, radius the ends of your hearth. As a visual aid, see Figs. 12-10 and 12-11. After all of these things are drawn, cut them out with a torch. Once the cutting is done, install the exterior air control and legs. See Fig. 12-11.

Following Fig. 12-12, draw the cut lines for the door opening. Cut it out with your cutting torch.

Draw a box around your door opening 1″ out from the edges of the opening. See Fig. 12-13. This will mark the locations of the door.

Mount the door using the guide lines you've just drawn. Once the door is in place, lay the trim along side the door and tack it into place. You must remember to leave a ¼″ space, between the door

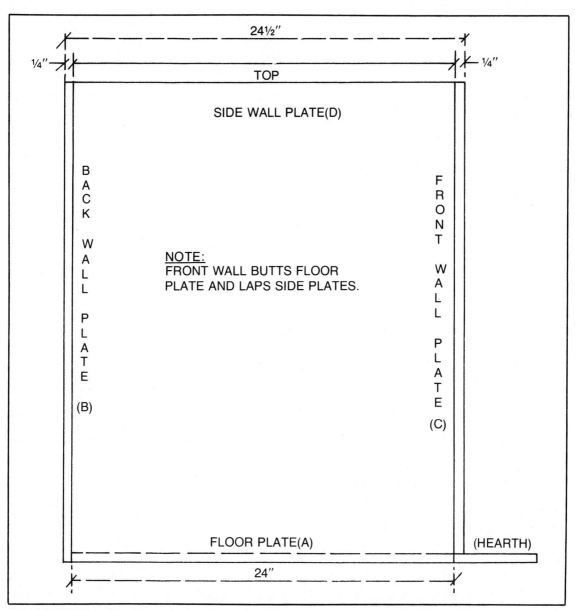

Fig. 12-5. Side view of the front wall assembly.

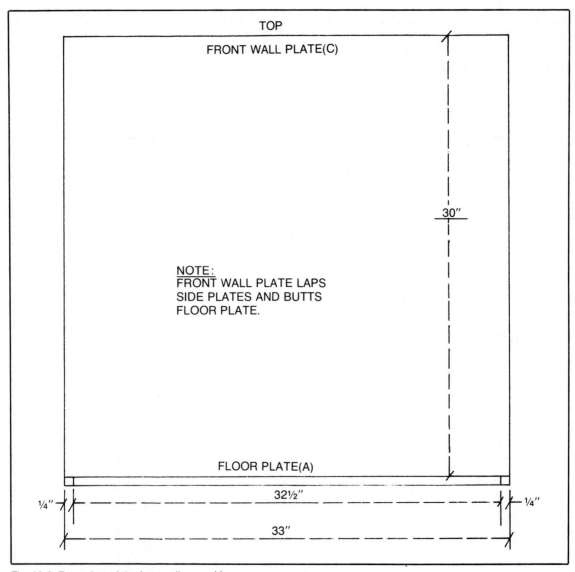

TOP

FRONT WALL PLATE(C)

30″

NOTE:
FRONT WALL PLATE LAPS
SIDE PLATES AND BUTTS
FLOOR PLATE.

FLOOR PLATE(A)

¼″        32½″        ¼″

33″

Fig. 12-6. Front view of the front wall assembly.

and the door trim, on the side (of the door) that the handle is on. This allows for the swing. See Fig. 12-14.

Put the pins in the hinges, and mount them, as shown in Fig. 12-14. When they are tack welded into position, remember to C-clamp the two sections of hinge together before you weld them to the stove and door. Once welded, allow the weld to cool before removing the C-clamp.

After the door is mounted, place the (door) locking wedge inside the door opening lip and weld. See Fig. 10-19.

Take the ½″-flat stock (about 46″ long) and, while the stove is on it's back, tack weld it to the front of the hearth in the same manner as you tacked the trim to the roof plate. When the hearth is trimmed, cut off the spare stock and attach the end to the angle iron leg.

Stand the stove in the upright position. Install the interior air control over the air opening, in your stove, and tack weld to the floor. Use tacks about 2″ long (one on each side and one in front). See Fig. 9-5.

Install the firebrick as shown in Fig. 12-15. If any cutting must be done on the brick, it can be done with a circular saw (with a masonary blade). Once the brick is installed, clean all slag off the welds. Scrape any spatter (from welding) off the stove and (using spray cans or a paint pad) paint the stove. Remember to use a high-heat paint; anything rated for over 1000° will due.

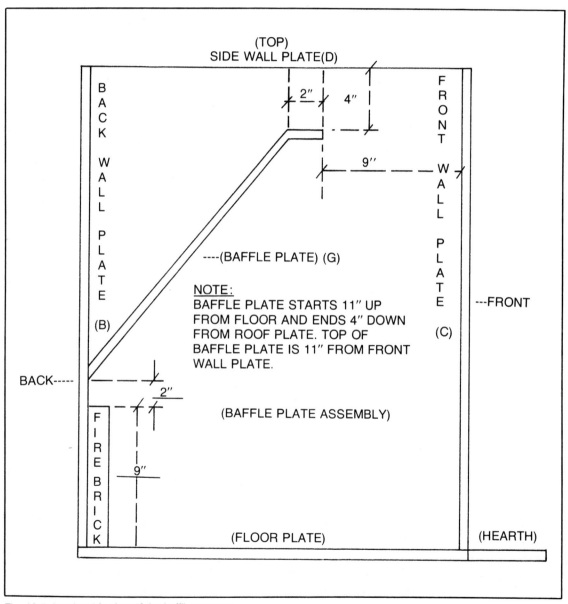

Fig. 12-7. Interior side view of the baffling system.

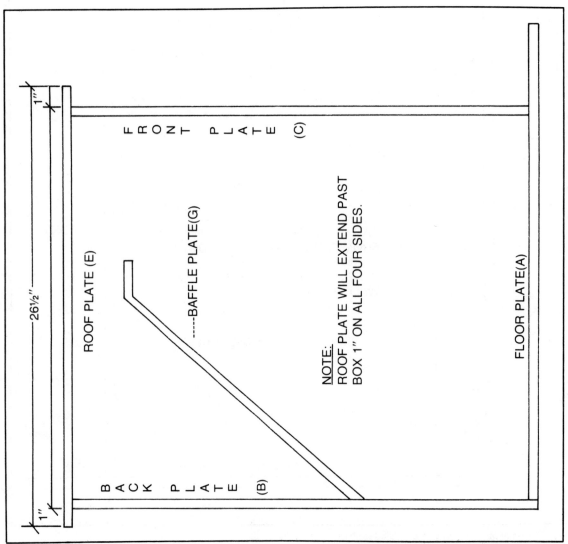

ROOF PLATE (E)

BAFFLE PLATE(G)

FRONT PLATE (C)

NOTE:
ROOF PLATE WILL EXTEND PAST
BOX 1" ON ALL FOUR SIDES.

FLOOR PLATE(A)

BACK PLATE (B)

26½"

1"

1"

Fig. 12-8. Side view of the roof installation.

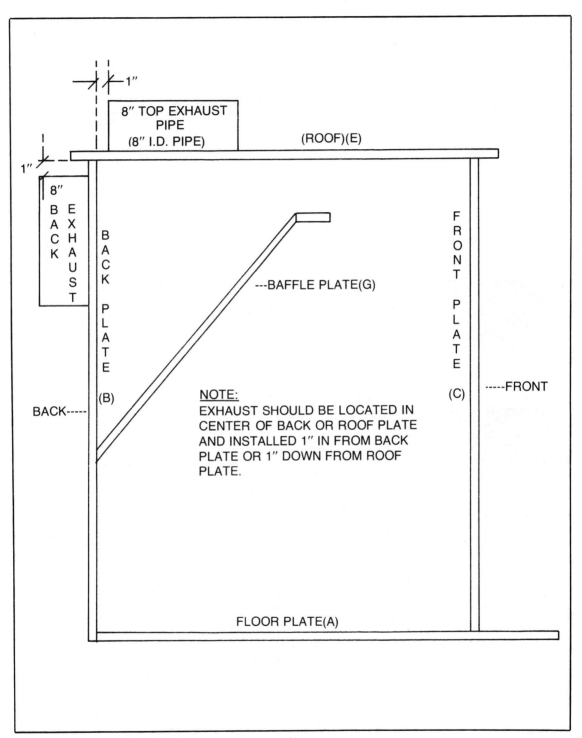

Fig. 12-9. Side view of the exhaust installation (top and back).

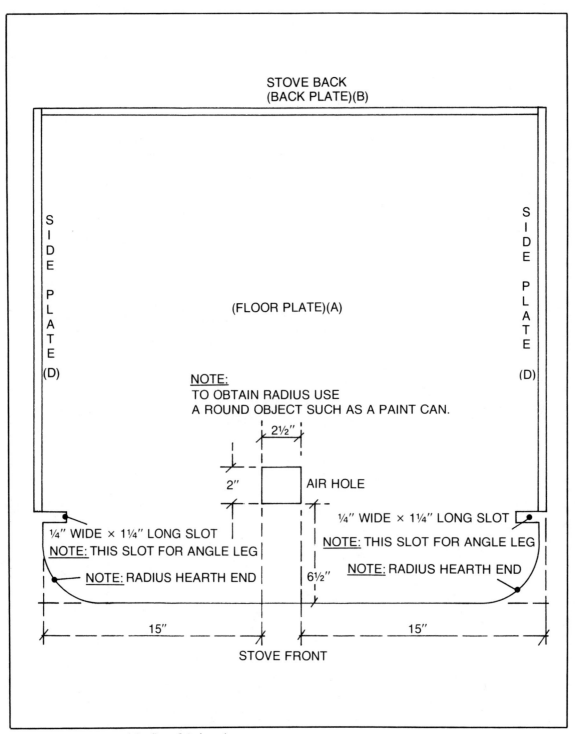

Fig. 12-10. Bottom view of the floor plate layout.

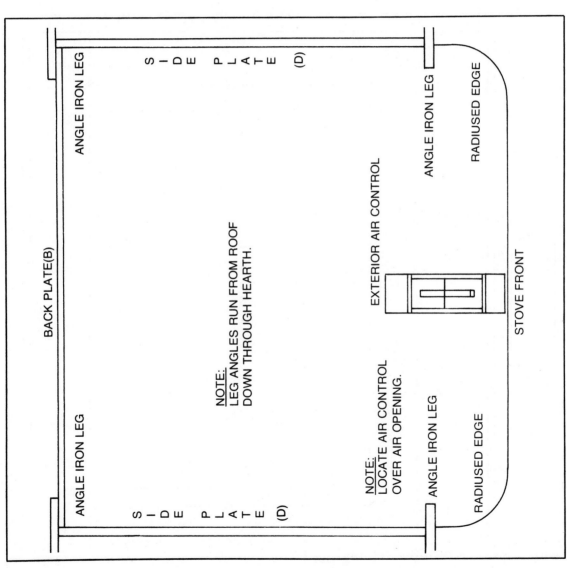

Fig. 12-11. Bottom view of the leg and air control installation.

117

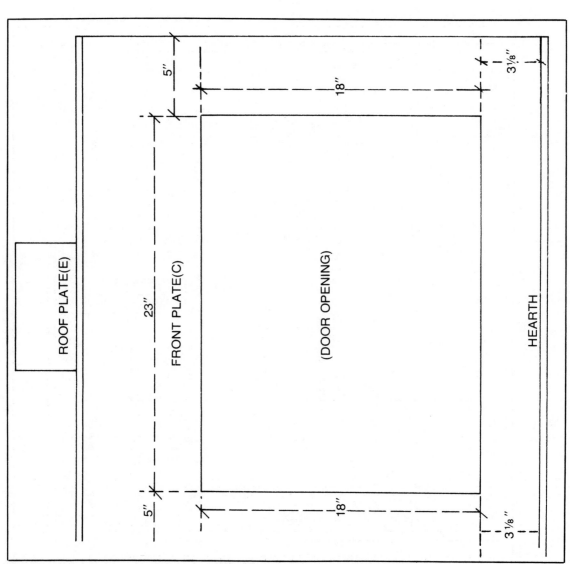

Fig. 12-12. Front view of the door opening.

ROOF PLATE(E)

FRONT PLATE(C)

(DOOR OPENING)

HEARTH

5"

5"

23"

18"

18"

3 1/8"

3 1/8"

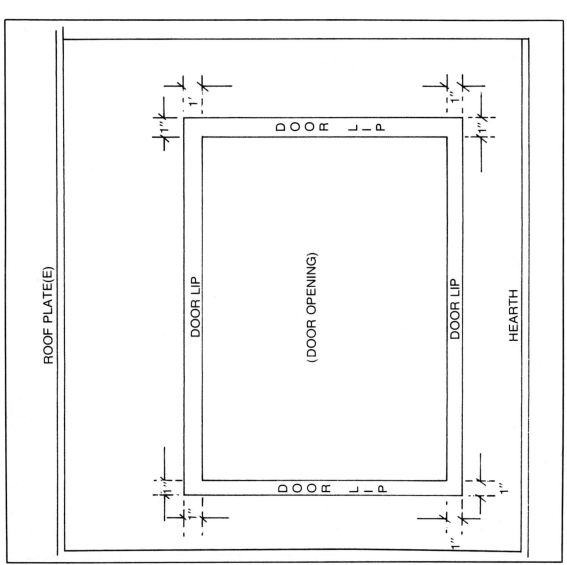

Fig. 12-13. Front view of the door opening.

119

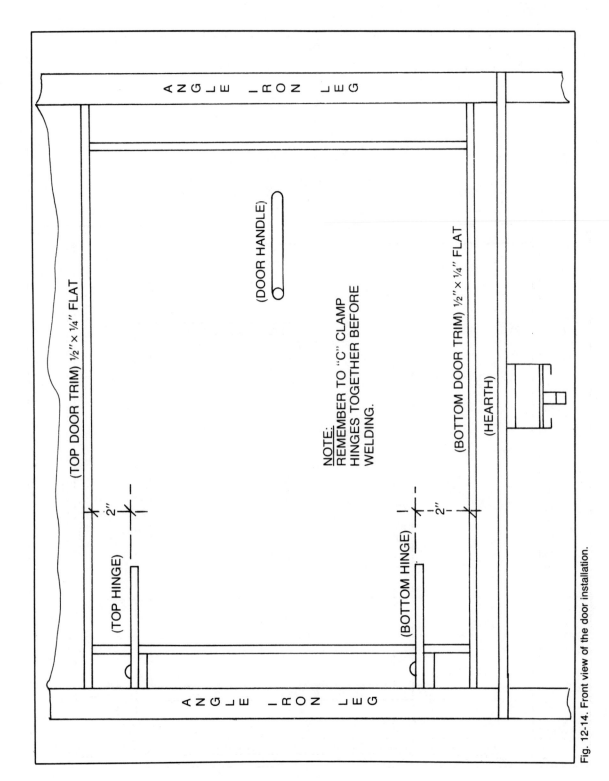

Fig. 12-14. Front view of the door installation.

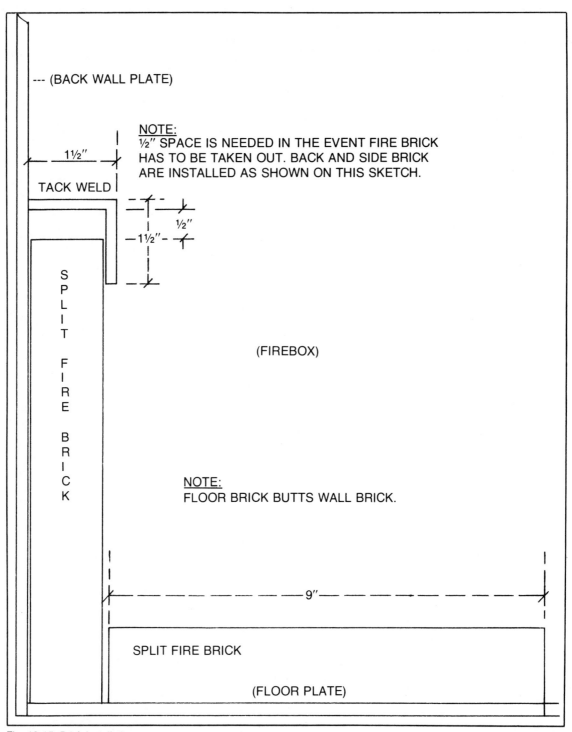

--- (BACK WALL PLATE)

NOTE:
½″ SPACE IS NEEDED IN THE EVENT FIRE BRICK
HAS TO BE TAKEN OUT. BACK AND SIDE BRICK
ARE INSTALLED AS SHOWN ON THIS SKETCH.

1½″

TACK WELD

½″

1½″

S
P
L
I
T

F
I
R
E

B
R
I
C
K

(FIREBOX)

NOTE:
FLOOR BRICK BUTTS WALL BRICK.

9″

SPLIT FIRE BRICK

(FLOOR PLATE)

Fig. 12-15. Brick installation.

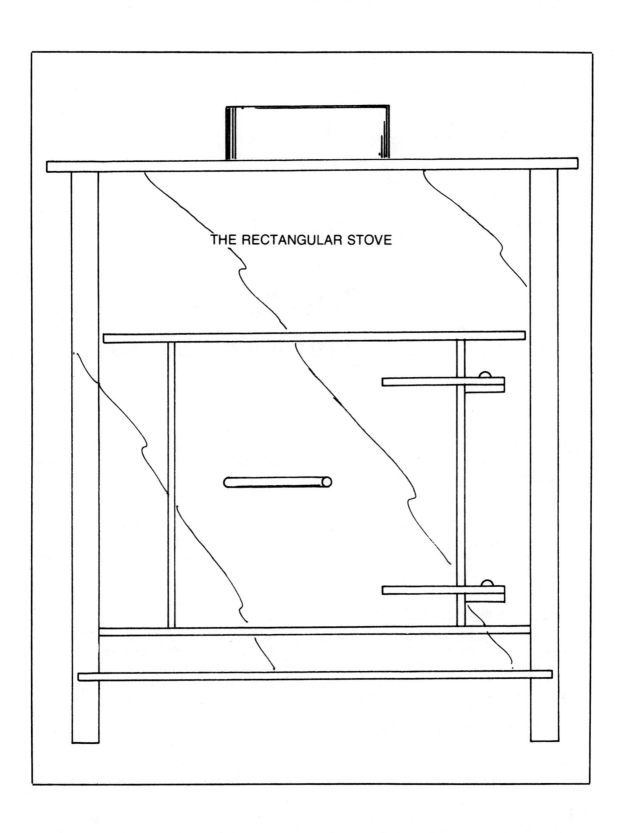

THE RECTANGULAR STOVE

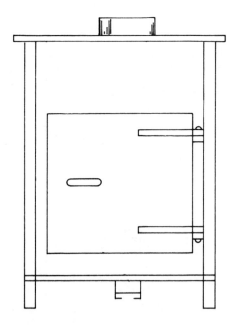

# Chapter 13

# Rectangular and Square Stoves

TWO TYPES OF BOX STOVES described in this chapter, the rectangular stove and the square stove, are the simplest stoves to build. The heating capacity and the location of the stove are factors for you to consider in choosing between these two models. The instructions for the fabrication of miscellaneous parts and stove fabrication are the same for both models. The only difference is in the depth of the firebox. See Tables 13-1, 13-2 and 13-3.

### FABRICATION OF MISCELLANEOUS PARTS

To start this project, begin with the fabrication of miscellaneous parts. You should have already decided on the following:

☐ The type of exhaust (top or back).
☐ The type of baffle that you are going to use.
☐ The type of solid fuel that you are going to burn.

You are now ready to follow the fabrication instructions for your stove.

A wood-burning unit requires an air slide in the bottom of the door. A unit that burns wood and coal, however, requires an air control system as shown in Figs. 10-1 through 10-6 and Figs. 10-8 through 10-11.

Turn to Chapter 9, the section of the book on air controls, and gather the parts shown in Figs. 9-1 and 9-2. Fabricate the illustrated interior air control. Instructions are given in Chapter 9 on how to do this.

Fabricate the exterior air control. Refer to Figs. 9-3 and 9-4.

Referring to the diagram of your stove, and depicting the mounting of the door (on your stove), you will see trim pieces around the door. Using this drawing, cut the door trim pieces according to the size shown on the sketch (Fig. 13-18).

Once the trim pieces are cut, refer to the door diagram (Fig. 10 .2) and find the door that corresponds with your stove. Lay out the door according to Fig. 10-2. Using Figs. 10-12 through 10-20, fabricate the parts that will be mounted on the door.

**Table 13-1. Square Stove Data.**

| | |
|---|---|
| Firebox height: | 24″ |
| Firebox width: | 24″ |
| Firebox depth: | 24″ |
| Heating Capacity: | approximately 1600 square feet |
| Fuel: | wood; can be converted to coal with a grate |
| Burn time: | on low burn, 10 to 12 hours |
| Fabrication time: | 8 hours (professionally) 12 to 16 hours (do-it-yourselfer) |
| Exhaust pipe: | 8″ Inside Diameter (ID) |
| Plate weight: | 295.55 pounds (approximately) |
| Log size: | 21″ |

Drill the door handle hole and cut the openings. Once the door is prepared, mount the slides and handles to the door.

Refer to Fig. 10-20 showing standard hinges. Fabricate the hinges using the sketch as a visual aid. Figure 10-20 shows one set of hinges. If you are using a single door on your stove, you will need two sets of hinges. If you are building a double-door stove, four sets of hinges will be needed. This stove was designed with one door.

If you decide you want to trim the edges of the roof plate, now is the time to do it. Take the roof plate, and measure it's width and length. Add the two measurements and multiply the answer by two. The answer gives you the length of the trim you'll need. Add 2 inches to the measurement for waste. Using the ½″-×-¼″ flat stock as the trim material, cut a piece that measures the sum of the four sides (plus 2″). Using a flat surface, lay the roof plate, upside down and, starting in a back corner, stand

**Table 13-2. Rectangular Stove Data.**

| | |
|---|---|
| Firebox height: | 24″ |
| Firebox width: | 24″ |
| Firebox depth: | 36″ |
| Heating capacity: | approximately 2500 square feet |
| Fuel: | wood; can be converted to coal with a grate |
| Burn time: | on low burn, 10 to 12 hours |
| Fabrication time: | 8 hours (professionally) 12 to 16 hours (do-it-yourselfer) |
| Exhaust pipe: | 8″ Inside Diameter (ID) |
| Plate weight: | 396.29 pounds (approximately) |
| Log size: | 33″ |

Table 13-3. Rectangular and Square Stove Material List.

**Table 13-3. Rectangular and Square Stove Material List.**

### Square Stove

| amount | size | letter mark | location | weight |
|---|---|---|---|---|
| 1 | 30" × 23½" × ¼" | A | floor | 49.99 lbs. |
| 1 | 24" × 24¼" × ¼" | B | back | 40.89 lbs. |
| 1 | 24" × 24" × ¼" | C | front | 40.41 lbs. |
| 2 | 24" × 24¼" × ¼" | D | sides | 81.68 lbs. |
| 1 | 26" × 26½" × ¼" | E | roof | 44.31 lbs. |
| 1 | 14" × 14" × ⅜" | F | door | 13.90 lbs. |
| 1 | 23¾" × 14½" × ¼" | G | baffle | 24.42 lbs. |
| | | | | Total Weight: 295.55 lbs. |

### Rectangular Stove

| amount | size | letter mark | location | weight |
|---|---|---|---|---|
| 1 | 42" × 23½" × ¼" | A | floor | 69.89 lbs. |
| 1 | 24¼" × 24" × ¼" | B | back | 40.84 lbs. |
| 1 | 24" × 24" × ¼" | C | front | 40.41 lbs. |
| 2 | 35¼" × 24¼" × ¼" | D | sides | 122.52 lbs. |
| 1 | 38" × 26" × ¼" | E | roof | 65.59 lbs. |
| 1 | 14" × 14" × ⅜" | F | door | 32.53 lbs. |
| 1 | 23¾" × 14½" × ¼" | G | baffle | 24.42 lbs. |
| | | | | Total Weight: 396.29 lbs. |

### Steel List for Both Stoves

| amount | length | description | use |
|---|---|---|---|
| 1 | 20' | 1½" × 1½" × ¼" angle iron | legs and brick stays |
| 1 | 20' | ½" × ¼" flat iron | roof, hearth, and door trim |
| 1 | 12' | 2" × ⅜" flat iron | hinges, top door trim, baffle |
| 1 | 14" | ½" round stock | door handle |
| 1 | 28" | 8" inside diameter | exhaust for stove |

Material needed for air controls is listed in Table 9-1.

### General Material for Both Stoves

| amount | description | use |
|---|---|---|
| 30 (box stove) | split firebrick | firebox and floor lining |
| 45 (rectangular stove) | split firebrick | firebox and floor lining |
| 60" | asbestos or spun-glass gasket | door gasket |
| 1 | small can of furnace cement | door gasket glue |
| 2 | ⅜" rivets | |
| 2 | 9/16" flat washers | |
| 3 | spray cans (or 2 quarts) of high-heat paint | |

the ½" flat stock on edge (the ½" side vertical to the roof). Place it against the edge of the roof. Once the trim is in place, tack it to the roof (tacking every 6") making sure that you are keeping the trim straight. When you reach a corner stop tacking.

Using your cutting torch, heat the trim at the corner. When the trim is red hot, slowly bend the trim around the corner. Once you have made the turn, begin tacking again until you reach the next corner. Then repeat the same procedure until you're back where you started. When you have reached that point, and the last tack is made, cut off the extra trim.

Using the 1½"-×-1½"-×-¼" angle iron, cut leg angles. Their length will be determined by the height of the firebox plus the height that you want the stove to be from the floor. To figure the length of the front stove legs (when partially sitting on a hearth), determine the height of the hearth and add 2 inches (for clearance) and take into account the height of the firebox. The length, (or height) of the back legs can be determined by the height of the firebox plus 2 inches (the clearance that was allowed in the front).

While cutting the leg angles, you might as well cut the brick stay angles. The length of these can be determined by the interior depth of the firebox and by the length of the back wall.

## FIREBOX PREPARATIONS

Now that you have completed the miscellaneous pieces, you can prepare to build your firebox. Before starting the actual fabrication of the stove, the plates should be laid out on the floor in order of the fabrication. This can be done very simply by:

☐ Sweeping down the area where you are going to be working.

☐ Laying your floor plate down in the middle of the floor.

☐ Laying your back plate on the floor just behind the floor plate.

☐ Laying the side plates along side the floor plate in their respective places.

☐ Laying the front plate just in front of the floor plate.

The roof plate door and miscellaneous steel parts should be laid out to the side of the work area in order to be close at hand when needed. Have all of your tools at hand to be ready for use. Make sure that all rules of safety apply before going any further.

## FABRICATION INSTRUCTIONS

With the plate in position, take the back plate B and place it against the back of floor plate A. Leave a ¼" overlap hanging past the floor plate on each side. When plate B is in place, tack weld it to floor plate A. Keep a 90° angle. See Figs. 13-1 and 13-2.

Once plate B is tacked, take side plate D and place it against the side of floor plate A. Butt plate D to back plate B. When side plate D is in position, tack weld it to floor plate A and back plate B. See Figs. 13-3 and 13-4.

Repeat the directions given in the preceding paragraph, on the opposite side. See Figs. 13-3 and 13-4.

Take front plate C, stand it on top of floor plate A, and lean it against (or butt it against) both plates D. When in position, tack weld to the floor plate and side plates. Pay attention to the alignment of the edges. See Figs. 13-5 through 13-8.

Using Jet rod, weld the floor of the stove to the walls. Once the floor is welded, lay the stove on it's side and weld the side plate to the front and back plate. Upon completion of this, lay the stove on it's opposite side and weld the other side plate to the front and back wall plates.

When welding your sides, you can also, as you finish welding each side, tack weld the brick stay angles into position. This can be done quite easily by taking a split firebrick and laying it into position. With the stove upright, the brick would be standing with the 9" side vertical. Take the angle, (one leg touching the wall, the other leg overlapping the brick by about ½") and tack the angle to the wall (using 2" long tacks). When tacking, the angle will lean away from the brick. This is preferred. It leaves room so that you can put in, or take out, the brick. See Fig. 12-15. With the brick stays in, the next thing to install is the baffle system. Refer to Figs. 11-1 through 11-3 and Fig. 13-10. Install your baffle.

Install the roof plate. To do this, take the roof plate and lay it on the floor, upside down. Take the firebox, turn it upside down, and place it on the roof. Pay strict attention to the following:

☐ That the firebox is square to the roof.

☐ That the firebox is centered to the roof.

Make sure that the distance from the box to the edge of the roof is equal on all four sides. Once the box is in position, tack weld the four sides. After the four sides are tack welded, weld all four sides solid. See Figs. 13-11 through 13-13.

After the roof plate is in place, install the exhaust pipe. When positioning the exhaust pipe, always keep the pipe centered and in 1" from the back wall plate, if top exhaust, or down 1" from the roof plate if the stove is a back exhaust.

To install the exhaust pipe, measure the length of the roof plate (or back plate) and draw a center

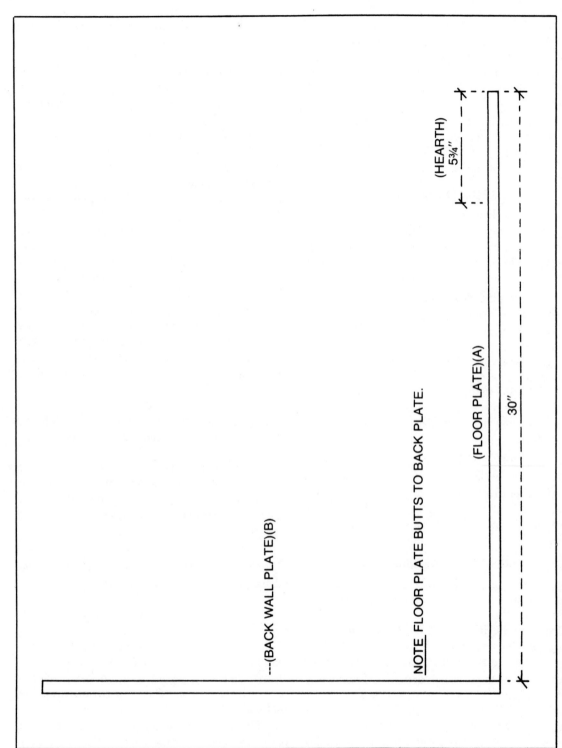

Fig. 13-1. Side view of the back wall assembly.

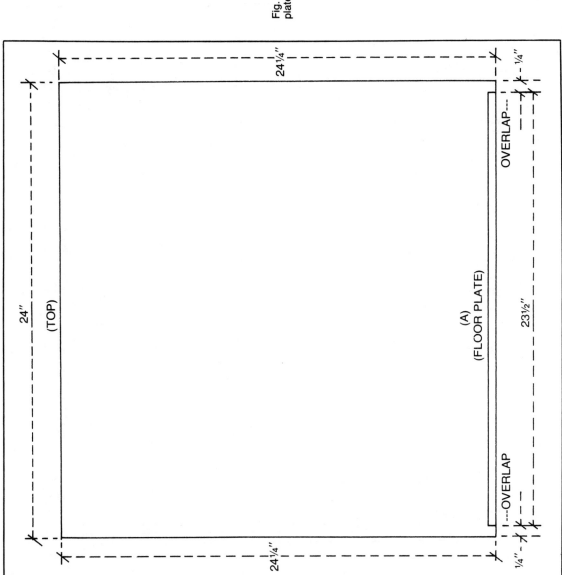

Fig. 13-2. Front view of the back wall plate.

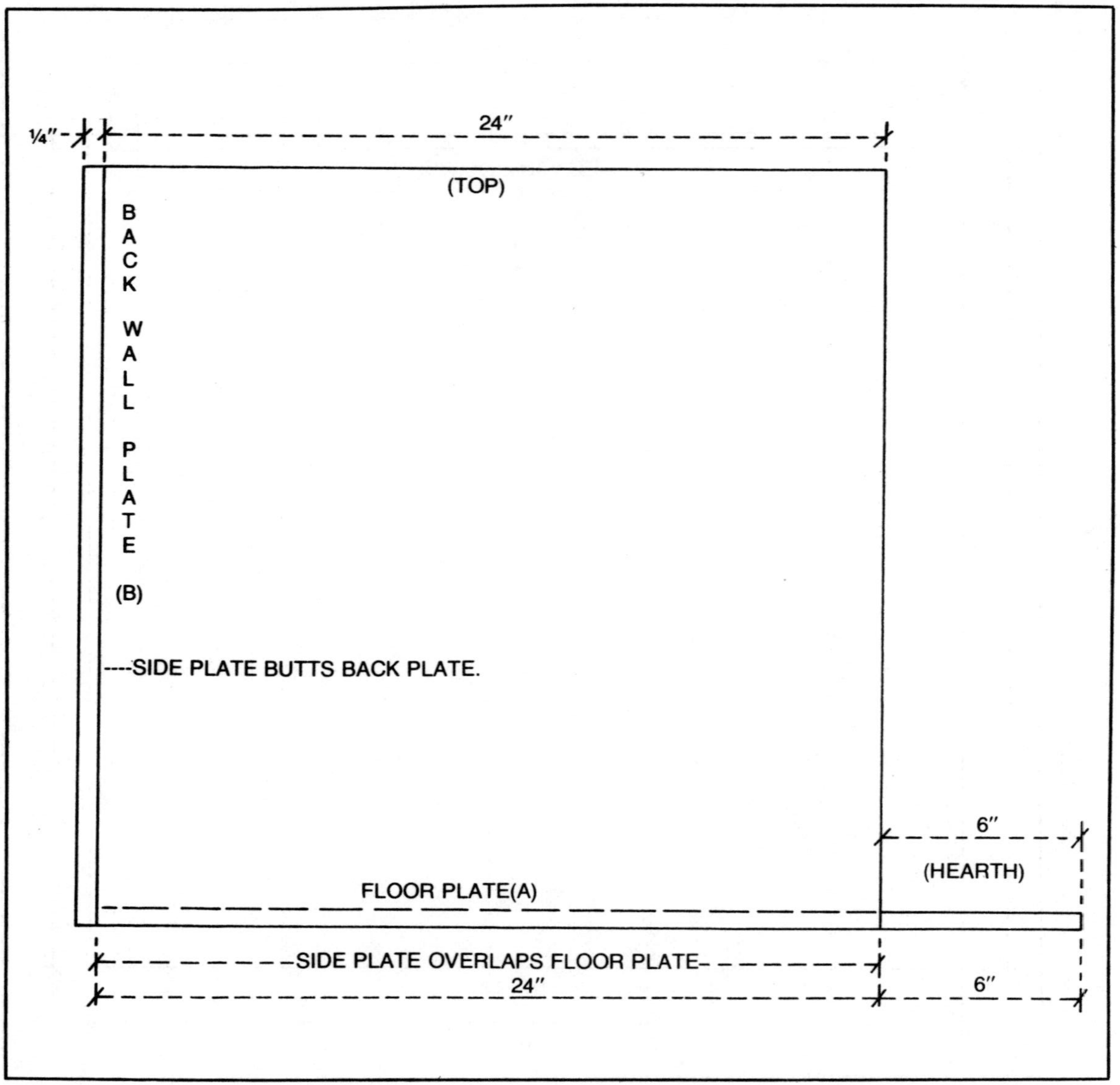

Fig. 13-3. Side view of the side plate assembly.

24″

(TOP)

¼″

BACK WALL PLATE (B)

SIDE PLATE BUTTS BACK PLATE.

FLOOR PLATE(A)

SIDE PLATE OVERLAPS FLOOR PLATE

24″

6″

(HEARTH)

6″

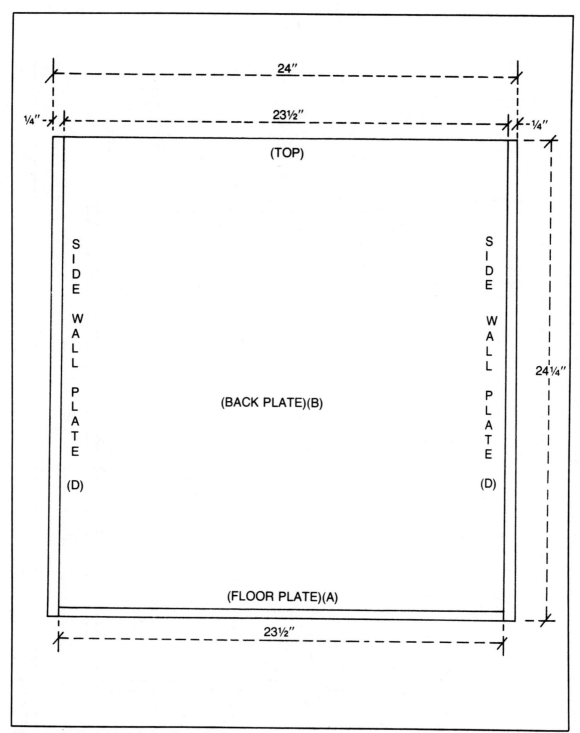

Fig. 13-4. Front view of the side wall assembly.

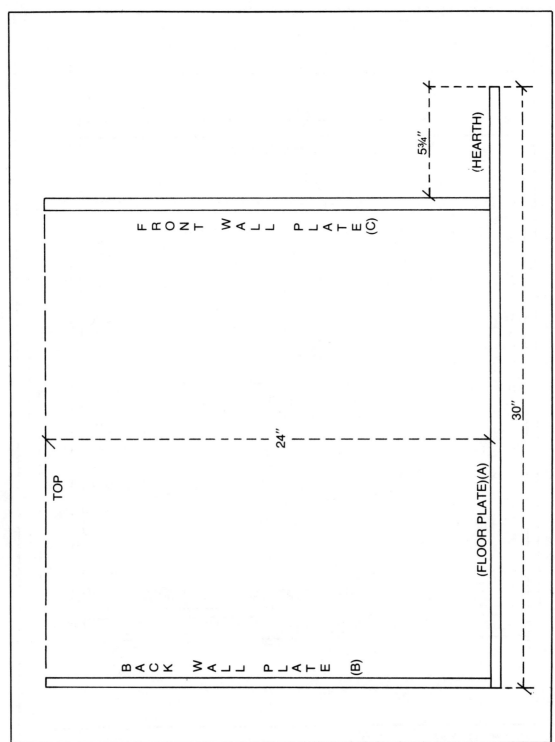

Fig. 13-5. Side view of the front plate assembly.

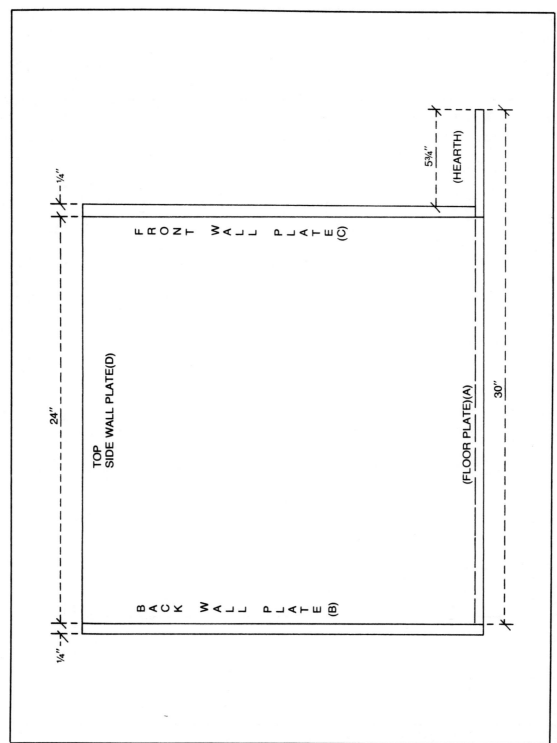

Fig. 13-6. Side view of the front plate assembly.

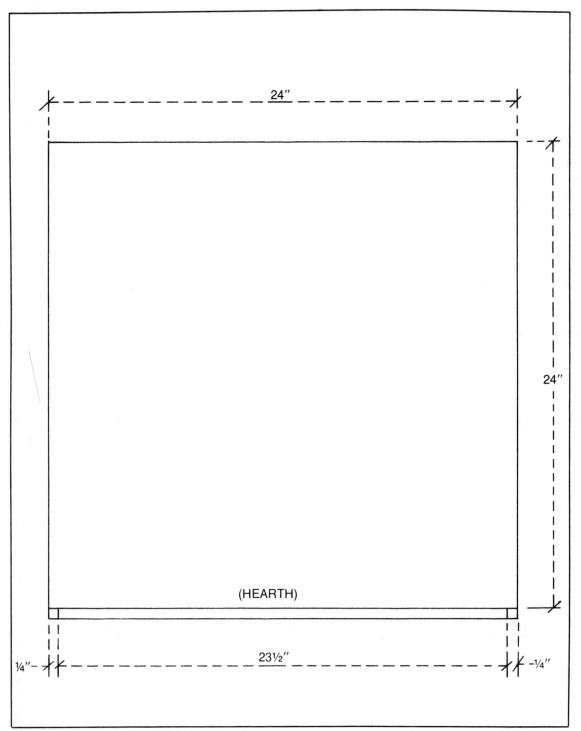

Fig. 13-7. Front view of the front plate assembly.

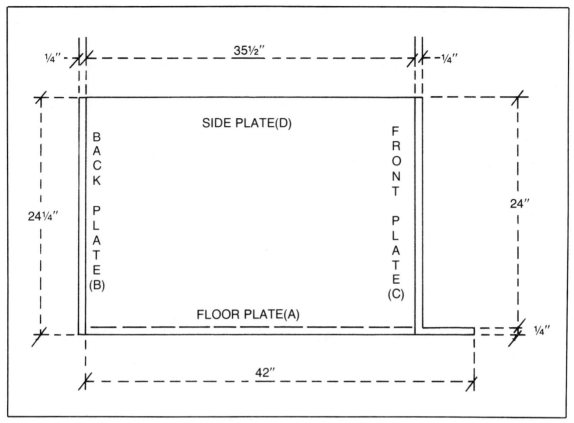

Fig. 13-8. Side view of the Square or Rectangular stove assembly.

line. Using the 1″ line as the one side of the box (you're about to draw), draw a square box with a length and width that equals the exhaust pipe's *outside diameter* (OD). In this example, it will be 8½″. The box will measure 8½″ × 8½″.

Once the box is drawn, place your exhaust pipe in it and draw a circle around the inside of the pipe, using as a guide. Remove the pipe, and cut the circle out, with your cutting torch. After cutting the circle out, place your exhaust pipe, back into position on the plate. Tack, in at least two places, and then weld it solid with your Jet rod. See Fig. 13-10.

The legs and the exterior air control are the next to be installed. To do this measure in 10¼″ from each side of the stove and draw a straight line. Measure back, from the front edge of the floor plate, 6″ and draw a line. Measure back, from the line you've just drawn, another 2″ and draw another line.

You should now have a 2″-×-2½″ box that is 6″ in from the front of your floor plate.

You can now draw the leg slots as shown in Fig. 13-14. Using a paint can as a guide, radius the ends of your hearth. As a visual aid, see Figs. 13-14 and 13-15. After all of these things are drawn, cut them out with a torch. Once the cutting is done, install the exterior air control and legs. See Fig. 13-15.

Following Fig. 13-16, draw the cut lines for the door opening. Cut it out with your cutting torch.

Draw a box around your door opening 1″ out from the edges of the opening. See Fig. 13-17. This will mark the locations of the door.

Mount the door using the guidelines you've just drawn. Once the door is in place, lay the trim alongside the door and tack it into place. You must remember to leave a ¼″ space, between the door

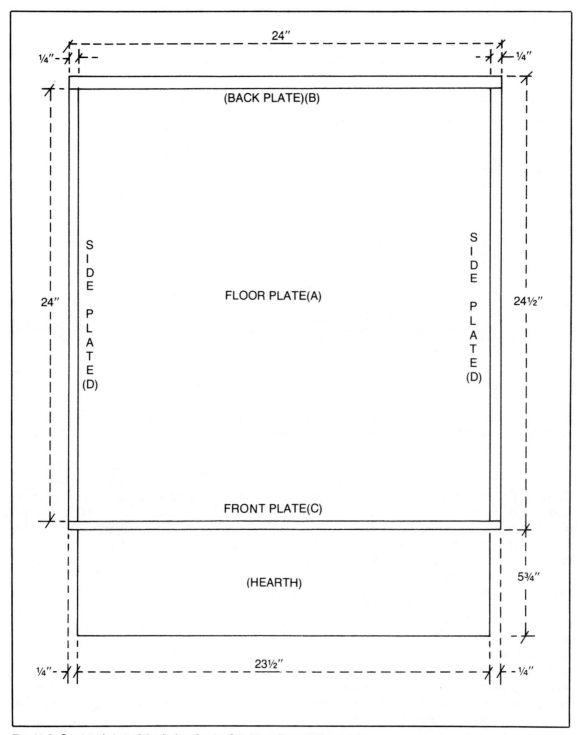

Fig. 13-9. Overhead view of the firebox for the Square or Rectangular stove.

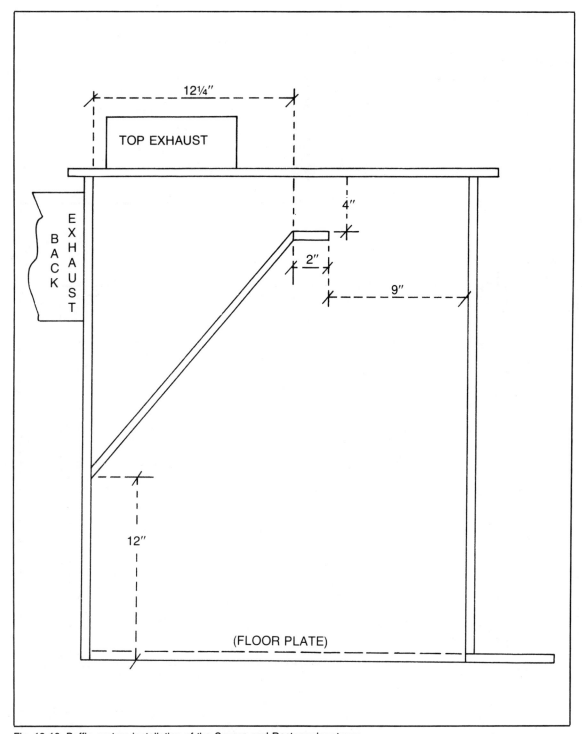

Fig. 13-10. Baffle system installation of the Square and Rectangular stoves.

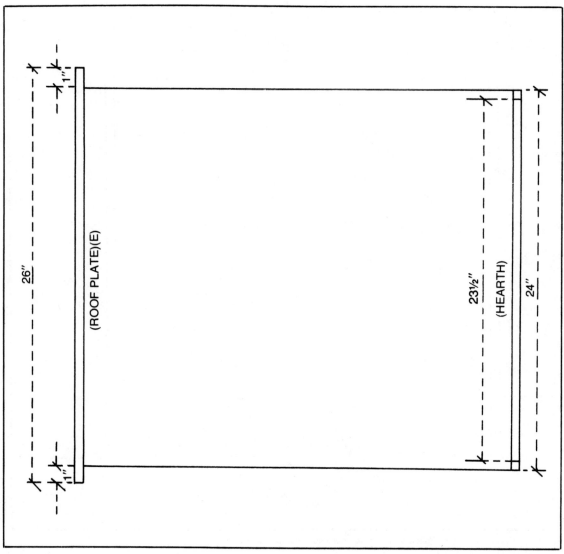

Fig. 13-11. Front view of the roof plate assembly.

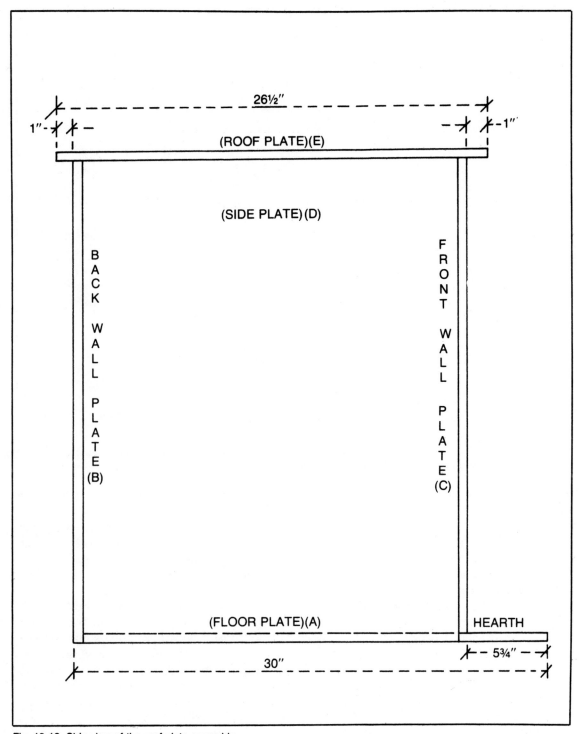

Fig. 13-12. Side view of the roof plate assembly.

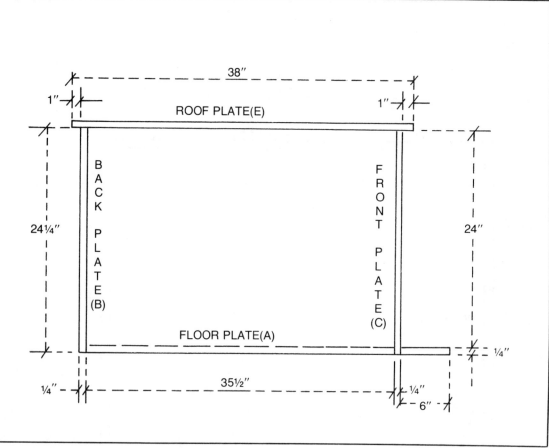

Fig. 13-13. Side view of the Square and Rectangular stoves.

and the door trim, on the side (of the door) that the handle is on. This allows for the swing. See Fig. 13-18.

Put the pins in the hinges, and mount them, as shown in Fig. 13-18. When they are tack welded into position, remember to C-clamp the two sections of hinge together before you weld them to the stove and door. Once welded, allow the weld to cool before removing the C-clamps.

After the door is mounted, place the (door) locking wedge inside the door opening lip and weld. See Fig. 10-19.

Take the ½"-flat stock (about 46" long) and, while the stove is on it's back, tack weld it to the front of the hearth in the same manner as you tacked the trim to the roof plate. When the hearth is

trimmed, cut off the spare stock and attach the end to the angle iron leg.

Stand the stove in the upright position. Install the interior air control over the air opening, in your stove, and tack weld to the floor. Use tacks about 2" long (one on each side and one in front). See Fig. 9-5.

Install the firebrick as shown in Fig. 12-15. If any cutting must be done on the brick, it can be done with a circular saw (with a masonry blade). Once the brick is installed, clean all slag off the welds. Scrape any spatter (from welding) off the stove and (using spray cans or a paint pad) paint the stove. Remember to use a high-heat paint; anything rated for over 1000° will do.

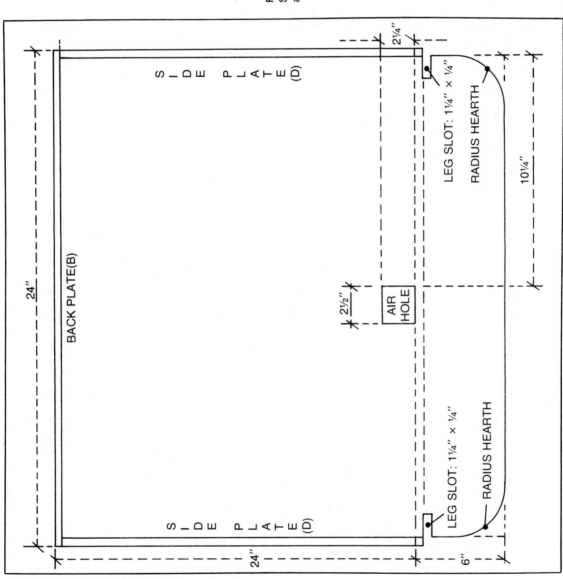

Fig. 13-14. Bottom view of the Square or Rectangular stove floor and hearth layout.

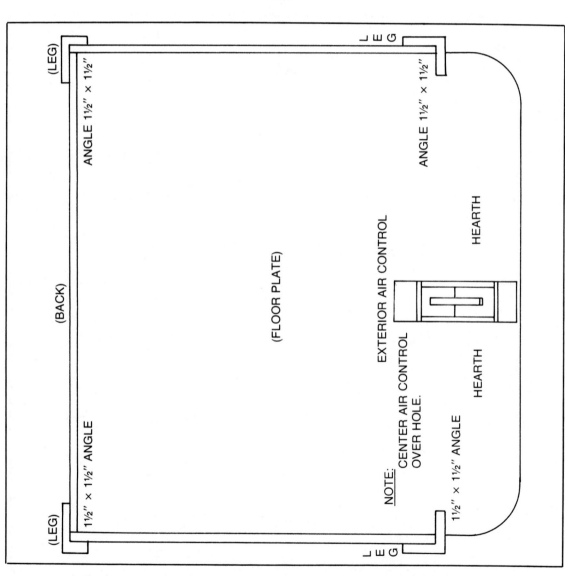

Fig. 13-15. Exterior air control and leg installation.

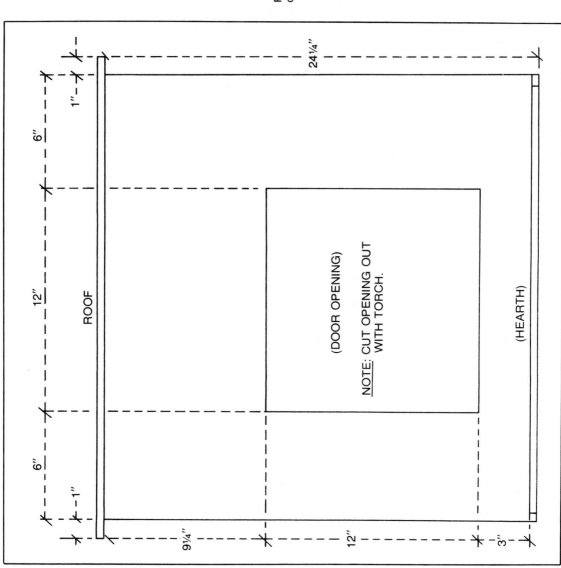

Fig. 13-16. Front view of the door opening cutout.

143

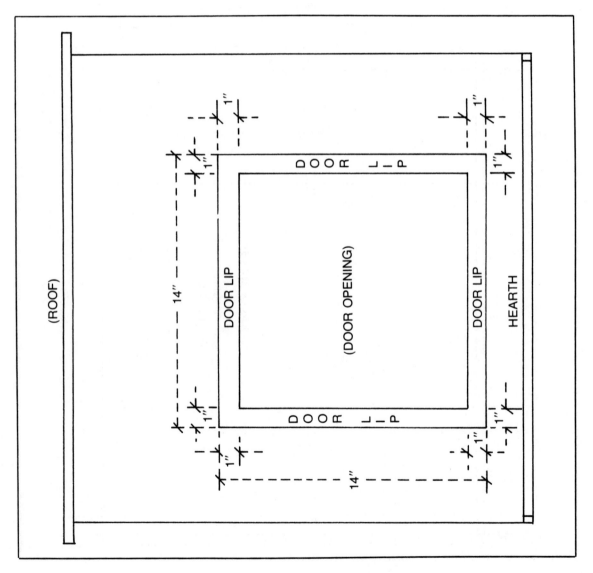

Fig. 13-17. Drawing depicting door location.

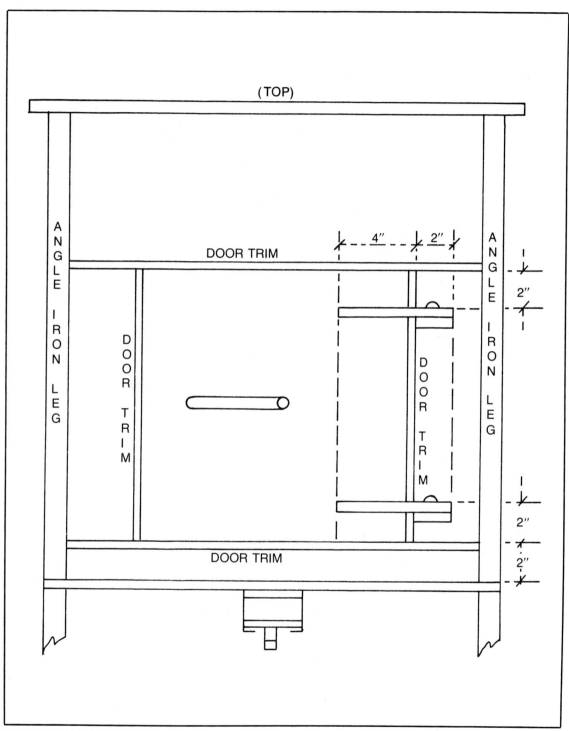

Fig. 13-18. Door installation.

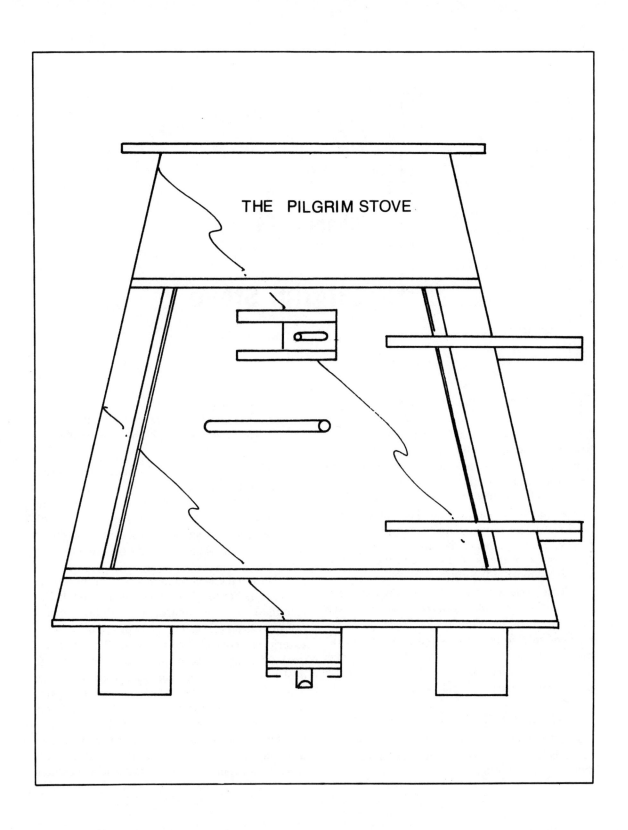

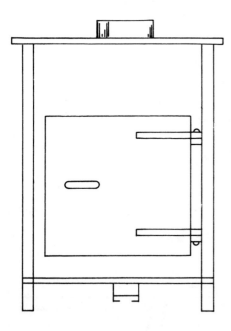

# Chapter 14

# Pilgrim Stove

THE PILGRIM IS A SMALL STOVE designed to heat two or three average size rooms or a small house. This stove is ideal for residents of summer homes who want to extend their stay into the fall months. It is almost amazing to experience the amount of heat that this little stove can produce.

The size of this stove makes it one of the better models for burning coal. This radiant stove has its own special interior air-control system and hinges. The diagrams of the stove are included in this chapter of the book and not in the chapters containing most of the other material.

**Note.** Due to the shape of the Pilgrim, extra cuts must be made when you are cutting the plate. See Fig. 14-A for sketches of these cuts. Remember to give the steel supplier a copy of the material list and a copy of cut sketch for this stove. The plates that have second cuts are B, C and F plates. See Tables 14-1 and 14-2.

### FABRICATION OF MISCELLANEOUS PARTS

To start this project, begin with the fabrication of miscellaneous parts. You should have already decided on the following:

☐ The type of exhaust (top or back).
☐ The type of baffle that you are going to use.
☐ The type of solid fuel that you are going to burn.

You are now ready to follow the fabrication instructions for your stove.

A wood-burning unit requires an air slide in the bottom of the door. A unit that burns wood and coal, however, requires an air control system as shown in Figs. 10-2 through 10-6 and Figs. 10-8 through 10-11.

Turn to the section in this chapter on air controls and gather the parts shown in Fig. 14-1. Fabricate the interior air control. You will find instructions in Chapter 9 on how to do this. Fabricate the exterior air control. Refer to Figs. 9-1 and 9-2.

Referring to the diagram, of your stove and depicting the mounting of the doors (on your stove), you will see trim pieces around the door. Using this drawing, cut the door trim pieces according to the size shown on the sketch (Fig. 10-3).

Once the trim pieces are cut, refer to the door diagram (Fig. 10-3), and find the door that corresponds with your stove. Lay out the door according

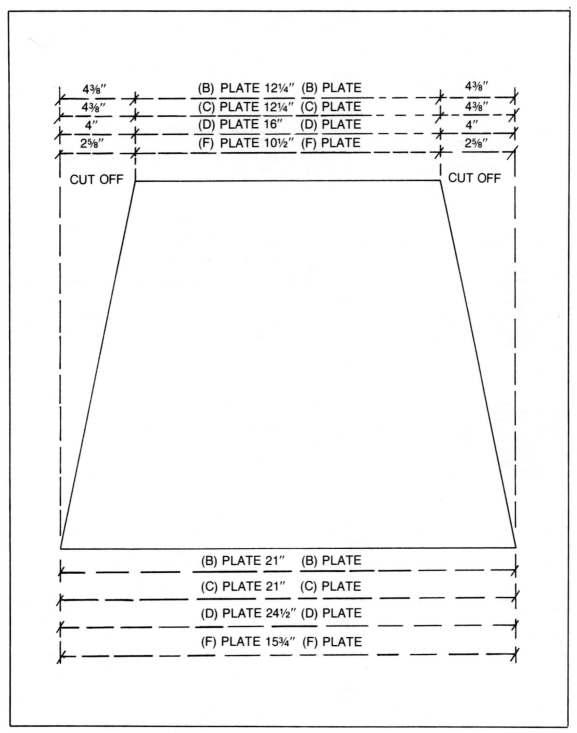

4⅜"    (B) PLATE 12¼" (B) PLATE    4⅜"
4⅜"    (C) PLATE 12¼" (C) PLATE    4⅜"
4"    (D) PLATE 16" (D) PLATE    4"
2⅝"    (F) PLATE 10½" (F) PLATE    2⅝"

CUT OFF        CUT OFF

(B) PLATE 21"    (B) PLATE

(C) PLATE 21"    (C) PLATE

(D) PLATE 24½" (D) PLATE

(F) PLATE 15¾" (F) PLATE

Fig. 14-A. Front view of cut sketches for plates B, C, D and F.

149

Table 14-1. Pilgrim Stove Data.

| | |
|---|---|
| Firebox height: | 18½″ |
| Firebox width: | 21″ |
| Firebox depth: | 24″ |
| Heating Capacity: | approximately 800 square feet |
| Fuel: | wood; can be converted to coal with a grate |
| Burn time: | on low burn 7 to 8 hours |
| Fabrication time: | 6 hours (professionally) 10 to 11 hours (do-it-yourselfer) |
| Exhaust pipe: | 6″ Inside Diameter (ID) |
| Plate weight: | 206.36 pounds |
| Log size: | 21″ |

Table 14-2. Pilgrim Stove Material List.

| amount | size | | | letter mark | location | weight |
|---|---|---|---|---|---|---|
| 1 | 22″ | × 33″ | × ¼″ | A | floor | 51.48 lbs. |
| 1 | 21″ | × 18⅜″ | × ¼″ | B | back | 27.17 lbs. |
| 1 | 21″ | × 18⅜″ | × ¼″ | C | front | 27.17 lbs. |
| 2 | 24″ | × 18½″ | × ¼″ | D | sides | 62.96 lbs. |
| 1 | 17½″ | × 15½″ | × ¼″ | E | roof | 19.23 lbs. |
| 1 | 15¾″ | × 11½″ | × ⅜″ | F | door | 18.35 lbs. |
| | | | | | Total Weight: | 206.36 lbs. |

NOTE: The baffle plate for this stove is the plate you will have when you cut out the door opening.

**Steel List**

| amount | length | description | use |
|---|---|---|---|
| 1 | 12″ | 3″ × 3″ angle iron | legs |
| 1 | 60″ | 2″ × ⅜″ flat iron | hinges |
| 1 | 13″ | 2″ × ¼″ flat iron | top door trim |
| 1 | 20′ | ½″ × ¼″ flat iron | door, hearth and roof trim |
| 1 | 14″ | ½″ round stock | door handle |
| 1 | 6″ | 6″ inside diameter pipe | exhaust pipe |
| 1 | 4″ | 3″ × 3″ × ¼″ angle iron | interior air control |
| 2 | | 2⅛″ × 3¼″ × ¼″ plate | interior air control |

The material for the exterior air control is listed in Table 9-1.

**General Material**

| amount | description | use |
|---|---|---|
| 20 | split firebrick | firebox lining |
| 60″ | asbestos or spun-glass gasket | door gasket |
| 1 | a small can of furnace cement | door gasket glue |
| 2 | 9/16″ flat washers | door handle stays |
| 2 | two quarts (or three spray cans of high-heat paint) | |

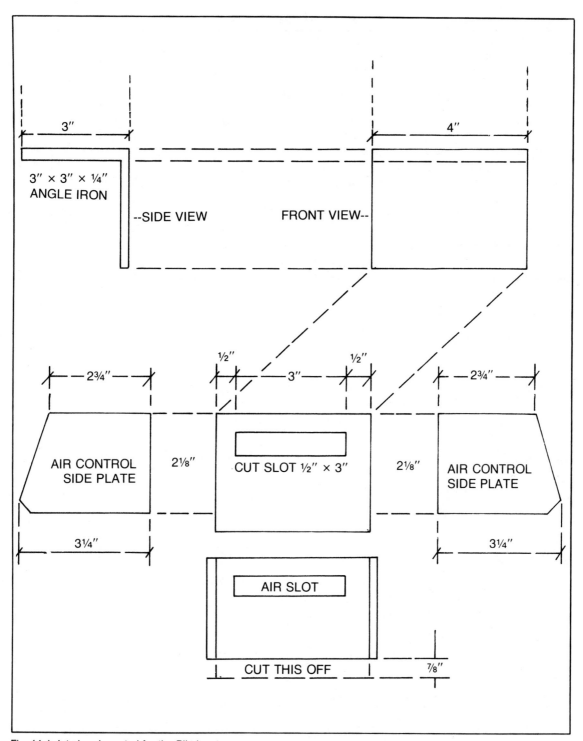

Fig. 14-1. Interior air control for the Pilgrim stove.

to Fig. 10-3. Using Figs. 10-12 through 10-14 and Figs. 10-17 through Fig. 10-20, fabricate the parts that will be mounted on the doors. Drill the door handle hole and cut the openings. Once the door is prepared, mount the slides and handles to the door.

Refer to Figs. 14-2 through 14-4 and fabricate the hinges, using the sketches as visual aids. Figures 14-2 and 14-3 show one set of hinges. If you are using a single door on your stove, you will need two sets of hinges. If you are building a double-door stove four sets of hinges will be needed. This unit has been designed with a single door.

If you decide you want to trim the edges of the roof plate, now is the time to do it. Take the roof plate and measure it's length and width. Add the two measurements and multiply the answer by two. The answer gives you the length of the trim you'll need. Add 2 inches to that measurement for waste. Using the ½″ × ¼″ flat stock, as the trim material, cut a piece that measures the sum of the four sides (plus 2″). Using a flat surface, lay the roof plate upside down and starting in a back corner, stand the ½″ flat stock on edge (the ½″ side vertical to the roof). Place it against the edge of the roof. Once the trim is in place, tack it to the roof (tacking every 6″) making sure that you are keeping the trim straight. When you reach a corner stop tacking.

Using your cutting torch, heat the trim at the corner. When the trim is red hot, slowly bend the trim around the corner. Once you have made the turn, begin tacking again until you reach the next corner. Then repeat the same procedure until you're back where you started. When you have reached that point, and the last tack is made, cut off the extra trim.

### FIREBOX PREPARATIONS

Now that you have completed the miscellaneous pieces, you can prepare to build your firebox. Before starting the actual fabrication of the stove, the plates should be laid out on the floor in order of the fabrication. This can be done very simply by:

☐ Sweeping down the area where you are going to be working.

☐ Laying your floor plate down in the middle of the floor.

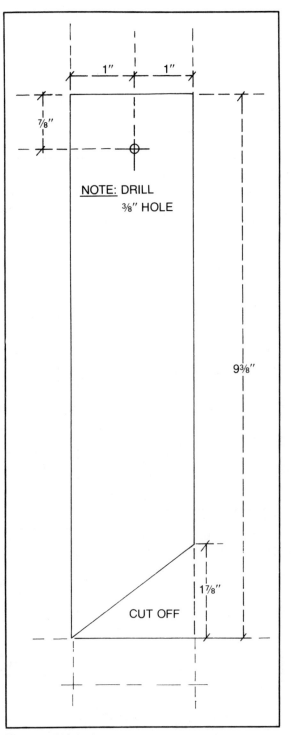

Fig. 14-2. Pilgrim door hinge.

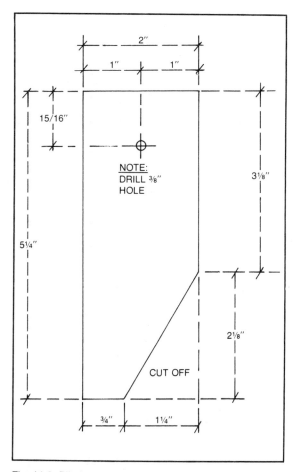

Fig. 14-3. Pilgrim top stove hinge.

☐ Laying your back plate on the floor just behind the floor plate.

☐ Laying the side plates along side of the floor plate in their respective places.

☐ Laying the front plate just in front of the floor plate.

The roof, the door, and miscellaneous steel parts should be laid out to the side of the work area in order to be close at hand when needed. Have all of your tools at hand to be ready for use. Make sure that all rules of safety apply before going any further.

## FABRICATION INSTRUCTIONS

Using a flat surface, stand the back plate B up and butt side plate D to it. Keep the bottom edges at a 90° angle to each other. This will keep your firebox square. See Figs. 14-5 and 14-6. Once in place, tack the sides together.

Repeat the instruction, given in the preceding paragraph, on the opposite side using the other (D) plate. See Figs. 14-7 through 14-9.

Attach front plate C to the two side plates D and tack weld. When completed, the firebox should resemble Fig. 14-10. Once plates B, D, and C are attached, take roof plate E and center it on the stove. Position the back of the plate flush to the

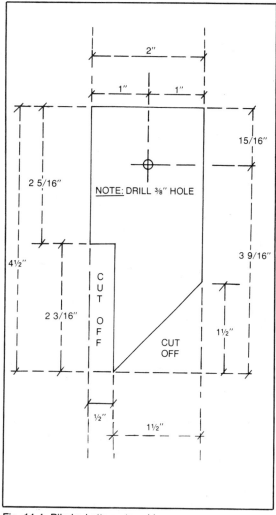

Fig. 14-4. Pilgrim bottom stove hinge.

153

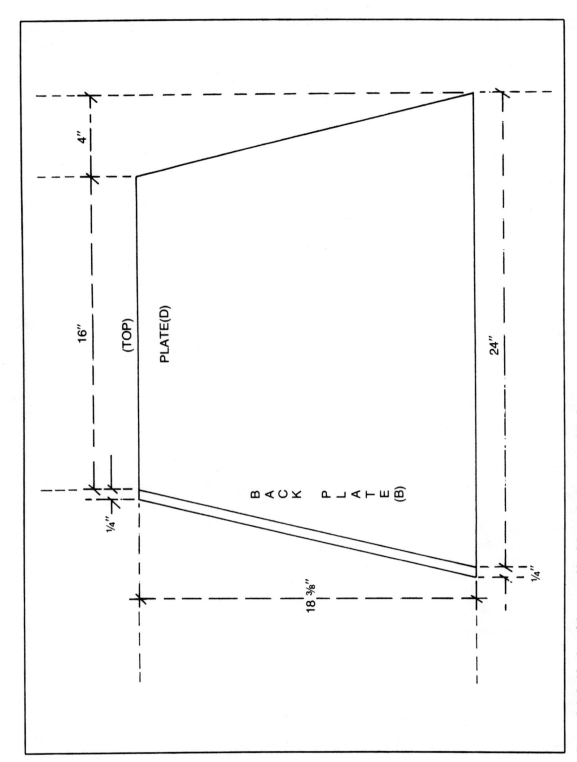

Fig. 14-5. Left side view of the assembly of the back plate to the side plate.

154

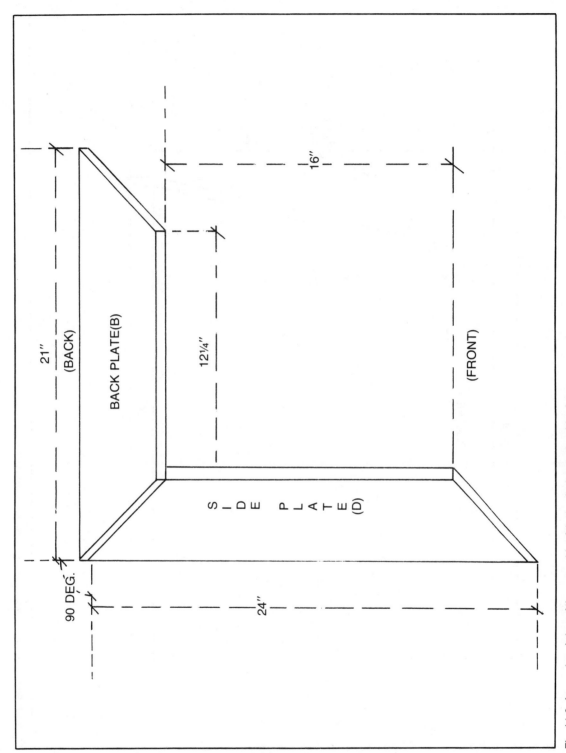

Fig. 14-6. An overhead view of the assembly of the back plate to the side plate.

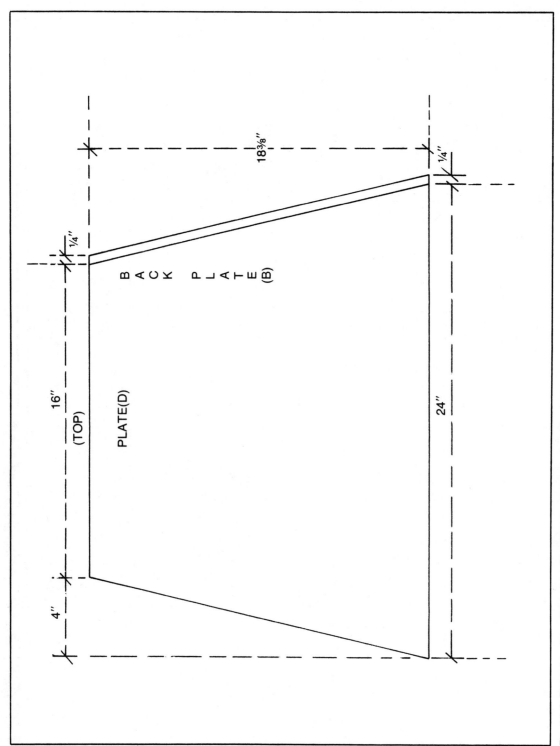

Fig. 14-7. Right side view of the assembly of the back plate to the side plate.

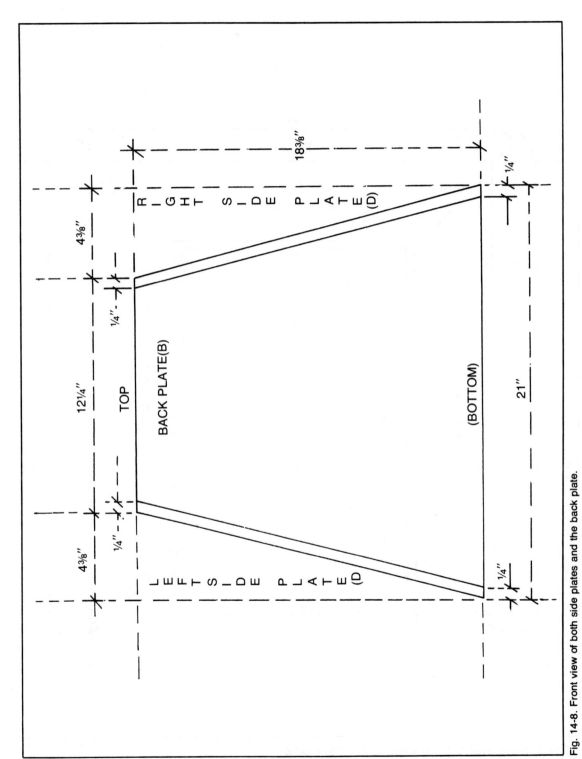

Fig. 14-8. Front view of both side plates and the back plate.

157

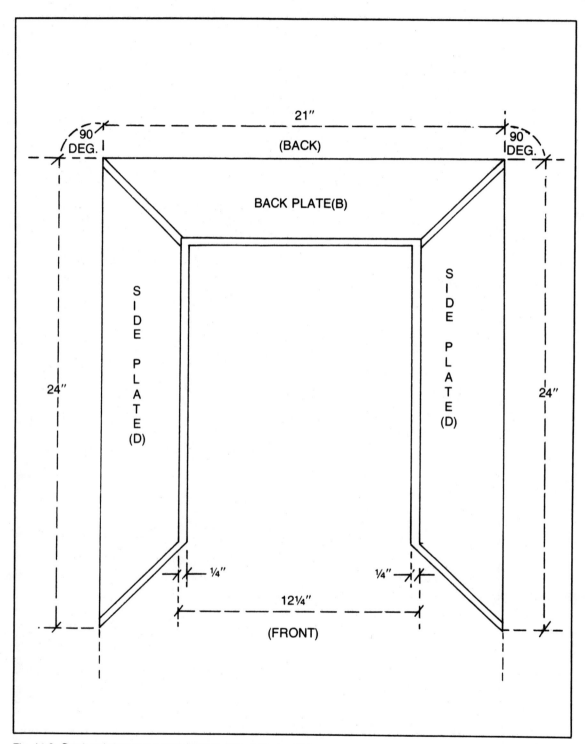

Fig. 14-9. Overhead view of the back plate to side plate assembly.

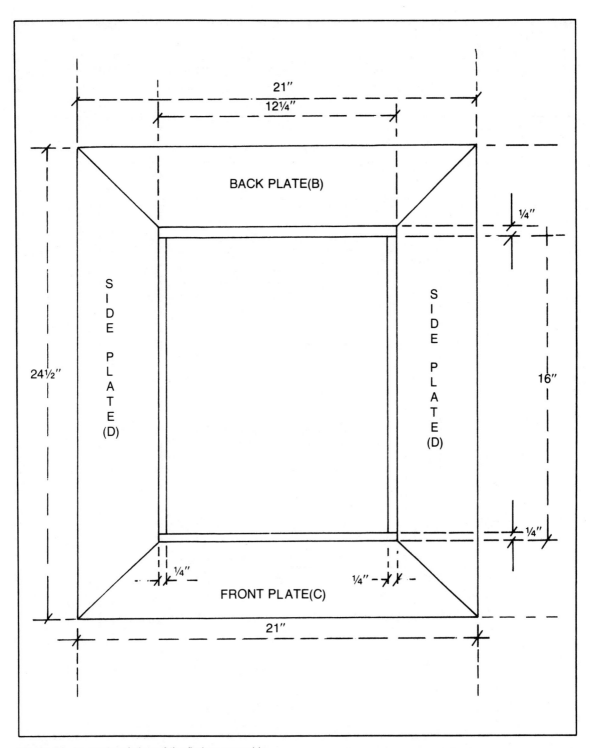

Fig. 14-10. An overhead view of the firebox assembly.

back of the stove. When plate E is in position, tack weld it to the box. See Fig. 14-11.

Once the roof plate is tacked on, turn the unit upside down and weld all inside joints. Use the Jet rod. You weld the inside in order to keep the box square. Lay the stove on a side and weld the two side joints. Repeat this on the opposite side.

When the box and roof are welded, set the box right side up on floor plate (A). Position it as shown in Fig. 14-12. Make sure you leave an edge or a

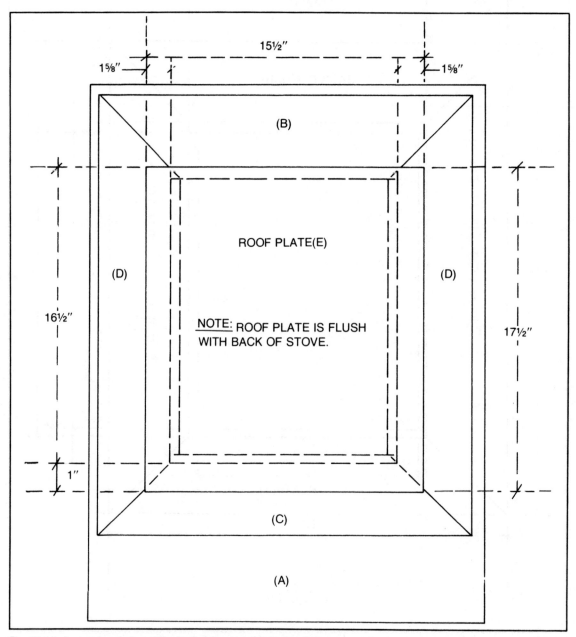

Fig. 14-11. An overhead view of the roof plate assembly to the stove.

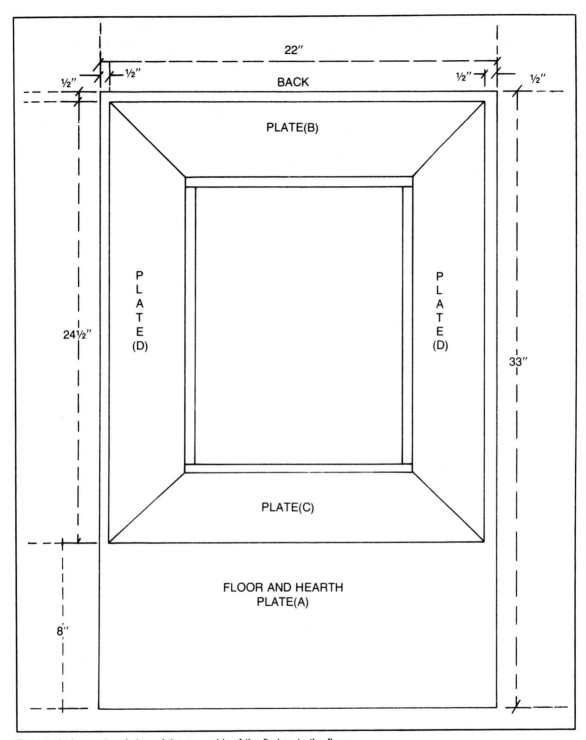

Fig. 14-12. An overhead view of the assembly of the firebox to the floor.

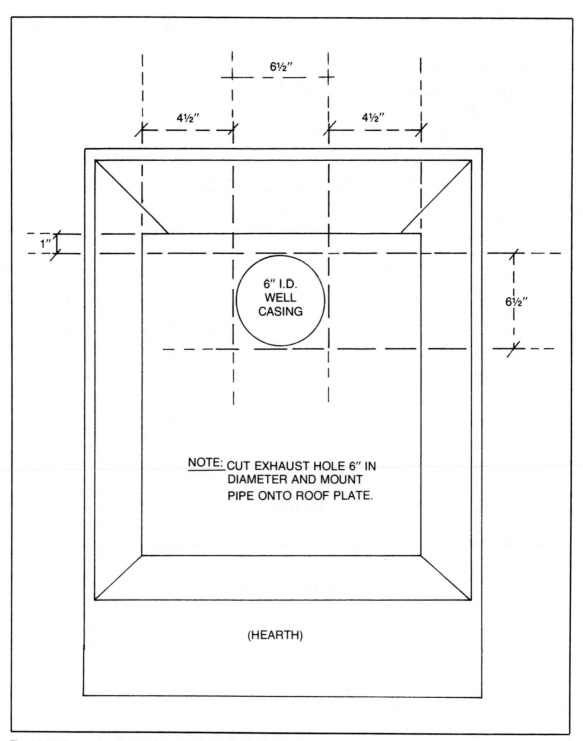

6½"

4½" 4½"

1"

6½"

6" I.D.
WELL
CASING

NOTE: CUT EXHAUST HOLE 6" IN
DIAMETER AND MOUNT
PIPE ONTO ROOF PLATE.

(HEARTH)

Fig. 14-13. An overhead view of mounting the exhaust (top).

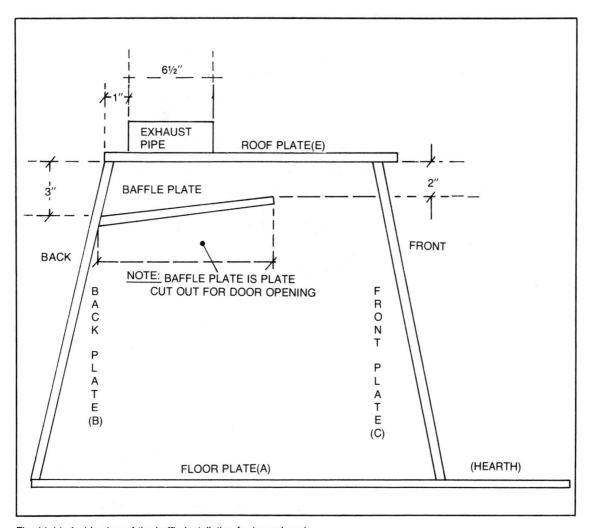

Fig. 14-14. A side view of the baffle installation for top exhaust.

space on the back plate and side plates to weld the box to the floor plate. When in position, tack weld to floor plate (A). Once tacked on four sides, weld solid with Jet rod.

Using the exhaust pipe as a guide, draw and then cut out the exhaust opening. Be sure not to make the opening any larger than 6 inches in diameter. Once the opening is cut, mount the exhaust pipe and weld it into place. See Figs. 14-13 through 14-16.

Turn the stove upside down and lay out the air control opening and hearth radius lines as shown in

Fig. 14-17. Once lines are laid out, cut out the air control opening and radius lines using your cutting torch (a paint can is a good guide to use).

Once the cutting is done, mount the exterior air control and legs as shown in Figs. 14-17 and 14-18. Once mounted, weld them into position.

Using Fig. 14-19 as a visual guide, lay out the door opening. Once the door opening is laid out, use the torch to cut out the door opening. The piece of plate that is left after the door has been cut out will become the baffle plate.

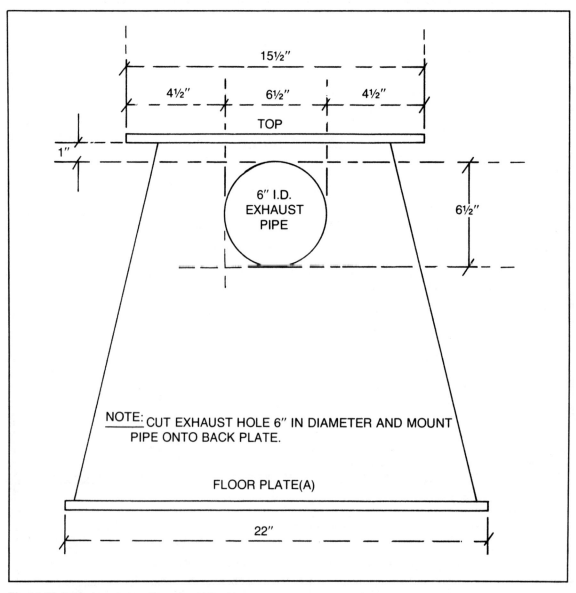

Fig. 14-15. Back view of mounting exhaust (back).

Using the piece of plate that you just cut out, mount the baffle. Use Figs. 14-14 and 14-16 as a visual aid to locate the baffle. Once in position weld it solid.

Once your baffle is installed, prepare to install the door. Draw a 1″ border around the door opening. This will mark the location of the door. Once the lines are drawn, lay the door into position.

Take the ½″ door trim and place it into position, around your door, and tack weld it to the stove. Remember to leave a ¼″ space on the side where you plan to put your door handle. This allows for swing.

Put pins in the hinges, and mount them, as shown in Fig. 14-20. When they are tack welded into position, remember to C-clamp the two sec-

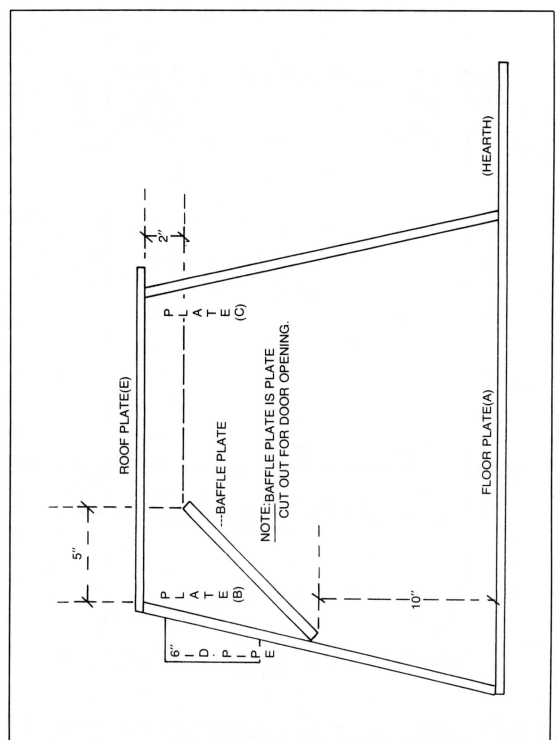

Fig. 14-16. Side view of baffle installation for back exhaust.

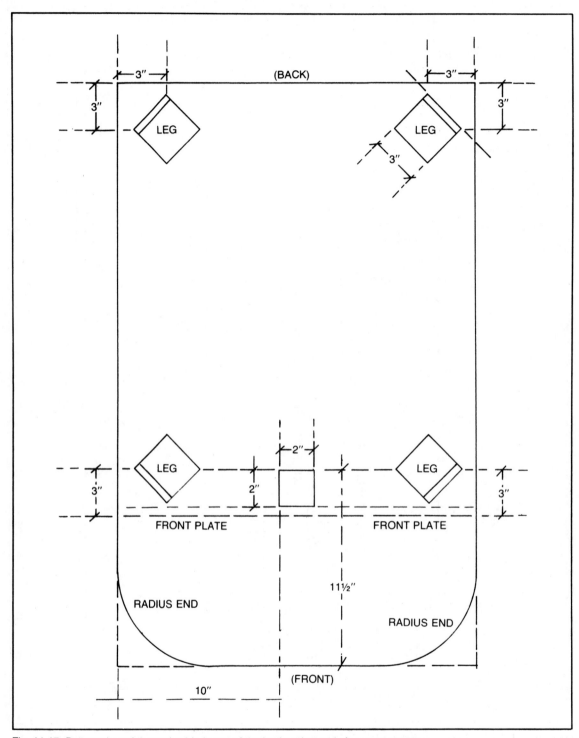

Fig. 14-17. Bottom view of the underside layout of the leg location and air control opening.

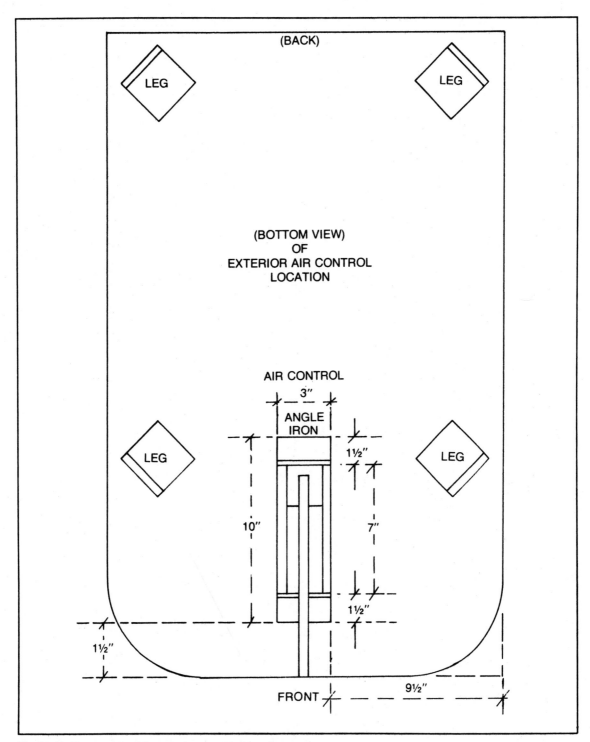

Fig. 14-18. Bottom view of the exterior air control location.

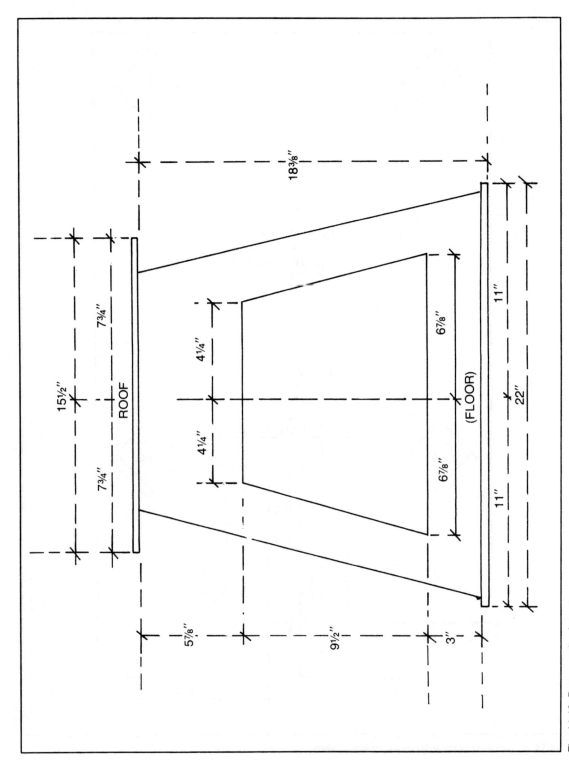

Fig. 14-19. Door opening layout.

168

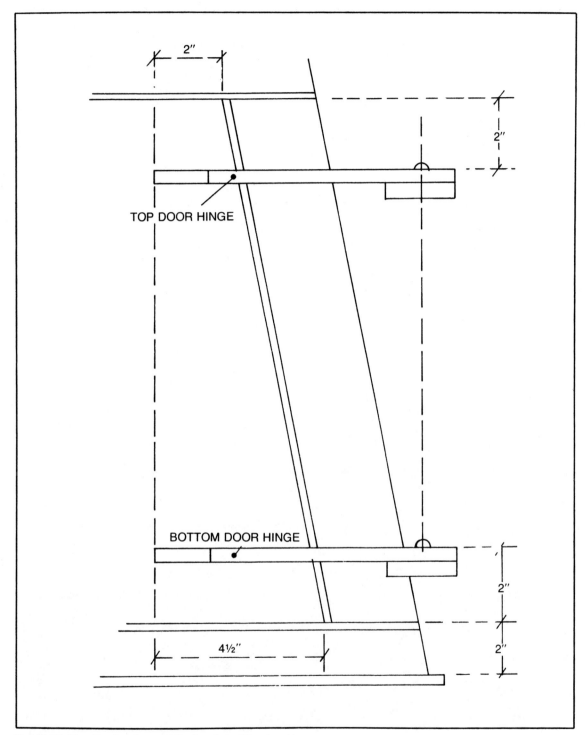

Fig. 14-20. Mounting the door and the location of the door hinges.

169

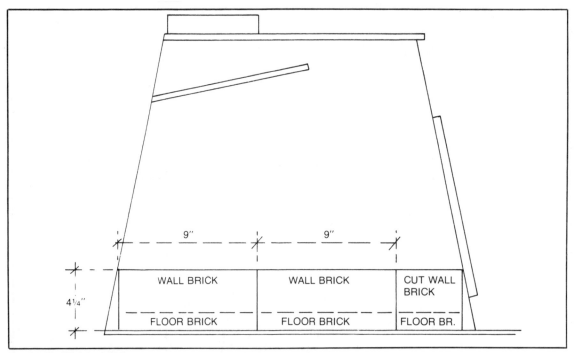

Fig. 14-21. Brick installation.

Fig. 14-22. A completed Pilgrim stove.

170

tions of hinge together before you weld them to the stove and door. Once welded, allow the weld to cool before you remove the C-clamps.

Measure the hearth and cut a piece of ½" flat stock and tack it to the hearth (to trim the edge).

Stand the stove in the upright position. Install the interior air control over the air opening, in your stove, and tack weld it to the floor. Use tacks about 2" long (one on each side and one in front). See Fig. 9-5.

Install the firebrick as shown in Fig. 14-21. If any cutting must be done on the brick, it can be done with a circular saw (with a masonry blade). Once the brick is installed, clean all slag off the welds. Scrape any spatter (from welding) off the stove and (using spray cans or a paint pad) paint the stove. Remember to use a high-heat paint; anything rated for over 1000° will due. See Fig. 14-22.

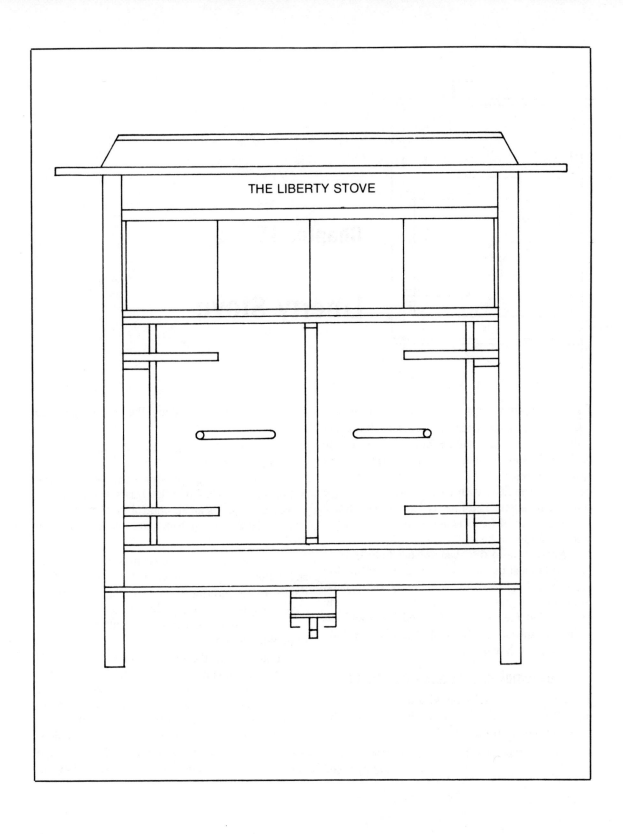

THE LIBERTY STOVE

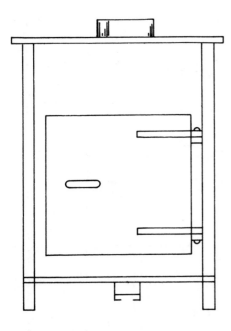

# Chapter 15

# Liberty Stove

THE LIBERTY IS DESIGNED TO heat bi-levels, small ranch houses and townhouses. It is especially useful in houses set up for electric heat. The design suits those that enjoy the aesthetic view of a stove that resembles a fireplace. Tiles give it a decor that can fit in with most homes or an eagle could be mounted. The Liberty has a large surface area that is ideal for cooking. It gives off a good amount of radiant heat.

**Note.** Due to the shape of the Liberty roof, extra cuts must be made when you are cutting the plate. See Fig. 15-A for sketches of these cuts. Remember to give the steel supplier a copy of the material list (see Tables 15-1 and 15-2) and cut sketch for this stove. The plates that have second cuts are plate E and plate H.

### FABRICATION OF MISCELLANEOUS PARTS

To start this project, begin with the fabrication of miscellaneous parts. You should have already decided on the following:

☐ The type of exhaust (top or back).
☐ The type of baffle that you are going to use.

☐ The type of solid fuel that you are going to burn.

You are now ready to follow the fabrication instructions for your stove.

A wood-burning unit requires an air slide in the bottom of the door. A unit that burns wood and coal, however, requires an air control system as shown in Figs. 10-2 through 10-6 and Figs. 10-8 through 10-11.

Turn to Chapter 9, the section on air controls, and gather the parts shown in Figs. 9-1 and 9-2. Fabricate the interior air control. You will find instructions in Chapter 9 on how to do this.

Fabricate the exterior air control. Refer to Figs. 9-3 and 9-4.

Referring to the diagram, of your stove and depicting the mounting of the door(s) on your stove, you will see trim pieces around the door(s). Using this drawing, cut the door trim pieces according to the size shown on the sketch (Fig. 15-20).

Once the trim pieces are cut, refer to the door diagrams Figs. 10-4 through Fig. 10-7 and find the door(s) that corresponds with your stove. Lay out

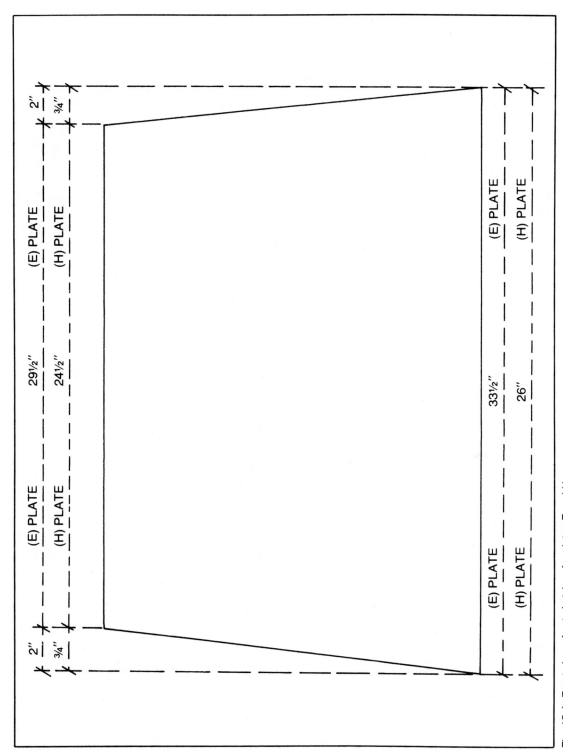

Fig. 15-A. Front view of cut sketches for plates E and H.

**Table 15-1. Liberty Stove Data.**

| | |
|---|---|
| Firebox height: | 25½″ |
| Firebox Width: | 27½″ |
| Firebox depth: | 25½″ |
| | |
| Heating Capacity: | approximately 1800 square feet |
| Fuel: | wood; can be converted to coal with a grate |
| | |
| Burn Time: | on a low burn, 10 to 12 hours |
| Fabrication time: | 8 hours (professionally) 15 to 18 (do-it-yourselfer) |
| | |
| Exhaust pipe: | 8″ Inside Diameter (ID) |
| Plate weight: | 357.5 pounds |
| Log size: | 24″ |

the door(s) according to that drawing. Using Figs. 10-12 through 10-20, fabricate the parts that will be mounted on the doors. Drill the door handle hole(s) and cut the openings. Once the door(s) is prepared, mount the slides and handles to the door(s).

Refer to Fig. 10-20 showing standard hinges. Fabricate the hinges using the sketch as a visual aid. Figure 10-20 shows one set of hinges. If you are using a single door on your stove, you will need two sets of hinges. If you are building a double door stove, four sets of hinges will be needed.

If you decide you want to trim the edges of the roof plate, now is the time to do it. Take the roof plate and measure it's length and width. Add the two measurements and multiply the answer by two.

**Table 15-2. Liberty Stove Material List.**

| amount | size | | | | letter mark | location | weight |
|---|---|---|---|---|---|---|---|
| 1 | 24″ | × | 27½″ | × ¼″ | A | floor | 47.00 lbs. |
| 1 | 28″ | × | 25¾″ | × ¼″ | B | back | 44.73 lbs. |
| 1 | 28″ | × | 25½″ | × ¼″ | C | front | 44.30 lbs. |
| 2 | 18″ | × | 25¾″ | × ¼″ | D | sides | 65.73 lbs. |
| 1 | 20″ | × | 33½″ | × ¼″ | E | roof | 47.50 lbs. |
| 1 | 27½″ | × | 10″ | × ¼″ | F | baffle | 17.01 lbs. |
| 2 | 10″ | × | 14″ | × ⅜″ | G | double doors | 29.77 lbs. |
| | | | | | or | | |
| 1 | 20″ | × | 14″ | × ⅜″ | G | single door | 29.77 lbs. |
| 1 | 26″ | × | 6″ | × ¼″ | H | shelf | 11.06 lbs. |
| | | | | | | Total Weight: | **307.10 lbs.** |

**Steel List**

| amount | length | description | use |
|---|---|---|---|
| 1 | 20′ | 1½″ × 1½″ × ¼″ angle iron | legs and brick stays |
| 1 | 12′ | 2″ × ⅜″ flat iron | hinges and top door trim |
| 1 | 26″ | 2″ × ¼″ flat iron | shelf back |
| 1 | 20′ | ½″ × ¼″ flat iron | roof, hearth, door shelf trim |
| 1 | 40″ | ½″ round stock | door handles |
| 1 | 24″ | 8″ inside diameter pipe | exhaust pipe |

Material needed for air controls is listed in Table 9-1.

**General Material**

| amount | description | use |
|---|---|---|
| 33 | split firebrick | firebox lining |
| 70″ | asbestos or spun-glass gasket | door gasket |
| 1 | small can of furnace cement | door gasket glue |
| 3 | 9/16″ flat washers | door handle stays |
| 3 | spray cans (or 2 quarts) or high-heat stove paint | |
| 4 | ⅜″ rivets | hinge pins |

The answer gives you the length of the trim you'll need. Add 2 inches to that measurement for waste. Using the ½"-×-¼" flat stock, as the trim material, cut a piece that measures the sum of the four sides plus 2". Using a flat surface, lay the roof plate upside down and starting in a back corner, stand the ½" flat stock on edge (the ½" side vertical to the roof). Place it against the edge of the roof. Once the trim is in place, tack it to the roof (tacking every 6") making sure that you are keeping the trim straight. When you reach a corner stop tacking.

Using your cutting torch, heat the trim at the corner. When the trim is red hot, slowly bend the trim around the corner. Once you have made the turn, begin tacking again until you reach the next corner. Then repeat the same procedure until you're back where you started. When you have reached that point, and the last tack is made, cut off the extra trim.

Using the 1½"-×-1½"-×-¼" angle iron, cut leg angles. Their length will be determined by the height of the firebox plus the height that you want the stove to be from the floor. To figure the length of the front stove legs (when partially sitting on a hearth), determine the height of the hearth and add 2 inches (for clearance) and take into account the height of the firebox. The length (or height) of the back legs can be determined by the height of the firebox plus 2 inches (the clearance that was allowed in the front).

While cutting the leg angles, you might as well cut the brick stay angles. The length of these can be determined by the interior depth of the firebox and by the length of the back wall.

## FIREBOX PREPARATIONS

Now that you have completed the miscellaneous pieces, you can prepare to build your firebox. Before starting the actual fabrication of the stove, the plates should be layed out on the floor in order of the fabrication. This can be done very simply by:

☐ Sweeping down the area where you are going to be working.

☐ Laying your floor plate down in the middle of the floor.

☐ Laying your back plate on the floor just behind the floor plate.

☐ Laying the side plates, alongside the floor plate in their respective places.

☐ Laying the front plate just in front of the floor plate.

The roof plate, the door(s), and miscellaneous steel parts should be laid out to the side of the work area in order to be close at hand when needed. Have all of your tools at hand to be ready for use. Make sure that all rules of safety apply before going any further.

## FABRICATION INSTRUCTIONS

With the plates in position, take the back plate B and place it against the back of floor plate A. Leave a ¼" overlap hanging past the floor plate on each side. When plate B is in place, tack weld it to floor plate A. Keep a 90° angle. See Fig. 15-1.

Once plate B is tacked, take side plate D and place it against the side of floor plate A. Butt plate D to back plate B. When side plate D is in position, tack weld it to floor plate A and back plate B. See Figs. 15-2 and 15-3.

Repeat the directions, given in the preceding paragraph, on the opposite side. See Figs. 15-4 and 15-5.

Take front plate C, stand it on top of floor plate A, and lean it against (or butt it against) both plates D. When in position, tack weld to the floor plate and side plates. Pay attention to the alignment of the edges. See Figs. 15-6 through 15-8.

Using Jet rod, weld the floor of the stove to the walls. Once the floor is welded, lay the stove on it's side and weld the side plate to the front and back plates. Upon completion of this, lay the stove on it's opposite side and weld the other side plate, to the front and back wall plates.

When welding your sides, you can also, as you finish welding each side, tack weld the brick stay angles into position. This can be done quite easily by taking a split firebrick and laying it into position. With the stove upright, the brick would be standing with the 9" side vertical. Take the angle, (one leg touching the wall, the other leg overlapping the brick, by about ½") and tack the angle to the wall (using 2" long tacks). When tacking, the angle will lean away from the brick. This is preferred. It

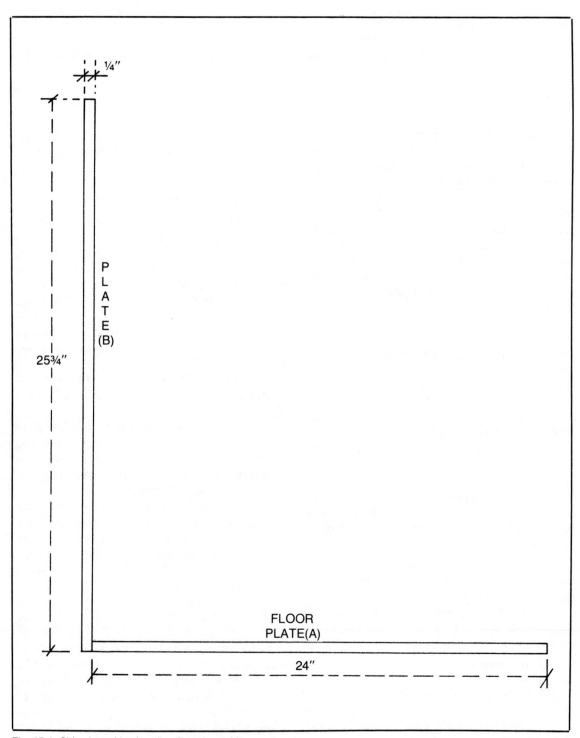

Fig. 15-1. Side view of back wall to floor assembly.

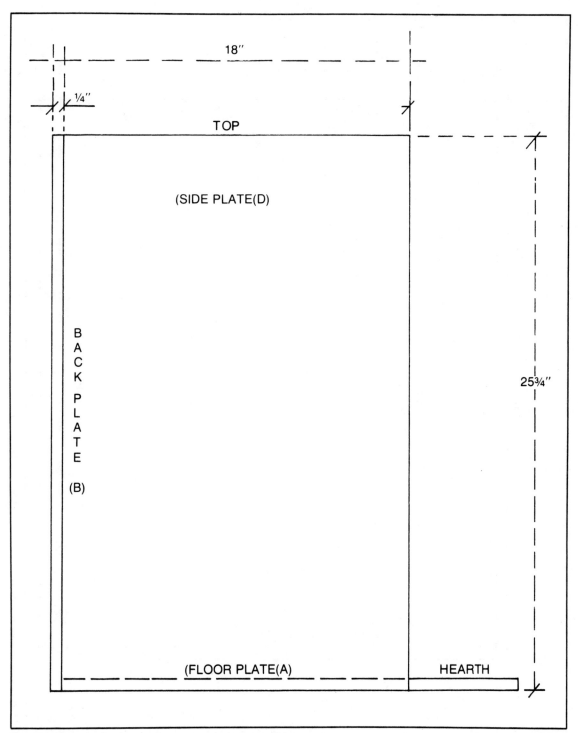

Fig. 15-2. Side view of side wall to back wall and floor assembly.

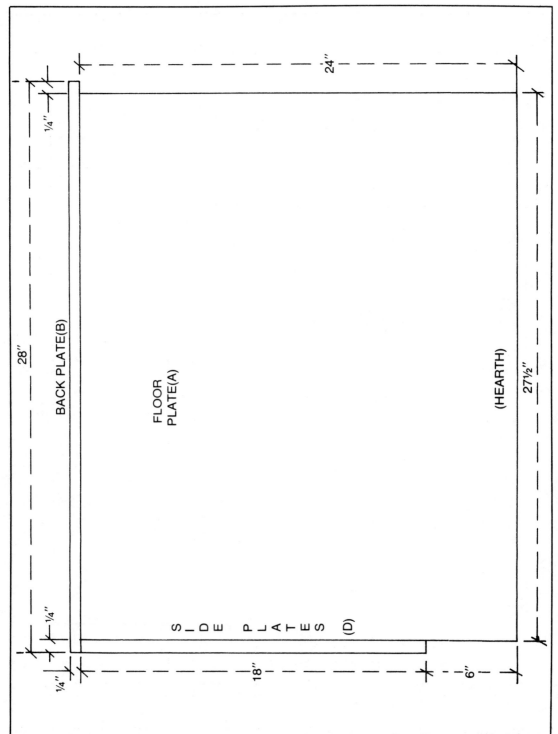

Fig. 15-3. Overhead view of side wall to back wall and floor assembly.

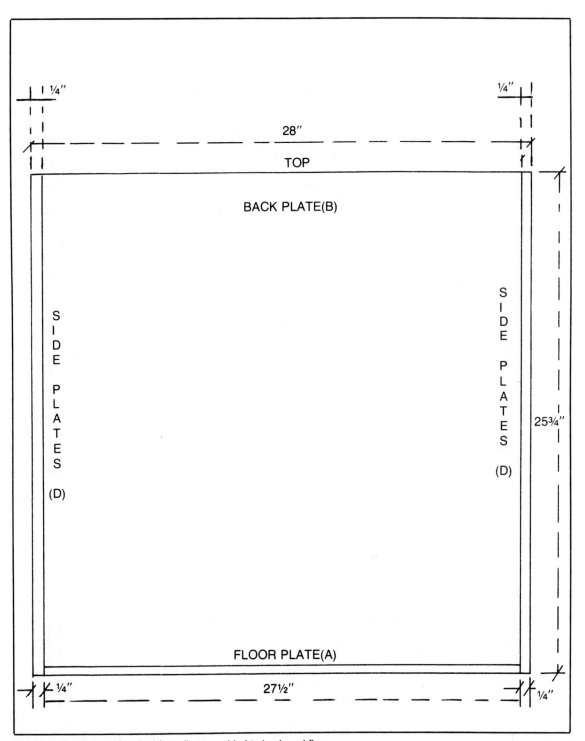

Fig. 15-4. Front view of both side walls assembled to back and floor.

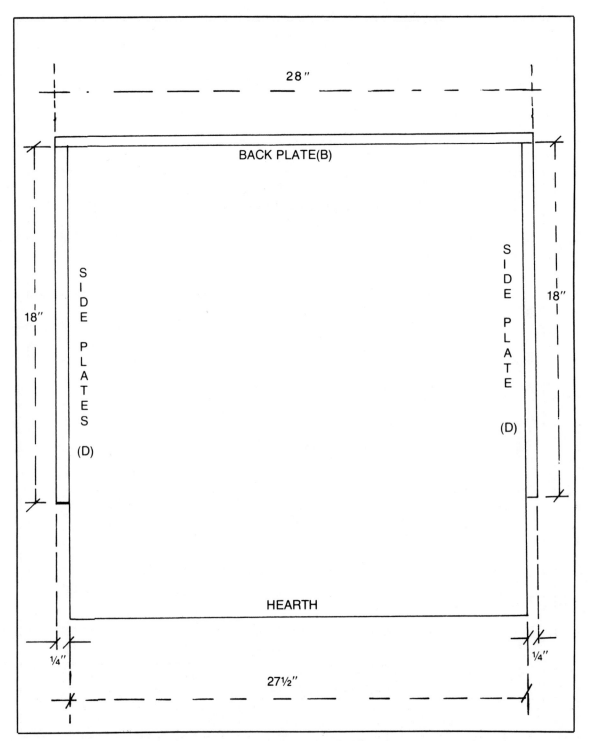

28"

BACK PLATE(B)

S
I
D
E

P
L
A
T
E
S

(D)

S
I
D
E

P
L
A
T
E

(D)

18"

18"

HEARTH

¼"

¼"

27½"

Fig. 15-5. Overhead view of both side walls assembled to back and floor.

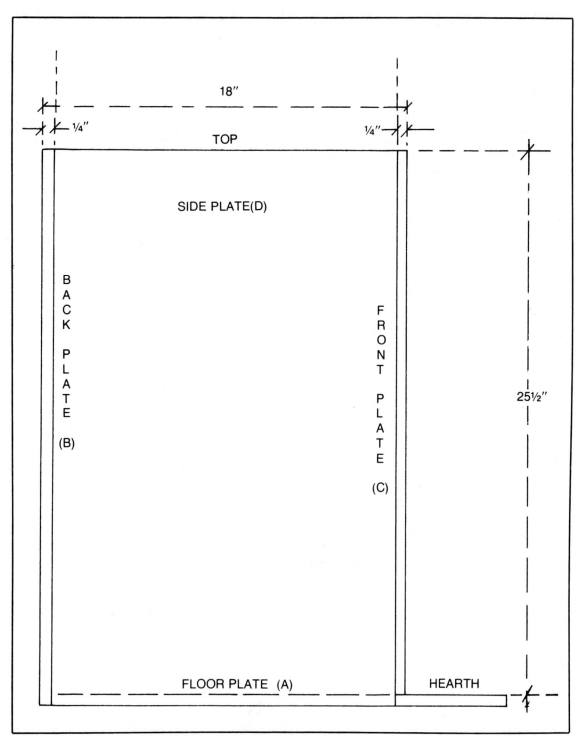

Fig. 15-6. Side view of front wall assembly to back sides and floor.

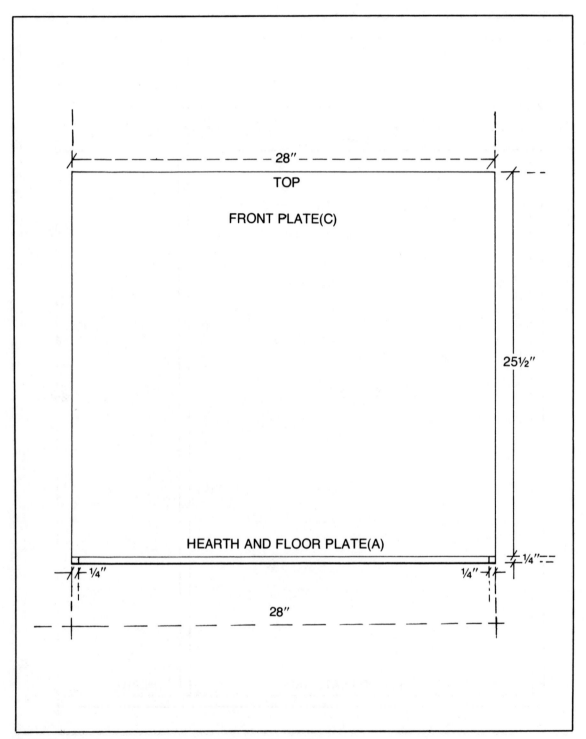

Fig. 15-7. Front view of front wall assembly to back, sides, and floor.

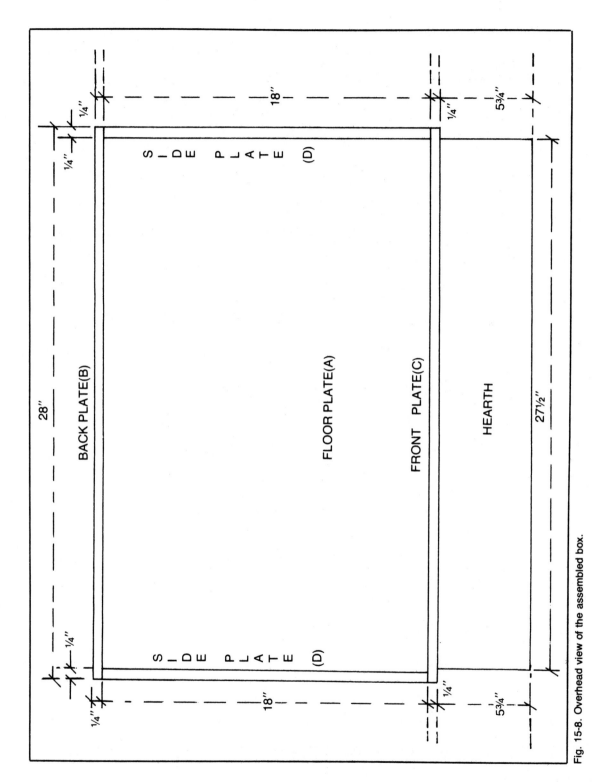

Fig. 15-8. Overhead view of the assembled box.

185

leaves room so that you can put in, or take out, the brick. See Fig. 12-15. With the brick stays in, the next thing to install is the baffle system. To do this, refer to the diagrams on baffling systems. Refer to Figs. 15-9, 15-11, and 15-13. Install your baffle.

Install the exhaust. If your Liberty stove has a back exhaust, follow the measurements given in Figs. 15-9 and 15-10. When you cut the opening, the diameter of the opening must equal the *outside* diameter (OD) of your pipe. This is because the

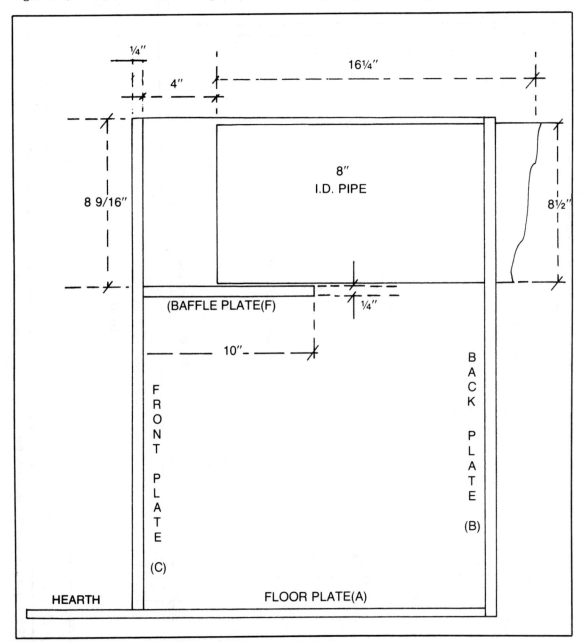

Fig. 15-9. Right side view of the baffle installation for the back exhaust.

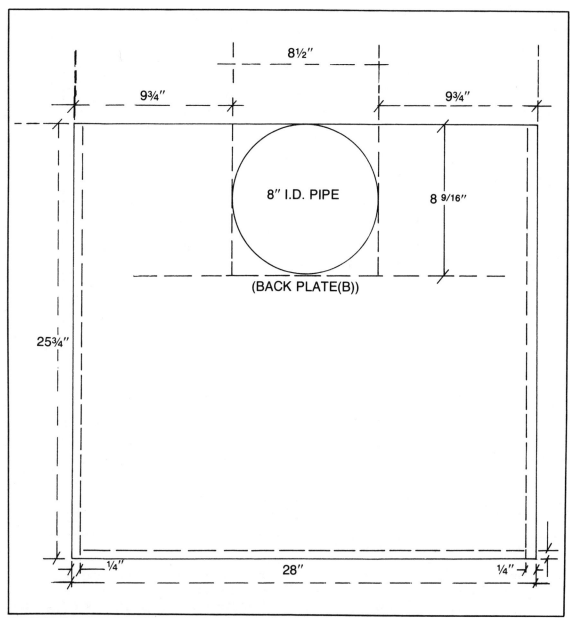

Fig. 15-10. Back view of the exhaust pipe installation for the back exhaust.

exhaust pipe slides through the back wall. See Fig. 15-10.

If your Liberty stove happens to have a top exhaust, refer to Fig. 15-12. Draw, and then cut out, the opening shown in Fig. 15-12. Start the box opening ½" from the top edge of back plate B.

Install the roof plate. To do this, take the roof plate, and lay it on the floor, upside down. Take the firebox and lay it, upside down, on top of the roof. Pay strict attention that the back of the firebox is flush to the back of the roof plate, and that the firebox is centered, lengthwise, to the roof plate.

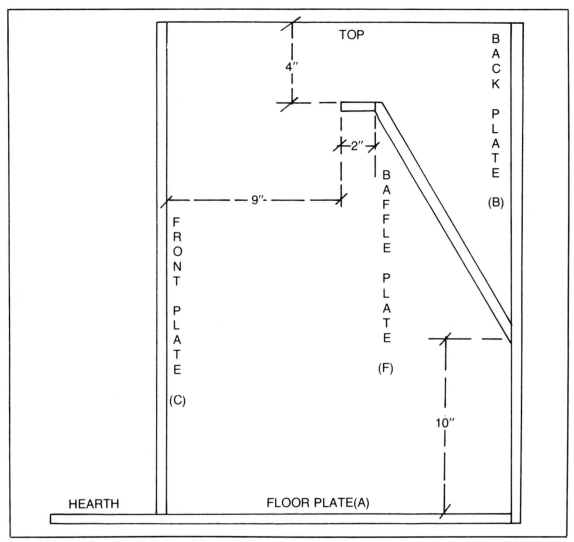

Fig. 15-11. Side view of the baffle installation for the top exhaust.

As a visual aid see Fig. 15-13. When positioned, tack weld the four sides. After the tack welding is completed, weld solid with Jet rod.

While your stove is upside down, lay out the floor plate. Use Fig. 15-14 as a guide. In this drawing you'll be laying out the air opening, the leg slots, and the radius lines on the hearth edges. Once these lines are laid out, take the cutting torch and cut out the pieces.

After the pieces have been cut out, mount the exterior air control, as shown in Fig. 15-15, and

weld it solid. Install the legs as shown in Fig. 15-15, and weld solid.

If your Liberty stove has a top exhaust, take the 8″ exhaust pipe and fabricate it as shown in Fig. 15-16. Once the exhaust pipe is fabricated, lay the stove face down, lay the exhaust pipe over the exhaust opening, and weld it in place. See Fig. 15-17.

Referring to Fig. 15-18, draw the cut lines for the door opening, and cut it out with your cutting torch.

Draw a box around the door opening 1″ out from the edges of the opening. See Fig. 15-19. This will mark the location of the door(s).

Mount the door using the guidelines you've just drawn. Once the door is in place, lay the trim alongside the door and tack it into place. You must remember to leave a ¼″ space, between the door and the door trim, on the side (of the door) that the handle is on. This allows for the swing. See Fig. 12-14. If you are installing a double door, remember to leave a ¼″ space between the two doors. This is to allow for swing. Put the pins in the hinges, and mount them, as shown in Fig. 15-20. When they are tack welded into position, remember to C-clamp

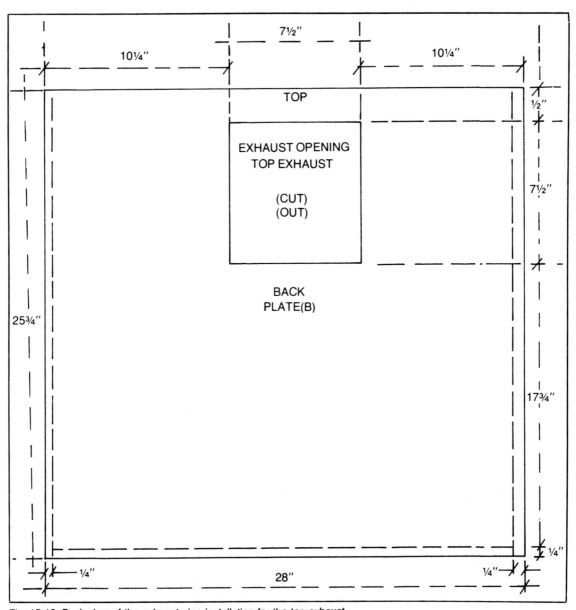

Fig. 15-12. Back view of the exhaust pipe installation for the top exhaust.

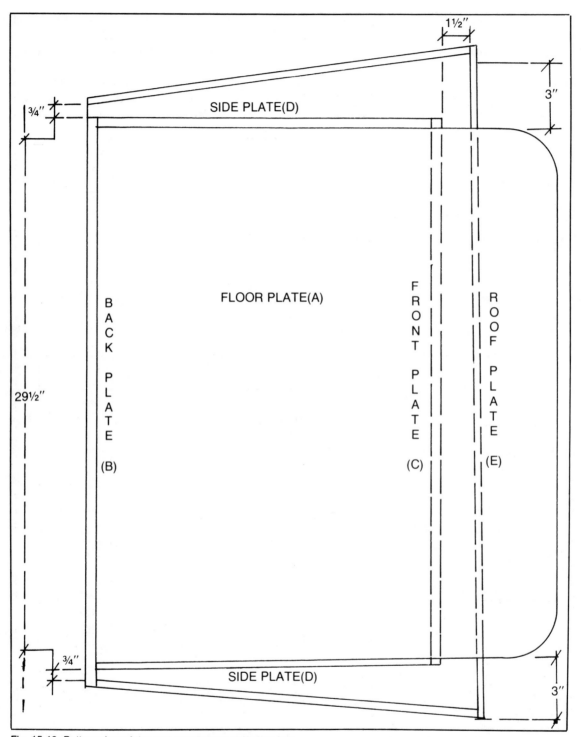

1½"

3"

¾"

SIDE PLATE(D)

B
A
C
K

P
L
A
T
E

(B)

FLOOR PLATE(A)

F
R
O
N
T

P
L
A
T
E

(C)

R
O
O
F

P
L
A
T
E

(E)

29½"

¾"

SIDE PLATE(D)

3"

Fig. 15-13. Bottom view of the roof assembly to the stove box.

190

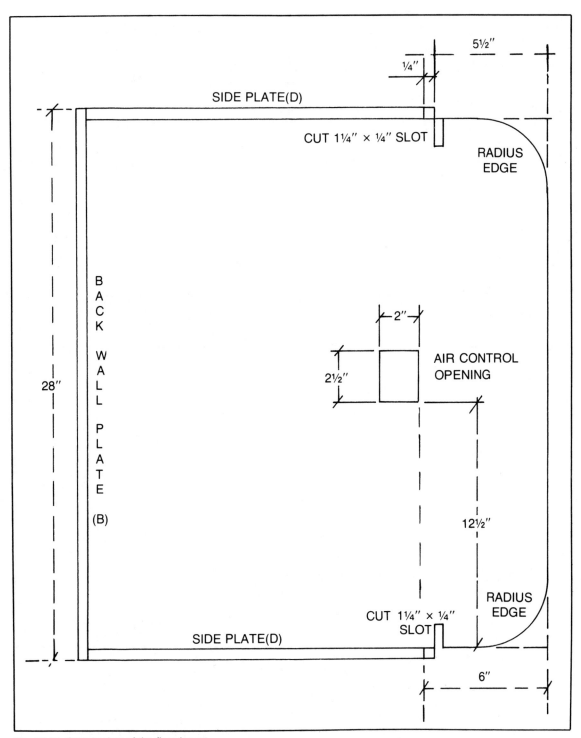

Fig. 15-14. Bottom view of the floor layout.

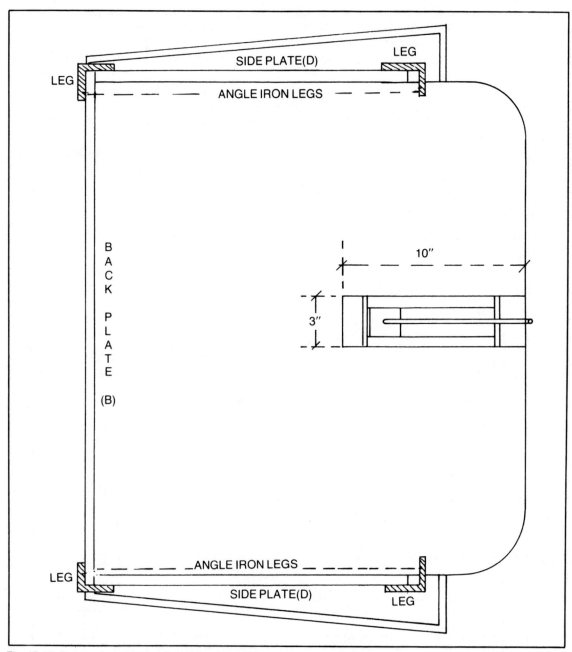

Fig. 15-15. Bottom view of legs and exterior air control.

the two sections of hinge together, before you weld them to the stove and door. Once welded, allow the weld to cool before removing the C-clamps.

After the door is mounted, place the (door) locking wedge, inside the door opening lip and weld. See Fig. 10-19 if you have installed a single door on your Liberty stove.

Take the ½″-flat stock (about 46″ long) and,

while the stove is on it's back, tack weld it to the front of the hearth in the same manner as you tacked the trim to the roof plate. When the hearth is trimmed, cut off the spare stock and attach the end to the angle iron leg.

Stand the stove in the upright position. Install the interior air control over the air opening, in your stove, and tack weld to the floor. Use tacks about 2" long (one on each side and one in front). See Fig. 9-5.

Using diagram (Fig. 15-21) as a visual aid,

fabricate and mount the second shelf and the tile tracks.

Install the firebrick as shown in Fig. 12-15. If any cutting must be done on the brick, it can be done with a circular saw (with a masonry blade). Once the brick is installed, clean all slag off the welds. Scrape any spatter (from welding) off the stove and (using spray cans or a paint pad) paint your stove. Remember to use a high-heat paint; anything rated at over 1000° will do. See Figs. 15-22 and 15-23.

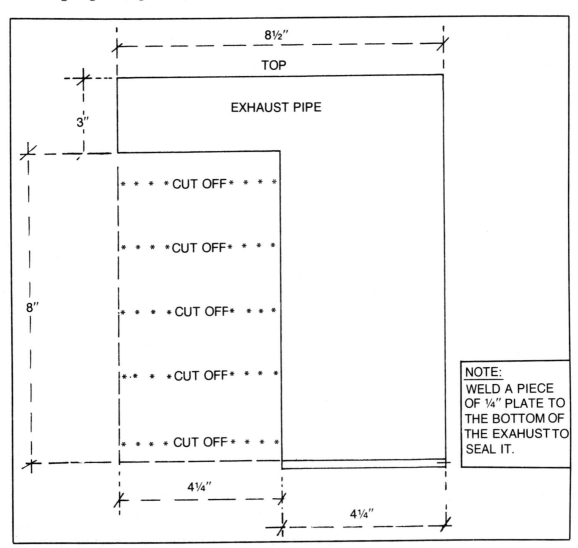

Fig. 15-16. Side view of the exhaust pipe for the top exhaust.

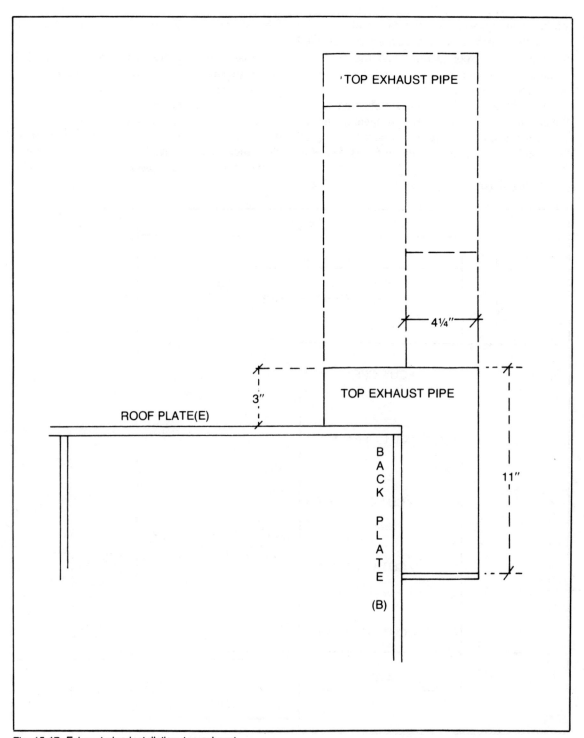

Fig. 15-17. Exhaust pipe installation, top exhaust.

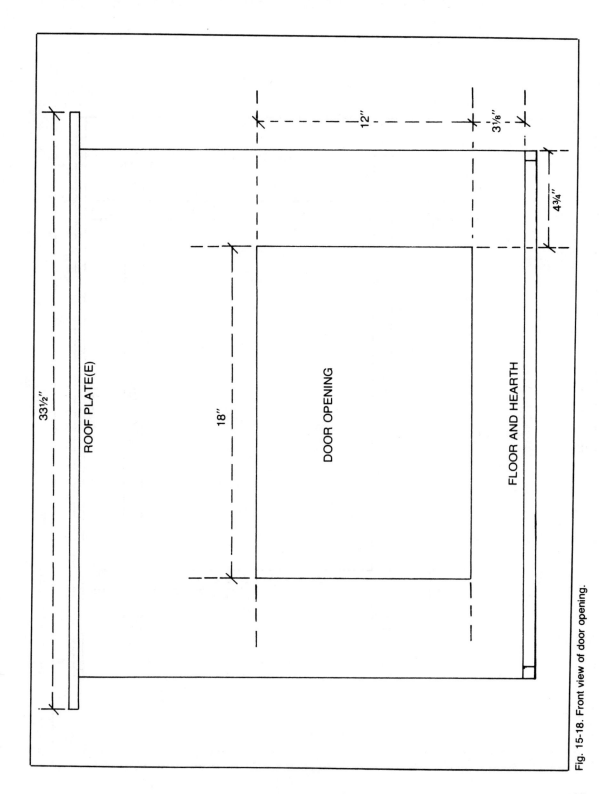

Fig. 15-18. Front view of door opening.

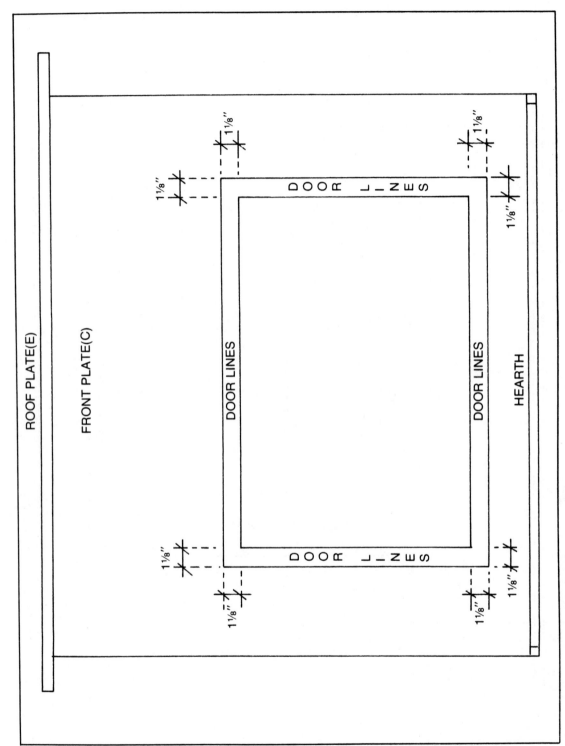

Fig. 15-19. Front view of door lines around door opening.

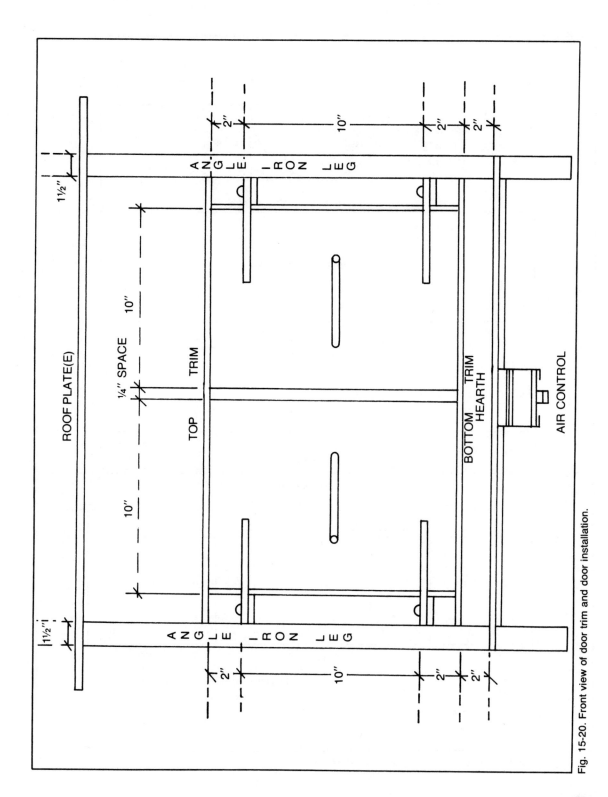

Fig. 15-20. Front view of door trim and door installation.

197

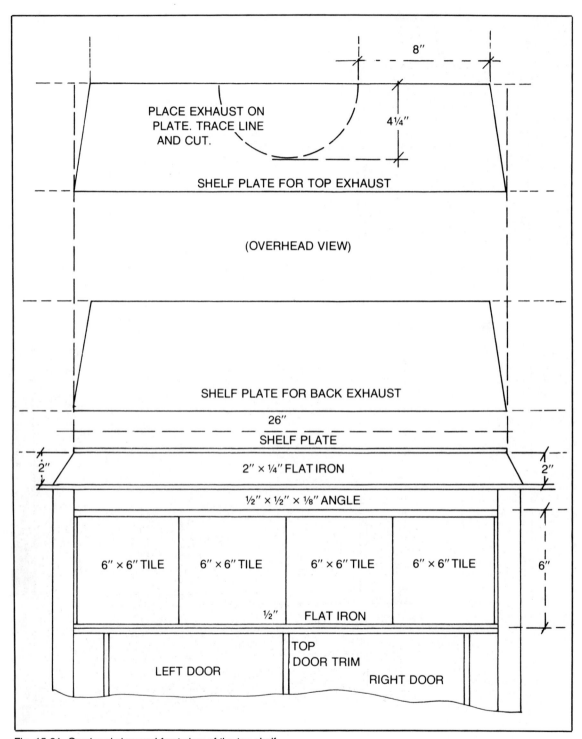

Fig. 15-21. Overhead view and front view of the top shelf.

Fig. 15-22. The Liberty stove.

Fig. 15-23. The Liberty stove.

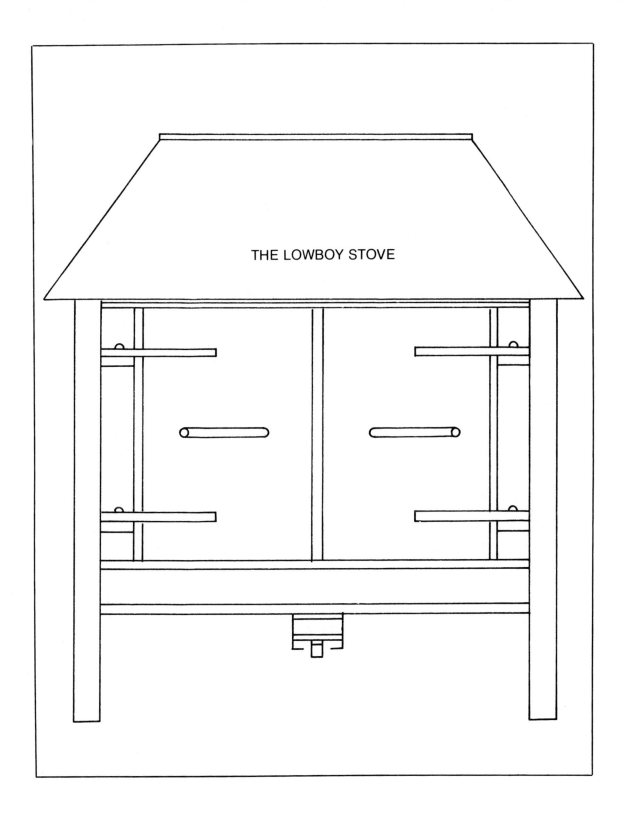

THE LOWBOY STOVE

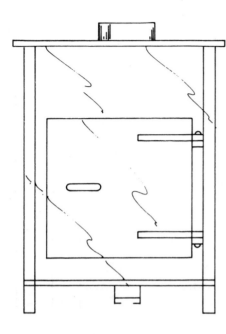

# Chapter 16

# Lowboy Stove

THE LOWBOY IS DESIGNED TO heat large ranch houses, split levels, raised ranchers, and two-story houses. This stove works very well in two-story farm houses; this is especially true for those that have not been well insulated.

If your home is broken up into small rooms—inhibiting the heat from being readily radiated—wall and ceiling registers can be installed throughout the house for faster, and more even, heat distribution. The Lowboy has the heating capacity to keep a home warmer than you have been previously with most existing heating systems.

This is the first model that I ever built. The heating capacity was too much for my two-story townhouse. My neighbors thought that I was crazy when I began my project. I built the stove on my patio in the middle of the summer and tested it in the midst of 90° heat. It worked. That was the beginning of my business.

It would be a very good idea to measure your doorways. Make sure that you will be able to fit the stove through doorways before you complete construction of the stove. Do not go through any un-

necessary aggravation. Before you begin to install registers, or mechanisms, run the stove for a few days to determine if any adjustments are needed to carry its heat further.

**Note.** Due to the shape of the Lowboy roof, extra cuts must be made when you are cutting the plate. See Fig. 16-A for sketches of these cuts. Remember to give the steel supplier a copy of the material list (see Table 16-1 and 16-2) for this stove. The plates that have a second cut are plates E and F.

### FABRICATION OF MISCELLANEOUS PARTS

To start this project, begin with the fabrication of miscellaneous parts. You should have already decided on the following:

- ☐ The type of exhaust (top or back).
- ☐ The type of baffle that you are going to use, and
- ☐ The type of solid fuel that you are going to burn.

You are now ready to follow the fabrication instructions for your stove.

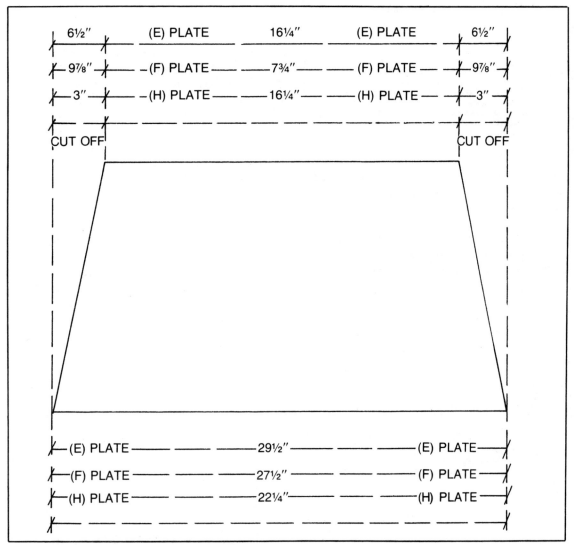

Fig. 16-A. Front view of cut sketches for plates E, F and H.

A wood-burning unit requires an air slide in the bottom of the door. A unit that burns wood and coal, however, requires an air control system as shown in Figs. 10-2 through 10-6 and Figs. 10-8 through 10-11. Turn to Chapter 9, the section of the book on air controls, and gather the parts shown in Figs. 9-1 and 9-2. Fabricate the interior air control. You will find instructions in Chapter 9 on how to do this.

Fabricate the exterior air control. Refer to Figs. 9-3 and 9-4.

Referring to the diagram, of your stove and depicting the mounting of the door(s) on your stove, you will see trim pieces around the door(s). Using this drawing, cut the door trim pieces according to the size shown on the sketch (See Fig. 16-25).

Once the trim pieces are cut, refer to the door diagrams Figs. 10-4 through 10-7 and find the door that corresponds with your stove. And lay out your door(s), according to that drawing. Using Figs. 10-12 through 10-20, fabricate the parts that will be

**Table 16-1. Lowboy Stove Data.**

```
Firebox height: 18″
Firebox width: 27½″
Firebox depth: 25½″
Roof height: 11⅜″
Heating capacity: approximately 3000 square feet
Fuel: primarily wood; the firebox will be too
      large to burn some varieties of coal
Burn time: on a low burn, 12 to 13 hours
Fabrication time: 9 hours (professionally) 16 to 21 (do-it-yourselfer)
Exhaust Pipe: 8″ Inside Diameter (ID)
Plate Weight: 357.5 pounds
Log size: 24″
```

mounted on your door(s). Drill the door handle hole(s) and cut the openings. Once the door is prepared, mount your slides and handles to the door(s).

Refer to Fig. 10-20 showing standard hinges. Fabricate the hinges using the sketch as a visual aid. Figure 10-20 shows one set of hinges. If you are using a single door on your stove, you will need two sets of hinges. If you are building a double door stove, four sets of hinges will be needed.

If you decide you want to trim the edges of the roof plate, now is the time to do it. Take the roof plate and measure it's length and width; add the two measurements and multiply the answer by two. The answer gives you the length of the trim you'll need. Add 2 inches to that measurement for waste. Using the ½″-×¼″ flat stock, as the trim material, cut a piece that measures the sum of the four sides (plus 2″). Using a flat surface, lay the roof plate upside down and starting in the back corner stand the ½″ flat stock on edge (the ½″ side vertical to the roof). Place it against the edge of the roof. Once the trim is in place, tack it to the roof (tacking every 6″) making sure that you are keeping the trim straight. When you reach a corner stop tacking.

Using your cutting torch, heat the trim at the corner. When the trim is red hot, slowly bend the trim around the corner. Once you have made the turn, begin tacking again until you reach the next corner. Then repeat the same procedure until you're back where you started. When you have reached that point, and the last tack is made, cut off the extra trim.

**Table 16-2. Lowboy Stove Material List.**

| amount | size | | | letter mark | location | weight |
|---|---|---|---|---|---|---|
| 1 | 31½″ | × 27″ | × ¼″ | A | floor | 60.30 lbs. |
| 1 | 27½″ | × 18″ | × ¼″ | B | back | 35.09 lbs. |
| 1 | 27½″ | × 17¾″ | × ¼″ | C | front | 34.61 lbs. |
| 2 | 25″ | × 18″ | × ¼″ | D | sides | 63.81 lbs. |
| 2 | 29½″ | × 13¾″ | × ¼″ | E | roof (front+back) | 57.52 lbs. |
| 2 | 27½″ | × 11⅜″ | × ¼″ | F | roof (sides) | 42.90 lbs. |
| 1 | 19″ | × 9″ | × ¼″ | G | roof (top) | 12.12 lbs. |
| 1 | 22¼″ | × 6″ | × ¼″ | H | baffle (roof) | 9.47 lbs. |
| 1 | 12″ | × 14″ | × ¼″ | I | baffle (exhaust) | 11.91 lbs. |
| 2 | 10″ | × 14″ | × ⅜″ | J | double doors | 29.77 lbs. |
| | | | | or | | |
| 1 | 20″ | × 14″ | × ⅜″ | J | single door | 29.77 lbs. |
| | | | | | Total Weight: | 357.50 lbs. |

| | | Steel List | | |
|---|---|---|---|---|

| amount | length | description | | use |
|---|---|---|---|---|
| 1 | 20′ | 1½″ × 1½″ × ¼″ angle iron | | legs and brick stays |
| 1 | 12′ | 2″ × ⅜″ flat stock | | hinges and top door trim |
| 1 | 20′ | ½″ × ¼″ flat stock | | roof, door, hearth trim |
| 1 | 40″ | ½″ round stock | | door handles |
| 1 | 6″ | 8″ inside diameter pipe | | exhaust pipe |

| | General Material | |
|---|---|---|

| amount | description | use |
|---|---|---|
| 42 | split firebrick | firebox lining |
| 70″ | asbestos or spun-glass gasket | door gasket |
| 1 | small can of furnace cement | door gasket glue |
| 3 | 9/16″ flat washers | door handle stays |
| 4 | ⅜″ rivets | hinge pins |
| 4 | spray cans (or 2 quarts) of high-heat paint | |

Using the 1½"-×-1½"-×-¼" angle iron, cut leg angles. Their length will be determined by the height of the firebox plus the height that you want the stove to be from the floor. To figure the length of the front stove legs (when partially sitting on a hearth), determine the height of the hearth and add 2 inches (for clearance) and take into account, the height of the firebox. The length (or height) of the back legs can be determined by the height of the firebox plus 2 inches (the clearance that was allowed in the front).

While cutting the leg angles, you might as well cut the brick stay angles. The length of these can be determined by the interior depth of the firebox and by the length of the back wall.

## FIREBOX PREPARATIONS

Now that you have completed the miscellaneous pieces, you can prepare to build your firebox. Before starting the actual fabrication of the stove, the plates should be laid out on the floor in order of the fabrication. This can be done very simply by:

☐ Sweeping down the area where you are going to be working.

☐ Laying your floor plate down in the middle of the floor.

☐ Laying your back plate on the floor just behind the floor plate.

☐ Laying the side plates along side the floor plate in their respective places.

☐ Laying the front plate just in front of the floor plate.

The roof plate, the door(s), and miscellaneous steel parts should be laid out to the side of the work area in order to be close at hand when needed. Have all of your tools at hand to be ready for use. Make sure that all rules of safety apply before going any further.

## FABRICATION INSTRUCTIONS

With the plates in position, take the back plate B and place it against the back of floor plate A. Leave a ¼" overlap hanging past the floor plate on each side. When plate B is in place, tack weld it to floor plate A. Keep a 90° angle. See Figs. 16-1 and 16-2.

Once plate B is tacked, take side plate D and place it against the side of floor plate A. Butt plate D to back plate B. When side plate D is in position, tack weld it to floor plate A and back plate B. See Figs. 16-3 and 16-4.

Repeat the directions, given in the preceding paragraph, on the opposite side. See Fig. 16-5. Take front plate C, and stand it on top of floor plate A, and lean it against (or butt it against) both plates D. When in position, tack weld to the floor plate and side plates. Pay attention to the alignment of the edges. See Figs. 16-6 and 16-7.

Using Jet rod, weld the floor of the stove to the walls. Once the floor is welded, lay the stove on it's side and weld the side plate to the front and back plates. Upon completion of this, lay the stove on it's opposite side and weld the other side plate to the front and back wall plates.

When welding your sides, you can also, as you finish welding each side, tack weld the brick stay angles into position. This can be done quite easily by taking a split firebrick and laying it into position. With the stove upright, the brick would be standing with the 9" side vertical. Take the angle, (one leg touching the wall, the other leg overlapping the brick by about ½") and tack the angle to the wall (using 2" long tacks). When tacking, the angle will lean away from the brick. This is preferred. It leaves room so that you can put in, or take out, the brick. See Fig. 12-15.

Begin to fabricate the roof by taking roof plate (E), and standing it up (the 16½" side up). Bring plate F in and butt it to plate E while laying plate E down on the plate F until both edges line up with each other. Using your 2-foot square, check to make sure bottom edges are at a 90° angle to each other. When these two plates (plate E and plate F) are in position, tack weld them. See Figs. 16-8 and 16-9. Repeat the directions given in the preceding paragraph, using the other plate (E). See Fig. 16-10. Taking the other plate (F) and connecting the two plates (E) together, make sure to line the edges up and (using a 2-foot square) make sure that all of the roof edges are square. Tack weld into position. See Figs. 16-11 and 16-12. Once all of the edges of the roof are tack welded, you can take roof plate G and

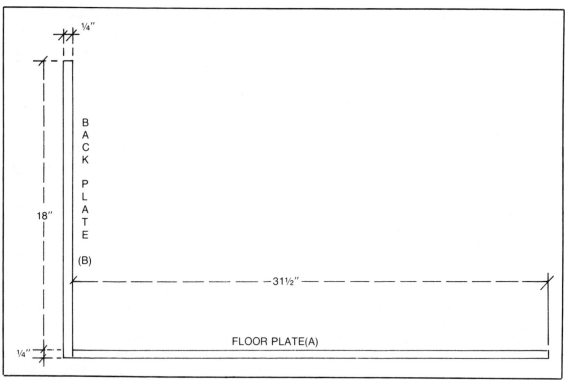

Fig. 16-1. Side view of back wall assembly to the floor.

lay it on top of the roof (squaring it to the roof). Once the plate G is in position, tack weld it into place. Once your roof is tacked, turn it over and weld all inside joints with Jet rod. See Fig. 16-13.

Take the roof baffle plate H and lay it out, according to Fig. 16-14. When plate (H) is laid out, cut the openings with your cutting torch.

Using Figs. 16-14 and 16-15, center the roof baffle H into your roof. When it is in position weld it into place.

Take the roof and lay it on the floor (upside down). Take the firebox (turning it upside down) and place it in the roof. See Fig. 16-16. Check to make sure the firebox sits square on the four corners of the roof. Once the firebox is aligned to the roof, tack the two together. Be sure to put at least four tacks in (one in the center of each side). Make them at least two inches long. You might notice at this point that your roof sides are bowed. This is due to the heat of welding. These bows should be filled in by ½″ flat stock. Cut some pieces to size

(the length of each side), and lay them flat in between the roof and box. Tack weld them to the box and roof. When the roof is in place, weld the roof to the box. See Fig. 16-16.

Using Figs. 16-17 and 16-18 as visual aids, cut the air opening in the floor plate. Lay out, and cut, the leg slots and hearth radiuses. Referring to Fig. 16-18, install the exterior air control and legs.

Laying the stove on it's back, and referring to Fig. 16-19, draw the cut lines for the door opening using your cutting torch.

Draw a box around the door opening 1″ out from the edges of the opening. See Fig. 16-20. This will mark the locations of the door(s). Referring to Fig. 16-21, if your stove is a back exhaust model or referring to Fig. 16-22 if your stove is a top exhaust model, lay out the exhaust opening. Cut it out with the cutting torch and install the exhaust pipe.

Using either Fig. 16-23 or 16-24 (depending on the direction of your exhaust), install baffle plate I.

Mount the door(s) using the guidelines you've

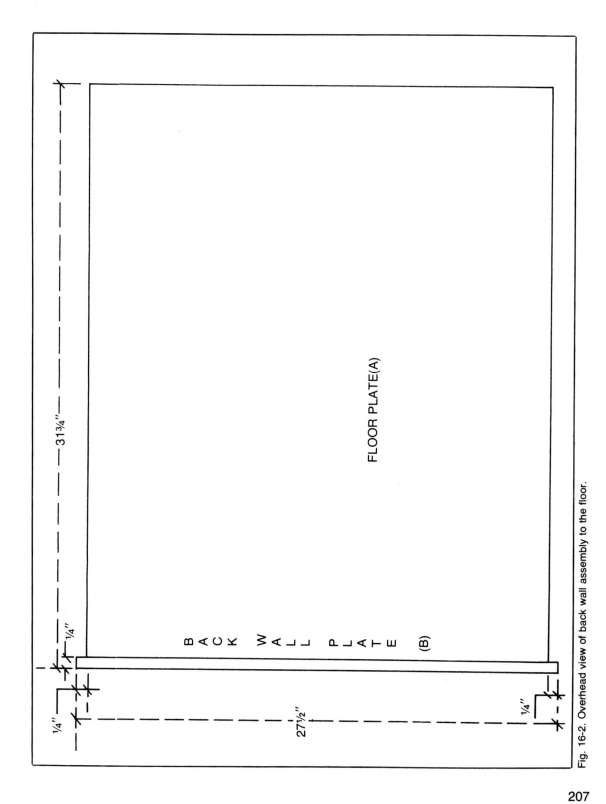

FLOOR PLATE(A)

BACK WALL PLATE (B)

31¾"

¼"

¼"

27½"

¼"

Fig. 16-2. Overhead view of back wall assembly to the floor.

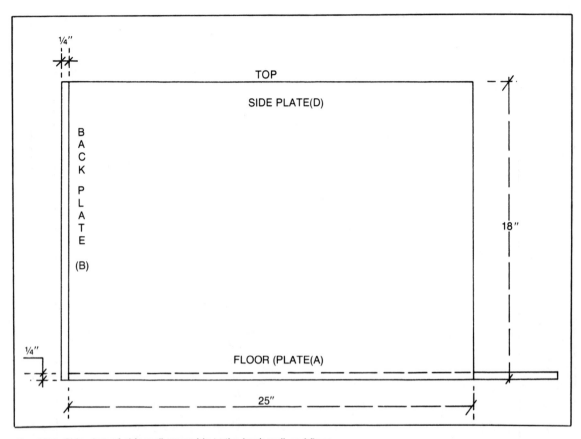

Fig. 16-3. Side view of side wall assembly to the back wall and floor.

drawn. Once the door is in place, lay the trim along-side the door and tack it into place. You must remember to leave a ¼″ space, between the door and the door trim, on the side (of the door) that the handle is on. This allows for the swing. See Fig. 12-14. If you are mounting double doors, be sure to leave a ¼″ space between the doors. This allows for expansion of the stove when hot. See Fig. 16-25.

Put the pins in the hinges, and mount them, as shown in Fig. 16-25. When they are tack welded into position, remember to C-clamp the two sections of hinge together before you weld them to the stove and door. Once welded, allow the weld to cool before removing the C-clamps. After the door is mounted, place the (door) locking wedge, inside the door opening lip and weld. See Fig. 10-19 (this is, only, for single-door models). Take the ½″ flat stock (about 46″ long) and, while the stove is on it's

back, tack weld it to the front of your hearth in the same manner as you tacked the trim to the roof plate. When the hearth is trimmed, cut off the spare stock and attach the end to the angle iron leg.

Stand the stove in the upright position and install the interior air control over the air opening, in the stove, and tack weld to floor. Use tacks about 2″ long (one on each side and one in front). See Fig. 9-5.

Install the firebrick as shown in Fig. 12-15. If any cutting must be done on the brick, it can be done with a circular saw (with a masonry blade). Once the brick is installed, clean all slag off the welds. Scrape any spatter (from welding) off the stove and (using spray cans or a paint pad) paint your stove. Remember to use a high-heat paint; anything rated at over 1000° will due. See Figs. 16-26 and 16-27.

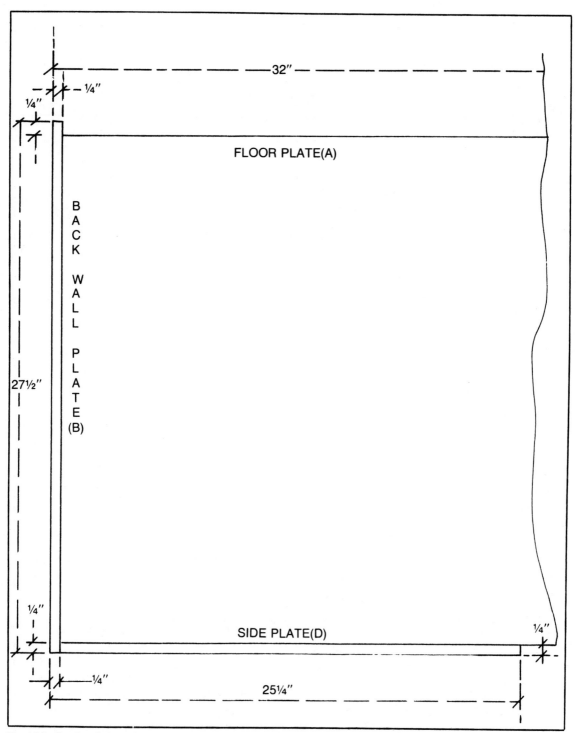

Fig. 16-4. Overhead view of side wall assembly to back wall and floor.

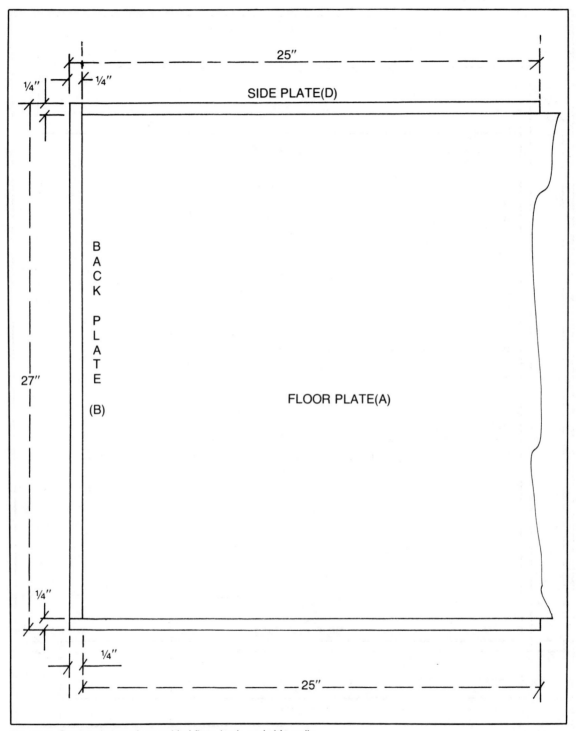

Fig. 16-5. Overhead view of assembled floor, back, and side walls.

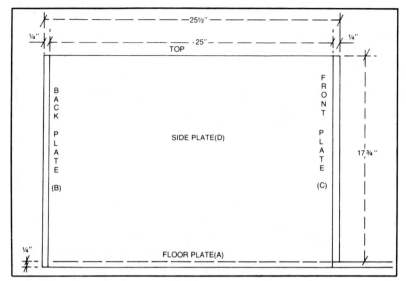

Fig. 16-6. Side view of the front plate to floor plate and side plates.

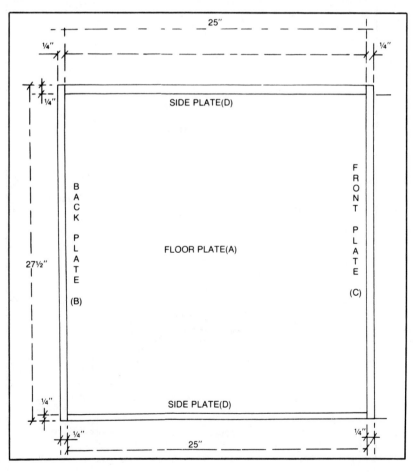

Fig. 16-7. Overhead view of the assembled firebox.

211

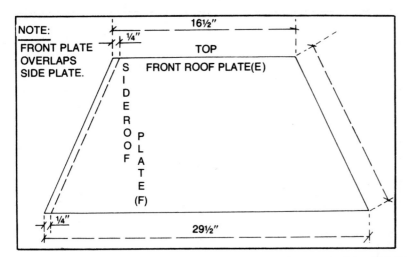

NOTE:
FRONT PLATE OVERLAPS SIDE PLATE.

¼″

16½″

TOP

S
I
D
E
R
O
O
F

FRONT ROOF PLATE(E)

P
L
A
T
E

(F)

¼″

29½″

Fig. 16-8. Front view of the front roof plate assembly to side roof plate.

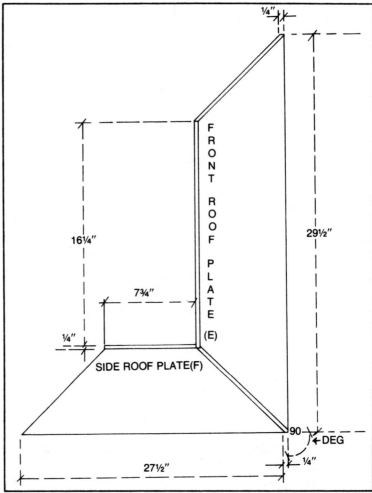

¼″

F
R
O
N
T

R
O
O
F

P
L
A
T
E

(E)

16¼″

7¾″

29½″

¼″

SIDE ROOF PLATE(F)

90

DEG

27½″

¼″

Fig. 16-9. Overhead view of the front roof plate assembly to the side roof plate.

212

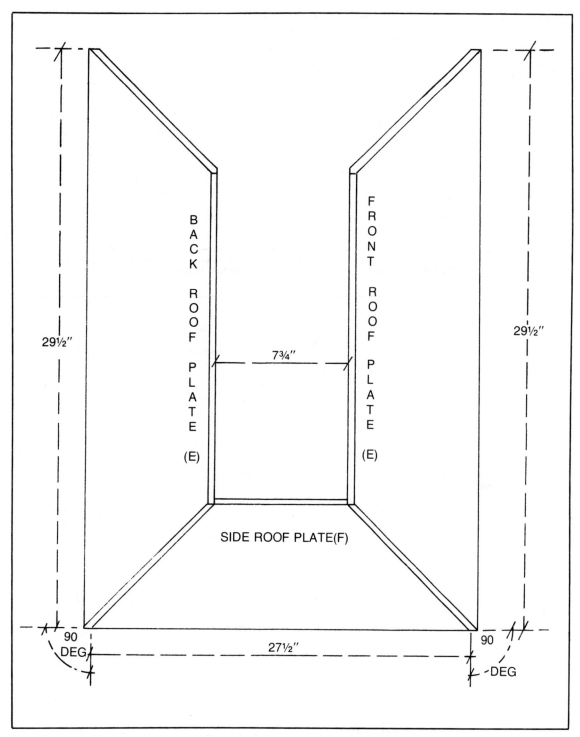

Fig. 16-10. Overhead view of the front roof plate and back roof plate assembly to side roof plate.

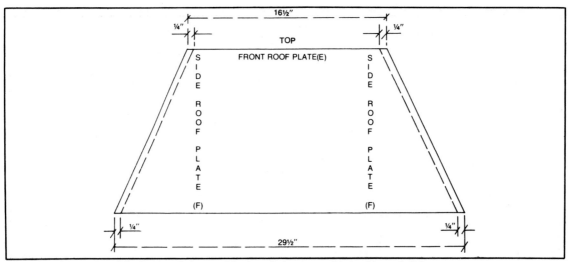

Fig. 16-11. Front view of the front roof plate and back roof plate assembly to side roof plates.

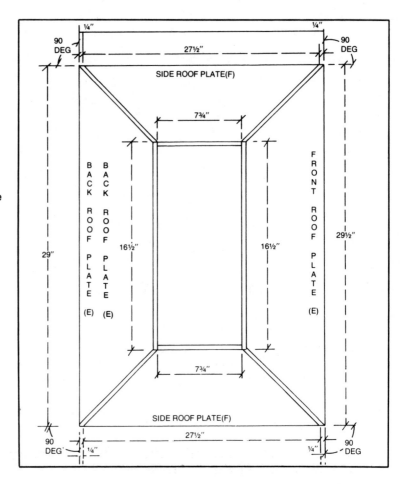

Fig. 16-12. Overhead view of the roof plate assembly.

214

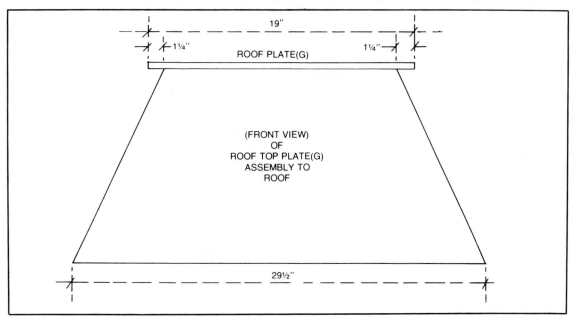

Fig. 16-13. Front view of the roof top plate assembly to the roof.

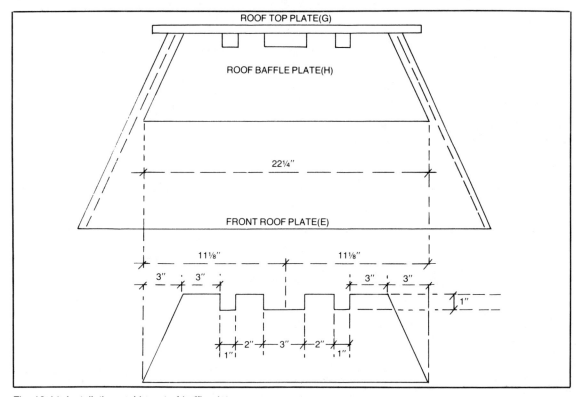

Fig. 16-14. Installation and layout of baffle plate.

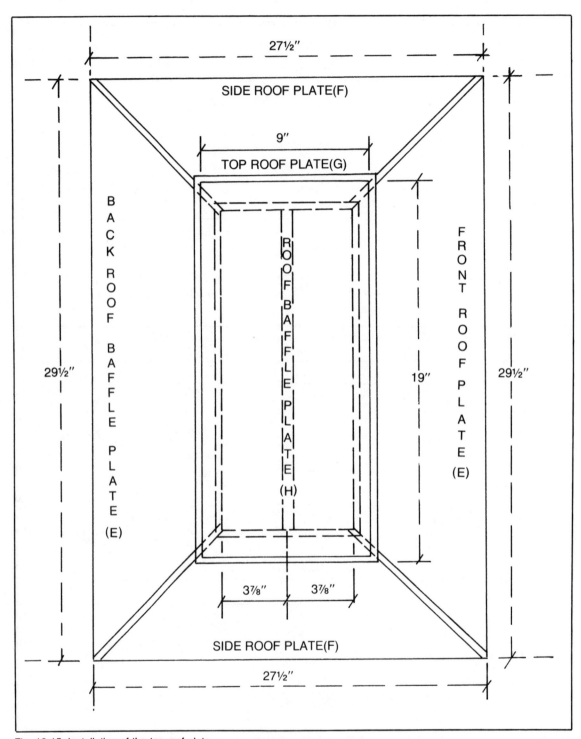

Fig. 16-15. Installation of the top roof plate.

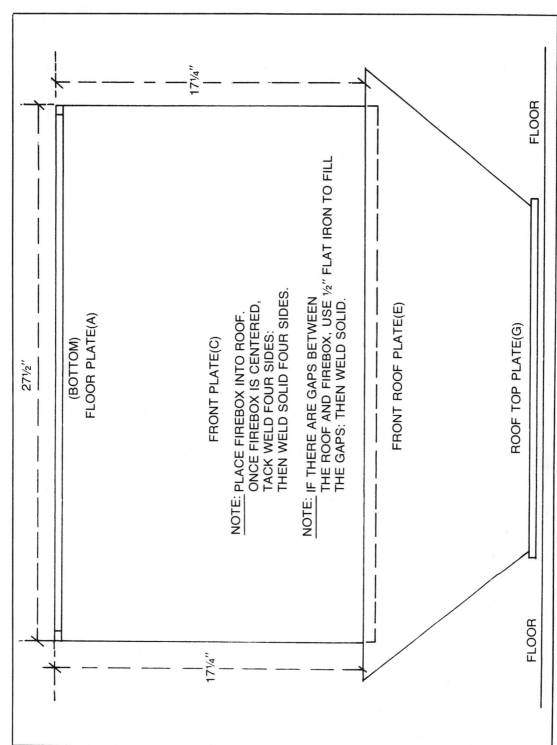

Fig. 16-16. Front view of the firebox assembly to the roof.

27½"

17¼"

17¼"

(BOTTOM)
FLOOR PLATE(A)

FRONT PLATE(C)

NOTE: PLACE FIREBOX INTO ROOF.
ONCE FIREBOX IS CENTERED,
TACK WELD FOUR SIDES;
THEN WELD SOLID FOUR SIDES.

NOTE: IF THERE ARE GAPS BETWEEN
THE ROOF AND FIREBOX, USE ½" FLAT IRON TO FILL
THE GAPS; THEN WELD SOLID.

FRONT ROOF PLATE(E)

ROOF TOP PLATE(G)

FLOOR

FLOOR

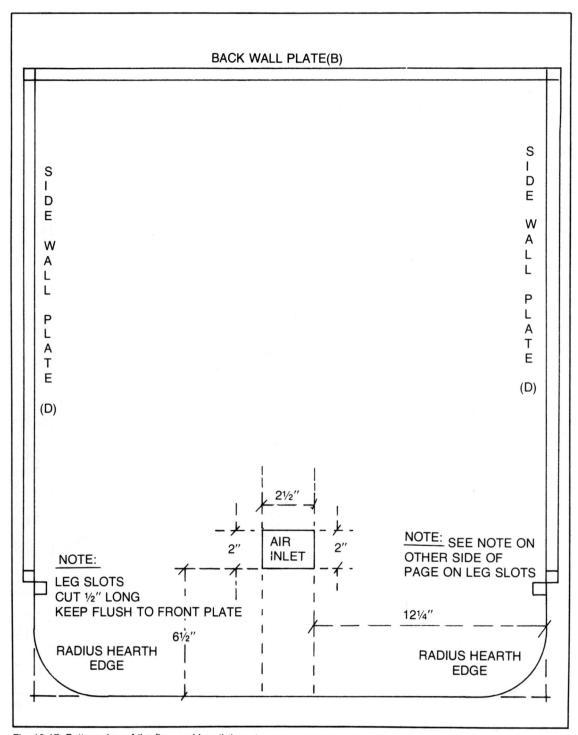

Fig. 16-17. Bottom view of the floor and hearth layout.

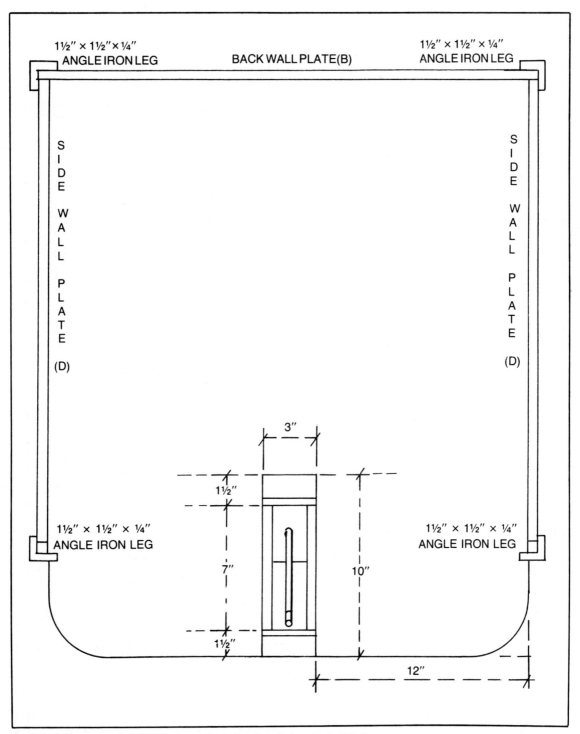

Fig. 16-18. Bottom view of the exterior air control and angle iron leg installation.

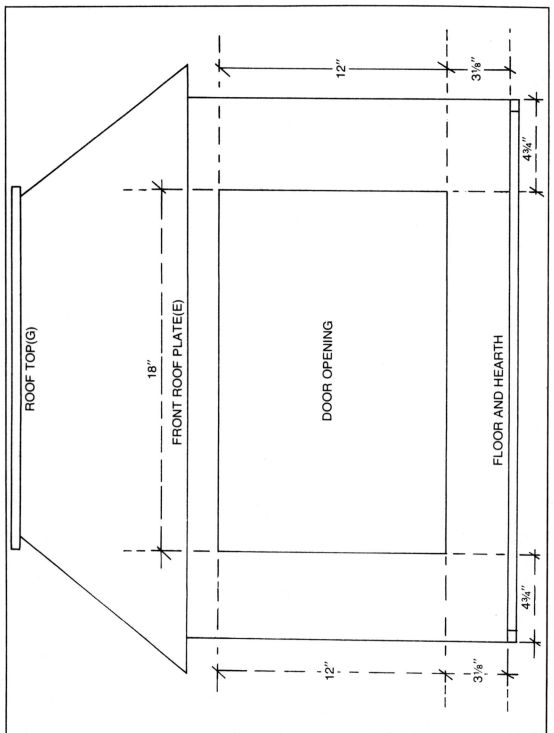

Fig. 16-19. Front view of the door opening layout.

ROOF TOP(G)

FRONT ROOF PLATE(E)

18"

DOOR OPENING

FLOOR AND HEARTH

12"

3 1/8"

4 3/4"

4 3/4"

12"

3 1/8"

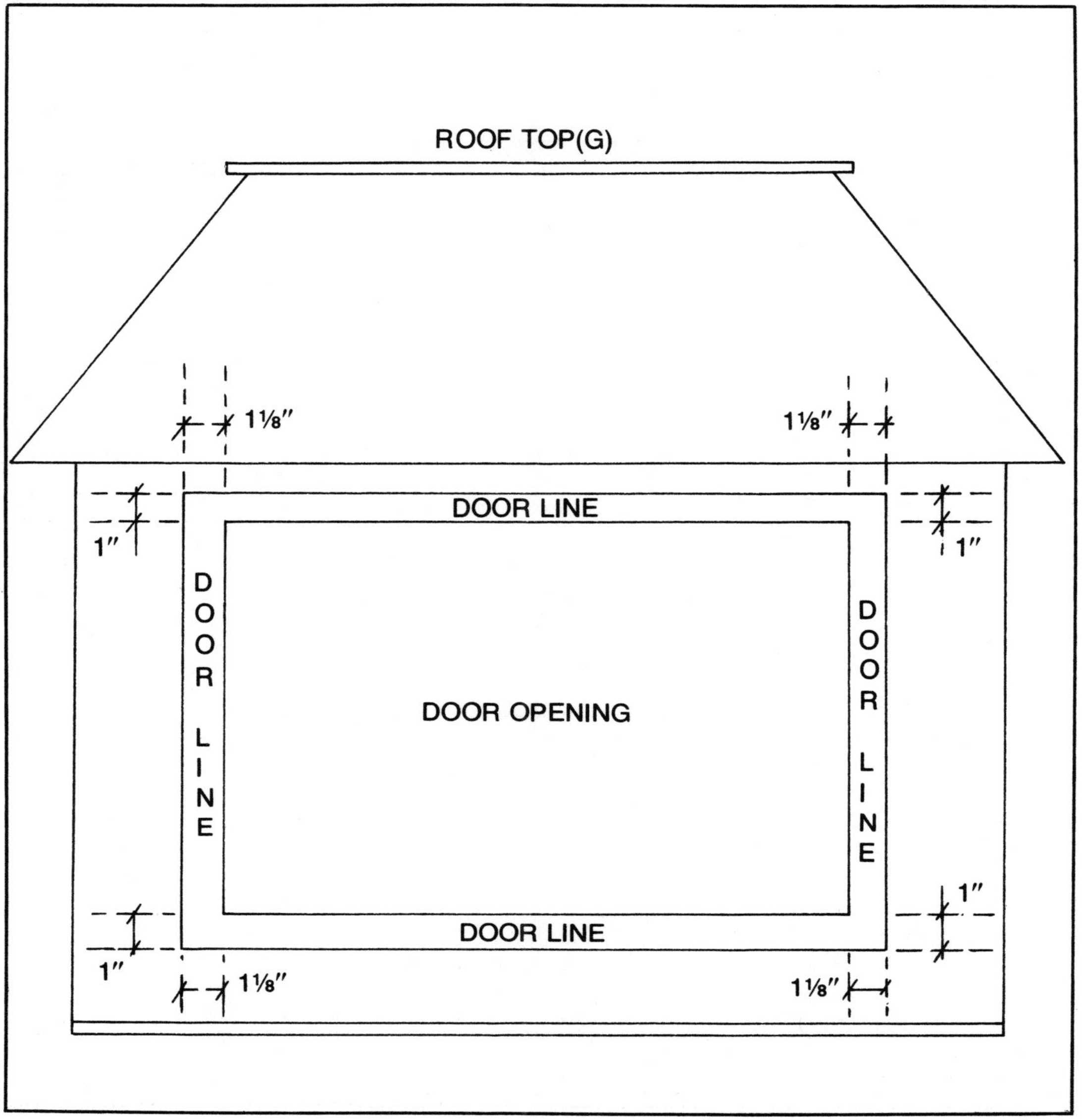

Fig. 16-20. Front view of the door lines layout.

ROOF TOP(G)

DOOR LINE

DOOR LINE

DOOR LINE

DOOR LINE

DOOR OPENING

1"

1"

1"

1"

1⅛"

1⅛"

1⅛"

1⅛"

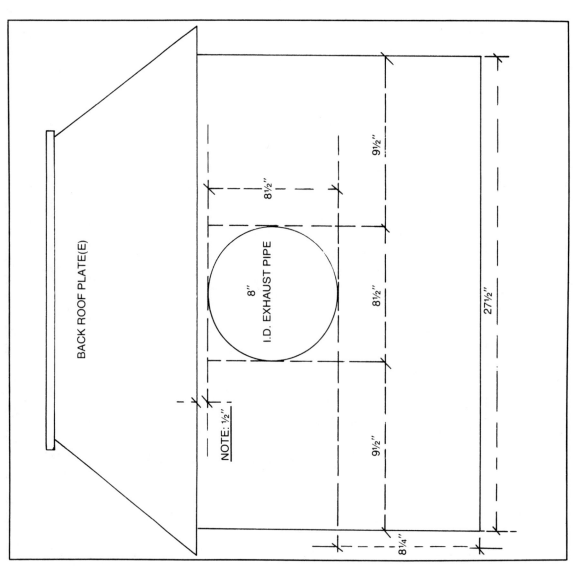

Fig. 16-21. Back view of the back exhaust installation.

BACK ROOF PLATE(E)

NOTE: ½"

8½"

9½"

8"
I.D. EXHAUST PIPE

8½"

9½"

27½"

8¼"

222

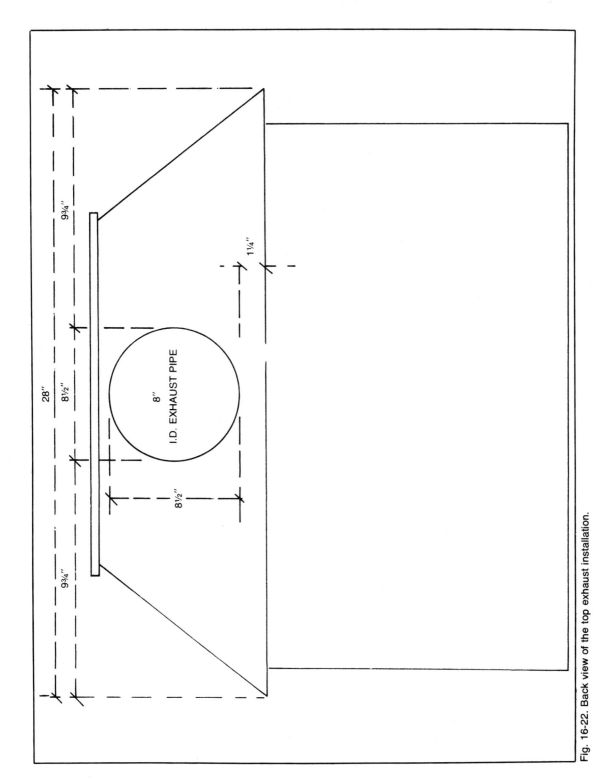

Fig. 16-22. Back view of the top exhaust installation.

223

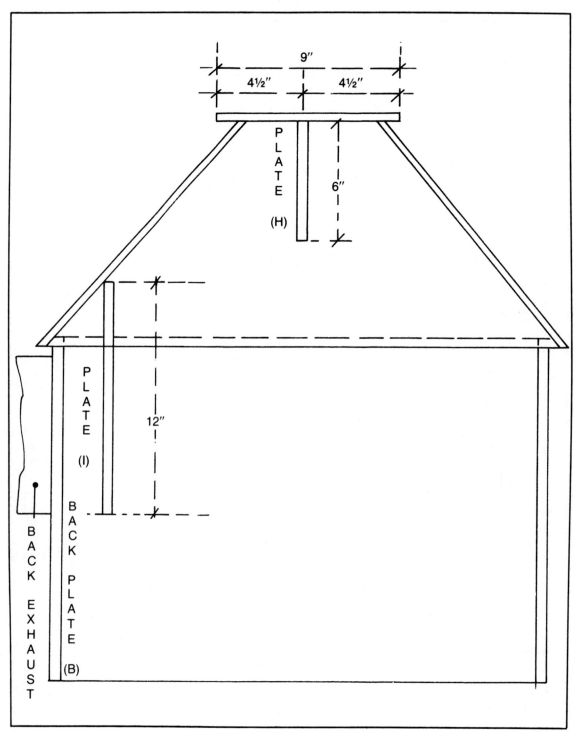

Fig. 16-23. Side view of the back exhaust baffle system.

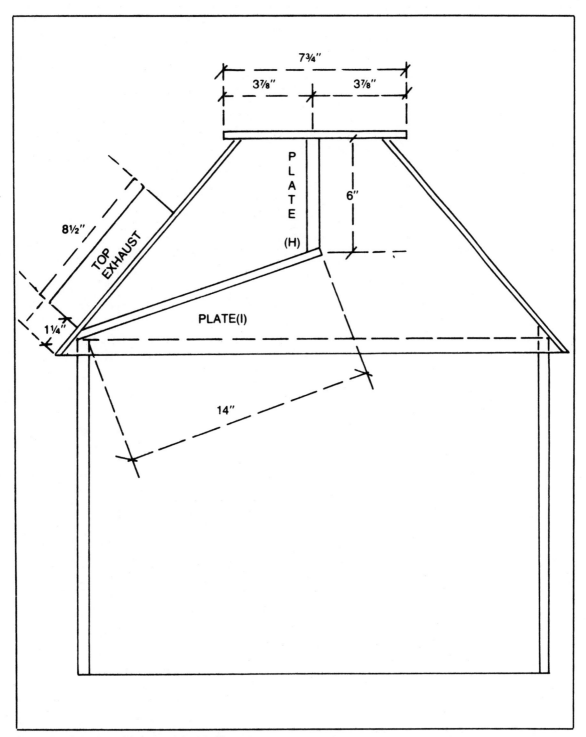

Fig. 16-24. Side view of the top exhaust baffle system.

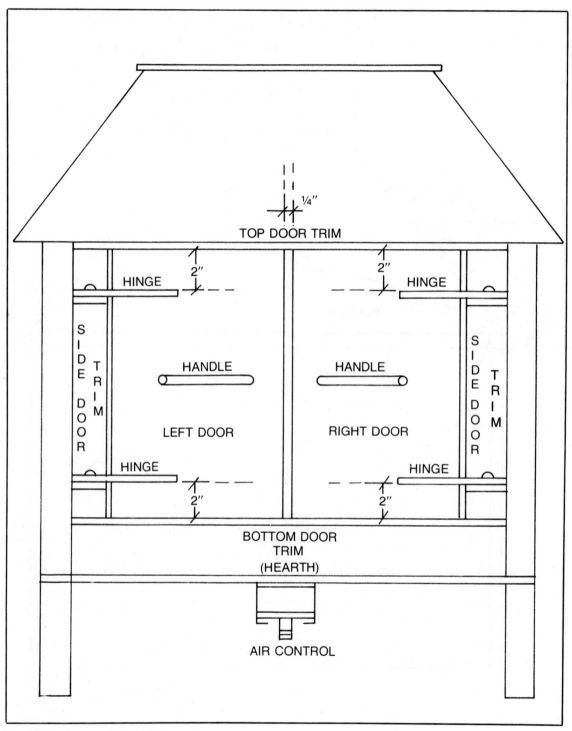

Fig. 16-25. Front view of the door installation.

226

Fig. 16-26. The completed Lowboy stove.

Fig. 16-27. The Lowboy stove with a fireplace cover.

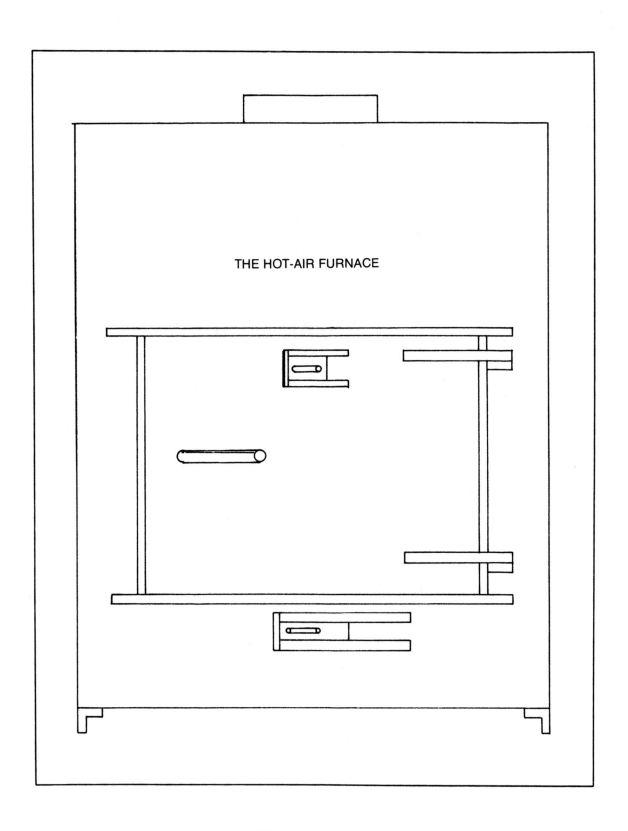

THE HOT-AIR FURNACE

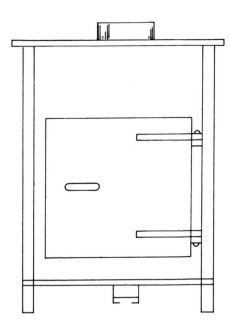

# Chapter 17

# Hot-Air Furnace

THIS HOT-AIR FURNACE IS designed for those who have an existing hot-air heating system in their home. It is hooked into the previously installed system and air is brought into the air jacket through two large air induction slots located under the unit. Air can be drawn in by normal convection and the use of an induction fan. You can install such a fan in your air duct connection pipe.

Air is drawn in and passed over the interior firebox (heating it). Hot air is then drawn into the air plenum and passed through the existing duct system to the rooms of your house.

## SUCCESSFULLY OPERATING THE UNIT

If the solid-fuel, hot-air furnace can supply enough hot air to heat your home, your thermostats will stay off (thus your first furnace will stay off). Successful operation of this unit, greatly depends on the following.

☐ Your house must be properly insulated. If all of the leaks in the house are not properly sealed, the efficiency of the unit will be reduced.

☐ If your cellar is normally cold, or even cool, during the heating season, the entire duct system should be insulated against the cold air. If this is not taken care of sufficiently, the cold air in the cellar will draw off the heat of the air in the plenum and ducts. This will result in only mildly heated air.

There are instructions on installing this unit in Chapter 24. If you follow these instructions and properly insulate the unit and ducts with fireproof insulation, you should have little trouble with the operation and efficiency of this unit.

This unit requires very little preparation for the actual fabrication of the unit. Because this unit is double-walled, most of your time will be spent welding the walls together. See Tables 17-1 and 17-2.

Begin by fabricating the door (Fig. 10-8), the lower air slide and the secondary air slide (Fig. 17-21), the door trim (Fig. 17-21) and the hinges (Fig. 10-20). Once these steps have been completed, and you have separated the plate (interior plates from the exterior plates), you are ready to begin construction of the stove.

## Table 17-1. Air Furnace Data.

| | |
|---|---|
| Height: | 36″ |
| Width: | 30½″ |
| Depth: | 25¾″ |
| Heating Capacity: | 2000 square feet |
| Fabrication Time: | 16 hours (professionally) 20 to 23 hours (do-it-yourselfer) |
| Fuel: | wood |
| Exhaust pipe: | 8″ Inside Diameter (ID) |
| Plate weight: | 705.18 pounds |
| Log size: | 27″ |

## FABRICATION INSTRUCTIONS

Lay interior floor plate A on a cleanly swept floor. Taking interior back plate B, butt plate B against the floor plate (the 25½″ side). Leave a ¼″ overlap hanging over each side of the floor plate. Once plate B is in position, tack weld it to floor plate A. See Figs. 17-1 and 17-2.

Once plate B is tacked, stand interior side plate C against the floor plate, and butt it against plate B overlap. Line up the corners of plate B and plate C. Make sure that they join together snugly. When in place, tack weld plate C to plate B and floor plate A. See Figs. 17-3 and 17-4.

Repeat the instructions given in the preceding paragraph, for the opposite side. See Fig. 17-5.

Take the other plate (A) and slip it into the top of the box; flush the plate to the top edges of plates B and C. When in position, tack weld to plates B and C. See Figs. 17-6 and 17-7. You have just made a 25½″-×-32″ box. This will become your firebox. Once the box is tacked together, using your Jet rod, weld all of the interior and exterior joints.

Using Figs. 17-8 and 17-9 as visual aids, install the sliding baffle tracks (with welds, 3 inches long, every 3 inches). Slide the baffle plate (G) into place and use C-clamps to hold it to the tracks. This will keep the baffle plate from sliding out when you have to roll the stove over.

Take exterior front plate D and lay it on the floor. Take the firebox (open side down) and lay it

## Table 17-2. Air Furnace Material List.

| amount | size | letter mark | location | weight |
|---|---|---|---|---|
| 2 | 25½″ × 23½″ × ¼″ | A | (interior) floor+roof | 84.98 lbs. |
| 1 | 26″ × 32″ × ¼″ | B | (interior) back | 58.00 lbs. |
| 2 | 23½″ × 32″ × ¼″ | C | (interior) sides | 106.64 lbs. |
| 2 | 30½″ × 36½″ × ¼″ | D | (exterior) front+back | 157.87 lbs. |
| 2 | 25¾″ × 30″ × ¼″ | E | (exterior) floor+roof | 109.54 lbs. |
| 2 | 25¾″ × 36½″ × ¼″ | F | (exterior) sides | 133.28 lbs. |
| 1 | 12″ × 24½″ × ¼″ | G | (interior) baffle | 20.85 lbs. |
| 1 | 20″ × 16″ × ⅜″ | H | door | 34.02 lbs. |
| | | | | Total Weight: 705.18 lbs. |

### Steel List

| amount | length | description | use |
|---|---|---|---|
| 1 | 5′ | ½″ × ¼″ flat stock | door trim and slide handles |
| 1 | 30″ | 2″ × ¼″ flat iron | top door trim and slides |
| 1 | 50″ | 2″ × ⅜″ flat stock | door hinges |
| 1 | 20″ | 4″ × 4″ × ¼″ angle iron | stove legs |
| 1 | 10′ | 1½″ × 1½″ × ¼″ angle iron | baffle tracks and brick stays |
| 1 | 10″ | 8″ inside diameter pipe | exhaust (air and smoke) |
| 1 | 14″ | ½″ round stock | door handle |
| 1 | 2′ | ½″ × ½″ × ⅛″ angle iron | slide tracks |

| amount | description | use |
|---|---|---|
| 33 | split firebrick | firebox lining |
| 1 length 80″ | asbestos or spun-glass gasket | door gasket |
| 1 | small can of furnace cement | door gasket glue |
| 2 | 9/16″ flat washers | door handle stays |
| 2 | ⅜″ rivets | hinge pins |
| 3 | spray cans (or 2 quarts) of high-heat paint | |

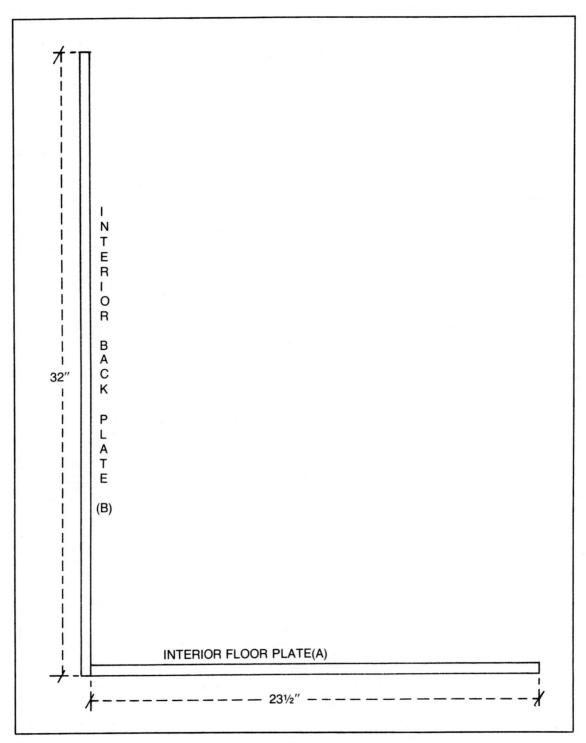

Fig. 17-1. Side view of the back plate and floor plate assembly.

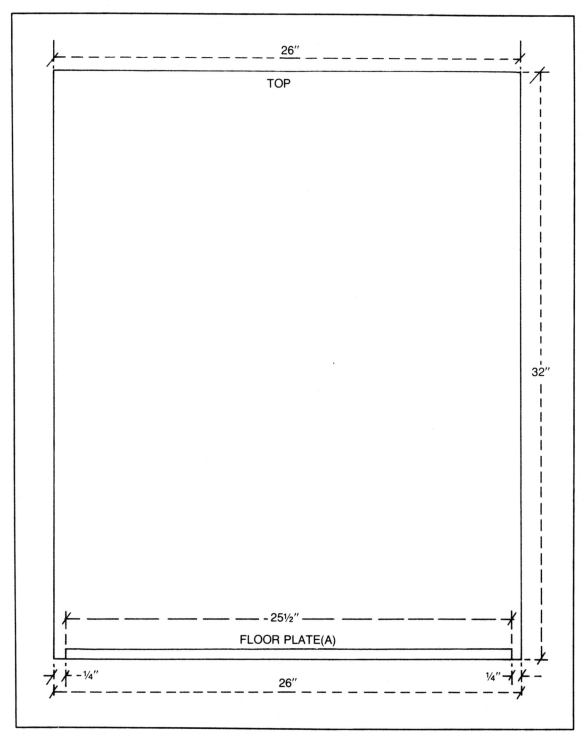

Fig. 17-2. Front view of the back plate and floor plate assembly.

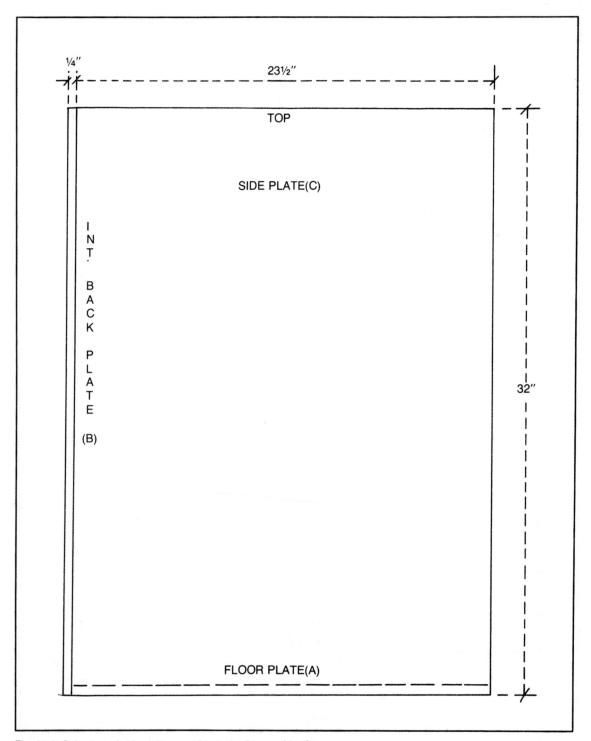

Fig. 17-3. Side view of side plate assembly to the floor and back.

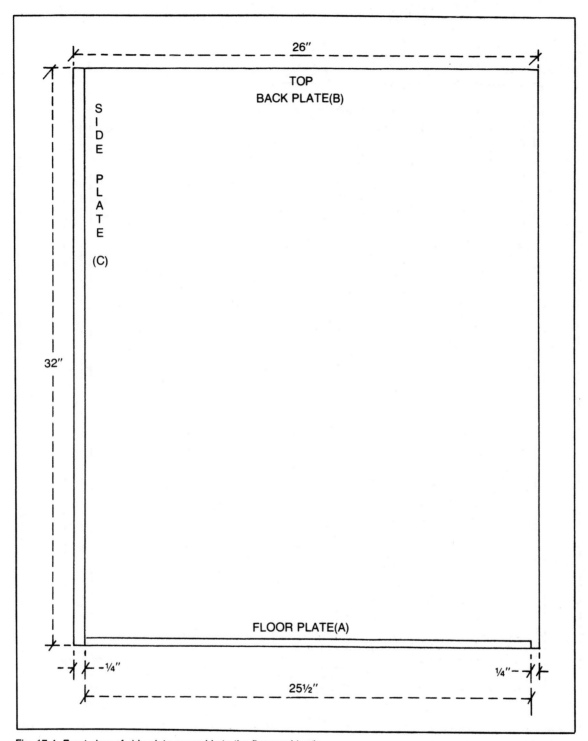

Fig. 17-4. Front view of side plate assembly to the floor and back.

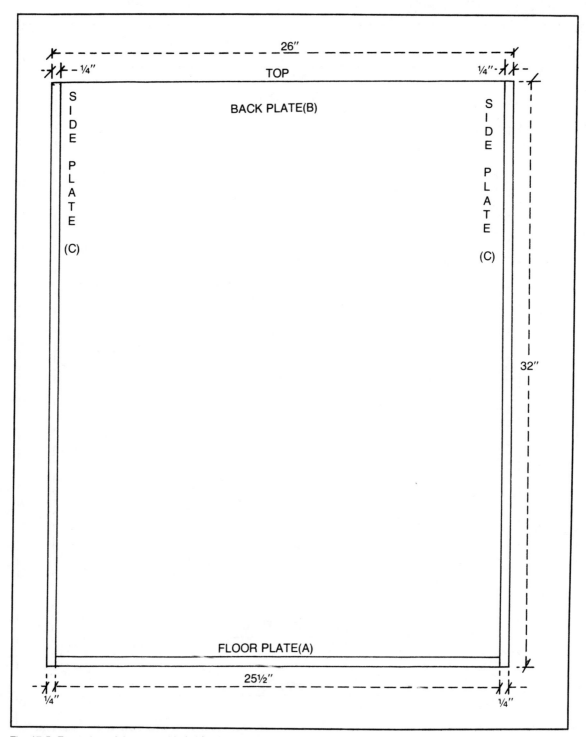

Fig. 17-5. Front view of the assembled side plates to the floor and back.

236

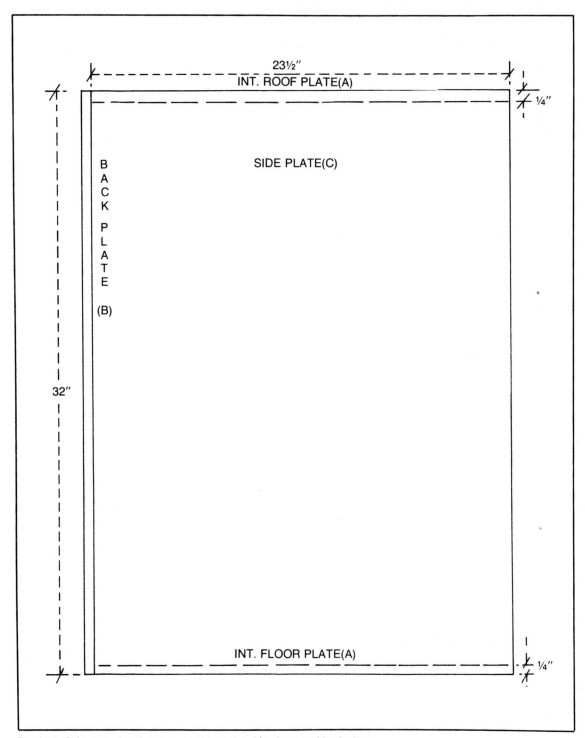

Fig. 17-6. Side view of roof plate assembly to the side plates and back plate.

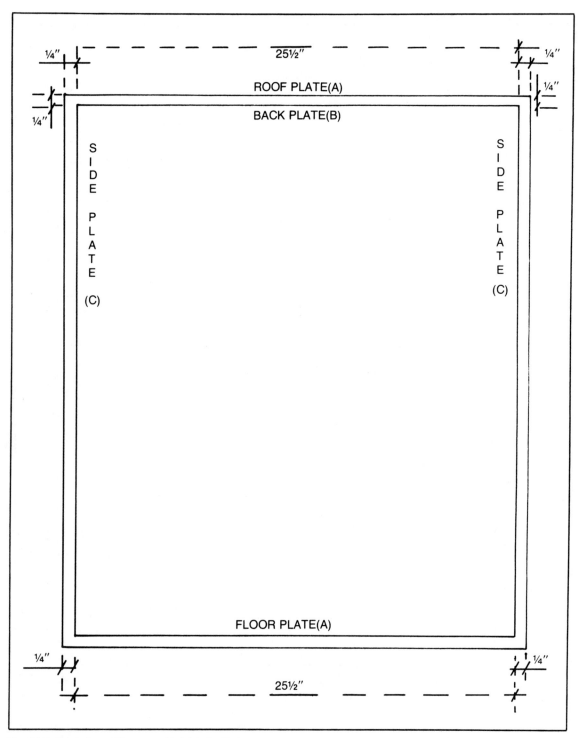

Fig. 17-7. Front view of the assembled interior firebox.

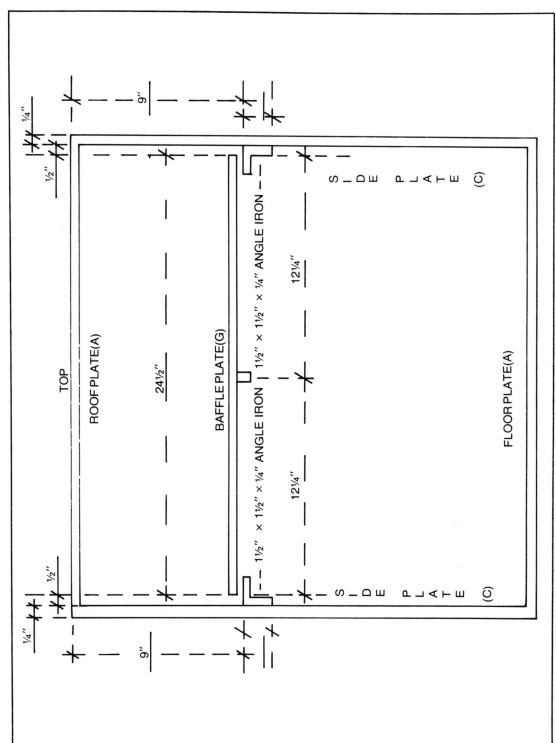

Fig. 17-8. Front view of the baffle plate installation into the firebox.

239

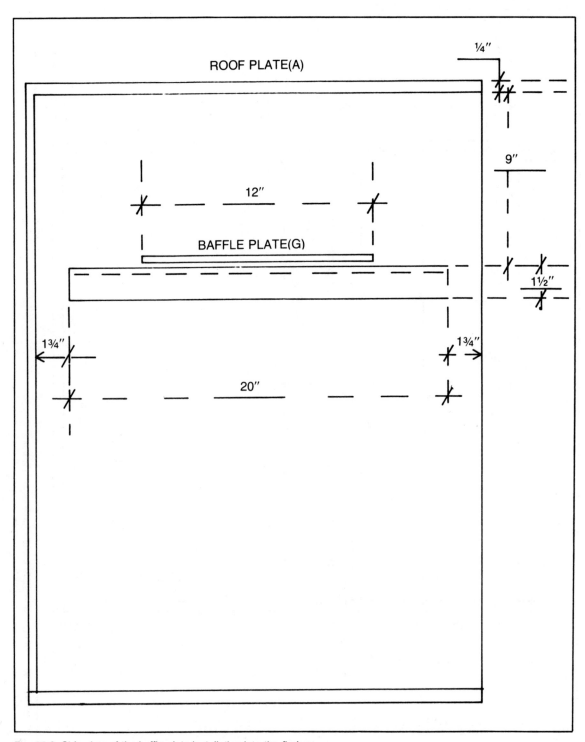

Fig. 17-9. Side view of the baffle plate installation into the firebox.

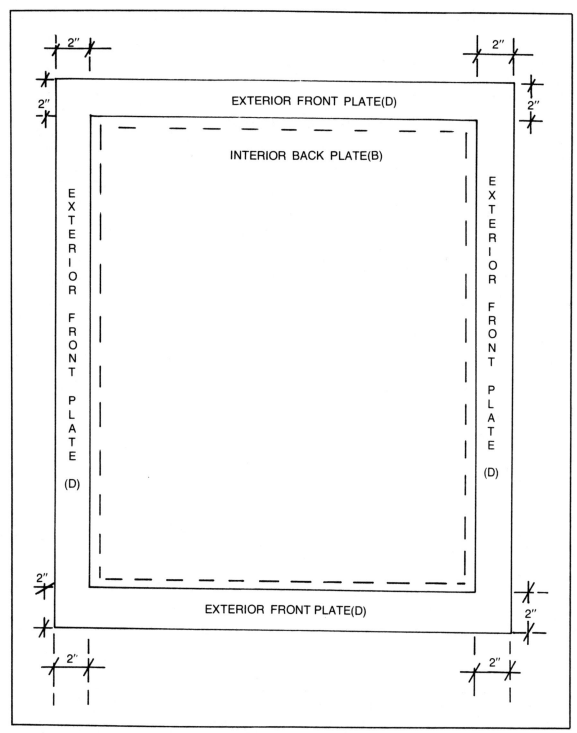

Fig. 17-10. Overhead view of the interior box mounted to the exterior front.

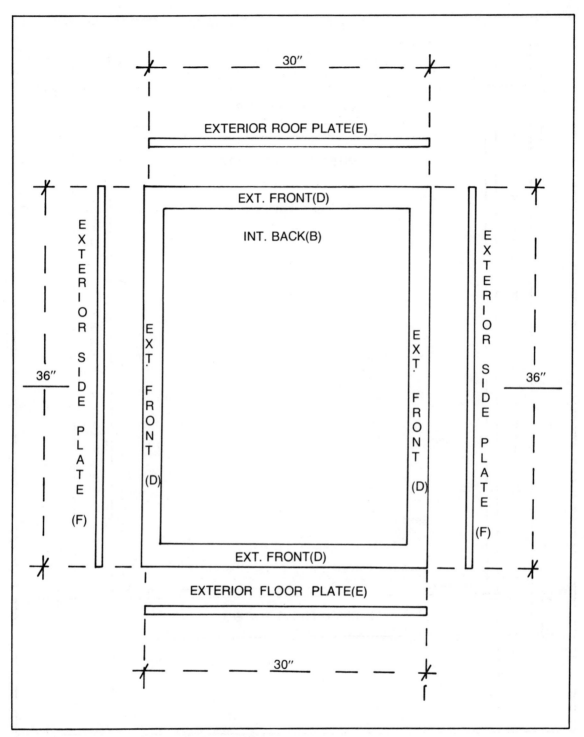

Fig. 17-11. Overhead view of the exterior box assembly.

on plate D. Leave a 2″ lip all around your firebox. Once the firebox is in position, tack weld four sides to plate D. After the tacking is completed, weld solid with Jet rod. See Figs. 17-10 and 17-11.

Referring to Figs. 17-11 through 17-14, attach the exterior plates. Remember that all exterior plates butt to front plate D. They do *not* overlap the side of plate D.

Figure 17-12 shows the exterior side of plate F butting to front plate D (running edge to edge). It also shows exterior roof plate E butting to plate D and plate F.

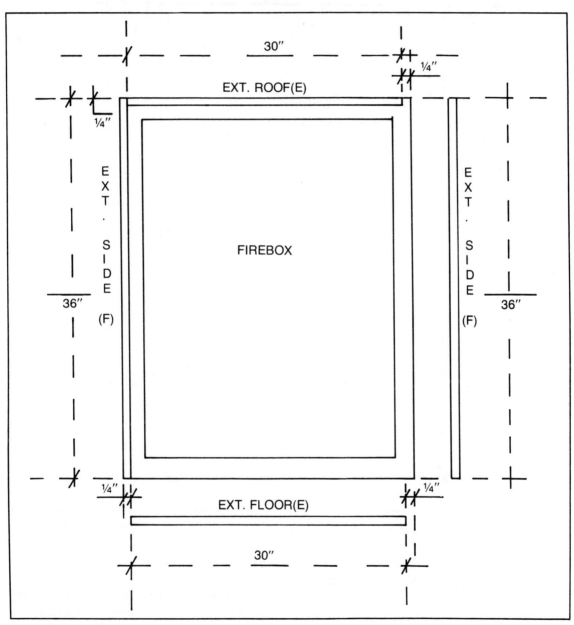

Fig. 17-12. Overhead view of the exterior box assembly.

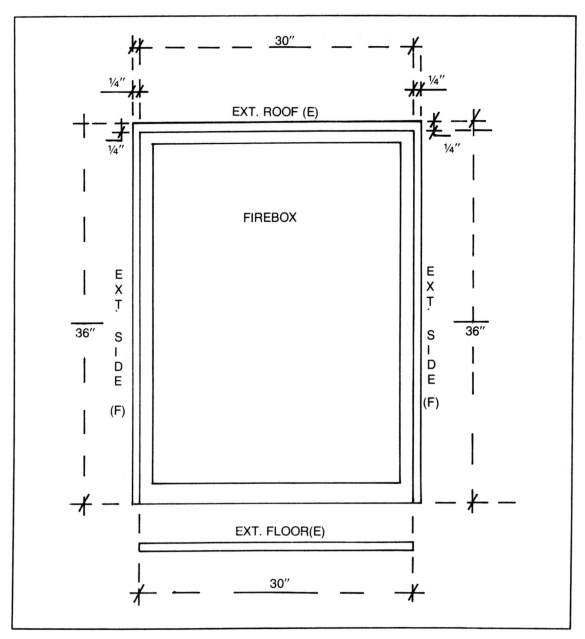

Fig. 17-13. Overhead view of the exterior box assembly.

Figure 17-13 shows the other exterior side plate (F) attached to plate E and plate D overlapping the edge of plate E and butting to plate D.

Figure 17-14 shows the installation of the other plate (E) butting both plates F and D. Once the outer box is tacked together, weld solid all joints.

Laying the stove face down, install the exhaust pipe in accordance with the measurements given in Fig. 17-15. Remember to cut an 8″ diameter hole and mount the exhaust pipe over it. When in place, tack weld the pipe to the interior back plate B. After it is tacked in two or three places, weld it solid with Jet rod.

Once the instructions in the preceding paragraph have been completed, take exterior back plate D, lay out, and then cut, the 8½"-diameter hole that your exhaust pipe will go through. See Fig. 17-16.

Sliding plate D over the exhaust pipe, fit plate D to the back of the furnace. Flush all sides to the furnace. Once in place, tack weld, and then weld solid.

Position and install the hot-air exhaust connection. Using another piece of 8" *inside diameter* pipe, position and install it as shown in Fig. 17-17. Once the hot-air exhaust is tack welded into place, weld it solid, with Jet rod.

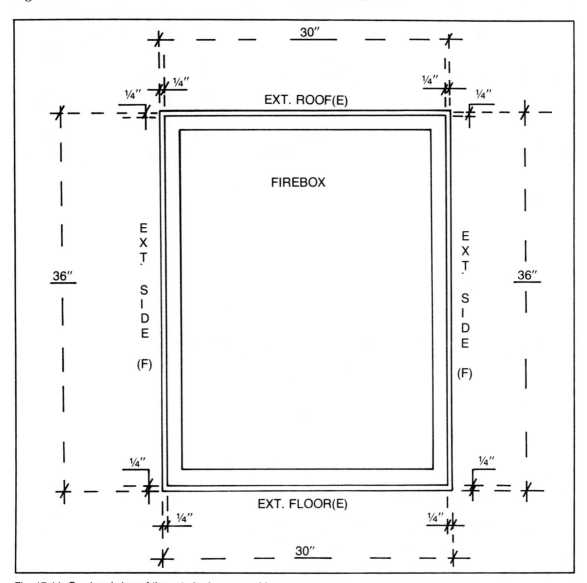

Fig. 17-14. Overhead view of the exterior box assembly.

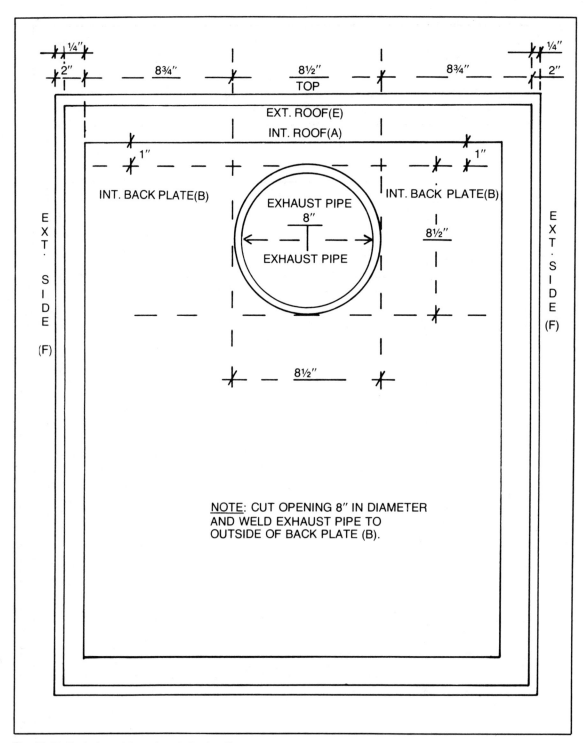

Fig. 17-15. Back view of the exhaust pipe location.

246

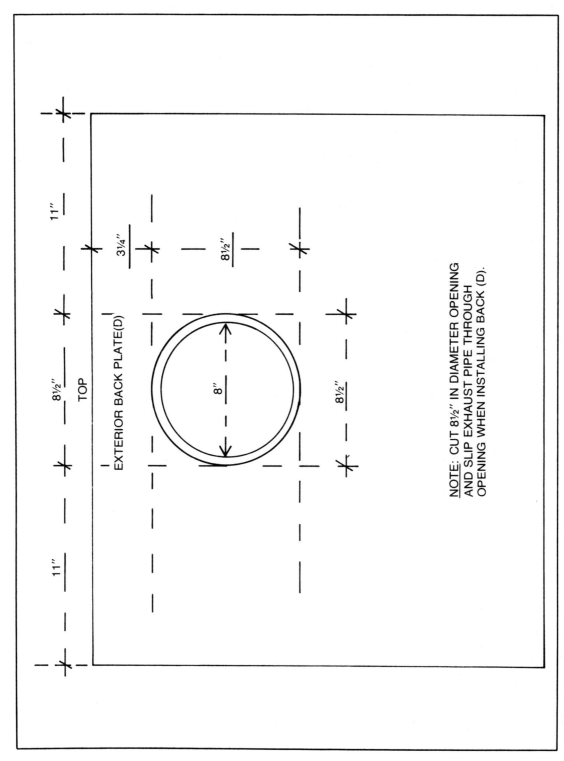

Fig. 17-16. Overhead view of the exterior back plate exhaust pipe opening layout.

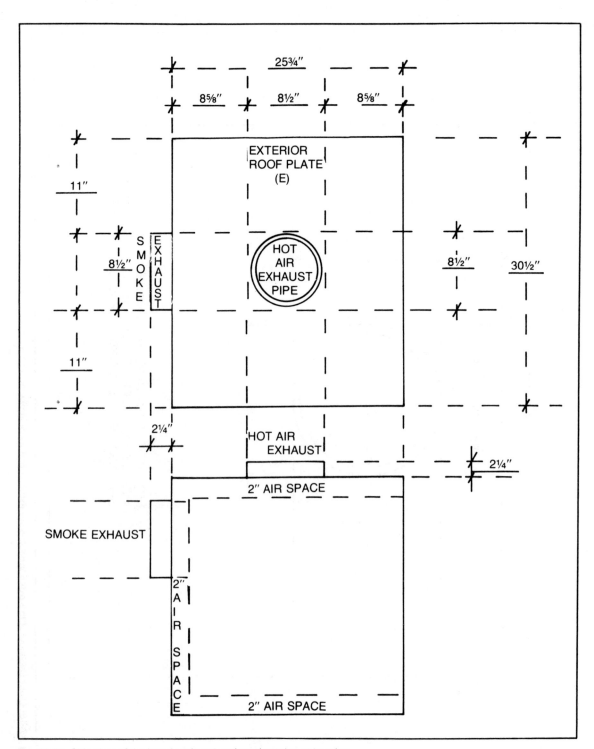

Fig. 17-17. Side view of the hot-air exhaust and smoke exhaust location.

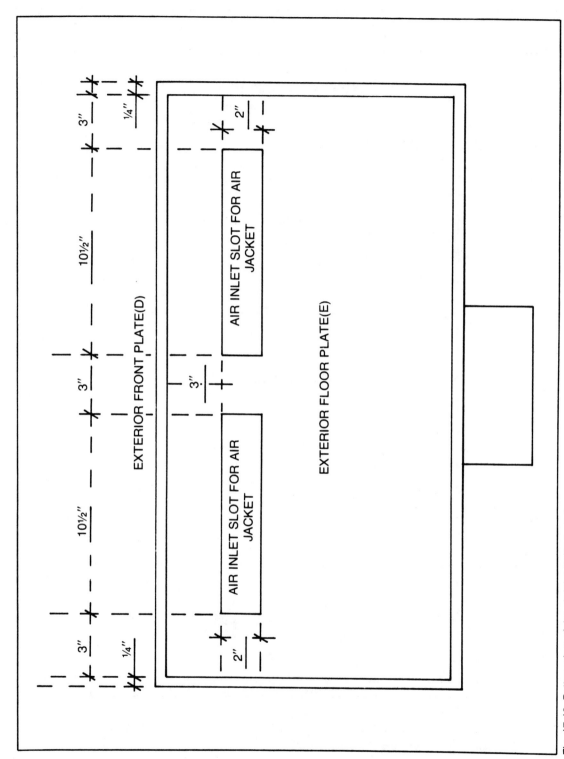

Fig. 17-18. Bottom view of the air inlet slides layout.

249

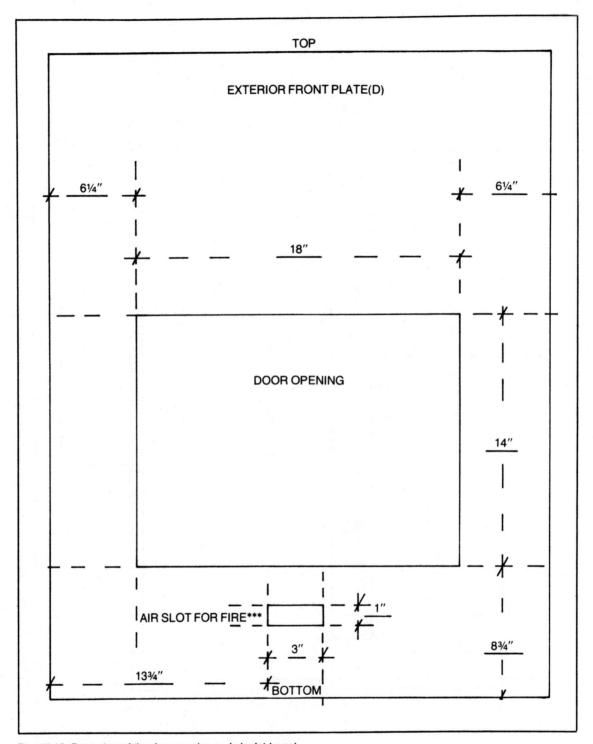

Fig. 17-19. Front view of the door opening and air slot layout.

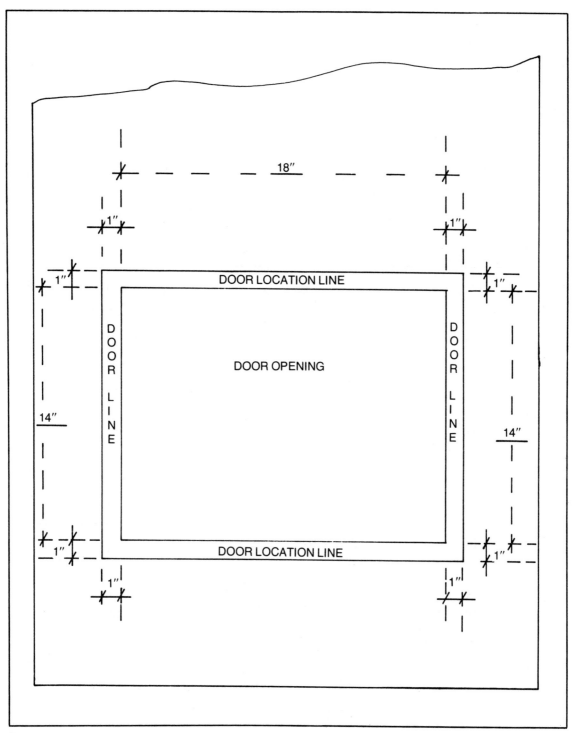

Fig. 17-20. Front view of the door location.

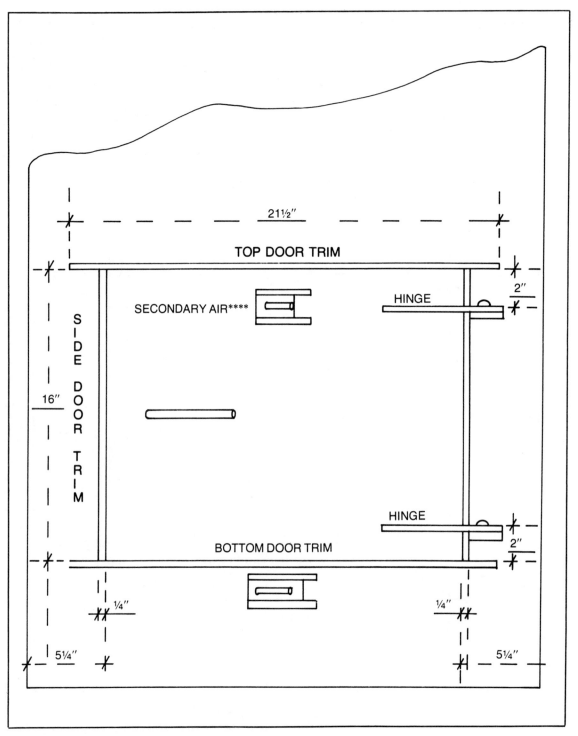

Fig. 17-21. Front view of the door and trim location.

Turn the unit upside down (bottom up), lay out, and cut two air inlets in the air jacket. Refer to Fig. 17-18 to locate these slots. A good idea is to place slides over these air jacket slots. By doing this, you can control the rate of speed the air will travel through the jacket. Just remember to make the slides at least 11″ long. If you decide to do this, make your slides similar to the slides shown in Fig. 10-17.

While the stove is upside down, position and weld legs on the unit. The legs should be similar to those shown in Fig. 14-18 of the Pilgrim stove described in Chapter 14. Referring to Fig. 17-19, position the door opening and firebox air control, and lay out the door location lines as shown in Fig. 17-20. Referring to Fig. 17-21, install the door, hinges, door trim, and air slide. Note: See 12-14 and Chapter 12 instructions for the Example stove. The order of installation is the same.

Install the firebrick. See Fig. 12-15. If you need brick stays, the length can be determined by the interior depth of the firebox and by the length of your back wall. Paint the unit with a high-heat paint.

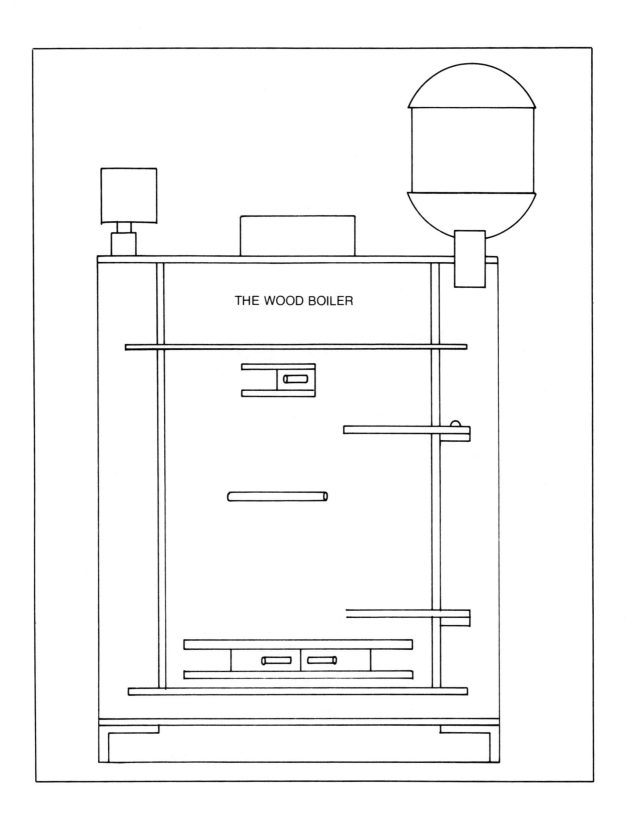

THE WOOD BOILER

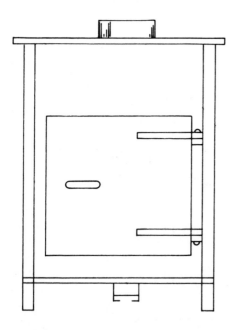

# Chapter 18

# Wood Boiler

THE WOOD BOILER DESCRIBED in this chapter is designed for homes heated with hot water. It is referred to as an *add-on boiler system* because it is added on to an existing heating system by tying it into feed and return line pipes. Installation can consist of hooking into the return line solely, tying into the feed line solely, or tying into both the feed line and the return line (see Chapter 24).

A domestic coil can be installed while you are fabricating your unit. This will preheat the water used by the household for bathing, laundry, etc. The average working pressure would be about 30 pounds. Notice that the size of the water jacket is ½″. The unit is specifically designed to heat the water as it runs through the jacket (½″ is more than sufficient). See Table 18-1.

This unit has been designed to work with the extra safety equipment listed in the material list (see Table 18-2). Even if you have all of these safety devices already on your system, it is essential to install all of this equipment in case your present system fails. You will then have a backup system.

The coil should contain at least 20 feet of tubing (or more). The more tubing you can install the more hot water you'll receive. When installing your coil, the coil must be filled with water to prevent the solder from melting because of the extreme heat caused by welding the coil mount plate into position.

Even though your existing hot water system has all the safety equipment listed in Table 18-2 a backup safety system must be installed for the unit described in this book. The unit described in this book is a solid-fuel burner. It will continually produce hot water whether your house needs it or not, and should have a way of pumping and storing excess hot water.

## FABRICATION PREPARATIONS

Anyone working on this project should have more than just a beginner's knowledge of welding. This cannot be stressed enough. The unit will have to

**Table 18-1. Wood Boiler Data.**

```
Firebox height: 25½"
         Width: 19"
         Depth: 24"
Heating capacity: approximately 3000 square feet
Water capacity: about 12 gallons
  Water temps: 160° to 180° plus
         Fuel: wood; if you want to burn coal, see
               the wood and coal boiler combination (Chapter 19)
    Burn time: on a low burn, 10 to 12 hours
Fabrication time: 16 hours (professionally) 20
               to 30 hours (do-it-yourselfer)
 Plate weight: 529.79 pounds
     Log size: 21"
```

stand up to a pressure test before it is hooked up. Be sure that all safety equipment has been mounted.

To begin, first fabricate all miscellaneous parts. This means that the door, the trim that is to go around the door, the hinges, and the brick stays (if you decide that you are going to brick the unit) will be completed before you begin the actual fabrication of the wood boiler.

The door fabrication should follow the examples shown in Fig. 10-9 and Fig. 18-26. Refer to Fig. 10-20 for the hinges. The door trim is shown in Fig. 18-26. If you need brick stays, the length can be determined by the interior depth of the firebox and by the length of the back wall. When all of the preceding has been completed, you will be able to concentrate on building the boiler. See Fig. 12-15.

All of the following instructions must be adhered to exactly, and in order. In addition, total care be taken in all of the welding involved in the project. After every weld has been run, all of the slag must be chipped and all of the welds must be wire-brushed so that you can visually check the welds for any holes.

The corners of the interior box (inside and out) should be double welded. If the unit leaks under pressure, it will usually leak in the corners. If a leak does appear (during testing), use NO. 6013 welding rod to seal it. If it is worth doing, then it is worth doing right!

## FABRICATION INSTRUCTIONS

Separate the plate into three piles. One pile should contain all of the interior plates (plates A, B, C, and

G. Another pile should contain all of the exterior plate (plates D, E, F, and H. The other pile should contain all of the miscellaneous parts previously fabricated.

Take one of the A plates and lay it on a cleanly swept floor. Take one of the B plates and lay it behind the A plate. Take the other B plate and lay it down on the opposite side of plate A. Take both C plates and lay them down (opposite of each other) on the remaining sides to plate A. You should now have plate A in the middle, plates B in front and back, and plates C on each side.

Take plate B and lay it against the edge of plate A (with the 25½" side vertical). Make sure that the ends of plate A and plate B are flush to each other. See Figs. 18-1 and 18-2. When in position, tack weld plate B to plate A.

Take plate C and lean it against plate B and plate A. Make sure that it's edges are flush with plate A and plate B. Once in position, tack weld plate C to plates A and B. See Figs. 18-3 and 18-4.

Repeat the instructions, given in the preceding paragraph, using the other plate C. See Fig. 18-5.

Install the remaining plate A into the top of the firebox. Flush plate A to the top edges of plate B and plates A. See Figs. 18-6 and 18-7. Once all of the plates have been tack welded into position, weld inside and outside seams with Jet rod.

Referring to Figs. 18-8 and 18-9, position, and install the sliding baffle. Tack weld the track angles (with tacks about 3" long, every 9"). After the baffle has been installed, C-clamp the baffle plate G to the tracks. This keeps the baffle in place when it is necessary to roll the unit around to do the welding.)

Fit the remaining plate (B) to the box—sealing it up. Make sure that all of the sides are flush with each other. Once in position, tack weld, and then weld solid. Be careful to watch for any holes that might be in the weld. You should now have a totally sealed box. See Fig. 18-10.

Referring to Fig. 18-11, lay the boiler on it's back. Note: the back will be the last plate (B) that you have just installed. Position, lay out, and cut (with your cutting torch) the door opening. When laying out and cutting the opening, be as accurate as possible.

**Table 18-2. Wood Boiler Material List.**

| amount | size | | | letter mark | location | weight |
|---|---|---|---|---|---|---|
| 2 | 24″ | × 19″ | × ¼″ | A | (interior) top+bottom | 64.60 lbs. |
| 2 | 25½″ | × 19″ | × ¼″ | B | (interior) front+back | 68.70 lbs. |
| 2 | 25½″ | × 24½″ | × ¼″ | C | (interior) sides | 86.80 lbs. |
| 2 | 26″ | × 21″ | × ¼″ | D | (exterior) top+bottom | 75.60 lbs. |
| 2 | 21″ | × 29″ | × ¼″ | E | (exterior) front−back | 82.20 lbs. |
| 2 | 25½″ | × 29″ | × ¼″ | F | (exterior) sides | 106.90 lbs. |
| 1 | 18″ | × 12″ | × ¼″ | G | baffle plate | 15.32 lbs. |
| 1 | 18″ | × 14″ | × ⅜″ | H | door | 26.79 lbs. |

Total Weight: 529.89 lbs.

**Steel List**

| amount | length | description | | | use |
|---|---|---|---|---|---|
| 1 | 20′ | ½″ | × ¼″ | flat stock | door trim |
| 1 | 5′ | 2″ | × ⅜″ | flat stock | door hinges |
| 1 | 2′ | 2″ | × ¼″ | flat stock | top door trim |
| 1 | 45″ | 1½″ | × 1½″ | angle iron | baffle plate tracks |
| 1 | 15″ | 3″ | × 3″ | angle iron | legs (3″ wide) |
| 1 | 14″ | | ½″ | round stock | door handle |
| 1 | 6″ | | 6″ | inside diameter | exhaust pipe |

**Plumbing Material**

| amount | description | use |
|---|---|---|
| 4 | ½″ pipe couplings (black iron) | expansion tank, aquastate, temp. gauge & drain |
| 2 | ¾″ pipe couplings (black iron) | safety valve and firebox safety |
| 2 | 1″ pipe couplings (black iron) | inlet and outlet connections |
| 3 | ½″ pipe plugs | for pressure test |
| 2 | 1″ pipe plugs | for pressure test |

**Domestic Coil**

| amount | length | description | use |
|---|---|---|---|
| 1 | ¾″ copper coil | copper tubing (bendable) | |
| 2 | ¾″ | couplings (black iron) | for going through side of boiler |
| 2 | ¾″ | thread to sweat adapters | to connect coil to ¾″ couplings |
| 1 | | 30-pound safety valve | blows off excess pressure when too much hot water is produced |
| 1 | | minicirculator pump | transfers extra hot water to existing furnace for storage |
| 1 | | small expansion tank | holds extra water from expansion |
| 1 | | L4006B Aquastate | turns minicircular to on /off by water temperature |
| 1 | | water & temperature gauge | reads water temperature and pressure |

**General Material**

| amount | description | use |
|---|---|---|
| 2 | ⅜″ rivets | hinge pins |
| 2 | 9/16″ flat washers | door handle stays |
| 1 (length 74″) | asbestos or spun-glass belt | door gasket |
| 1 | small can of furnace cement | door gasket glue |
| 20 | split firebrick | for firebox lining |
| 3 | spray cans (or 2 quarts) of high-heat paint | |

Once the preceding has been completed, take a piece of ½″ flat stock, 58″ long, and stand it up on edge. Trim the door opening by tacking it to the front plate. Keep it flush to the edge of the door opening. Remember to heat the flat stock before bending it around corners. After you have trimmed the door opening, cut off the extra piece, at the end, and weld the trim solid to plate B. When you have completed the welding, again check for holes. See Figs. 18-12 through 18-14.

Take the exterior front plate (D) and, using Fig. 18-15 as a visual aid, lay out and then cut out the door opening. Once the door opening has been cut out, clean all of the slag off of the back of the cut. Slag will prevent a snug fit. If you have a disc grinder, grind the back of the cut until it is flush.

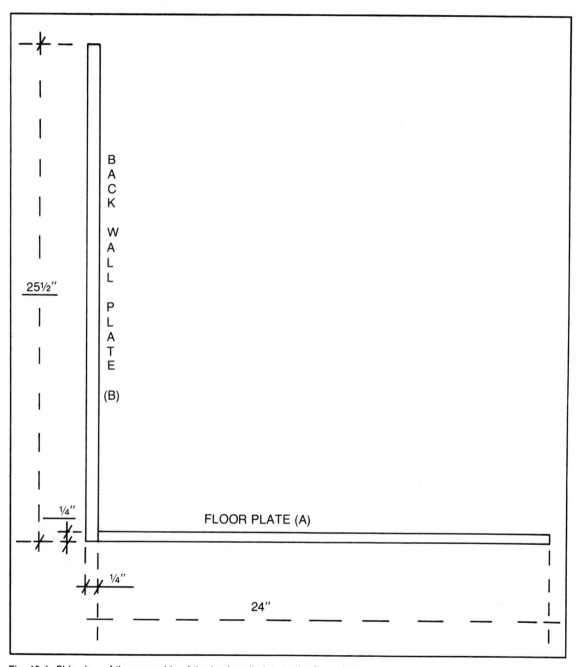

Fig. 18-1. Side view of the assembly of the back wall plate to the floor plate.

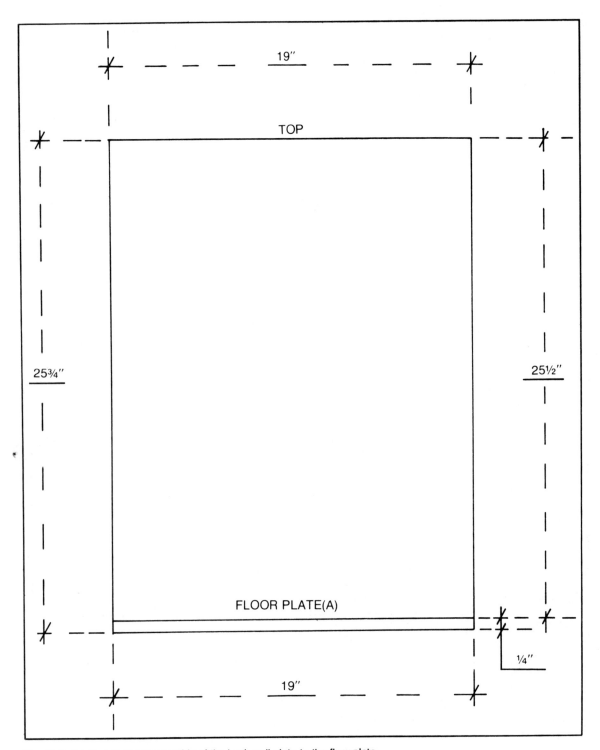

Fig. 18-2. Front view of the assembly of the back wall plate to the floor plate.

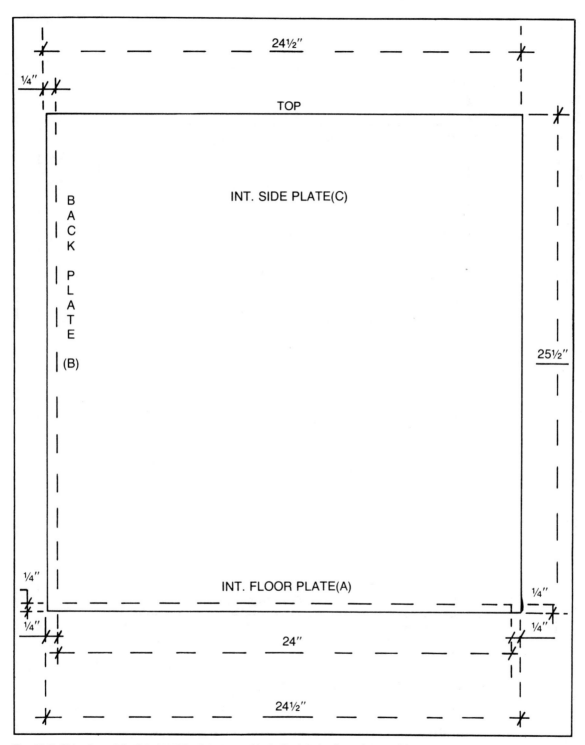

Fig. 18-3. Side view of the interior side plate assembly to the interior floor plate and the interior back plate.

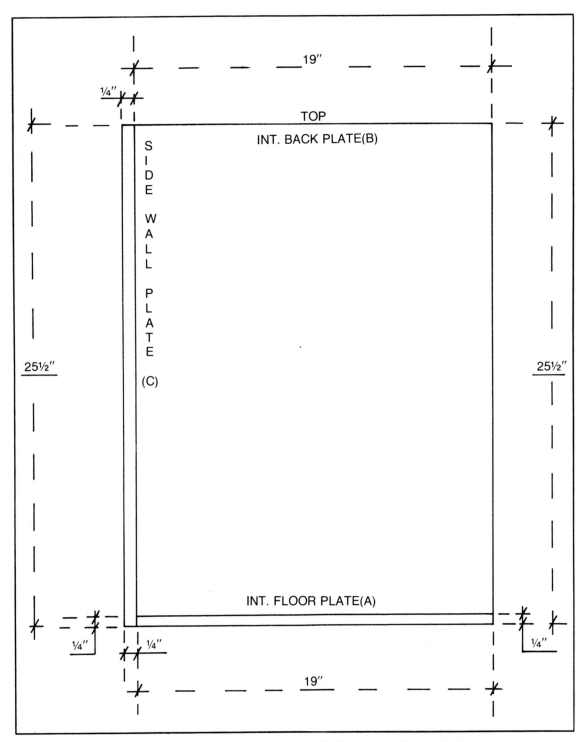

Fig. 18-4. Front view of the interior side plate assembly to the interior floor plate and interior back plate.

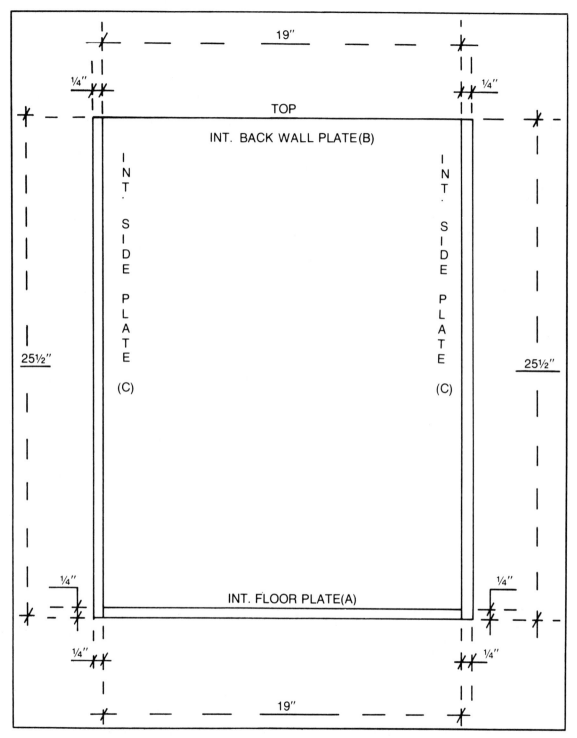

19″

¼″          ¼″

TOP

INT. BACK WALL PLATE(B)

I          I
N          N
T.         T.

S          S
I          I
D          D
E          E

P          P
L          L
A          A
T          T
E          E

25½″       25½″

(C)        (C)

¼″                              ¼″

INT. FLOOR PLATE(A)

¼″                              ¼″

19″

Fig. 18-5. Front view of the assembled interior side plates to the interior back plate and interior floor plate.

263

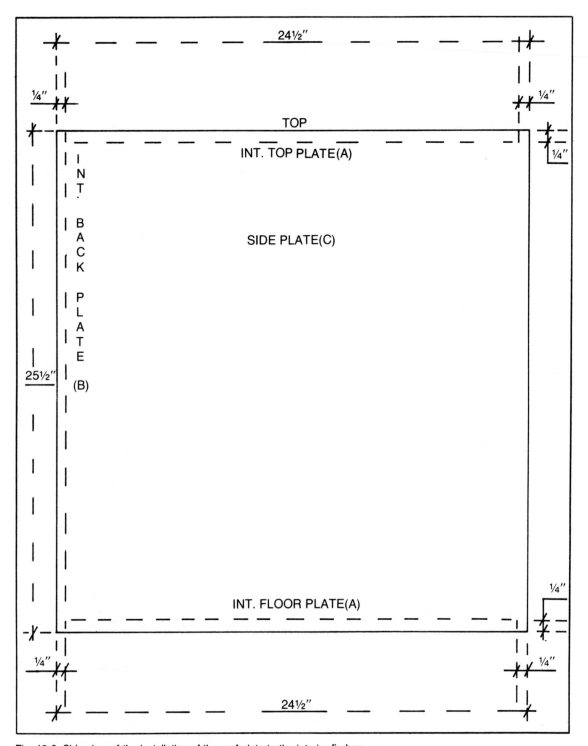

24½"

¼"    TOP    ¼"

INT. TOP PLATE(A)    ¼"

INT. BACK PLATE (B)

SIDE PLATE(C)

25½"

INT. FLOOR PLATE(A)    ¼"

¼"    ¼"

24½"

Fig. 18-6. Side view of the installation of the roof plate to the interior firebox.

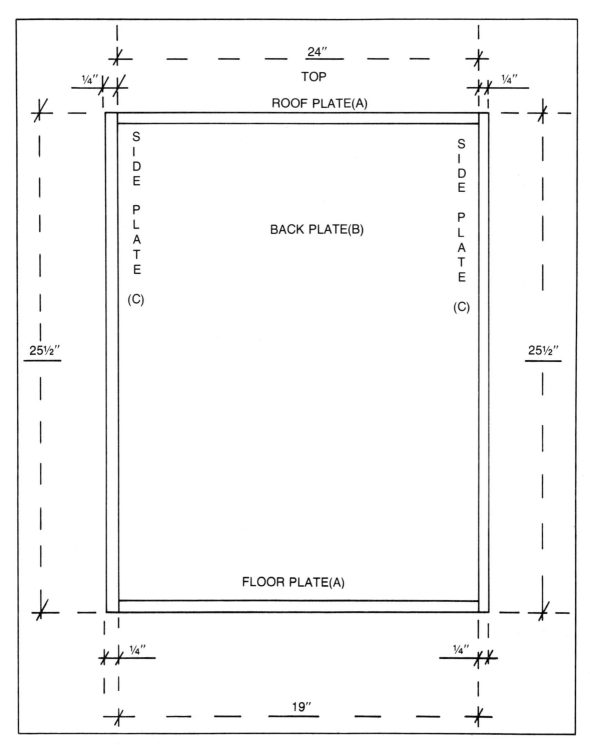

Fig. 18-7. Front view of the installed roof plate.

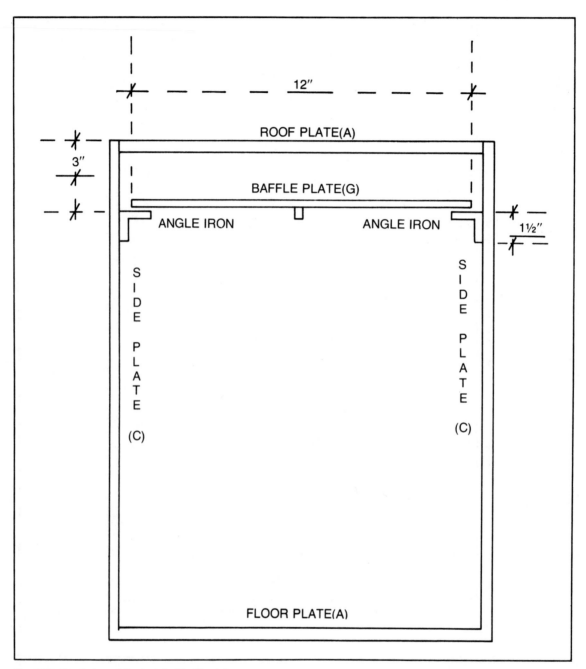

Fig. 18-8. Front view of the installed baffle plate.

Take plate D and lay it on the door opening trim (lining up the two openings). When in place—using at least two C-clamps—clamp plate D to the door opening. Check to make sure that the opening is flush to the ½″ flat stock. Using your tape measure, check to make sure that each end of the bottom is the same measurement from the box. Once the plate is in position, tack weld it in at least four

266

places to the ½″ door trim. Make the tacks about 2″ long. Once plate (D) is firmly tacked to the door opening, remove the C-clamps. While the stove is still in position, reach down and weld the interior joints of the back wall. See Fig. 18-16.

Check your local building codes. You might be required to follow the ASME codes. This code requires that spacers be welded to the interior box, extending through the exterior box, and also, be welded to the exterior walls before being installed

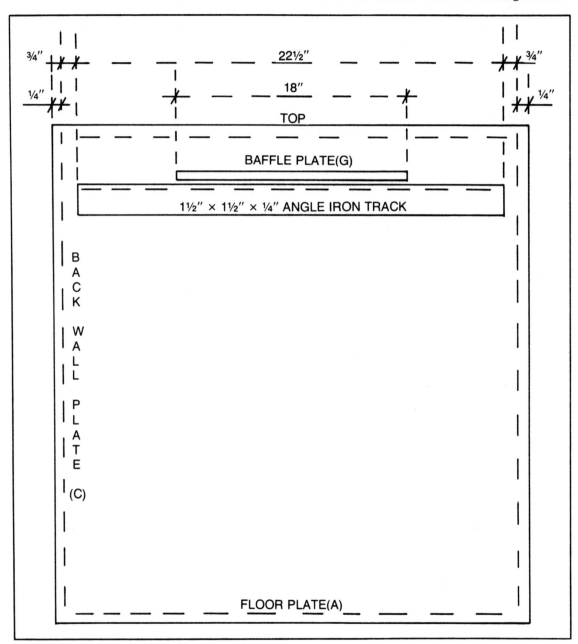

Fig. 18-9. Side view of the installed baffle plate.

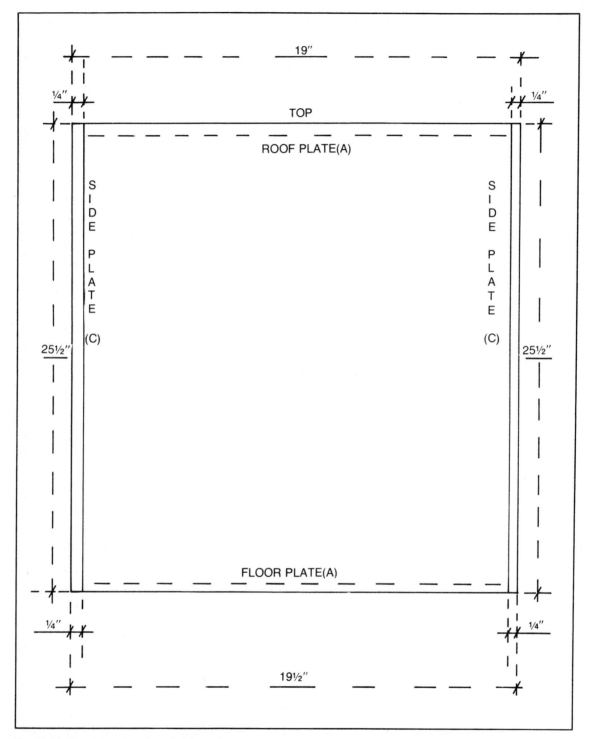

Fig. 18-10. Front view of the installed front plate.

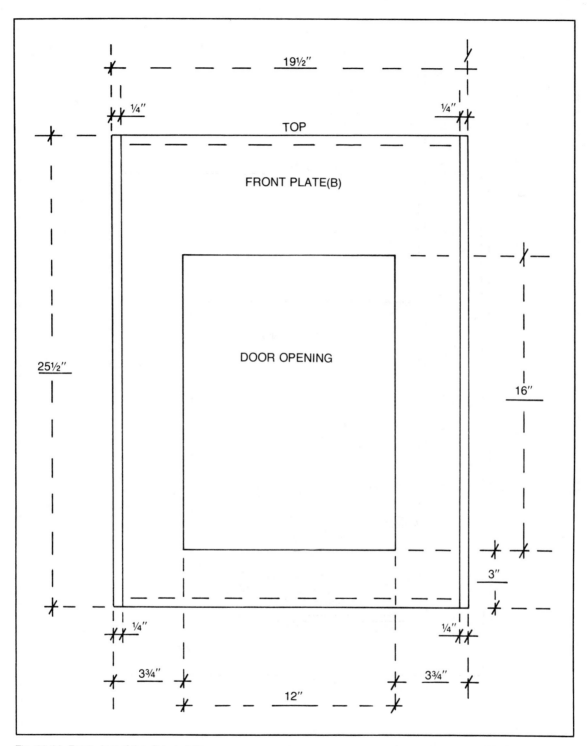

Fig. 18-11. Front view of the door opening.

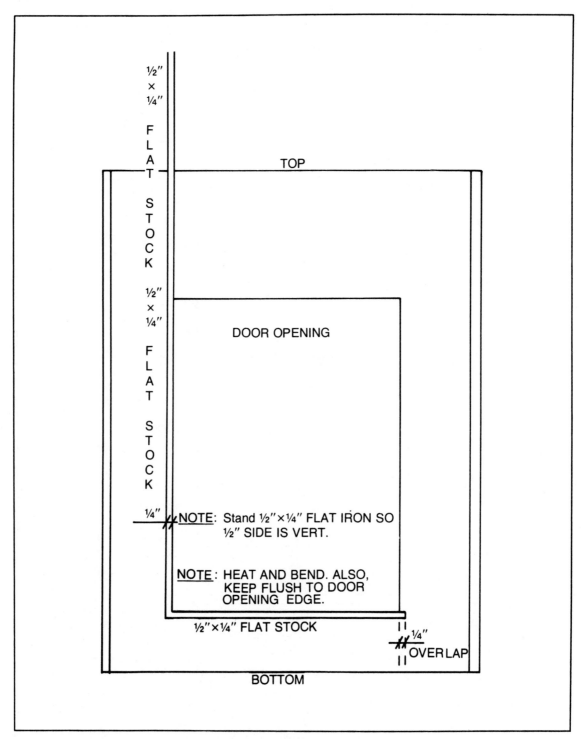

Fig. 18-12. Overhead view of the mounting door water-jacket spacer.

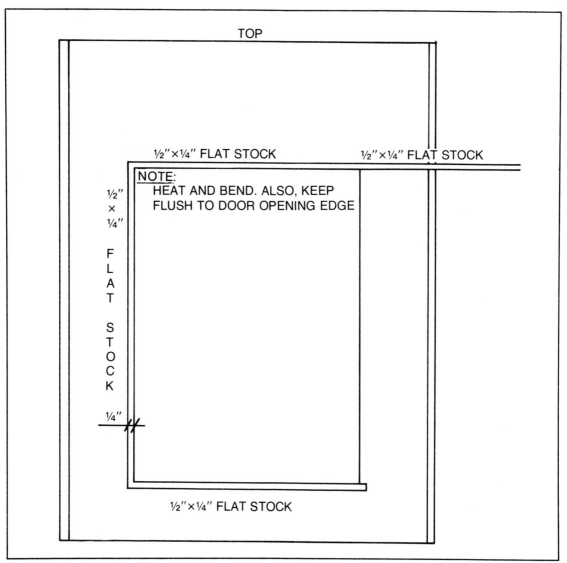

Fig. 18-13. Overhead view of the mounting door water-jacket spacer.

in your home. This is the point in the fabrication procedure to do it. If these spacers are necessary, refer to Fig. 18-27. If it is not required, move on to the next step.

Turn your box over, face down. Taking plate F (with the 25½″ side vertical), set it up on the edge of plate E. Match the ends of plate F to the ends of plate E. When in position, tack weld plate F to plate E. See Figs. 18-17 and 18-18.

Repeat the instructions, given in the preceding paragraph, for the opposite side. Use plate F.

Once this has been done, refer to Fig. 18-19, position and cut a ¾″ hole (as shown in Fig. 18-19. Once the hole has been cut, a ¾″ piece of (black iron) pipe coupling over the hole. When the coupling is in position, weld it solid to plate B. After welding, check for holes. This will be the safety drain tie in the connection.

Take plate D and lay it against the edges of plates F and plate E. Line up all the edges. Once

271

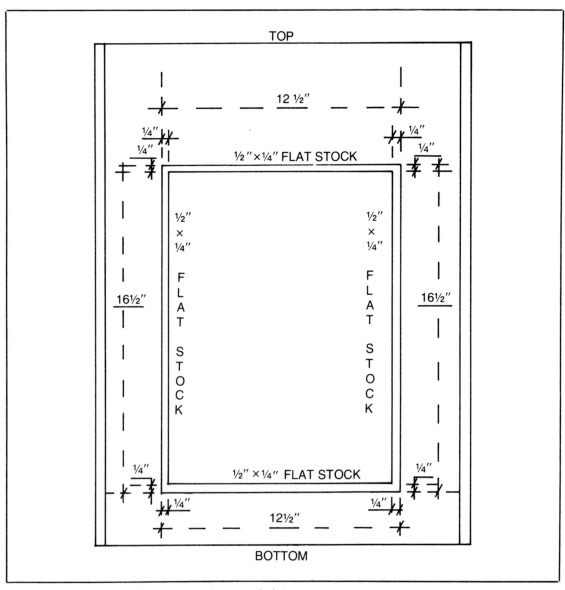

TOP

12 ½"

¼"
¼"

½" × ¼" FLAT STOCK

½"
×
¼"

F
L
A
T

S
T
O
C
K

½"
×
¼"

F
L
A
T

S
T
O
C
K

16½"

16½"

¼"
¼"

½" × ¼" FLAT STOCK

¼"
¼"

¼"
¼"

12½"

BOTTOM

Fig. 18-14. Overhead view of the mounting door water-jacket spacer.

all of the edges are flush, tack weld plate D to plates F and plate E. This is the bottom plate. See Fig. 18-20.

Take the last plate (E), and referring to Fig. 18-21, position and cut a 1⅛" diameter hole. To make an accurate hole to accept your safety drain connection, take another ¾" coupling and trace a circle around it (on the plate). See Fig. 18-21.

Once the preceding instructions have been completed, mount plate E into position. Butt bottom plate D and overlap side plates E. Once in place, tack weld all sides; also tack weld to the coupling.

Once the back plate is on, refer to Fig. 18-22 and position, lay out, and cut the exhaust opening. Position the exhaust pipe and, with soapstone, draw

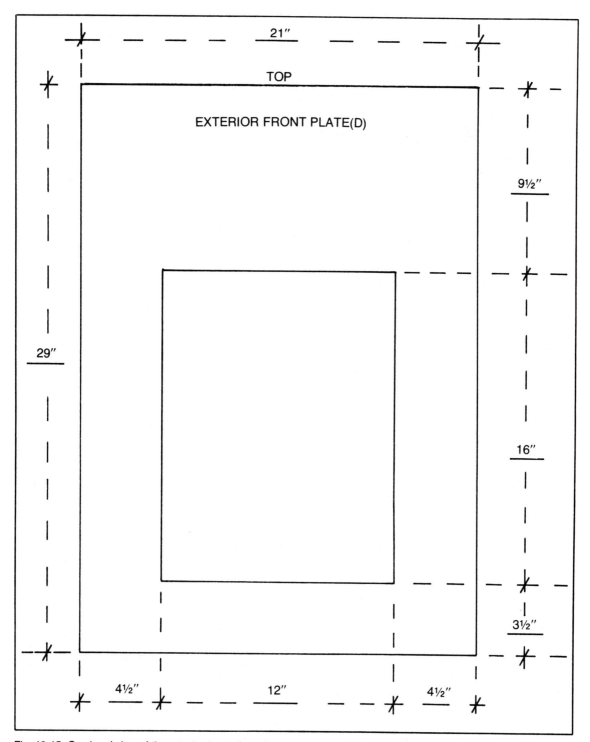

Fig. 18-15. Overhead view of the exterior front plate, door-opening layout.

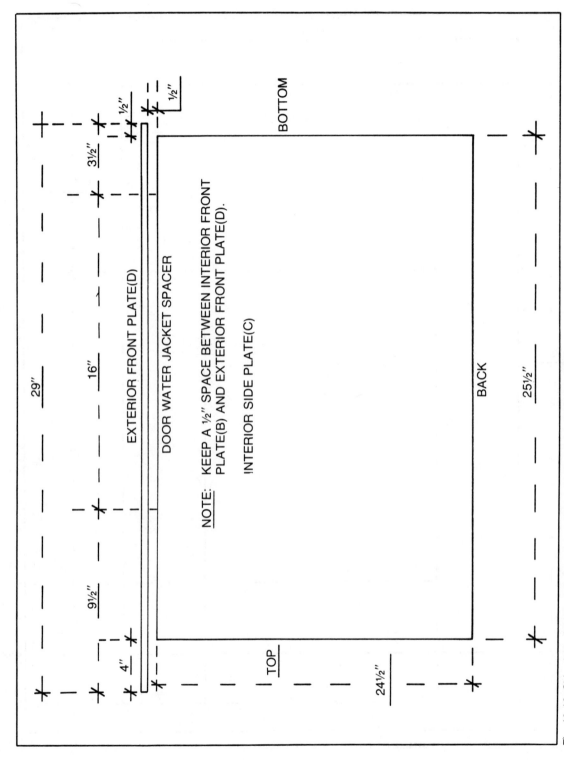

Fig. 18-16. Side view of the installation of the exterior front plate to the interior firebox.

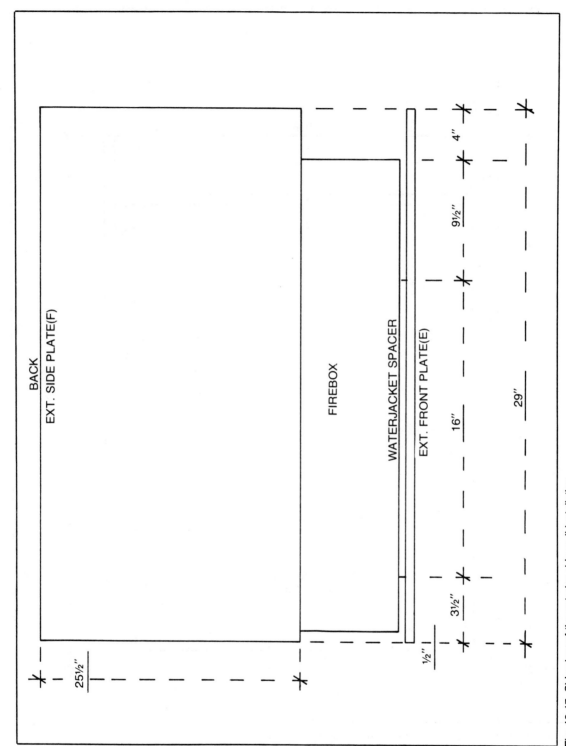

Fig. 18-17. Side view of the exterior side wall installation.

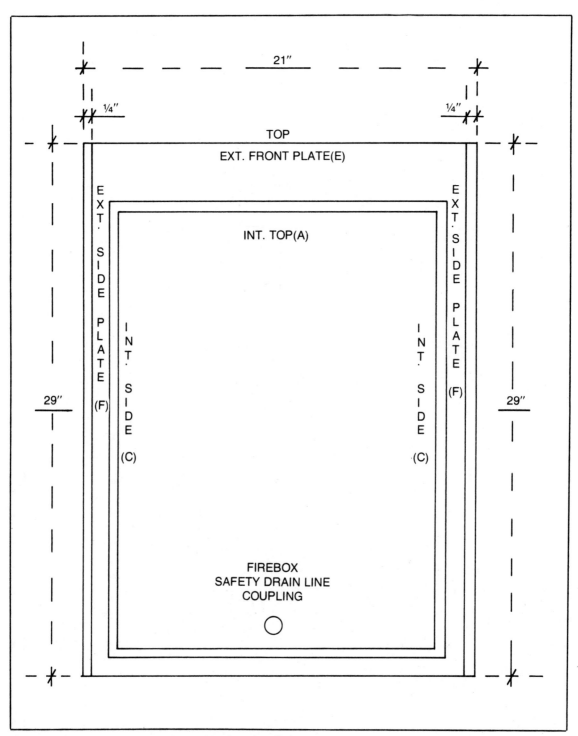

Fig. 18-18. Overhead view of the exterior side plates installed.

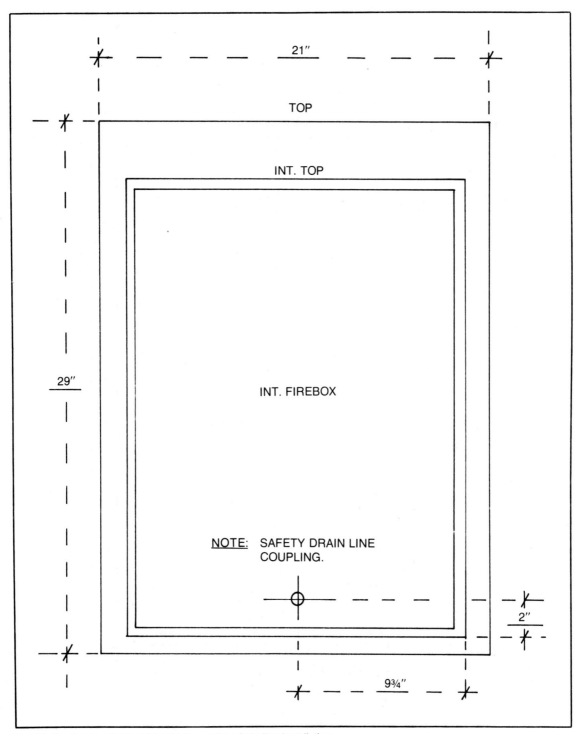

Fig. 18-19. Overhead view of the firebox safety drain line installation.

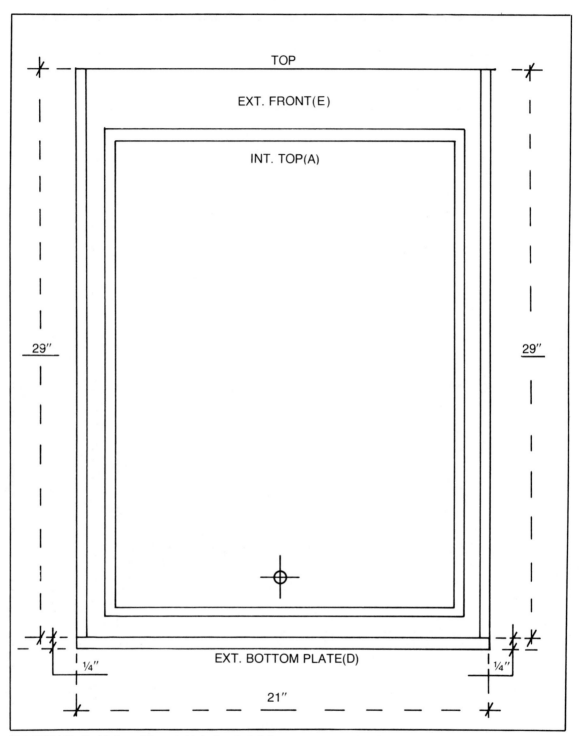

Fig. 18-20. Overhead view of the exterior bottom installation.

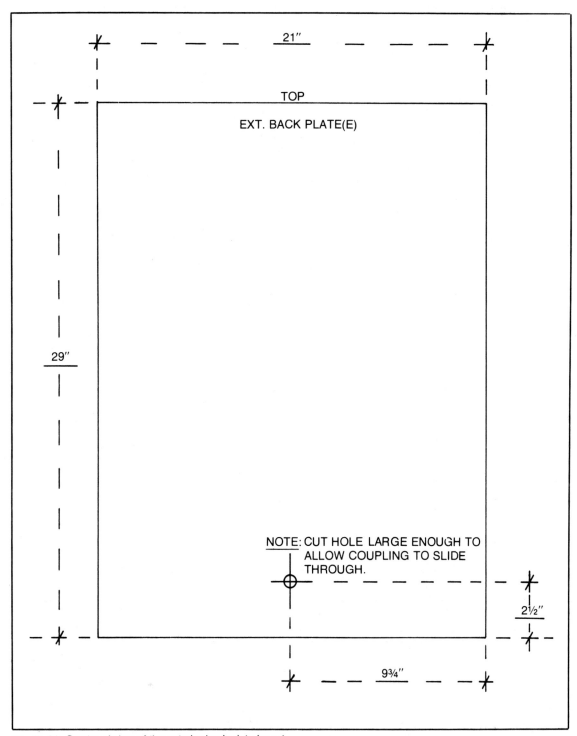

Fig. 18-21. Overhead view of the exterior back plate layout.

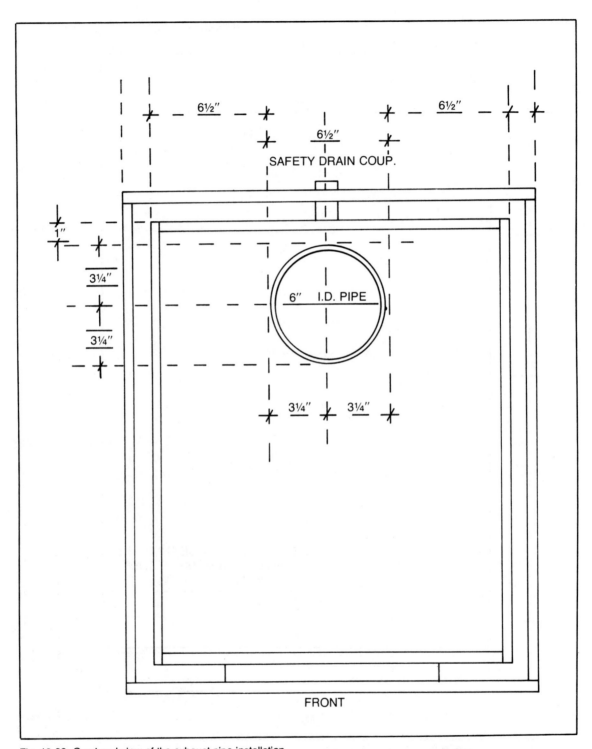

Fig. 18-22. Overhead view of the exhaust pipe installation.

a circle using the *interior* diameter of the pipe as a guide. Once the circle is drawn, cut it out with your torch.

Take the remaining plate (D), and referring to Fig. 18-23, position, lay out, and cut the exhaust pipe hole. Use the exhaust pipe as a guide; but this time trace the circle using the *outside* diameter.

Once the preceding has been completed, mount the exhaust pipe over the hole, on your boiler, and weld it solid to plate A.

Take plate D (with the hole in it) and mount it on the stove, slipping it over the exhaust pipe. Once it is in position, tack weld it.

When the exterior is totally together, begin welding all the exterior seams. In addition, check for any holes in the welds.

Once all of the seams have been welded and checked, refer to Fig. 18-25, position, lay out, and cut the coupling holes. Remember to keep the holes a little smaller than the coupling you will place over it. After all of the holes have been cut, mount the couplings and weld into place.

Referring to Fig. 18-24, lay the unit over (face down) and locate, lay out, and cut the inlet coupling hole. Be sure to make the hole a little smaller than the coupling. Once the hole is cut in plate E, mount and weld in the inlet coupling. Once the coupling has been welded, screw a nipple or a plug into the inlet connection. This will prevent damaging the connection when the unit has to be rolled over.

Using Fig. 18-26 as a visual aid, mount the door (making sure your gasket is on). Set the door; let it overlap the opening 1″ on all sides. When the door is in place, mount the door trim. Leave a ¼″ gap between the trim and the door (on the side where the handle is).

Once the trim is in place, mount the hinges as shown in Fig. 18-26.

If you prefer, brick the floor and brick the sides. If you want to attach legs, angle iron can be welded under the boiler (as in the Pilgrim model). Once all of the welding and bricking has been completed, paint the unit using a paint that will stand up to a high heat. See Fig. 18-28.

Pressure test the boiler before you hook it up.

## PRESSURE TESTING A BOILER UNIT

Once a (wood or wood and coal) boiler has been constructed, it is necessary to test the unit for leaks. Do this test before you hook it into your heating system. In the event you come across a leak, it can easily be repaired while your unit is still in the fabrication area (where your welding machine is). It will only take a matter of minutes to repair.

You can run the test on your unit very easily by using a garden hose connection valve. Because the garden hose valve obtains its water from your domestic water system it should be pressurized with 30 pounds pressure. This makes it perfect for testing.

You will need the following plumbing supplies to test your boiler; two ½″ threaded pipe plugs, two 1″ threaded pipe plugs, one ½″ threaded garden hose valve, one double-female hose adapter, and the garden hose. A double-female hose adapter is a short piece of garden hose, about an inch or two long, that has the type of end that can screw into your hose valve at each end. You will also need a 30-pound safety valve.

Once you have gathered all of the equipment, you can begin as follows:

☐ Connect the 30-pound safety valve to the ¾″ coupling on the boiler unit. Using the plugs and garden hose valve, seal the boiler unit for testing.

☐ Connect the garden hose to the garden-hose valve on the boiler using the garden hose and the double-female adapter. Make sure that the garden hose valve is closed.

☐ Turn on the garden hose valve in your home.

☐ Slowly open the garden hose connection at the boiler while manually lifting the safety valve. This bleeds the air out of your water jacket which, in turn, allows the water into the jacket. Keep the safety valve manually open until water comes out. When this does happen, release the safety valve. The safety valve might leak some, but that's what it is designed to do. Don't worry.

☐ Now that the boiler is full, leave the garden hose valve on. This will maintain the 30-pound pressure. Visually check the interior for leaks. If

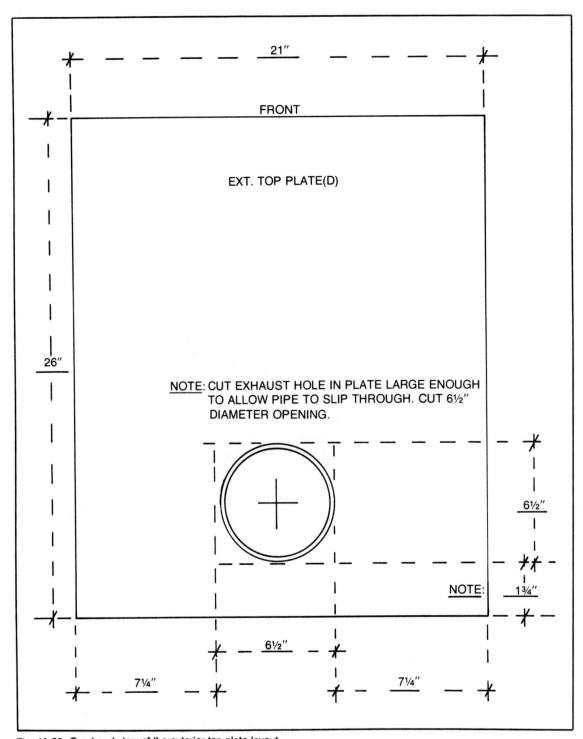

Fig. 18-23. Overhead view of the exterior top plate layout.

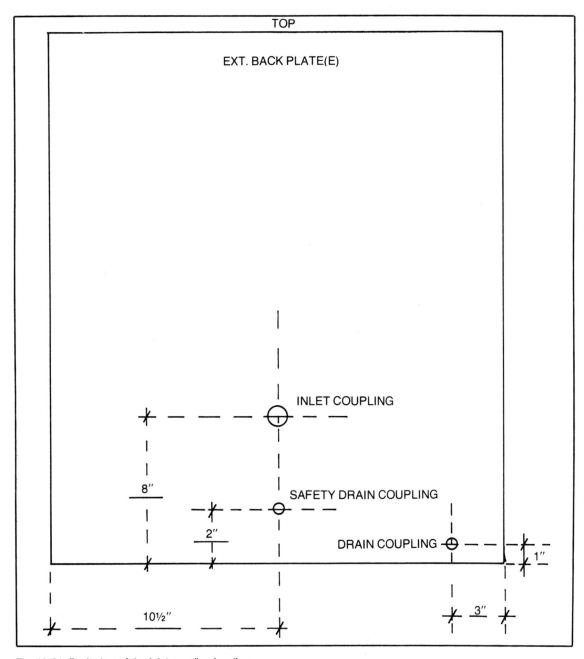

Fig. 18-24. Back view of the inlet coupling location.

you find one, circle the leak with soapstone. After you have finished checking the inside for leaks, check the exterior for leaks in the same manner. Circle any leaks you find with soapstone.

☐ To complete the test, close the garden hose valve on the boiler and in the house.

☐ Disconnect the garden hose at the house hose valve. Release the built-up pressure in the

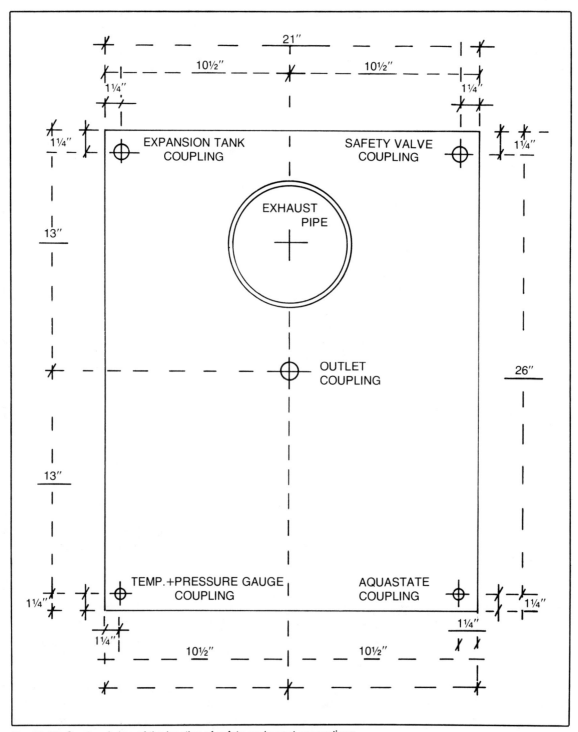

Fig. 18-25. Overhead view of the location of safety equipment connections.

284

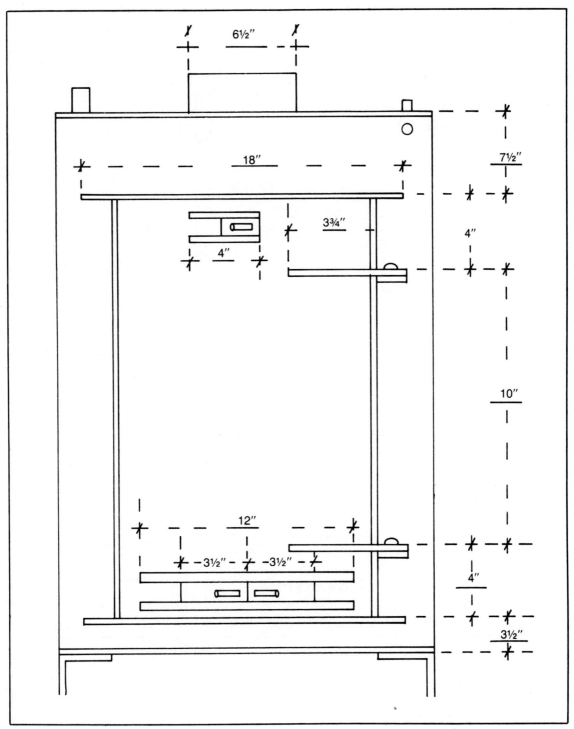

Fig. 18-26. Front view of the door installation.

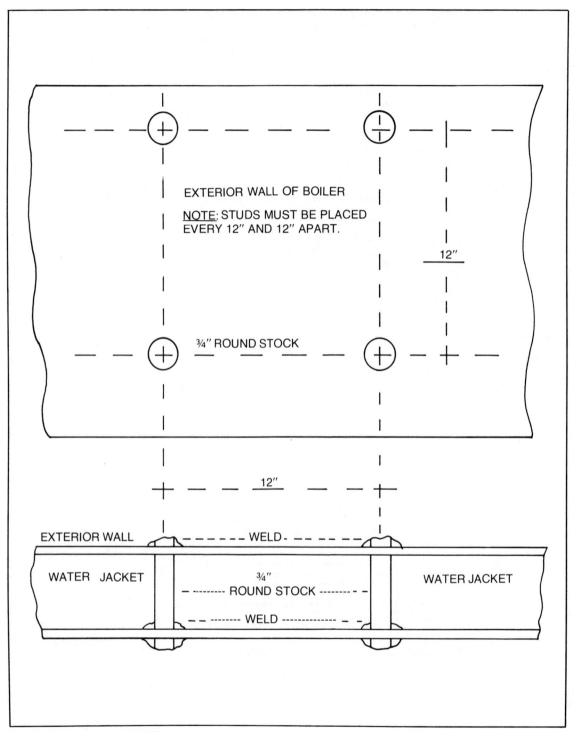

EXTERIOR WALL OF BOILER

NOTE: STUDS MUST BE PLACED
EVERY 12″ AND 12″ APART.

12″

¾″ ROUND STOCK

12″

EXTERIOR WALL ——— WELD

WATER JACKET
¾″
——— ROUND STOCK ———
——— WELD ———
WATER JACKET

Fig. 18-27. An example of ASME spacers.

Fig. 18-28. A completed wood boiler.

boiler by slowly opening the garden hose valve on your boiler unit. When all of the pressure has been drained, remove the plugs.

If you do come across a leak, repair it and test your unit again. Bear in mind that you cannot repair a leak while there is water leaking out of it. If you find a leak in the upper part of your boiler unit, you have to drain the water down, below the leak, and weld it closed. This will be the supreme test of how carefully the boiler has been welded.

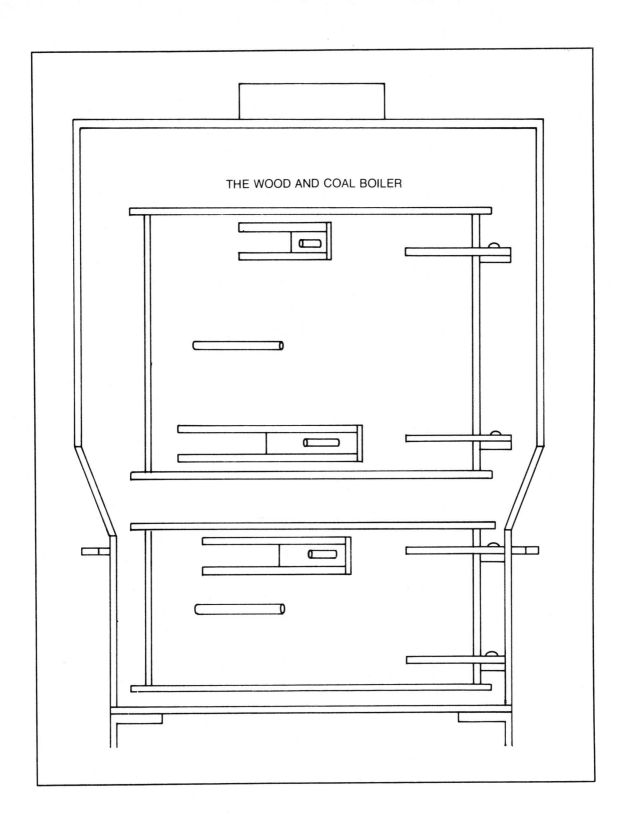

THE WOOD AND COAL BOILER

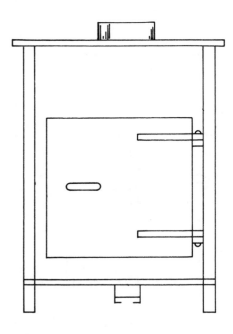

# Chapter 19

# Wood and Coal Boiler

THIS UNIT WAS ORIGINALLY designed for commercial use in restaurants, factories, and other large buildings. It is ideal for use in hard-to-heat, poorly insulated homes. This is because of the ample size of the firebox and the capacity of water that it holds (28 gallons). See Table 19-1.

If the unit will be placed in a cold cellar, insulate the unit with fireproof insulation. You can hook this unit into your inlet and outlet heating pipes as described in Chapter 24.

This is another unit that is referred to as an add-on boiler system (as is the wood boiler). It is added on to your existing system by tying it into the feed and return line pipes (See Chapter 24). You will have to make a decision whether to hook up your unit to the return line solely, tying into your feed line solely, or tying into both the feed line and the return line.

A domestic coil can be installed while you are fabricating your unit. This will preheat the water that is used by the household for bathing, laundry, etc. The average working pressure would be about 30 pounds.

Remember that this unit has been specifically designed to burn wood and coal. It requires special instructions due to the additional air slides and the sliding baffle. It will burn either wood or coal efficiently.

To burn wood, close the secondary air slide located at the top of the firebox door. Also close the two slides located on each side of the boiler and the upper slide on your ash door. Place firebrick on the grate. This keeps the smaller pieces of unburned wood from falling through.

Slide the baffle plate over the exhaust-pipe opening. This will make smoke turbulent and help burn off the gases in the smoke. Once the fire has been started, close the firebox door and control the firebox air using only the bottom slide in the firebox door.

To burn coal, slide the baffle plate out of the way of the exhaust. Take the brick off the grate if you previously have been burning wood. Close the air slide on the bottom of the firebox door. Once you close this slide, open the slides on top of the firebox door (the secondary air slide). Also, open the two

**Table 19-1. Wood and Coal Boiler Data.**

| | |
|---|---|
| Height: | 37″ |
| Width: | 26″ |
| Depth: | 31″ |
| Heating capacity: | approximately 3000 square feet commercially or 5000 square feet residentially |
| Water capacity: | about 28 gallons |
| Water temps: | 160° to 180° |
| Fuel: | wood: firebrick on grate and sliding baffle over your exhaust pipe opening. Coal: firebrick removed from grate and sliding baffle out of the way of the exhaust. |
| Burn time: | residentially (on a low burn) 12 to 14 hours with wood and (on a low burn) 10 to 12 hours with coal. |
| Fabrication time: | 24 hours (professionally) 30 to 40 hours (do-it-yourselfer) |
| Plate weight: | 628.87 pounds |
| Log size: | 24″ |

slides (one on each side) located on the sides of the boiler. Now open the air slide on the ash door. All of these slides (other than the secondary air slide) will supply your coal with combustion air. If you find that you are burning more on one side of grate, adjust the slides accordingly. Once your coal fire is burning well, the secondary air slide can be closed. You do not need to open it again, until you refuel. Keep in mind, the following when you are burning coal:

☐ Read Chapter 4 on how to heat with coal.

☐ The efficiency in burning coal is greatly affected by the grade and classification of the coal that you burn.

☐ Once you add coal to your fire, keep the doors closed. Every time you open the door you affect the draw of air to your coal fire.

Before you begin to burn any solid fuel, it is important that you realize that this unit has been set up to work with the extra safety equipment listed in Table 19-9. This is true even if all of these devices are on your existing system. It is essential to install all of this equipment in the case that your present system fails. You will then be assured of a total backup system.

Provide your steel supplier with a copy of the extra cut sheet for interior back wall plate E. See Fig. 19-A.

## FABRICATION PREPARATIONS

Anyone working on this project should have more

than just a beginner's knowledge of welding. This cannot be stressed enough. The unit will have to stand up to a pressure test before it is hooked up. Be sure that all safety equipment has been mounted.

To begin, first fabricate all miscellaneous parts. This means that the door, the trim that is to go around the door, and the hinges will be completed before you begin the actual fabrication of the wood and coal boiler.

The door fabrication should follow the examples shown in Figs. 10-10 through 10-18. Refer to Fig. 10-20 for the hinges. The door trim is shown in Fig. 19-26. When all of the preceding has been completed, you will be able to concentrate on building the boiler.

All of the following instructions must be adhered to exactly and in order. In addition, total care be taken in all of the welding involved in the project. After every weld has been run, all of the slag must be chipped and all of the welds must be wire-brushed so that you can visually check the welds for any holes.

The corners of the interior box (inside and out) should be double welded. If the unit leaks under pressure, it will usually leak in the corners. If a leak does appear (during testing), use No. 6013 welding rod to seal it. If it is worth doing, then it is worth doing right!

## FABRICATION INSTRUCTIONS

Separate the plate into two piles. One pile should contain plates A through E. The other pile should contain plates F through M.

Begin by taking plate A and laying it on your work bench. Using soapstone and a combination square—starting at the 26″ end—draw a line up 1¾″ in, from each end; make the line 13½″ long. Measure up 9¼″ and draw a line across the plate. From this line, measure up another 4¼″, and mark this measurement at the edge of each side of plate A. Using a ruler, draw a line from the 4¼″ mark to the 9¼″ mark. Do this on both sides. Use Fig. 19-1 as a visual aid to do the preceding layout. Using your cutting torch, cut off the two pieces you have just laid out. See Fig. 19-1. Repeat instructions,

## Table 19-2. Wood and Coal Boiler Material List.

| amount | size | | | letter mark | location | weight |
|---|---|---|---|---|---|---|
| 2 | 37″ | × 26″ | × ¼″ | A | front & back | 136.41 lbs. |
| 1 | 24″ | × 30″ | × ¼″ | B | (interior) roof | 51.05 lbs. |
| 2 | 14″ | × 30″ | × ¼″ | C | (interior) sides | 59.55 lbs. |
| 2 | 30″ | × 6½″ | × ¼″ | D | (interior) sides | 27.65 lbs. |
| 1 | 20¼″ | × 23½″ | × ¼″ | E | (interior) back wall | 34.46 lbs. |
| 2 | 30½″ | × 23¼″ | × ¼″ | F | (exterior) sides | 98.09 lbs. |
| 2 | 30½″ | × 4⅝″ | × ¼″ | G | (exterior) sides | 20.04 lbs. |
| 1 | 30½″ | × 26″ | × ¼″ | H | (exterior) top | 55.30 lbs. |
| 1 | 18″ | × 8½″ | × ⅜″ | I | (ash door) | 16.27 lbs. |
| 1 | 18″ | × 14″ | × ⅜″ | J | (main door) | 26.79 lbs. |
| 2 | 30½″ | × 9¼″ | × ¼″ | K | (exterior) sides ash box | 39.02 lbs. |
| 1 | 30½″ | × 22½″ | × ¼″ | L | (exterior) floor ash box | 48.66 lbs. |
| 1 | 22″ | × 10″ | × ¼″ | M | baffle | 15.60 lbs. |
| | | | | | Total Weight: | 628.87 lbs. |

### Steel List

| amount | length | description | use |
|---|---|---|---|
| 1 | 20′ | ½″ × ¼″ flat stock | door trim |
| 1 | 10′ | 2″ × ¼″ flat stock | top door trim |
| 1 | 10′ | 2″ × ⅜″ flat stock | hinges |
| 1 | 10′ | 1″ × ¼″ flat stock | water jacket spacer |
| 1 | 52″ | 2″ × 2″ × ¼″ angle iron | baffle plate tracks |
| 1 | 60″ | 3″ × 3″ × ¼″ angle iron | legs |
| 1 | 28″ | ½″ round stock | door handles |

NOTE: See Chapter 10 for the miscellaneous steel parts you will need to fabricate air slides.

| amount | description | use |
|---|---|---|
| 4 | ½″ pipe couplings (black iron) | expansion tank, aquastate, temp. gauge & drain |
| 2 | ¾″ pipe couplings (black iron) | safety valve and firebox safety |
| 2 | 1″ pipe couplings (black iron) | inlet and outlet connections |
| 3 | ½″ pipe plugs | for pressure test |
| 2 | 1″ pipe plugs | for pressure test |

### Domestic Coil

| amount | length | description | use |
|---|---|---|---|
| 1 | ¾″ copper coil | copper tubing (bendable) | |
| 2 | ¾″ | couplings (black iron) | for going through side of boiler |
| 2 | ¾″ | thread to sweat adapters | to connect coil to ¾″ couplings |
| 1 | | 30-pound safety valve | blows off excess pressure when too much hot water is produced |
| 1 | | minicirculator pump | transfers extra hot water to existing furnace for storage |
| 1 | | small expansion tank | holds extra water from expansion |
| 1 | | L4006B Aquastate | turns minicirculator on/off by water temperature |
| 1 | | water & temperature gauge | reads water temperature and pressure |

### General Material

| amount | length | description | use |
|---|---|---|---|
| 1 | 12″ | 8-inch inside diameter pipe | exhaust pipe |
| 20 | | split firebrick | firebox lining |
| 1 | 8′ | asbestos or spun-glass gasket | door gasket |
| 1 | | small can of furnace cement | door gasket glue |
| 4 | | 9/16″ flat washers | door handle stays |
| 4 | | ⅜″ rivets | hinge pins |
| 4 | | spray cans (or 2 quarts) of high-heat paint | |

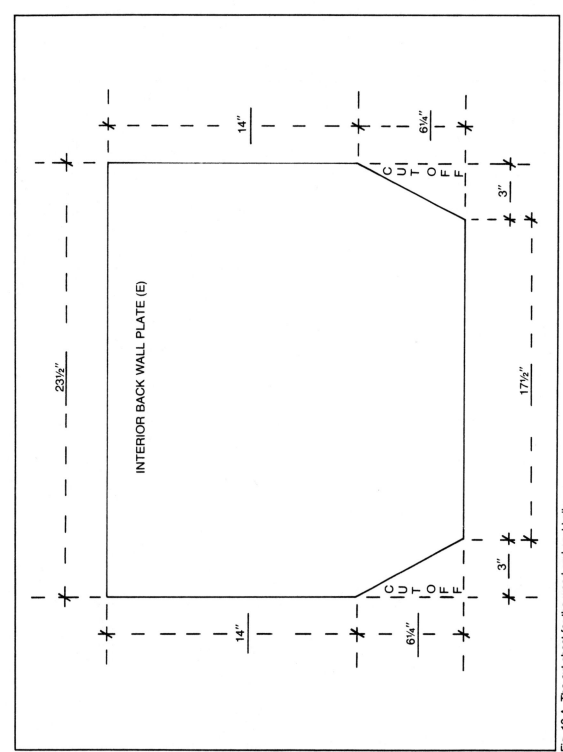

Fig. 19-A. The cut sheet for the wood and coal boiler.

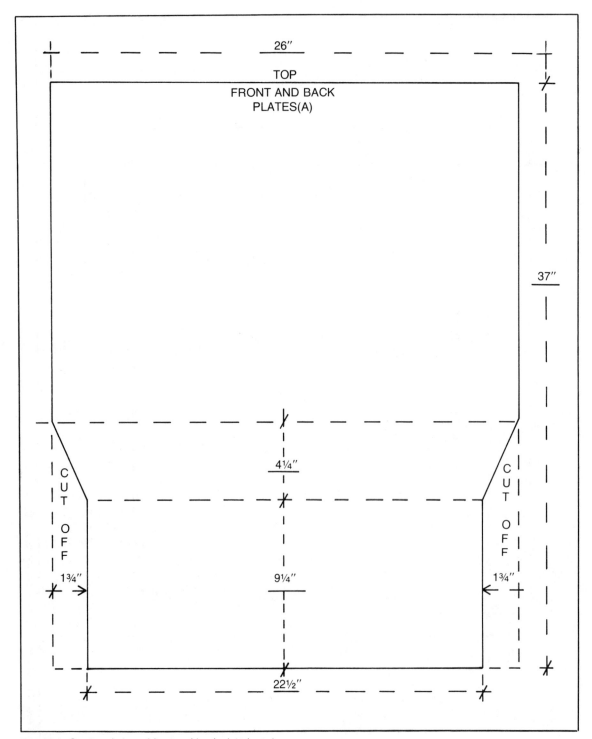

Fig. 19-1. Overhead view of front and back plate layout.

given in the preceding paragraph, using the other plate (A).

Once both plates A have been cut, lay out the location lines for plates B, C, and D. First, come down (from the top of the plate) 7 inches and draw a line across the plate. This is the location of plate B. Draw a line down each side of plate A 1 inch in from each side, making the line 14″ long, starting the line from your 7″ mark. This is the location line for plates C. Go down to the 9¼″ line and, from the cut edge, measure in 1 inch and mark. Do this on both sides. Using a ruler, draw a line connecting the end of the 14″ line to the 1″ mark on your 9¼″ line. (This will give you a 6″2″ line.) Do this on both sides. This is the location of plate D. Use Fig. 19-2 as a visual aid.

Repeat the instructions, given in the preceding paragraph, for the other plate (A).

Once all the location lines are drawn, take one of the plates A and put it aside. (It won't be needed for awhile.) Using the other plate A, take plate B (the 30″ side is vertical) and place it on the inside of the 7″ line. Keeping plate B at a 90° angle to plate A. Once in position, tack weld it to plate A. See Fig. 19-3.

Take plate C (the 30″ side is vertical), and place it on the inside of your 14″ line; butt the edge to plate B. Keeping plate C at a 90° angle to plate A, and while flushing plate C, to the edge of plate B, tack weld plate C to plates A and B. See Fig. 19-4.

Repeat the instructions, given in the preceding paragraph, for the opposite side of the plate A, using your other plate (C).

Take plate D (the 30″ side is vertical) and place it on the inside of the 6½″ line, butting the edge to plate C. Keeping plate D at a 90° angle to plate A, once plate D is in position, tack weld it to plates A and C. See Fig. 19-5.

Repeat the instructions given in the preceding paragraph, for the opposite side of plate A, using the other plate (D). Take a piece of 1″ flat stock (17½″ long) and, with the 1″ side vertical, place it between the plates D, tacking it to plate A and plates D. This will become the bottom of your back wall water jacket. Take another piece of 1″ flat stock (10″ long) and place it near the center top of the interior box.

Tack weld it to plate A. This will be used as a spacer to help keep the interior plate 1″ away from the exterior plate (creating your back water jacket.) See Figs. 19-6 and 19-7.

Using Jet rod, weld solid plates B, C, and D to plate A. As you are doing this welding, weld solid the piece of 1″ flat stock to plate A. Remember to clean and then check your welds for holes.

When you have completed the welding, take plate E and slip it down between plates B, C, and D, and rest it on your 1″ flat stock. Some trimming might be needed on plate E to adjust it into position. Once in position, tack weld it to plates B, C, and D. Once tacked, weld it solid to plates B, C, and D. Also, weld solid to 1″ flat stock. You have now, installed the back wall water jacket. See Fig. 19-8.

Take two pieces of 1″ flat stock (30″ long) and stand them on end. Attaching them to the sides of plate (D), tack welding them to plates D and plate A. See Fig. 19-9.

Once the 1″ flat stock is tacked, use Jet rod to weld the exterior sides of plates B, C, and D to plate A. Remember to clean and then check the welds for holes.

Once the welding is completed, take the other plate A and lay it on top of plates B, C, and D. Line plate A up according to the location lines you have drawn earlier. Remember that both plates A must be aligned with each other. Take your time with this step. If mounting this plate is not done properly, it will cause many problems later in the fabrication. See Figs. 19-10 and 19-11. Once plate A is in position, tack weld plate A to plates B, C, and D.

Using your cutting torch, cut slots through plates B, C, and D; keep the slots between plates A and E. These slots will allow the water to flow from the back jacket to the side jackets. Remember, do not cut slots in the 1″ flat stock. See Fig. 19-12.

Turn the unit over so that the last plate (A), you have just installed, is laying flat on your bench or floor. When in position, use Jet rod to weld solid plate A to plates B, C, and D. Remember to check for holes.

Now is the time to mark the front and back. The plate (A) that you have just welded is the front of the boiler. The other plate A (with the water

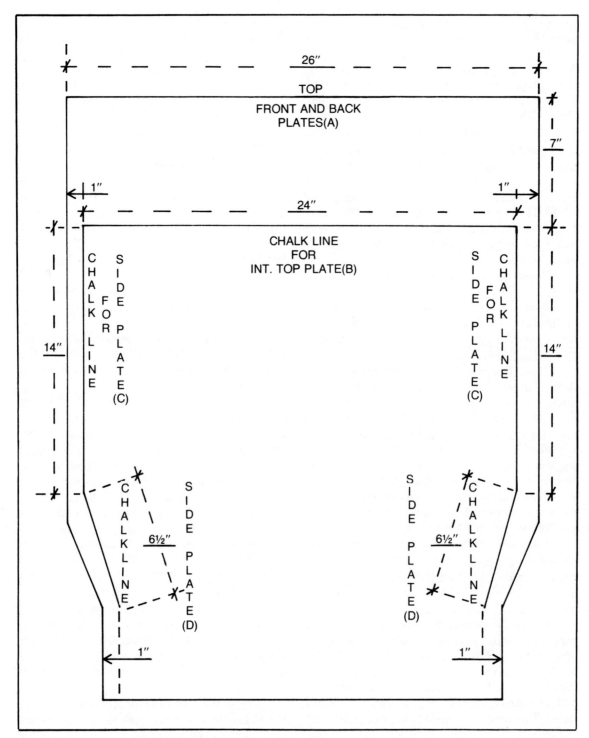

Fig. 19-2. Overhead view of interior plate location.

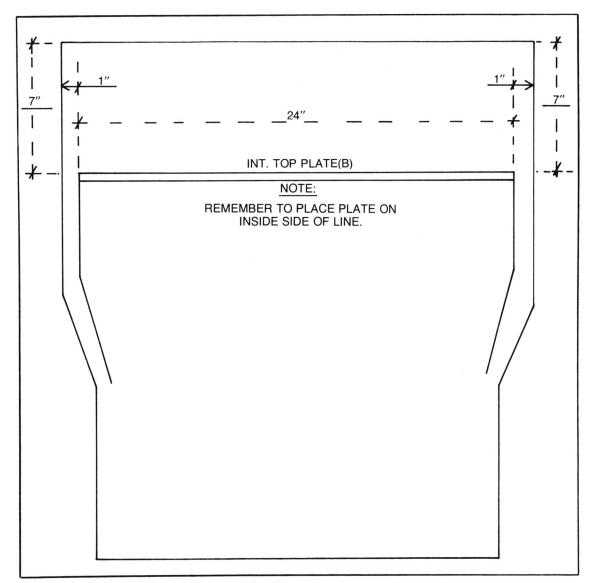

Fig. 19-3. Overhead view of interior top plate location.

jacket) is the back of your boiler. Mark these plates now. If you don't, when all of the plates are in position, you might lose track of which is the back and which is the front.

Check your local building codes. You might be required to follow the ASME codes. This code requires that spacers be welded to the interior box, extending through the exterior box, and also, be welded to the exterior walls before being installed in your home. This is the point in the fabrication procedure to do it. If these spacers are necessary, refer to Fig. 18-27. If it is not required, move on to the next step.

Take plate F and lay it against the side of the two plates A (with the 30½″ side vertical). Flush the top to plate A and align the edge to the ends of plates A. When in position, tack weld it to plates A. See Fig. 19-13.

297

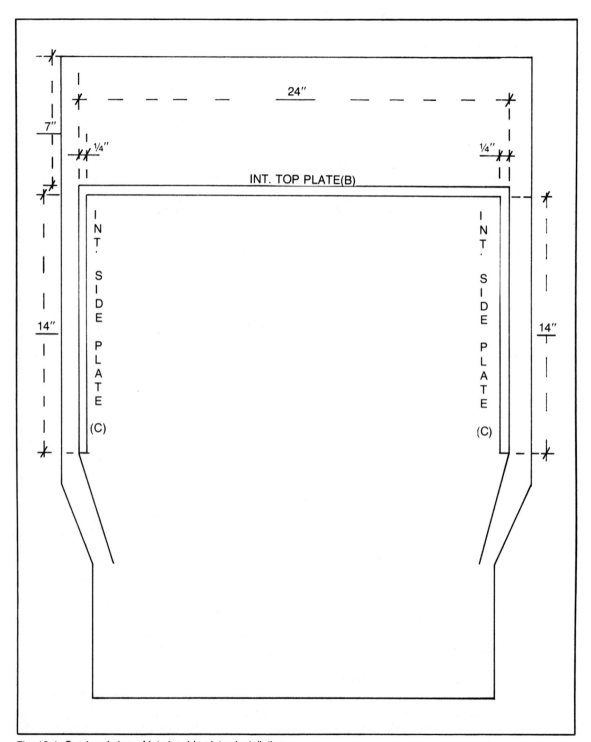

Fig. 19-4. Overhead view of interior side plates installation.

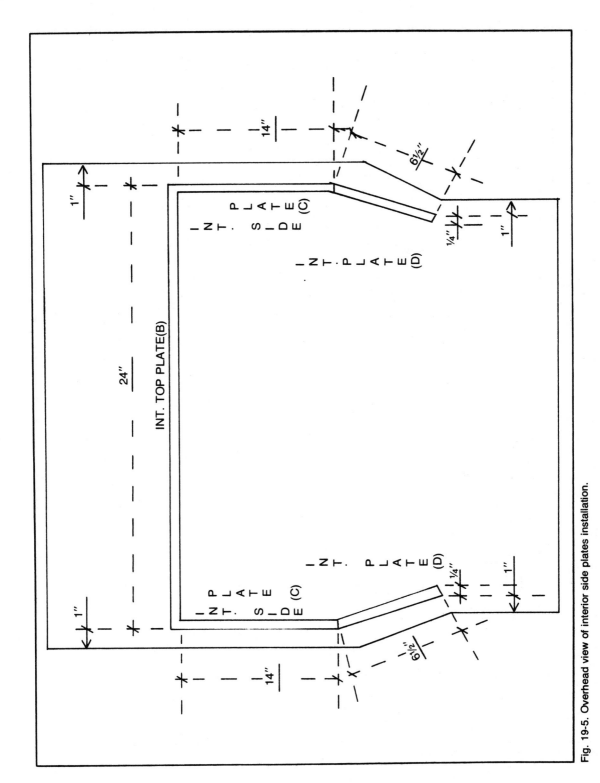

Fig. 19-5. Overhead view of interior side plates installation.

299

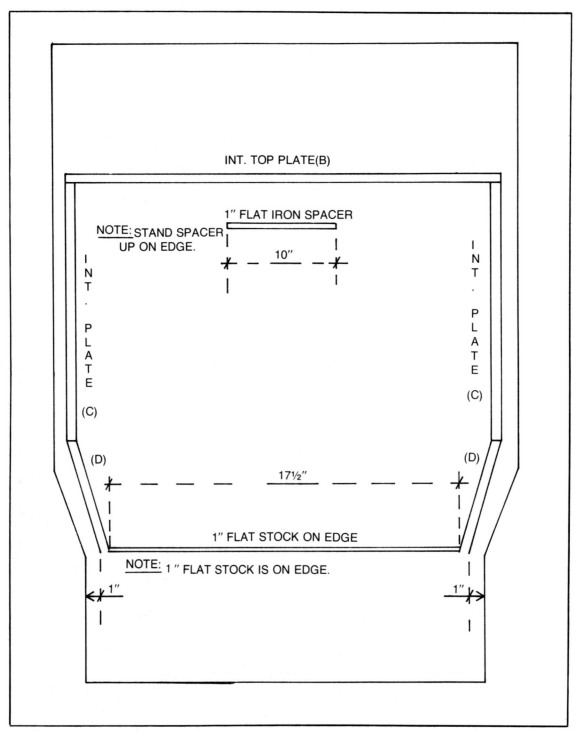

Fig. 19-6. Overhead view of spacer installation.

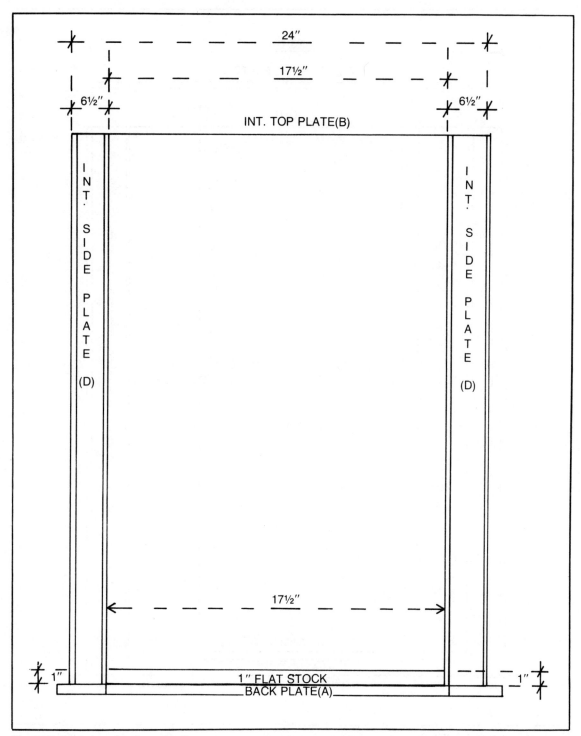

Fig. 19-7. Front view of bottom of boiler.

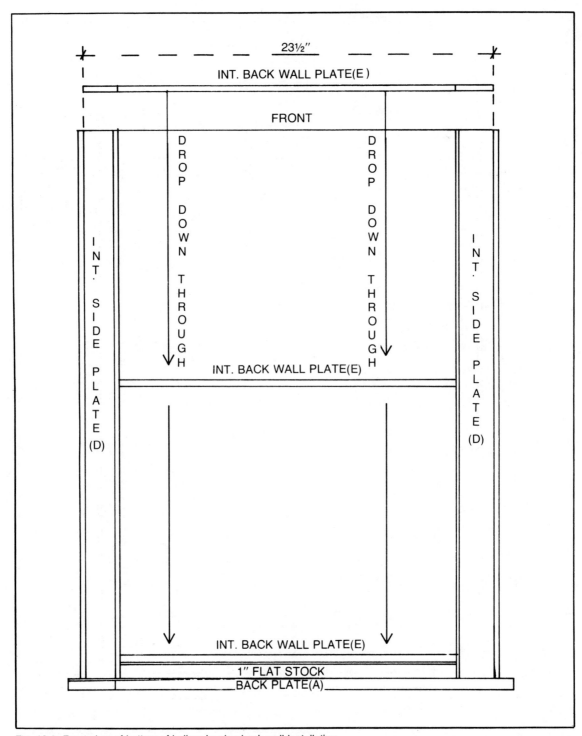

Fig. 19-8. Front view of bottom of boiler showing back wall installation.

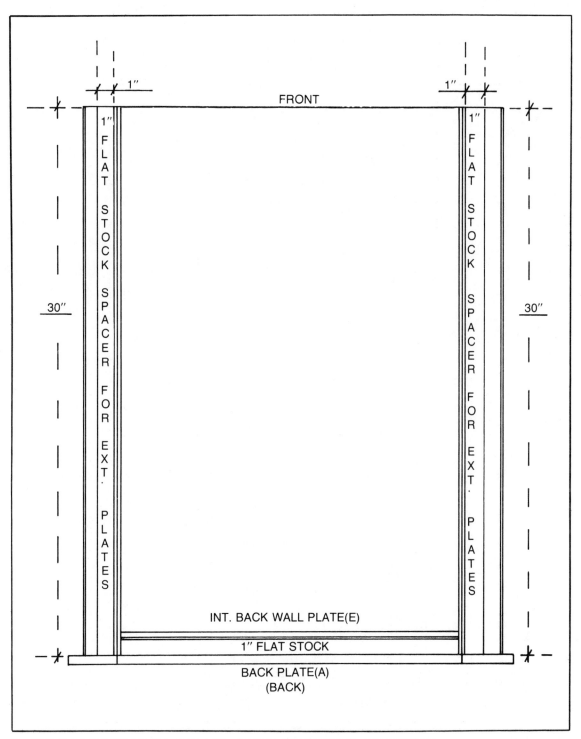

Fig. 19-9. Front view of the bottom of the boiler showing space location for side wall plates.

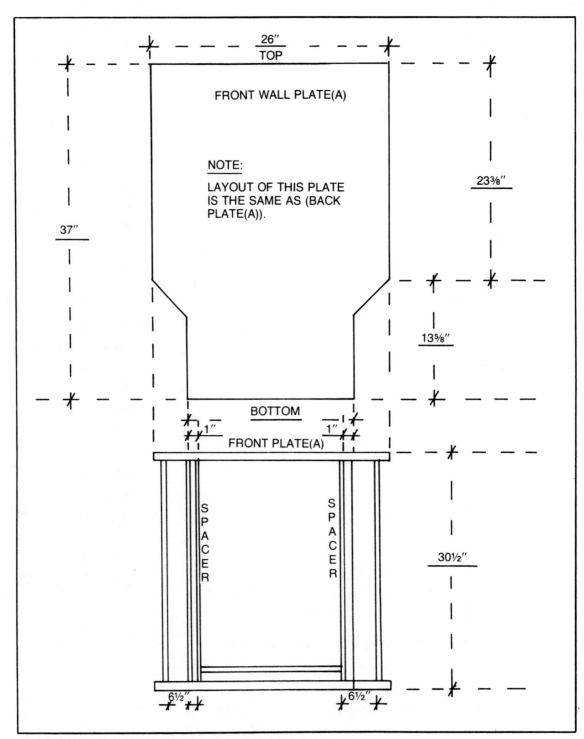

Fig. 19-10. Overhead view and front view of the front plate installation.

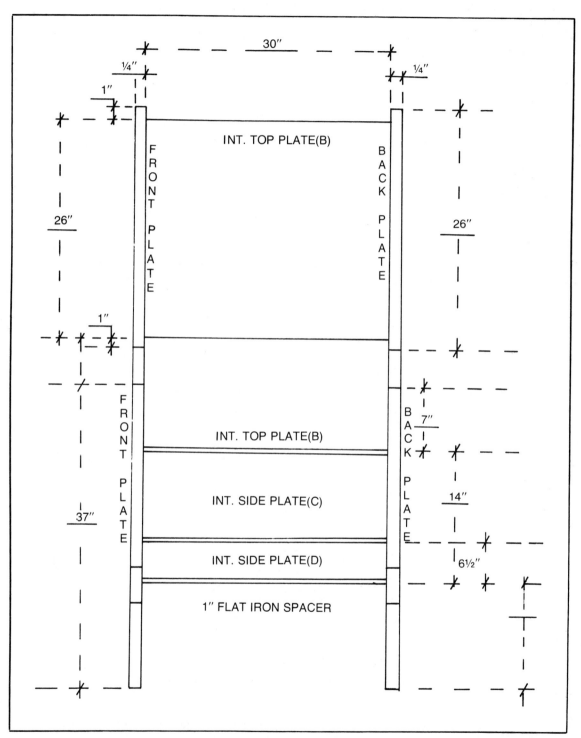

Fig. 19-11. Overhead and side view of the interior boiler box.

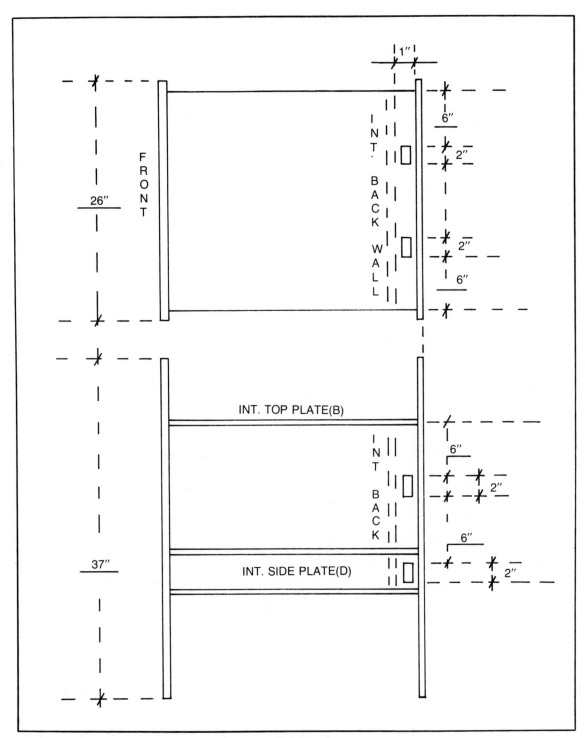

Fig. 19-12. Overhead view and side view of the back wall slot locations.

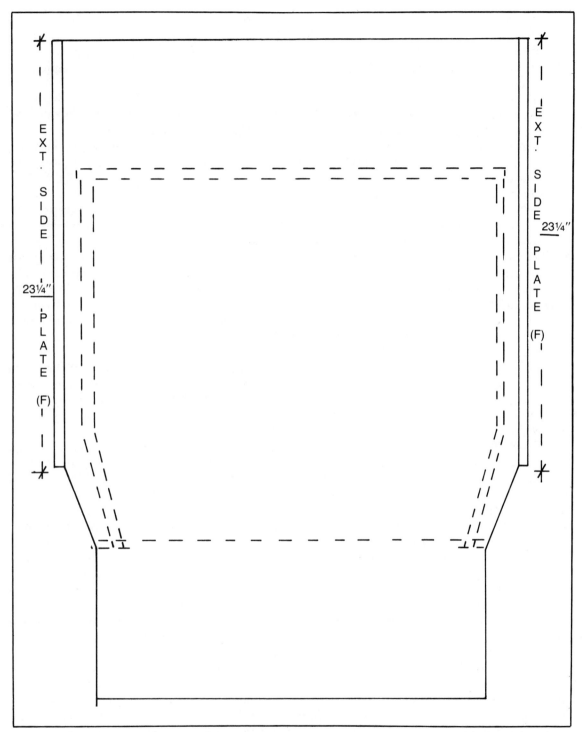

Fig. 19-13. Overhead view of the exterior side plates location.

Repeat the instructions, given in the preceding paragraph, for the opposite side. See Fig. 19-13.

Take plate G and (with the 30½" side vertical) fit it to plates A; butt it against the edge of plate F. Once in position, tack weld plate G to plates A and plate F. See Fig. 19-14.

Repeat the instructions, given in the preceding paragraph, for the opposite side. See Fig. 19-24.

Take plate K and (with the 30½" side vertical) fit it to plates A and plate G, butting the edge of plate K to the edge of plate G. See Fig. 19-15. Once in position, tack weld it to plates A and G.

Repeat the instructions, given in the preceding paragraph, for the opposite side. See Fig. 19-15.

Once plates F, G, and K are tack welded into position, weld all of the joints solid using Jet rod. Roll the boiler over as needed. A hint here is to do the rolling over in such a way that, when you make your last roll, you end up with the front of the boiler face up.

Remember to check to make sure that you have the front of the boiler face up. Using Fig. 19-16 as a visual aid, position, lay out, and cut out the main door opening and the ash door opening.

Using Fig. 19-17 as a visual aid, lay the boiler on it's side, and position lay out, and cut out the side air opening.

Repeat the instructions, given in the preceding paragraph, for the opposite side. See Fig. 19-17.

Referring to Fig. 19-18, fabricate and install the side air control slides. When mounting the slide, use a 9/16" washer, tacked to the side of plate K, as a guide for the air control handle. This will keep the handle straight, when the boiler is standing upright, and it will also make the slide action operate smoothly.

Repeat the instructions, given in the preceding paragraph, for the opposite side. See Fig. 19-18.

Laying your boiler on it's back, measure up 10½" from the bottom of the boiler, on the inside of the firebox, and draw a line across the back water jacket. This is the location for the 2"-×-2"-×-¼" angle iron. Once the line is drawn, position the angle and tack it into place (using 2"tacks every 6"). When positioning the angle, remember to keep it centered to the back wall. See Fig. 19-19.

Roll the boiler over on it's side. Using the 1½"-×-1½" angle iron, tack weld the angle, along the bottom edge of the side water jacket, with the one leg facing up. This will hold your firebrick. See Fig. 19-19.

Rolling the boiler over, front down, Repeat the instructions given in the paragraph before the preceding paragraph. See Fig. 19-19.

Rolling the boiler over on the last remaining side, repeat the instructions given in the paragraph before the preceding paragraph. See Fig. 19-19.

Rolling the boiler over on it's top, lay two firebricks on the ceiling of the firebox. On top of the firebrick, lay baffle plate M. On top of baffle plate M, lay the 2"-×-2" angle iron (26" long). Lay the one leg flat, on the baffle, and the other leg against the side wall. Do the same on the opposite side. Once the angles are in place, tack weld them to the side walls (using tacks 2" long every 5"). When you have finished this procedure, slide the baffle out of the way and remove the firebrick. (This is your sliding baffle.) See Fig. 19-20.

Take the piece of 3" channel (30" long) and drill, or burn, a series of holes, ½" in diameter, down the middle of the channel. Keep them about 2" apart. After the holes are in, take the channel and place it on the 2" angles. Center it in the middle of the boiler. When it is in place, weld it to both 2"-×-2"-×-¼" angle irons. See Fig. 19-21. Take two, 3" channels (11½" long) and drill, or burn, a series of ½" holes down the center (keeping them about 2" apart). Next, install them into the boiler; line them up to the side air controls and the center of the existing channel. When in place, weld them solid to the side water jackets and the existing channels. Once the channels are welded in place—using your cutting torch—cut away the sides of the long channel that block the small channels. These channels will guide the incoming air so that all the wood or coal will receive air. This will give you a total and even burn. See Fig. 19-22.

Turn the boiler upright. Using Fig. 19-23, *locate* position, lay out, and cut the exhaust opening. Use the 8" *inside* diameter pipe to draw the 8" circle. Remember to trace the inside of the pipe, (not the outside).

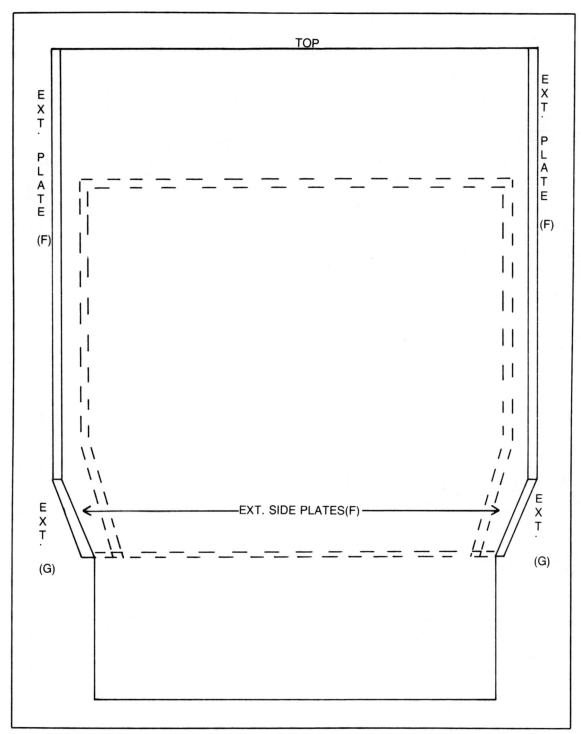

Fig. 19-14. Overhead view of the exterior side plates location.

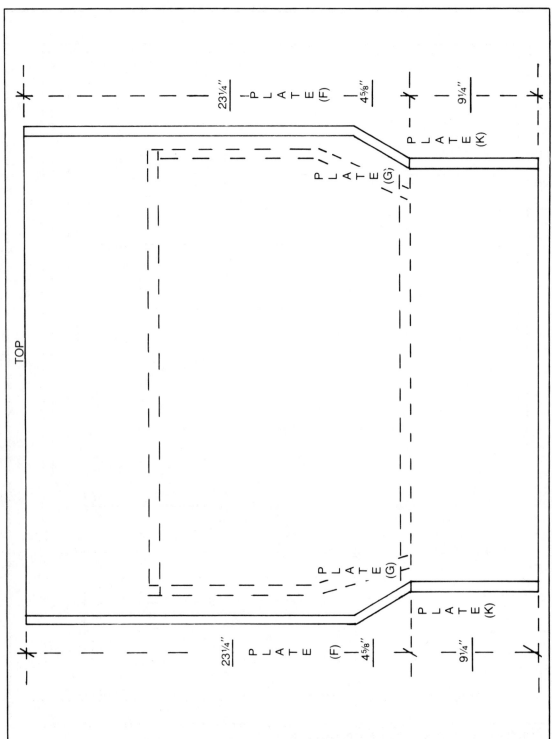

Fig. 19-15. Overhead view of the exterior side plate location.

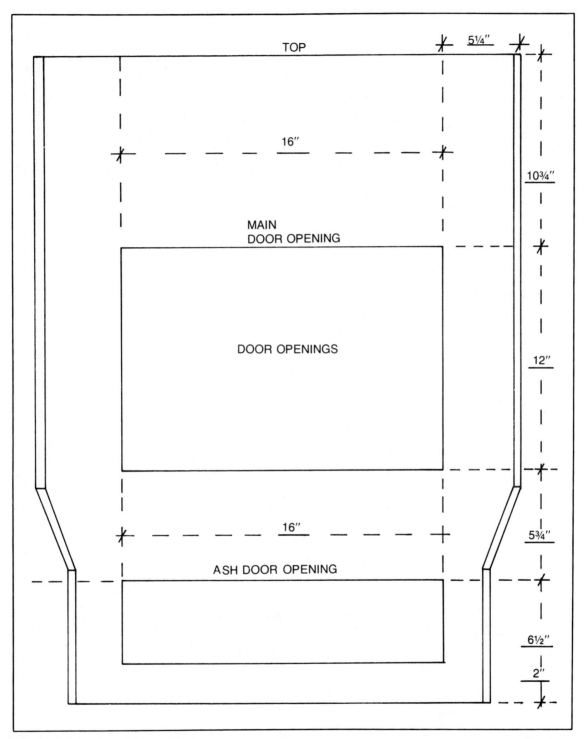

Fig. 19-16. Front view of door openings.

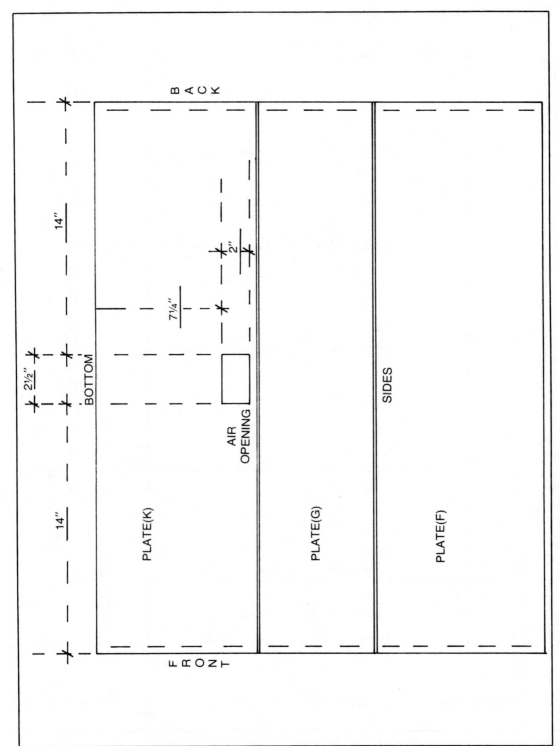

Fig. 19-17. Side view of side air openings for left and right sides.

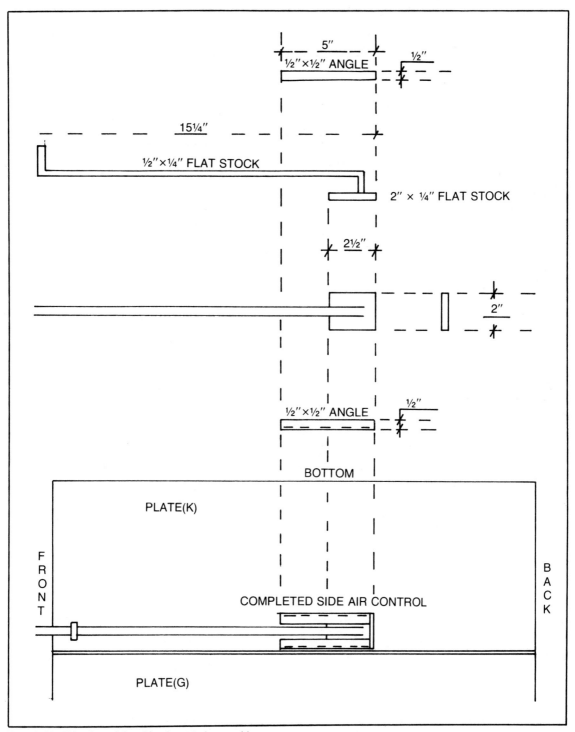

Fig. 19-18. Side view of the side air control assembly.

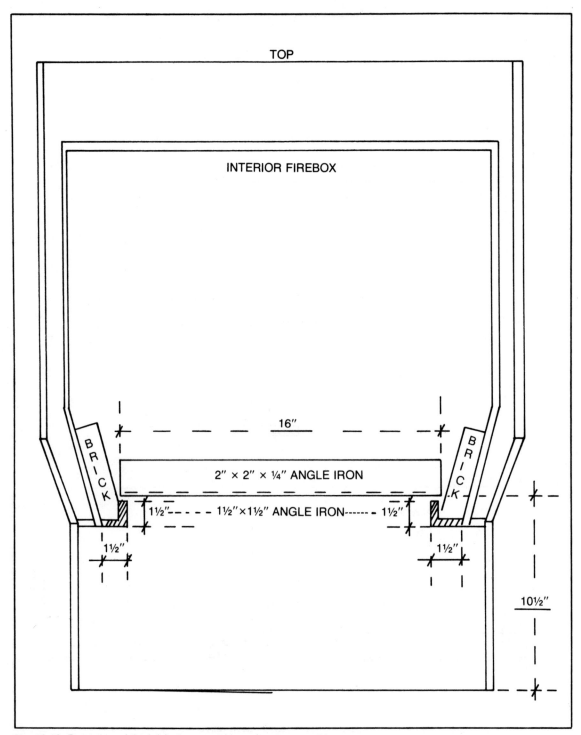

TOP

INTERIOR FIREBOX

BRICK

BRICK

16″

2″ × 2″ × ¼″ ANGLE IRON

1½″ — 1½″ × 1½″ ANGLE IRON — 1½″

1½″

1½″

1½″

10½″

Fig. 19-19. Front view of the brick stay assembly and grate assembly.

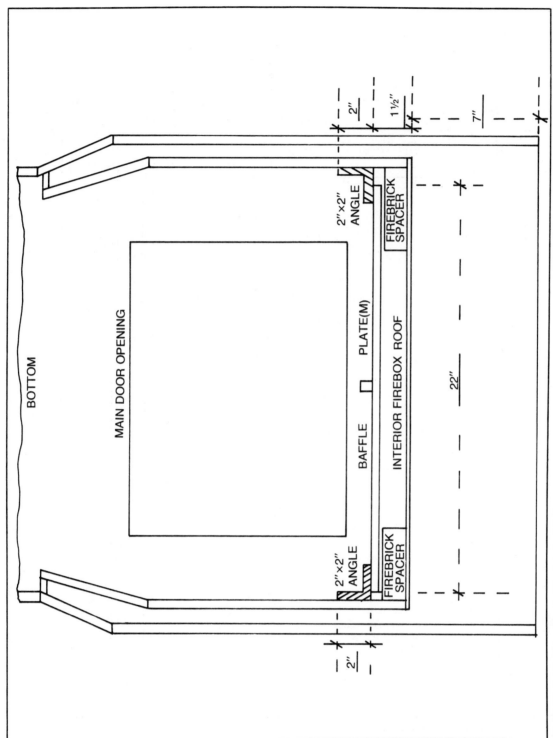

Fig. 19-20. Front view of the baffle plate installation.

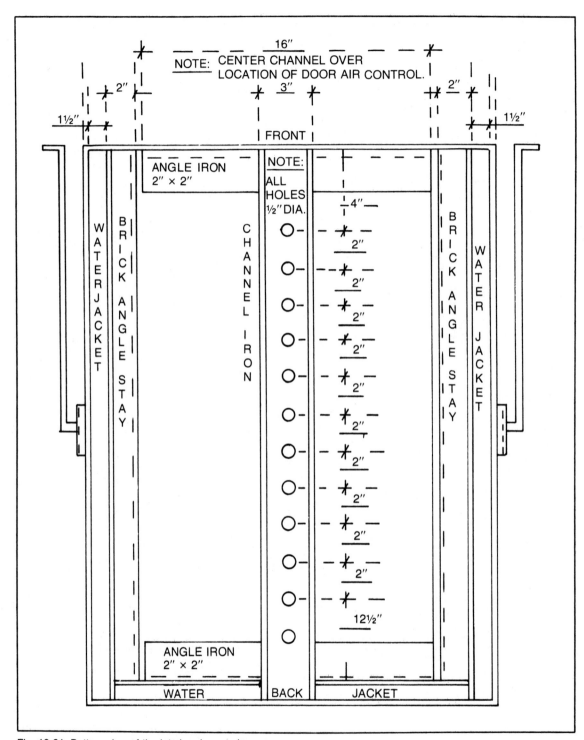

Fig. 19-21. Bottom view of the interior air controls.

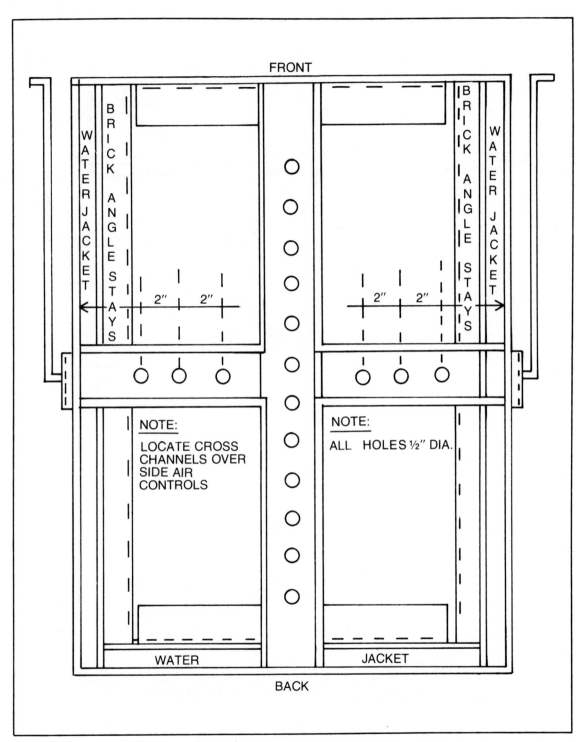

Fig. 19-22. Bottom view of the interior air controls.

317

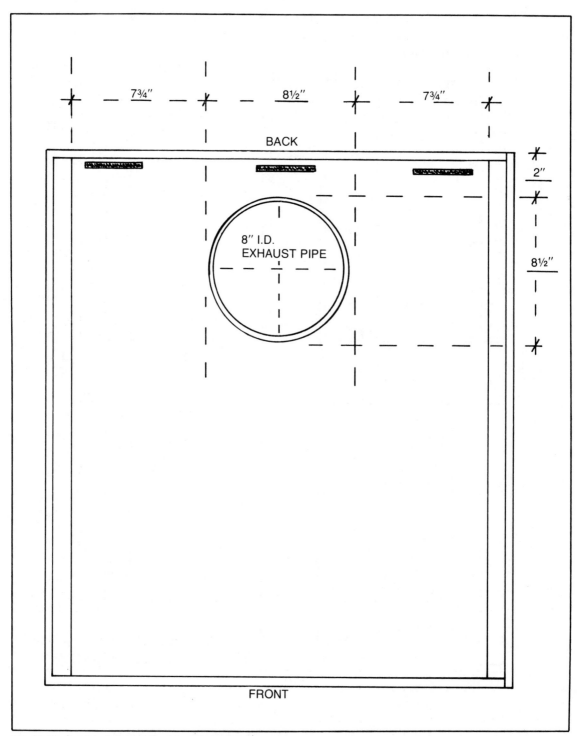

Fig. 19-23. Overhead view of the exhaust pipe location.

Using Fig. 19-24 and your 8″ pipe, take roof plate H and position, lay out, and cut an 8½″ diameter opening. This time use the *outside* diameter of your pipe to trace the line.

Take the exhaust pipe and weld it solid to the interior roof. Take the roof plate H and slip it over the exhaust. Square it to the sides of the boiler and tack it into position. Once tacked, weld it solid to the boiler and exhaust pipe. Remember to check for holes after the welding is completed. See Fig. 19-25.

Roll the boiler upside down. Take plate L and lining it up to the sides of your boiler. Tack weld it in place. Once it has been tacked, weld it solid to the bottom of the boiler. After the floor is on, take two pieces of 2″-×-2″-×-¼″ angle iron (25″ long) and tack weld one on each side of the floor. Use tacks, about 2″ long, every 6″. These are the legs. See Fig. 19-25.

Using Fig. 19-26 as a visual aid, take the (previously fabricated) firebox door and ash door and lay them over the door openings. Make sure that the doors overlap the door openings 1″ on all sides.

Once the doors are in position, install the door trim on both doors. Leave a ¼″ space on the side that the handle is located on. Once the trim is in place, tack weld it in position.

Referring to Figs. 12-14 and 19-26, mount the hinges to the boiler. Once the hinges are welded in place, open the doors and install the locking wedges on the inside edge of your door opening. See Fig. 10-19.

Once all of the seams have been welded and checked, refer to Fig. 18-25, position, lay out, and cut the coupling holes. Remember to keep the holes, a little smaller than the coupling you will place over it. After all of the holes have been cut, mount the couplings and weld into place. Referring to Fig. 18-25, lay the unit over (face down) and locate, lay out, and cut the inlet coupling hole. Be sure to make the hole a little smaller than the coupling. Once the hole is cut in plate E, mount and weld in the inlet coupling. Once the coupling has been welded, screw a nipple or a plug into the inlet connection. This will prevent damaging the connection when the unit has to be rolled over.

Laying the boiler face down, cut a hole, ⅞″ in diameter, in the exterior back wall. Measure up (about) 11″ and center it in the middle of the back plate. Once the hole has been cut, take a 1″ black iron coupling, place it over the hole (you've just cut) and weld it in solid. This is the boiler inlet.

Once all the couplings have been welded into position, the boiler can be bricked, cleaned, and painted. See Fig. 19-27.

You will have two things left to do on your wood and coal boiler. First the grate will have to be made. The instructions and drawings for this can be found in the Chapter 21. Second, an ash pan will be needed for the coal boiler. The box should be made, at a sheet-metal shop, out of heavy gauge sheet metal. It will be also easier, and less costly, to let someone else make the pan for you. You will need a box that is 15½″ wide, 26″ long, and 6″ high. Once the grate and ash pan are installed, the boiler is complete. Anyone who completes this project deserves credit. This is a very time-consuming project.

Pressure test the boiler unit before you hook it up.

### PRESSURE TESTING A BOILER UNIT

Once a (wood or wood and coal) boiler has been constructed, it is necessary to test the unit for leaks. Do this test before you hook it into your heating system. In the event you come across a leak, it can easily be repaired while your unit is still in the fabrication area (where your welding machine is). It will only take a matter of minutes to repair.

You can run the test on your unit very easily by using a garden hose connection valve. Because the garden hose valve obtains its water from your domestic water system it should be pressurized with 30 pounds pressure. This makes it perfect for testing.

You will need the following plumbing supplies to test your boiler: two ½″ threaded pipe plugs, two 1″ threaded pipe plugs, one ½″ threaded garden hose valve, one double-female hose adapter, and the garden hose. A double-female hose adapter is a short piece of garden hose, about an inch or two long, that has the type of end that can screw into

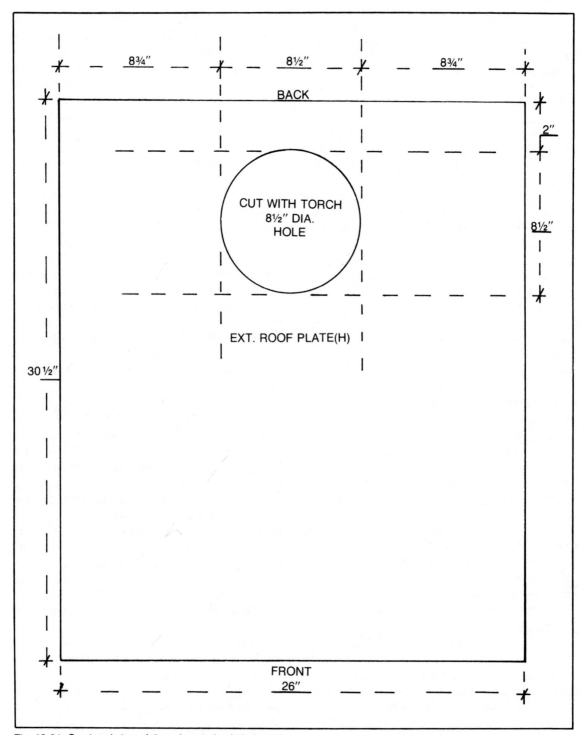

Fig. 19-24. Overhead view of the exhaust pipe hole location.

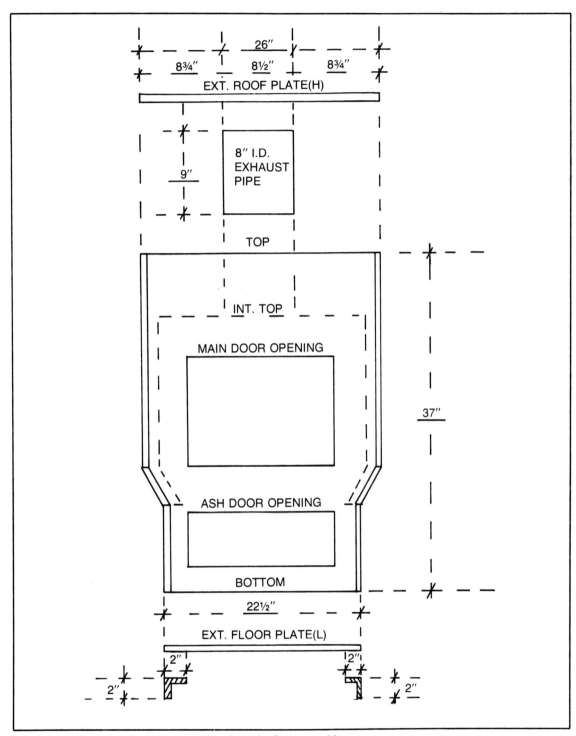

Fig. 19-25. Front view of the roof assembly and exterior floor assembly.

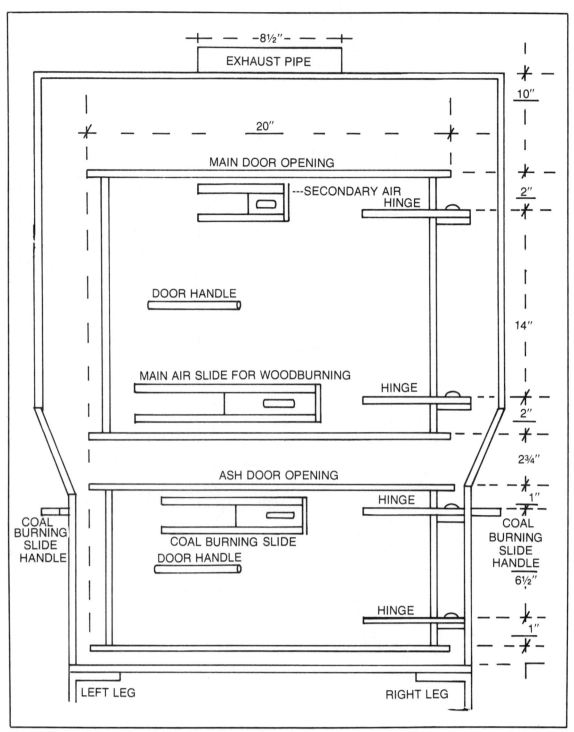

Fig. 19-26. Front view of the door location and assembly.

Fig. 19-27. An installed wood and coal boiler.

your hose valve at each end. You will also need a 30-pound safety valve.

Once you have gathered all of the equipment you can begin as follows:

☐ Connect the 30-pound safety valve to the ¾″ coupling on the boiler unit. Using the plugs and garden hose valve, seal the boiler unit for testing.

☐ Connect the garden hose to the garden-hose valve on the boiler using the garden hose and the double-female adapter. Make sure that the garden hose valve is closed.

☐ Turn on the garden hose valve in your home.

☐ Slowly open the garden hose connection at the boiler while manually lifting the safety valve. This bleeds the air out of your water jacket which, in turn, allows the water into the jacket. Keep the safety valve manually open until water comes out. When this does happen, release the safety valve. The safety valve might leak some, but that's what it is designed to do. Don't worry.

☐ Now that the boiler is full, leave the garden hose valve on. This will maintain the 30-pound pressure. Visually check the interior for leaks. If you find one, circle the leak with soapstone. After you have finished checking the inside for leaks, check the exterior for leaks in the same manner. Circle any leaks you find with soapstone.

☐ To complete the test, close the garden hose valve on the boiler and in the house.

☐ Disconnect the garden hose at the house hose valve. Release the built-up pressure in the boiler by slowly opening the garden hose valve on your boiler unit. When all of the pressure has been drained, remove the plugs.

If you do come across a leak, repair it and test your unit again. Bear in mind that you cannot repair a leak while there is water leaking out of it. If you find a leak in the upper part of your boiler unit, you have to drain the water down, below the leak, and weld it closed. This will be the supreme test of how carefully the boiler has been welded.

323

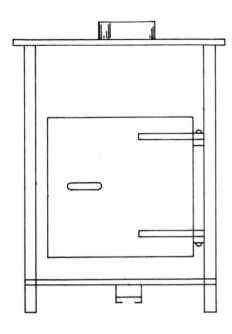

# Chapter 20

# Fabricating a Protective Screen

**O**NE OF THE BENEFITS OF A RADIANT stove is the beauty of an open fire. For maximum safety, you will need a protective screen. The screen will prevent hot embers from popping out of the stove. Such embers can cause a fire, or at the very least, burn holes in a rug or floor.

It probably would be very difficult for you to find a manufactured screen that would fit properly. Building your own screen yourself is not a particularly difficult procedure. You won't even need very much material. All that is required is 7 feet of 1″ × ¼″ flat stock and, if you are unable to purchase fireplace screening, radiator protection screen. Radiator screen can be purchased from most building supply stores. Such screen is made with a sheet of aluminum that is perforated with holes or a pattern of designs. The sheets come in various sizes. For this project, you'll need a piece about 23″ long and 20″ wide. The fabrication instructions are as follows.

Measure the door opening. Take that measurement and add 1½″ to the length and 1½″ to the width. This will make the screen overlap the door opening. Example: the Liberty model door opening measures 18″ long and 12″ wide. For this stove, the screen would measure 19½″ long and 13½″ wide. This will make the screen (when centered) overlap the opening ¾″ on each side.

Using a cutting torch or hacksaw, cut the pieces of the screen frame as is shown in Fig. 20-1.

Fit the pieces together, as shown in Fig. 20-1 using your 2 foot carpenter square. Make sure that you keep all of the sides at a 90° angle (or square) and tack weld them together. Once you have all four corners tack welded, fit the frame to the stove. Make sure that it fits. Once this last check is made, weld the frame together only on the one side.

Take the screen and lay the frame on it. Mark the cut lines. Remember to take into account for the extra material that you will need when folding (or wrapping) the screen around the frame.

Cut lines having previously been marked, use a pair of tin snips to cut the screen. After the screen has been cut, lay the frame on the screen. Center it

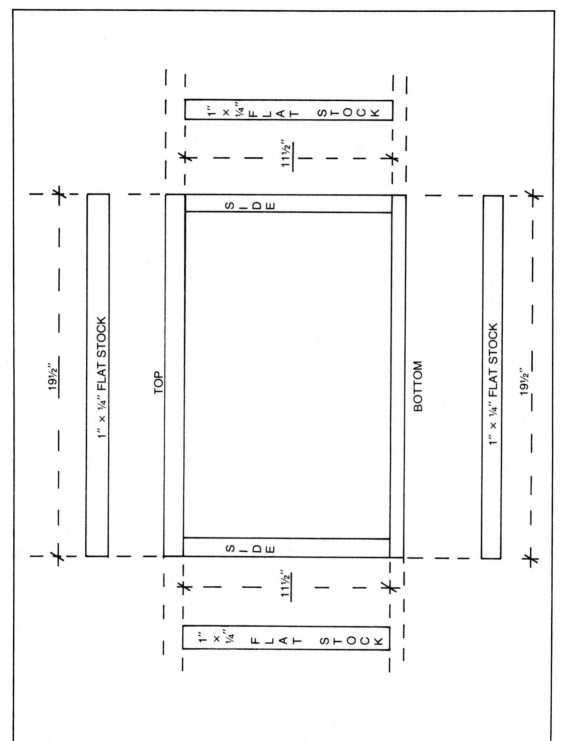

Fig. 20-1. Screen frame for the Liberty stove and Lowboy stove.

325

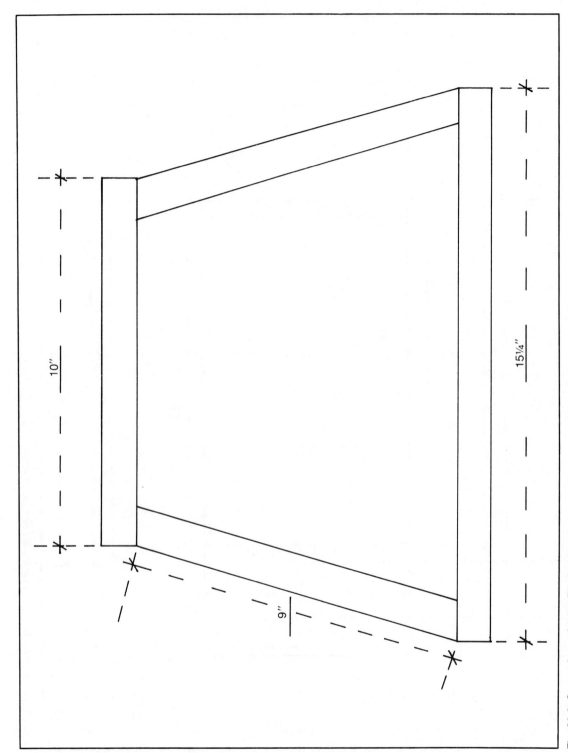

10"

15¼"

9"

Fig. 20-2. Screen frame for the Pilgrim stove.

326

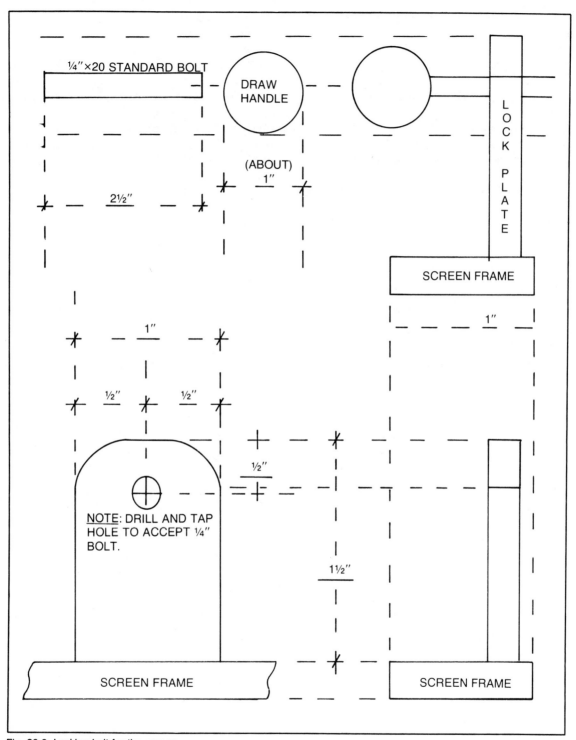

Fig. 20-3. Locking bolt for the screen.

and begin to fold over the edges of the screen (thus attaching the screen to the frame). Trim edges as you go. Be sure to keep the bends tight to the frame. Make sure that it is snug.

Take a piece of 1″ flat stock, no longer than 1¼″ long, and drill a hole through it as is shown in Fig. 20-3. Tap the hole out so that a ¼″ bolt will thread into it. Take this piece of flat stock and mount it as is shown in Fig. 20-3. This will be the locking device that will keep the screen in place when it is being used.

After the screen is completed, check for proper fit. You can spray the screen with high-heat paint once the screen fits properly.

Don't be worried about using aluminum as a screen. Aluminum transfers heat very quickly and the chances of the screen burning out are very small. When you want to watch the fire, you will only want a minimum amount of wood in the stove. If you fully load the stove and then put the screen on it, you would create too much heat. You would also be unable to control the amount of air that reaches the fire.

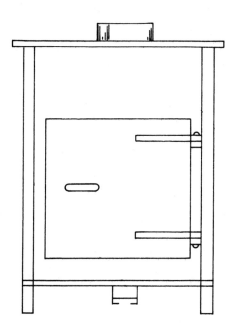

# Chapter 21

# Grates and Ash Pans

T O BURN COAL IN THE EXAMPLE stove, the Square stove, the Rectangular stove, the Pilgrim, the Liberty, the Lowboy, or the Wood and Coal Boiler, you need a grate and an ash pan. This chapter includes instructions and sketches to aid you in fabricating the grate and fitting an ash pan.

A manufactured cast iron grate that will fit your stove will be extremely difficult to find. You can, however, make a grate out of steel. It would be a good idea to also make a spare grate because a steel grate will eventually warp. By building two grates, you will have a spare ready when the original grate has warped beyond use.

General fabrication instructions follow for building a grate and a stand for the grate. There are sketches of grates for each stove model, and a general method for hooking an ash pan under the floor plate of the radiant stoves.

The ash pan can be fabricated in a sheet-metal shop. It is much simpler and less costly to have it done this way. It should be made out of not less than ⅛" thick sheet metal, and it should have a lip extending out from the top edges on three sides.

## GENERAL MATERIALS

One 10′ length of 1½"-×-1½"-×-¼" angle iron for the grate mount.

One 10′ length of ½"-×-½"-×-⅛" flat stock for ash pan tracks.

Three to four 20′ lengths of 2"-×-⅜" flat stock for grate material.

The following are the sizes of the ash pans required for each unit. All of the radiant stoves require a ½" lip out from all top sides. No lip is required for the ash pan for the Wood and Coal Boiler. See Figs. 21-1 and 21-2.

☐ Example stove: 32" long × 18" wide × 5" deep.

☐ Square stove: 23½" long × 18" wide × 5" deep.

☐ Rectangular stove: 23½" long × 28" wide × 5" deep.

☐ Pilgrim stove: 20" long × 16" wide × 5" deep.

☐ Liberty stove: 25" long × 14" wide × 5" deep.

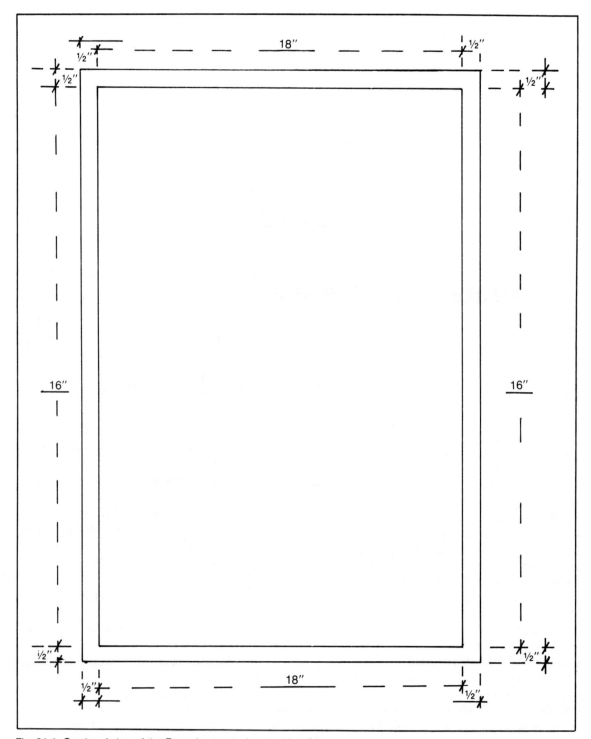

Fig. 21-1. Overhead view of the Example stove ash pan with ½" lips.

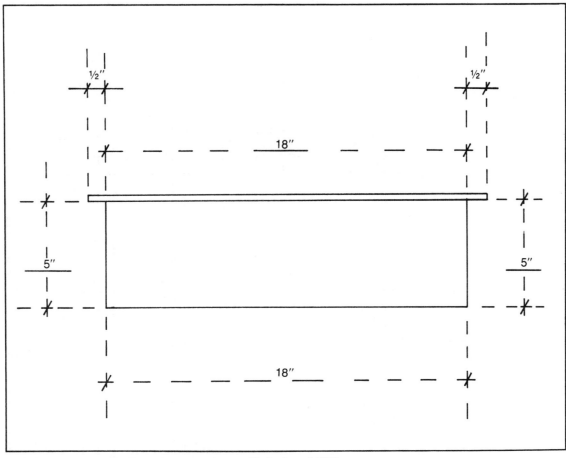

Fig. 21-2. End view of the Example stove ash pan with depth and ½″ lips.

☐ Lowboy stove: 20″ long × 18″ wide × 5″ deep.

☐ Wood and Coal Boiler: 26″ long × 15½″ wide × 6″ deep.

### FABRICATION INSTRUCTIONS

See Figs. 21-6 through 21-13 and find the grate that corresponds with your stove. The sketches show the length and width of the grate and the length of the center pieces.

Cut to size the four outside edge pieces. Then cut to size the center pieces. Before you begin to cut, remember to count the number of center pieces you will need. This can be easily accomplished by drawing the grate out and counting the center pieces.

Once all of the pieces are cut and cleaned, take the four side pieces and put them together (with the 2″ side vertical). When they are tacked (at equal spaces), insert the center pieces (keeping them ¾″ apart). Use a piece of wood, ¾″ wide, as a spacer. As you insert the center pieces, tack them in place. After your grate has been tacked together, weld all parts solid.

Once the grate is complete, take the 1½″-×1½″-×-¼″ angle iron, refer to Fig. 21-3, and fabricate the grate stand.

Now that the grate stand has been fabricated, turn the stove upside down and cut a 3″-×-3″ opening in the center of the firebox floor. See Fig. 21-4. Once the opening is cut, lay the pan upside down over the opening. When the pan is in position, lay

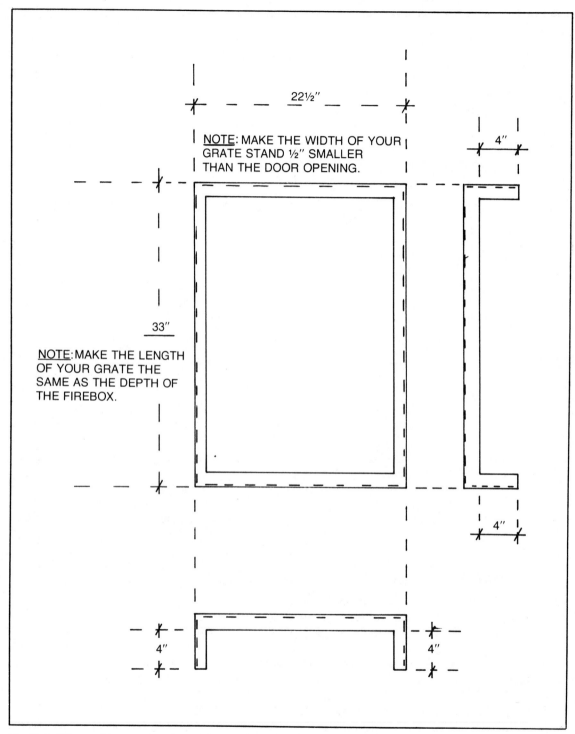

Fig. 21-3. Orthographic projection of a grate stand for the Example stove; overhead, side, and end views are shown.

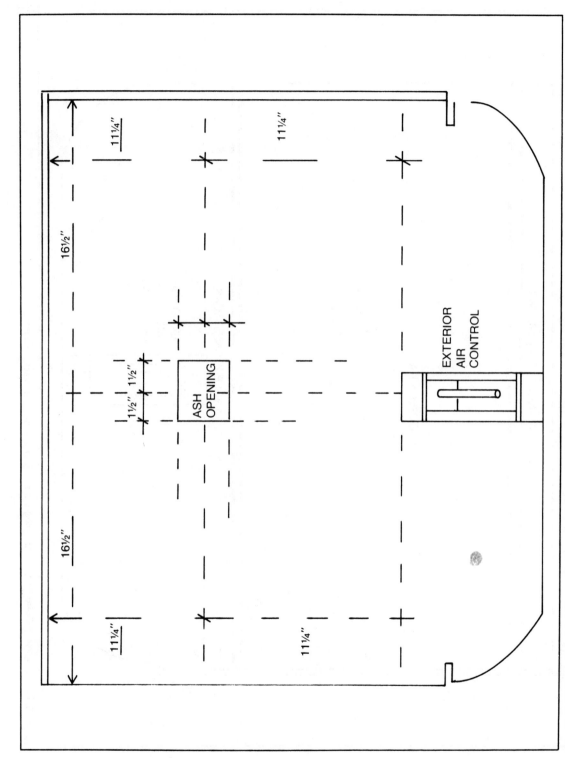

Fig. 21-4. Bottom view of the Example stove showing the centering and layout of the ash opening.

333

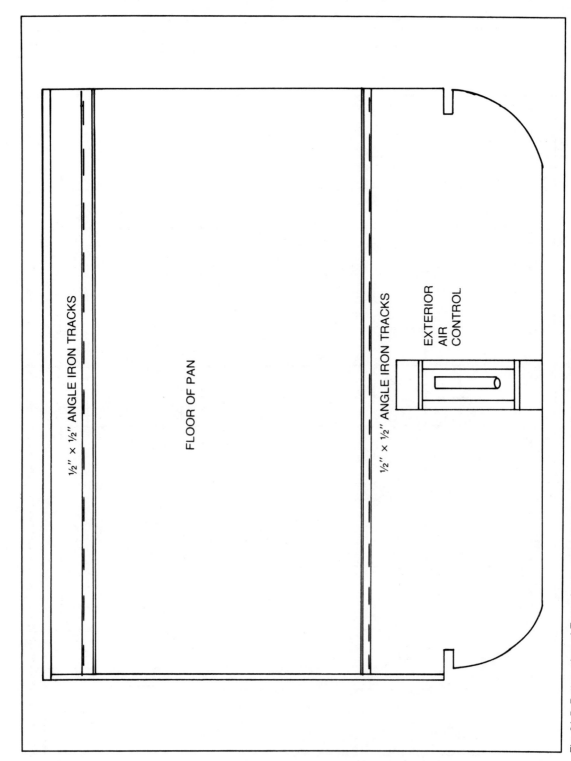

½" × ½" ANGLE IRON TRACKS

FLOOR OF PAN

½" × ½" ANGLE IRON TRACKS

EXTERIOR
AIR
CONTROL

Fig. 21-5. Bottom view of Example stove showing the ash pan and ash pan tracks mounted.

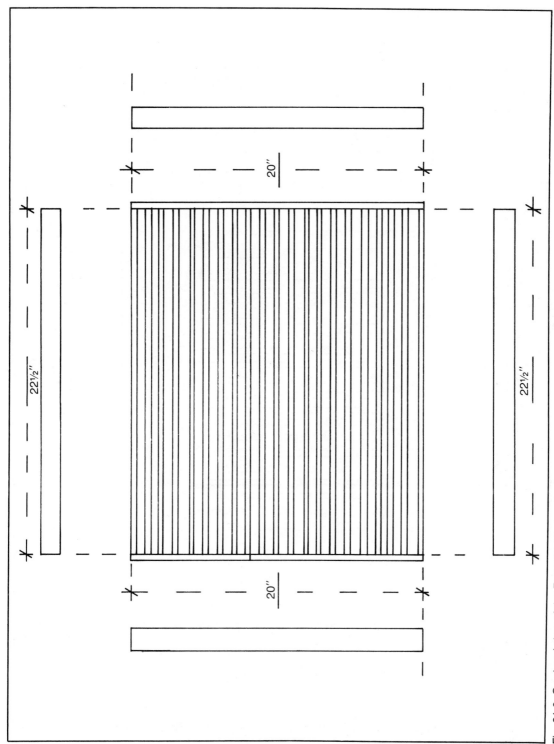

Fig. 21-6. Overhead view of the Example stove grate.

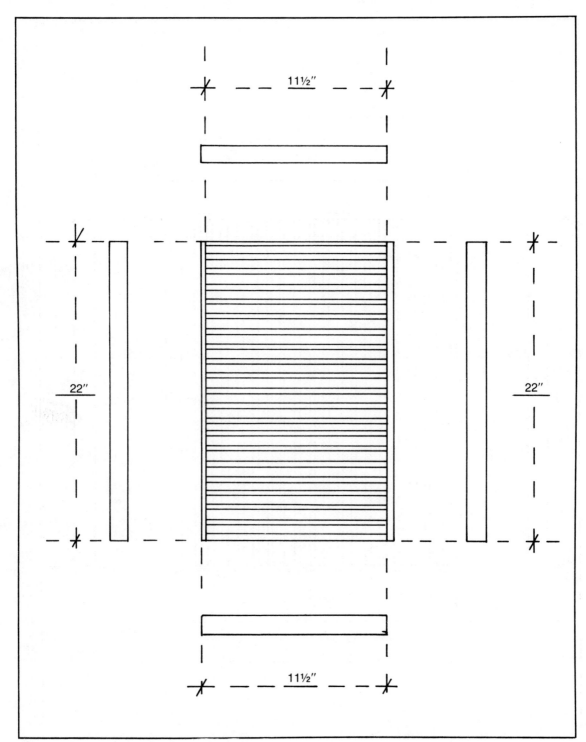

Fig. 21-7. Overhead view of the Square stove grate.

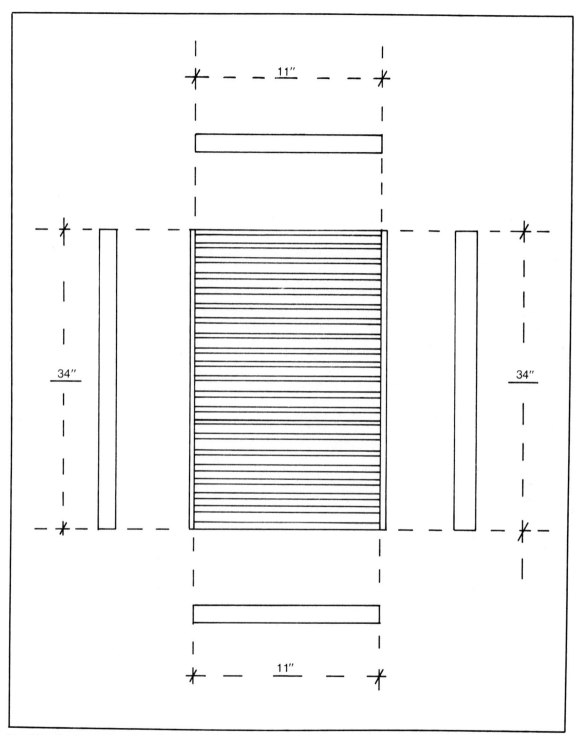

Fig. 21-8. Overhead view of the Rectangular stove grate.

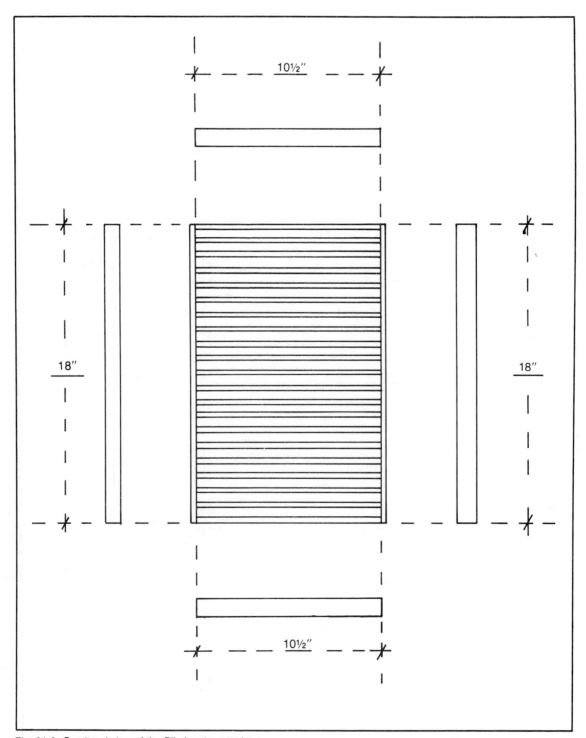

Fig. 21-9. Overhead view of the Pilgrim stove grate.

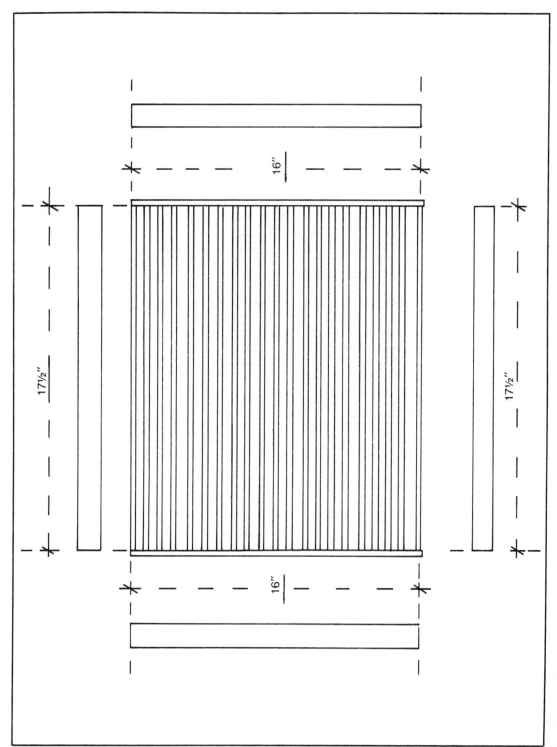

Fig. 21-10. Overhead view of the Liberty stove.

339

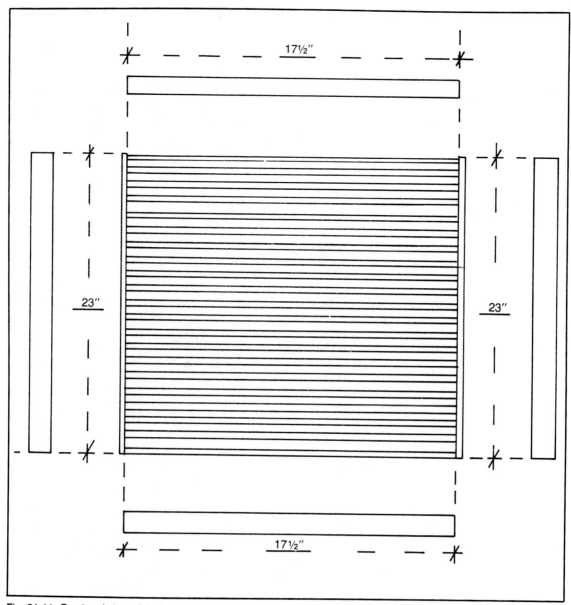

Fig. 21-11. Overhead view of the Lowboy stove grate.

the ½″ angle over the lips of the two sides. Tack them in place. These are your pan tracks. When the tacking is completed, turn the stove right side up. See Fig. 21-5.

You are ready to burn coal when the stove is right side up and the grate stand is inserted with the grate on the stand. You will occasionally want to shake down ashes. You can do this by sliding the grate forward and backward on the stand (in a rocking action). Make a small hook out of some scrap material and use it to shake the grate. The design is up to you. Make a shaker rod that is comfortable to use and at the same time gives the proper shaking action.

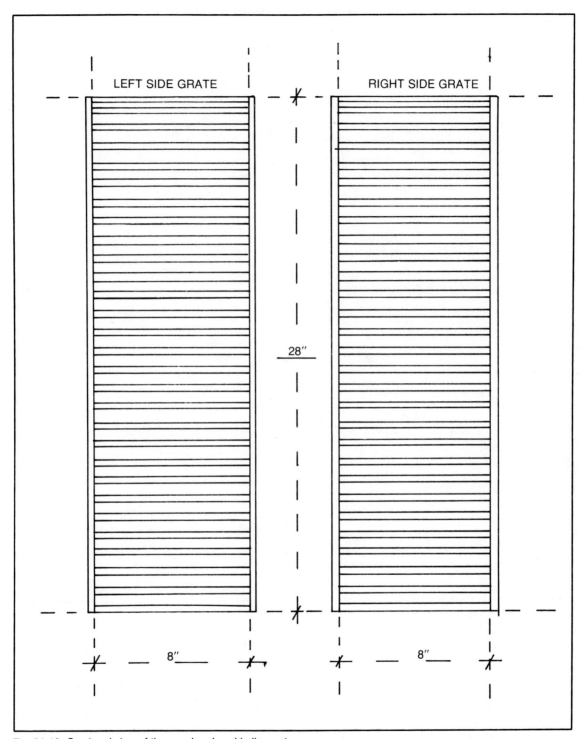

LEFT SIDE GRATE

RIGHT SIDE GRATE

28"

8"

8"

Fig. 21-12. Overhead view of the wood and coal boiler grate.

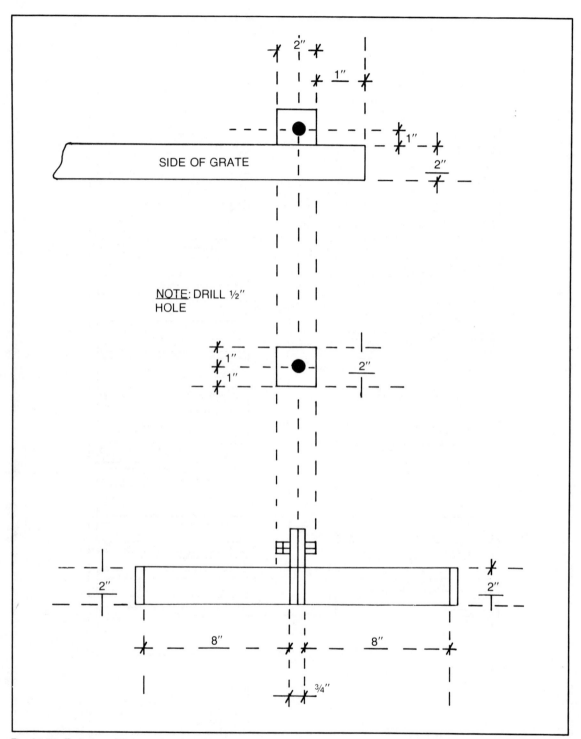

Fig. 21-13. End view of the wood and coal boiler grate.

# Part 3
## After
## Building Your
## Solid-Fuel Unit

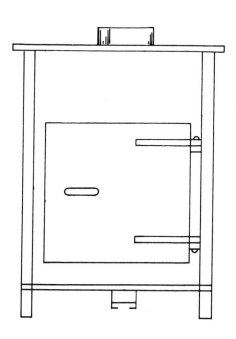

# Chapter 22

# Safety Procedures

**T**HE FIRST THING TO KEEP IN mind is that you have to be careful with the fuel that you are going to use. If you are going to burn coal, there will be no problem as long as you use the secondary air system installed in the stove. This system is specifically designed with the intention of burning coal. See Fig. 10-2 as an example. This will eliminate the coal gases from entering the room.

### MAINTAINING YOUR CHIMNEY

For wood fire safety tips, refer to the section on laying and maintaining a fire. Be aware of creosote buildup when burning with wood. Always remember that seasoned wood is your best bet. Some of the woods that can be burned green, if you find it necessary to do so, are white ash, cherry, maple, beech, sumac and some birches.

If you are going to burn green wood, you will have a large creosote build up in your chimney. Check your chimney on the average of once every week. Remember, burning green wood is not recommended.

If you are burning seasoned wood, there will be much less of a chance of considerable creosote buildup. The only time that creosote has a chance of building up, when you are burning seasoned wood in an air-tight stove, is during the course of a night. This is the time when you will more than likely be shutting the stove down to a lower setting. This drops the temperatures way down.

When you first begin to burn wood, check the chimney every couple of weeks. This will give you a good idea of the estimated rate of creosote formation. You will probably be able to lengthen the intervals between these inspections once you are aware of the burning pattern that leads to a creosote buildup.

If the conditions under which you are operating your stove change, it would be wise to resume the biweekly inspections. Using a new batch of wood might change the burning pattern that you have previously established. There are also some installations that would warrant cleaning on a monthly basis. Be aware of the circumstances that would require the continuous cleaning of a chimney.

Never intentionally create a creosote fire to burn out creosote that's attached to the lining of the chimney. This is a foolish chance to take. Besides the fact that the fire could get out of hand, you stand the chance of cracking the flue liner. If you run the unit with the air control wide open for at least 10 to 15 minutes a day, this will dry up most of any creosote buildup. It will flake off and fall to the bottom of the chimney. This is why the tile-lined chimneys and pipe chimneys are preferred.

Creosote is a black tar-like substance that results from the condensation of wood gases not burned in the combustion process. There is no way to totally prevent the formation of creosote, but it can be minimized by avoiding smoldering fires, burning only seasoned hardwoods, and using quality interior chimneys.

If a fire is burning below 1100° F, volatile gases escape and condense on relatively cool surfaces. There will always be some amount of creosote, but, it is only when it is allowed to accumulate in large quantities that it becomes the fuel that ignites a chimney fire. Once you become familiar with operating a radiant stove, you will have no problem in regulating maintenance procedures.

Water-jacketed boiler units will build up more creosote due to their efficiency. You will have to check the pipes for creosote often. The water or air absorbs a tremendous amount of the heat from the smoke. Have a fire extinguisher of some type on hand. It will prove itself invaluable in the case of a chimney fire or a creosote fire. A chimney fire will occur when large deposits of creosote are exposed to very high temperatures.

You will know if you have a chimney fire or a creosote fire. It sounds like a 747 flying about 3 feet over the roof of your house. You will also see black smoke come out of the chimney and sparks, or possibly even flames, will be thrown out. This depends on how long the fire goes unnoticed and if it has a chance to get going.

Sparks and burning debris can spread such a fire to adjacent roofs and walls. In the case that you don't have a fire extinguisher handy, keep the stove's doors shut and shut down the air controls. In a relatively airtight stove, this will suffocate the fire due to the lack of oxygen.

It is just as important to make sure that the chimney is airtight. If the stovepipe and stove con-

nections are tight and secure, and if there is only one stove connected to the flue, you will be able to shut the fire down.

If you have a fire call the fire department. Do not assume once the fire has burned out that your problems are over. After such a fire, the chimney should be checked carefully before it is again used. The high temperatures can crack the lining and violent forces can shake it apart. Without careful attention, a second chimney fire will finish the job the first fire started. Before the fire department even gets there, wet down the roof and adjacent areas to prevent the fire from spreading further.

## HOW TO CLEAN A CHIMNEY

There are chemical cleaners available that can be used to break down creosote. Although they serve as an aid to the prevention of large amounts of creosote deposits, they should not be relied upon as the sole method of cleaning. These types of products are best used between the regulated manual cleaning of your chimney. Their use can be consindered a type of preventative medicine.

If you do not feel capable of cleaning the chimney yourself, a professional chimney sweep should be hired. In some cases the job, of cleaning a chimney is a simple enough procedure to do yourself. People have been known to come up with a wide range of methods for chimney cleaning. You will not get very good results from hanging chains in the flue, to be banged back and forth, or from pulling a small tree up and down the flue. It is best to use the wire brush method with a brush especially designed for the sole purpose of chimney cleaning.

Before you begin cleaning your chimney, make sure that you have all of the necessary equipment such as proper lighting, an ash bucket, a shovel, a whisk broom, brushes for the flue with extension handles, and a wire brush. A drop cloth can help keep clean the area in which you are working.

Begin by reaching into the connection of the chimney flue and checking it for creosote with the aid of a flashlight and mirror. If you find any creosote, examine it to see if it breaks off in slabs or just resembles a tar-like substance. Creosote can be found in either state and both states of creosote require cleaning.

If you are going to clean the chimney, from the inside of the house, you will have to remove the damper in the fireplace and keep the opening covered. Cut a slit in the cover just large enough to allow the insertion of a brush. Clean the creosote by scraping the creosote with the brush up through the flue and up through the chimney. Add extension handles as necessary. There are many sizes and shapes of brushes. You should be able to find one to fit any flue and chimney.

Another method that can be used is the rope system. Two ropes are pulled up and down the chimney. One person pulls from up the roof and the other pulls down from below. In lieu of the second person, the rope can be weighted. This method is outdated due to the manufacturing of all the new shapes and sizes of brushes for cleaning flues and chimneys.

Work your way up the chimney, scraping the sides as you go, and remove any substance that has attached itself on the inside of the chimney. The job can become easier if you install cleanout T's in the stovepipe and chimney. Well placed T's can make this chore not more than a 5-minute job.

Even if you have been burning coal as a solid fuel, rather than wood, there is a chance that fly ash has adhered itself to the inside of the chimney. It too must be brushed away.

A chimney sweep should be contacted for cleaning a tile-lined chimney. He will have the equipment to clean this type of chimney without doing any damage to the masonry.

## SAFE STOVE LOCATION

A radiant stove should be 36" from combustible material to best prevent fires from the radiated heat. You must be aware that the sides, bottom, and stovepipe will attain various temperatures while the stove is in operation. The only time that a stove can be placed closer to a wall than the 36" is if a noncombustible material is spaced at least 1" away from the wall. This will allow air to circulate behind the material and carry the heat away. Placing a noncombustible material directly on the wall will have no real value because the material will easily conduct heat to the wall behind it (which creates a very dangerous condition).

There are many beautiful noncombustible surfaces designed specifically for use behind stoves. They are not all that expensive.

Never enclose a solid-fuel unit in a confined area such as a closet. The concentration of heat in a small room presents the danger of the ignition of the walls surrounding the unit. Wallpaper has a low ignition temperature. It is always best to place a radiant stove in an open area to allow it to perform at it's maximum efficiency and allow for it's safest installation. Remember, curtains and drapes are made of combustible materials. You will also have to take the placement of furniture into consideration. Don't take chances; lives might depend on your decisions. Be careful not to place kindling wood and newspapers, too close to an operating unit. Anything that will heat up quickly can also ignite quickly.

Safe floor clearances for a wood-burning radiant stove are smaller than those recommended for wall spacing because the heat that is radiated from the bottom of a stove will be, generally, less than that from either of the sides or the top. A coal fire radiates it's heat in such a way that the legs and floor of the unit will get very hot and will conduct heat to the floor. If a fire should occur, the ashes fall to the bottom of a stove. This has an insulating affect and will resist the flow of heat downward. The average stove's leg length is approximately 6" to 18" so you will want at least 18" of clearance to a combustible material. A 24-gauge layer of sheet metal over a ¼" layer of noncombustible material is a safe measure. A metal plate would provide the same protection. It is advisable to use either the metal plate or the noncombustible material with attractive material such as stone, brick, or tile.

A brick hearth is also a very attractive mount for your solid-fuel unit. The safety problems of falling embers and sparks that sometimes pop from the burning wood, especially if it is wet from being outside in the elements, is sometimes ignored. To avoid this potential problem, extend the floor protection a good 18" from the front of the stove and 6" around the sides and back. This will afford you reasonable protection, but does not mean that you still do not have to take precautions when tending to the stove. This is just as important a factor as ever. Try to take care that ashes and hot coals fall only on the protected area. It only takes one spark to burn down a house.

## SAFETY EQUIPMENT

Be prepared in case hot coals spill or sparks fall into an unprotected area. Always keep a pair of gloves, a brush, a metal bucket, and a small shovel within reach. Try to immediately shovel the coals back into the firebox. If this is impossible, make sure that you have a fire extinguisher on hand. You will defi-nitely want it to be in handy reach in case of a chimney fire (or a creosote fire). The extinguisher that would be best used for a chimney fire is the flair type. You ignite the flair, throw it in the stove, shut the door, and shut down the air controls. It will suffocate the fire in the chimney. They are inexpensive and very worthwhile having around.

Smoke detectors should be placed in various places throughout the house. Do not allow yourself a false feeling of safety by totally relying upon their use. Continue to take precautions. Remember, the smoke has to rise enough to be caught by the detector. If you can catch a fire before it reaches that stage, it probably will not amount to much.

The phone number of the fire department or fire dispatcher should be located near each phone.

# Chapter 23

# Solid-Fuel Unit Efficiency

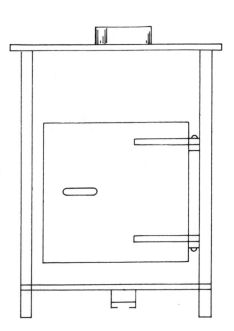

SOLID-FUEL UNIT EFFICIENCY is evaluated according to just how much heat from the unit is transferred to the area that is to be heated and the amount of burnable substance that is safely used.

A radiant stove does not have the operating convenience of oil or gas heat, and especially not that of electric heat. An add-on boiler unit does allow more control than with a radiant stove. This is especially true with the aid of an automatic stoker when you are burning coal.

You cannot just set a stove and forget it. It will require periodic attention to obtain the proper heating temperatures. Once you have learned many of the techniques for efficient operation of a solid-fuel unit, you will be able to operate your unit with fewer demands made upon you. Time and practice will be your best teachers. You will probably find that you will even enjoy this process of discovery.

The terms *draft* and *draw* are used throughout this chapter. Draft is air that is pushed through or pulled through the solid-fuel unit, or chimney, by the air control system, the door being opened, or the outside air flow that is pushed down the chimney (possibly) in the form of a *back draft* caused by too much wind pushing it's way down the chimney. Consider the draft to be the turbulence or the speed of air that is allowed to pass through, or is pushed through, the solid-fuel unit or chimney. The amount of air or the amount of draft that is allowed to the fire, is the chief factor in determining the temperatures of the fire or the height of the blaze. An adequate amount of draft must be provided through the air feed inlet (the draft control or the air control system), and pulled through the firebox and up through the chimney.

The draw is the means by which the air (usually referred to as a draft) is pulled. Hot air is drawn to cold air or the path that you choose to create a draw. A draw can be created by providing higher temperatures within the flue to draw the hot gases out through the chimney (hot air rises).

Draft is the air flow and the draw is the path the air flow takes. When building up a fire, shutting one door creates a concentrated amount of air, or draft, to be drawn to the fire. This builds up a fire faster.

If your only experience burning an alternate source of energy has been with burning wood in a fireplace, you are in for a very pleasant surprise.

The aesthetic view of a fireplace is most rewarding. You can have the same luxury with a radiant stove without denying yourself efficiency and heating capacity. You will use much less wood than a fireplace consumes. Operate the stove with the doors closed during the hours that you are unable to relax in front of the fire. There is no need to worry about runaway fires as there is when a fireplace is left burning.

There is a lack of efficiency in burning wood in a stove with the doors open for any length of time. You will use up a great deal more wood in addition to creating very high heating temperatures. The difference in efficiency of a radiant stove, burning wood with the doors open, and a fireplace is that the stove will be able to radiate it's heat for more heat distribution.

The more oxygen that is allowed to the fire the hotter it will burn and the higher the blaze. Imagine how fast the wood is being burned up in a fireplace. The most distressing point in fireplace operation is that the gases cannot be burned and most of the heat cannot be directed into the room. Approximately 90 percent of the heat is drawn up the chimney.

Unless radiation takes place, the proper amount of heat distribution cannot take place. Most of the heat from the stove comes from the radiation. The heat expands from the stove top and sides. If the stove is restricted, such as being inserted inside a fireplace opening (as is what is done with a unit that is referred to as a *fireplace-insert*) the heat has no place to be transferred. It will just be drawn up the chimney along with the gases.

Burning wood in a fireplace can draw heat out of the room and up the chimney. Depending upon the kind of draw that the flue, (inside the fireplace) has a sucking action can take place. This draws the heat to the flue and draws it up the chimney.

### REGULATING TEMPERATURES

Before you can control the heating temperatures of a stove, you will have to understand the combustion process (refer to Chapter 3 for additional information). Light and heat is created from the energy that is released during combustion. The various stages of combustion can all be occurring at the same time in various parts of the fire. Regulating the temperature of a solid-fuel unit is simply learning to control the variables that cause the combustion process: solid fuel, oxygen, and a high ignition temperature.

The energy content of a solid fuel is of prime importance. The second ingredient that is essential to the combustion process is oxygen. The dampers, referred to as the air-feed inlets or the air-control system, is the primary source of the oxygen that can be supplied to the fire. If the solid-fuel unit is airtight, the air controls, being shut way down, will cause the fire to burn slowly. By opening the air control wider, you will be allowing more oxygen to be introduced to the fire and a hotter fire will be produced.

The air-control system primarily controls the efficiency of the burning process. It also is the primary means by which ignition temperatures are reached. In an airtight unit with the air controls shut way down (where a draft does not interfere with the airflow from the primary air-feed inlets) the fire will not be able to burn efficiently. If an insufficient amount of oxygen is allowed to the fire, a valuable amount of heat will be lost.

A fire that is being burned with a wide open air control is hot enough to burn the gases, but the high temperatures will create a draft strong enough that the heat will be lost up the chimney before it can be used efficiently. The extent of the two extremes might make efficient heating seem to be a hopeless cause. But there is definitely a compromise that will prove to be effective. A position in between will provide the best and most efficient burn.

### PROLONGING BURN TIME

Until you feel confident enough to extend your stove's burn time for a night's duration, allow your furnace or existing heating system to be of some assistance. Set your thermostat for 55° or 60°. In case the stove fire does burn out, you will not wake up to a cold house.

Before retiring for the night, you can use thermal momentum to keep the temperatures of the house from dropping too low by the next morning. This is simply a matter of overheating the room. By creating an intense fire, and allowing it to burn for no less than 15 to 20 minutes, you will be allowing some of the creosote to dry up and flake off if you are burning with wood. The heat radiated by this intense fire will warm the area. Even if the area cools down 15° or 20° overnight, it will not be too uncomfortable in the morning hours.

Save those magazines with glossy paper. The paper contains a lot of filler that will not burn all that well. And it leaves behind it a large amount of ash. Too much ash will interfere with the burning of the fuel. To slow an intense fire, lay about 10 to 15 pages of the glossy paper on the fire. The idea is for it to burn and also to leave a thick layer of ash on the top of the solid fuel. The reduced amount of air that can get to the fuel will slow down the burn rate of the fire.

If you are cutting and using wood as your solid fuel, you will more than likely come across large pieces, known as *knotty wood*, that seems to defy the hammer and wedge. These pieces are good to set aside for overnight use—especially on a cold night. Using wood pieces of this type, along with other denser woods will ensure a slow burn.

If you leave the air controls open, just a crack, you can derive a longer burn time. Do not concern yourself with the possibility of unburned gases. This will be compensated for by a better heat transfer between the fire and the walls of the solid fuel unit. Just remember that these are the combined gases that end up as creosote that can adhere to the flue pipe or interior chimney walls. It is important to periodically check the flue pipe for creosote buildup—and *clean it.*

Setting a burning schedule will allow for a more complete burn. There should be a period of time, usually at bedtime or in the morning hours, when the fire has been allowed to burn down to a bed of coals. This will ensure that a fuel change can be expected to last for a maximum period of time.

If you are very careful, you can mix greener wood with seasoned wood. This will slow down a fire, for a longer burn time, and allow the fire to burn at lower temperatures. Whenever you are creating the circumstances that will make for the formation of creosote, you must maintain careful checks.

On very cold nights, especially when there is an outside draft allowing more oxygen to the fire, the fire will burn more intense thus not lasting as long, and it might burn out during the course of the night. The alternative to allowing the fire to die out, before you are up to stay, is to get up during the night and stoke the fire and go back to sleep. This also can be done on nights when it is not cold enough outside to build up a fire to temperatures that would be considered hot in the house. If you do not want to go this route, make sure that the thermostat is set to automatically turn on the heat, in case the temperatures in the house drop down too low.

You will eventually have to remove the ashes that have built up in the firebox of your solid-fuel burner or they will interfere with the complete burning of fuel. Use a heavy metal bucket. You can expect to find some live coals mixed in the ashes while shoveling out ashes. Don't be careless. Never dispose of the ashes in the garbage or even close to any combustible surface or material. Let ashes sit in the bucket for at least 24 hours. You can eventually use the ash, from burning wood, as fertilizer. If you are not going to save the ashes, filter through the bucket to make absolutely sure that there will be no chance of something smoldering upon their disposal.

## STOVE PLACEMENT AND HEAT RADIATION

The placement of a stove plays one of the most important roles in how and where the heat will radiate. You might have little choice as to where the stove will sit. This is especially true if you have a chimney and flue already set into place or if the rearrangement of furniture is not practical. It would, however, be most ideal to place the stove in the center of the house at the lowest possible level. This will allow the heat from the stove to circulate at it's best if there are no leaks to draw it's radiant heat away through windows and walls. Heat rises. The upper floors can be heated as well as the bottom floors.

If a radiant stove is placed near a staircase, the heat will be drawn up the stairs to the next floor. But it might not be drawn into the other parts of the house on the same level where the stove has been placed. It might be wiser to install a register in the ceiling of the lower level to draw the air to the second floor at a faster rate. In other words, provide a shortcut and place the stove in the center of the house if that is feasible.

If the stove must be placed at the end of the house, you can still obtain the necessary radiation of heat by placing a small fan in the vicinity to push the radiant heat in the proper direction. Wall registers can be used to carry the rising heat quickly to other parts of the house.

Consider using wall or ceiling registers to draw the heat to a particular room. The heat will first be drawn to the place where it is needed most. You can purchase registers that can be opened and closed. This offers the convenience of better regulating the amount of heat that will be drawn into a particular room or area. It could also add some privacy. Room doors can be closed at night when you are sleeping. If a room is not in use, close the register.

The best placement of a radiant stove is in a carpeted room that is most used by your family. It would be wise to place the stove out of major traffic areas within the household. You don't want to be bumping into it or have to fear that a small child might fall into it. A radiant stove is not anywhere near as dangerous as most people are inclined to believe where a small child is concerned. Athough an accidental fall is a very real possibility, you can block off the area with railings or other barriers. Children are often more aware of situations than we readily give them credit for and they learn very fast to stay away from an area that is dominated by heat. If you allow them to experience the rays of heat that are thrown from the unit, they will be less inclined to experiment on their own.

Make sure that you have chosen the right size radiant stove to take care of your heating needs. There are pros and cons for using a stove that is considered to have too large a heating capacity for the area or to make a smaller stove work harder. The theory behind pushing a smaller stove to run hot is that it will operate more efficiently and that smoldering fires will not be a potential hazard. I

never really endorsed that theory. I do not feel that there is any reason why you should be compelled to completely fill the firebox of a larger unit. That way you can still avoid the constant smoldering fires. The advantage is that when more heat is being called for you will have the capabilities of providing it.

There is no reason that a larger unit has to drive you out of your house, due to its tremendous heat, if you know how to operate it. The difference in cost between the larger units and the smaller units is almost negligible. The heating capabilities *can* make the difference in heating comfort. This is especially true if you have leaks that draw the heat out.

## CAPTURE A MAXIMUM AMOUNT OF HEAT

To take advantage of all of the radiant heat that your stove is capable of producing, you should learn how a stove radiates it's heat. Basically, it flows in a circular motion, rises up to the ceiling, and, then flows outward. As it meets the chill of the walls, it will bounce back down to the floor, rise, and warm up again. It is interesting to note that a radiant stove functions opposite that of most types of central heating systems. Radiators and registers, being located along outer walls, circulate warmth up and down the wall to keep the wall and adjacent air warm. A radiant stove, being a source of circulating radiant heat, will emit it's heat directly at whatever is close by. A great deal of it's energy flows straight up, until it reaches that cold spot, and then down again.

You will want your stove to be positioned where it's warmth can be best used. Remember that the cold air, at the extremes of the circulated motion of heat, is only comparatively cool when you consider that the heating temperatures, inside the stove, will rise to over 1000°. If you choose a radiant stove with enough heating capacity, your worries will be few.

Obtaining the utmost heat from a solid-fuel unit is simply a matter of proper distribution. When a fire is restricted inside the firebox, the heat over the stove begins to expand and push out in a circular motion. When the cooler air bounces to the floor (warms, and rises again) it is convection that has caused this action. If the heat is directed to other areas of the house, mechanical convection would be it's means of transmission.

If possible, do not depend upon any means that must be electrically operated to transmit the heat through your house. If you do so, you might be spending more money than necessary on utility bills. And in the case of an electrical outage, you would not be able to provide enough heat within your house.

### PROVIDING AN ADEQUATE DRAFT

You will have to create a draft to the solid-fuel unit if the draft within the house is not sufficient. Older homes seldom have this kind of "problem." But with so many more conscientious people using energy saving types of insulation and with houses now being built specifically for electric heat, some houses are simply so airtight that fresh air must be supplied from the outdoors. Cracking open a window, near the solid-fuel unit, might be all that is necessary to supply the needed draft. If this is not feasible in your case, then a pipe can be vented to provide more of a draft. It is very important that you are able to control the amount of air coming in from the outside. You certainly do not want to create a chill.

### INSTALLATIONS AND HEATING EFFICIENCY

The installation of the flue is important in order to operate your solid-fuel unit at maximum efficiency. A flue is a guide that takes advantage of the natural tendency of hot air to rise by insulating it's warmth and directing it up and out through the chimney. Hot air will rise faster if it is kept warm. The higher the flue the greater the possibility is of a stronger exhaust and a better draw. When you are starting a new fire, the flue should be preheated to prevent smoke from chilling and being emitted into the room. Once the flue has obtained the proper temperatures, it will not cool the rising air and a good draw will be created.

The best way to derive a good draft from the installation of a proper flue is to offer a negligible amount of impediments to the natural upflow of the warm air. The chimney or stack should be installed as straight up as possible and as high as practicality will allow. Keep the top free from any barriers that could interfere with the air flow. If your chimney is not airtight, cracks can let cold air in or sparks out. It only takes one spark to burn down a house.

To prevent hot gases from pouring out of the stove, plan the direction of the stovepipe. Stovepipe will heat up to it's hottest points at the elbows and any place where the pipe takes a change of direction such as from horizontal to vertical or any other directional change.

For the stove to function at it's best, make sure that all of the stovepipe is connected firmly. If you are not sure of it's airtightness, insert a flashlight into the stove. Close the doors, close the air controls, and shut off the lights in the room. The light should not be able to beam out if the connections are as tight as they should be. Airtightness can be maintained if the stovepipe is installed at a slightly upward slope from the stove to the connection. Remember that the stovepipe radiates as much heat, if not more, than the stove. Keep this in mind when you are planning the installation of the stovepipe. You will also have to take into consideration the capacity of the solid-fuel unit and it's heat output. Make sure that the stovepipe is never too hot to the touch.

Chimney's are affected by air currents, the outside temperature, and any obstructions to the free flow of a natural draft. For example, a house located at the bottom of a hill will encounter chimney problems because too much air can pour in to create too much of a draft and a faster burning fire. There will be a great loss of efficiency. A strong current of air can affect any chimney. You will have to take this into consideration when you are evaluating the probable burn rate of a fire on a cold or windy night. Increasing the height of the chimney will help prevent such downdrafts. Nevertheless, it might be better to remove obstructions rather than to build such a high unattractive chimney.

A chimney cap can deflect air. A revolving type of chimney cap might be able to turn the wind velocity to your advantage. Consulting a professional to access your situation would be the best advice. Each circumstance is very different from the next, and there can never be any hard and fast rule that could be applied in all situations.

## BACKPUFFING

You will have to accept a little *backpuffing* from your solid fuel unit every now and again. The popping noise might take you by surprise. If you understand the cause of backpuffing, you will not be bothered by it very often. It is in no way an indication that your solid-fuel unit is going to "blow up."

Backpuffing can occur under a variety of circumstances such as too much baffling or a wet piece of wood. The overall cause is from an insufficient amount of oxygen being allowed to the fire. The solid fuel will burn at smoldering levels. When a rush of fresh oxygen is allowed to the fire, such as by opening the door(s), air coming through the draft control, or from a downdraft within the chimney, gases ignite and the noise, that results can be startling. Sometimes smoke is emitted into the room from the solid-fuel unit or the stovepipe.

Too much baffling can be a cause of backpuffing. Too much baffling allows an excessive amount of gases to remain in the firebox, and they can ignite. When too much moisture has to be burned off the solid fuel, such as with a wet piece of wood, smoldering fires occur.

You might be able to eliminate some of the circumstances that result in backpuffing by stoking the fire with less wood, at any one given time, and using larger pieces when you do. Before opening the doors, if you allow a little more air to be emitted through the air control system, the fire will begin to burn with more of a blaze and you will not be taken aback by the great gush of air that will rush to the fire. Always stand to the side of the door when you open it. It would be a good idea not to look in on a fire until it is blazing, and all of the possibilities of backpuffing have probably been eliminated.

## SMOKING

Smoke results, most of the time, from inadequate draft. The draft in an airtight stove is dependent on the intake of air through the air control inlet(s). It can also be dependent on the draw that is created in the chimney.

By heating the flue, you are not allowing the smoke and gases to be cooled off too quickly (which could result in it thrusting the smoke back into the room). Most people will, however, experience some semblance of this problem with the first fire of the season or with the very first fire they make with the solid-fuel unit. This will only be a temporary problem. The flue might need more time and hotter heating temperatures before it functions efficiently. In addition, the paint on a new stove, or a newly painted stove, needs some time to bake on.

Inferior grades of solid fuel or wet wood will be a cause of smoke. Do not blame the solid-fuel burner for it. Always allow enough circulation of the air between the solid fuel. If enough oxygen is allowed to complete the combustion process, the solid fuel will not smolder.

## MAXIMUM COAL-BURNING EFFICIENCY

The draft that is required for burning coal is different from the draft that is required for burning wood. First, you need more of it. A coal fire burns from the center and from the bottom up. It seems that the draft that is fed to the unit from the bottom (underneath the grate) would be a stronger one than that of a draft that feeds the air from the top. If you do not have a precise draft it would be difficult to burn hard coal with any amount of efficiency. You would only be able to burn soft coal that does not require as much direct air feed.

Remember that soft coal has a tendency to smoke. It might even possess low fusion temperatures that could cause clinkers.

One of the differences between heating with wood and heating with coal is the time it takes to build a good coal fire. It takes very little time to get a wood fire blazing. You can just open the air controls or one of the doors to create a super good draw. With a coal fire, it takes at least an hour before you can benefit from it's warmth. When you turn the stove or add-on boiler down for the day (as you probably would do when there is not going to be anyone in the house during that time), you have to anticipate this lag time upon returning home. If you are using an add-on boiler unit, you will have the choice of whether to set the furnace to automatically turn on and use your main source of heat or bear with the lag time in providing warmth to the area to be heated.

Shaking the grate properly is one of the main points of coal fire regulation and efficiency. By shaking the coals down, you are supplying more oxygen to the fire. If properly done, this will cause hotter coal fire temperatures. But if you overshake it, you could lose some of the burnable substances. Ideally, you will shake just enough of the ash down to allow the remaining coal and burnable remains to continue to burn efficiently. On the other side of the coin is that by undershaking the coal you will not allow the much-needed oxygen supply to circulate the coal bed. Therefore, the coal cannot adequately complete it's combustion.

After an overnight burn, it is probably the best procedure (when burning coal) to open the draft control for a period of time, before rebanking it, and after cleaning the accumulated ash. Bank the unit, within about 40 minutes, and regulate the air controls accordingly. Leave the secondary air open long enough to burn off the gases. Leave open the air feed inlet, under the grate, to allow for the burn rate that is required. Take into consideration the outside temperatures, the wind velocity, and the heat output with regard to the day's needs. Always leave an amount of coal exposed to aid in quickly burning off the gases.

To obtain the most efficient burn with coal, use anthracite coal that is low in ash content, fusion temperature, moisture, sulfur content, and volatile gases, and that is high in fixed carbons.

Before using your coal-burning solid-fuel unit to provide total heating capacity, it is wise to slowly break it in. Start with a kindling fire and add only a small amount of coal. Allow it to burn until it is glowing. Shut the air controls totally down and allow the firebox to cool down. Overnight would be good. Then build a new fire, but this time allow it to burn for a longer period of time. Again shut it down and allow the firebox to cool down. This procedure will give you a fire of long endurance, and your grate

will be seasoned. You will not have to worry about warping the grate after building a fire with high temperatures.

## ENERGY CONSERVATION METHODS

Most energy conservation methods apply to the operation of a solid-fuel unit unless you seal the area to be heated too tightly.

If there is no way for the heat to escape, more will be captured within this area and circulated. Insulate your attic and any exterior walls. Caulk and weather strip any cracks around doors and windows. If you are unable to install storm windows, cover the windows with a heavy sheet of plastic. You would be amazed how much heat is allowed to escape through an inadequate storm door. It is more than worth the investment. Make sure that the door is a tight fit, but allow for some expansion if the door is near concrete or other surface that could expand with moisture.

To get more heating capacity out of the stove of your choice, close off any rooms that are not being used. You might find that ceiling heights are more than you bargained for when calculating heating costs of solid-fuel unit capacity. If this becomes a real problem, and you are unable to lower the ceilings, then, I would recommend ceiling fans. They are attractive and they can aid heating efficiency and in circulating cooler air during the warm months of the year.

## OPERATING AN ADD-ON BOILER

Exactly how your add-on boiler will function depends upon the type of installation that you choose. Made sure that you refer to Chapter 24. You will now begin to see all of your hard work pay off in satisfaction and in cash. In most cases, boilers and their installation costs usually pay for themselves within one normal heating season. Even if you must buy the wood, you can expect a tremendous savings by the beginning of the second season.

## OPERATING SAFELY

Safety should always be on the operator's mind. Remember that a solid-fuel unit is a piece of equipment just as is your lawnmower or welding machine. It should be respected. You shouldn't be afraid of it. You simply should pay strict attention to what you are doing while any piece of equipment is in operation. Start your unit as follows.

□ Open the inlet and outlet valves. Using the lever on the safety valve, and domestic coil check valves, bleed all of the air out of the solid-fuel burner as it fills with water. Also close the bypass valve between the two T's in the line. If you don't you will probably melt all of the solder in the lines and you could run the risk of destroying the accessories (aquastate, circulator, temperature pressure gauge, etc.).

□ Start the fire as you would normally start a fire—using wood—whether you are going to be burning wood or coal. Once the fire is going, coal should be added.

□ While the fire is getting started, take the time to label the inlet and outlet check valves with a tag labeled *wood (or coal) boiler, leave on*. This is to ensure that no one turns these valves off by accident. This situation would isolate your unit. It would have no place to expel or receive water, and it would become hazardous. A safety valve is part of the add-on boiler package. Built up steam pressure can be drawn off or relieved. This will prevent a possible explosion of the water jacket. You will, however, still run the risk of the destruction of your accessories and also experience a very wet floor.

□ Once the unit is burning normally, watch the temperature gauge. You should start to cut the fire back (using your air control system) at about 140°. Bring the air slide to the half-closed position. This should show the rise in temperature. You can estimate that it will take about 10 minutes before you see the change on your indicator.

□ Using a screwdriver, turn the temperature adjustment control down on the aquastate until the circulator comes on. This is how you test the aquastate and circulator. Once this safety test has been completed, set the aquastate somewhere between 160° and 180°. Later this may have to be raised or lowered; it depends on your needs and the degree of insulation in your house. The setting will be the temperature that will activate the circulator to transfer the hot water to the furnace or the house.

□ Locate the low limit control on your aquastate for your furnace. Set that aquastate about 10° lower than the aquastate on your solid fuel unit. This will complete your parallel hookup.

□ All that needs to be attended to now is your fire. It would be most advisable to run your unit a little hotter, during the evening hours, when there will be more of a demand for hot water to be used in meal preparation, clean up, and bathing. Before retiring for the evening, load the unit as full as you are able to and cut the air control down until it is only open a crack—to give you a low burn. In the morning, reload the unit. Open the air control and allow it to run hot for about 10 minutes. This raises the water temperature (for the coming demands of the day), and keeps the creosote level (when burning wood) down in your chimney. This is a good time to check the water temperatures to be sure everything is operating as it should. Once the system is functioning, normally, you will become accustomed to taking charge of it's operating procedure as you would with any other solid-fuel burner.

If you do not understand *all* of the starting procedures that are involved in the operation of your unit, call a reliable plumber and let him instruct you. It is of utmost importance that you follow the proper procedures when you are starting the unit and you are also testing the safety equipment. You are also bringing it into line and adjusting it in conjunction with your existing furnace and heating system.

After you have been running the unit for a couple of days, you might find that some fine adjustment is required of your aquastate in order to increase the efficiency of your unit to your individual needs. Usually, all of these adjustments can be made within one week. From then on, all that you will have to do is tend to the fire and clean out the ashes every now and again.

This system is not that difficult to understand. It simply operates by heating the water in your existing system by passing the returning heating system water through the solid-fuel unit (passing over the firebox). By keeping the water hot with the solid-fuel boiler, you keep your existing furnace off.

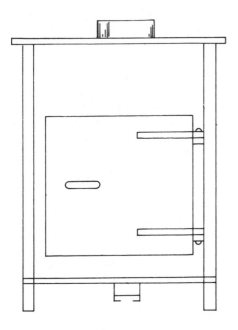

# Chapter 24

# Installations

**T**HERE ARE MANY WAYS TO HOOK up a stove or a boiler to a house. The quality of the chimney is just as important as the efficiency of the solid-fuel unit. A chimney must perform the very basic function of creating a draft that supplies fresh air to the fire. It must also vent the rising heat that draws the gases and smoke to safety. Airtightness in the chimney is crucial. In an airtight wood or coal stove, the draw of the chimney can become a major factor in the efficiency of the stove. All the air that is needed to exhaust through the chimney must be drawn through the stove. If this is done, then you have a stove that functions as it should.

## INSPECT A CHIMNEY FOR SAFETY

If you are not constructing a new chimney, it would be best to have your existing chimney inspected for safety. You cannot be sure of the workmanship and the materials unless you check it yourself while it is being built. Ask the local fire department to send someone out. In some cases, it is required by law. If it is not required by law, the department will proba-

bly be most willing to comply. A mason can also perform this task.

For homes built approximately 75 to 100 years ago, in an age when there was no knowledge of tile-lined chimneys, have a chimney sweep or mason inspect the chimney before the stove is hooked up. More than likely the chimney will have to be cleaned.

When chimney is in good condition, the stove can be hooked into it without worry. If the chimney is in poor condition, make the necessary improvements.

You can begin by checking out some of the chimney safety features on your own. This will give you an idea of what to expect. A masonry block chimney should be tile lined. The safety value of this lining has been proven. The tile lining is similar in material to that of a clay flower pot, but it is made of a harder substance. If you look down the chimney, with a flashlight, the flue will seem smooth and uniform. Upon scraping the surface of the tile lining, you will discover that it is much harder than brick. If the tile lining has not previously been installed, it would be advisable to do it now. The tile lining is available on the market. It is a ceramic tile usually in the form of a square or a circular shape. It creates a hard, smooth surface that creosote is unable to cling to, and will aid in making the chimney airtight.

If a tile lining has been provided, make sure that it is in good condition. You do not want the hot gases and creosote to be allowed to escape the flue prematurely and possibly start a fire. The lining and chimney must be checked for cracks. If the tile lining is not already provided in the existing chimney, the chimney might have to be completely rebuilt.

Because the flue tiles are brittle they can crack. A smoke test can be performed. This can be done by building a smokey fire in the fireplace or stove. By covering the top of the flue, the smoke from the fire will be forced through any cracks or holes. If smoke leaks out, the chimney must be repaired or it should not be used. If you do use this test, you must be prepared for smoke being emitted into the house.

The concrete might have to be repointed. This is the process of adding more concrete between the blocks or bricks. You can find loose mortar by scraping between the bricks. If the mortar crumbles easily, the old mortar will have to be scraped out. The brick must be removed and new mortar installed before the brick is replaced.

## GENERAL CHIMNEY SAFETY

Be aware of other safety hazards. Do not use a masonry chimney if it has been supported by shelves or brackets. The brackets have a tendency to weaken. You would be taking a chance that the chimney could fall while it is in use. It would be totally inadvisable to use a chimney that is also used to support the framing of the house. The heat that is conducted to the frame could eventually start a fire.

An interior chimney must have a clearance of a full 2 inches between any combustible material that is required in the building of a chimney. A zero clearance is only acceptable if the chimney is a full 8″ thicker at this point. These are standard safety precautions. Some areas have their own regulations. Check the safety codes that would pertain to you. Some safety codes will allow an exterior chimney to have one side in contact with exterior sheathing.

If more than one appliance is to be connected to a flue, you might experience backdrafts of carbon monoxide into your home. To install a fireplace flue in a stove, the fireplace opening must be entirely closed off by a noncombustible material.

It would be wise not to use a snap-in type of cover for any of the chimney pipe inlets that are not in use. If you take this chance, the heat from a chimney fire could easily cause them to pop out. Fill in these holes with the same masonry material or tile that you use to build or repair your chimney. Make sure that care is taken to build this up to the same thickness as the existing chimney.

Although a reducer can be used, with no expected problems, to connect a large flue to a smaller stove pipe as installed in a solid-fuel unit, it is not recommended that you use a chimney with a flue area twice the size or more than the required size stove pipe of the stove or boiler unit. Backdrafts can result from such use.

The height of the existing chimney, or the new one to be built, is also an important area of inspection. It is a relatively simple task for a mason or installer to extend a chimney that does not meet the minimum standards of common safety practice or those required by state or local building codes. Extend your chimneys at least 3 feet above a flat roof and at least 2 feet above the highest point of a pitched roof within 10 feet of the installation. This safety precaution is to prevent downdrafts and fires that could result from sparks.

It should be a constant concern to keep the safety of the chimney always up to the standards required by law, simple common sense, and safety practices. A chimney must be inspected on a yearly basis. Just because a chimney is in good working order at the beginning of a burning season, does not necessarily mean that it will be in the same shape after a season of use. It is best to inspect a chimney for loose bricks, and the possibility of the mortar becoming weakened, settled, or cracked.

During the summer when the chimney is not in use, birds may find it a perfect place to build their nest. Bees have been known to build their hives in chimneys. At the beginning of each season, inspect the chimney, make repairs, and make sure that it is cleaned. No heating season should begin before you account for all safety precautions. Chimney caps or cleanout T's might help to prevent some problem.

## WHAT TYPE OF CHIMNEY TO BUILD

At one time, an insulated pipe chimney was always less expensive than a block chimney. This is not necessarily the case anymore. Due to rising costs, within the industry and it's success, a masonry block chimney is economical to purchase. Labor costs are the differentiating factor. A pipe chimney can be put up by almost any homeowner. A block chimney requires some knowledge of the masonry trade.

You will have to investigate the costs of material and potential labor costs. A block chimney will have to be tile lined. Aside from the hard, smooth surface that is a great aid to the prevention of creosote build up, the lining helps in creating the airtightness that is necessary for solid-fuel burning efficiency.

Be aware of confusing the terms *stovepipe* and chimney. They are not interchangeable; they are two different things. Stovepipe—used for the inside of the house—is referred to as a single-wall stovepipe. The pipe used in building a chimney is referred to as insulated stovepipe.

## INSULATED STOVEPIPE

If you decide to use a pipe chimney, all the pipe going through the wall—or that which is mounted on the exterior side of the house—must be insulated stovepipe. There are various types on the market; the brand names are endless. Use a chimney that is round and stainless steel.

Check for the minimal clearance required in the installation of insulated pipe. If the pipe is well insulated, it will only require a 2″ clearance from combustible material. Make sure that it will survive a safety test where the flue gases have temperatures far higher than you will probably ever obtain in the normal use of your solid-fuel unit.

Insulated pipe must be used on the outside of a chimney for it's corrosion resistant properties, but it is primarily used to insulate the smoke from being cooled by the outside air. If single wall stovepipe is used on the exterior of the house, very serious conditions can occur. The cooling process, created inside the single wall stovepipe, will build up creosote rapidly, and weather elements such as wind and rain will cause corrosion of the pipe. Consequently, this situation presents little protection against a fire.

The insulated pipe should be able to keep the smoke at least 220° or above. The insulation will allow the smoke to stay a gas, rise, and go out of the chimney. In the event that the smoke cools below 220°, the smoke will begin to turn back into its liquid state (water, tree sap, and etc.). This condensation is creosote. Creosote cannot be left unattended or uncleaned. Creosote is basically a petroleum product and it burns the same as gas and oil. When you use stovepipe (chimney pipe), on the exterior part of the house, this buildup can be partially eliminated. You will still have to take safety precautions both in operating your unit and in building and using your chimney.

## SINGLE-WALL STOVEPIPE

Inside a house, a lot of people prefer the use of single-wall stovepipe because single-wall stovepipe will radiate as much heat, if not more, than the stove itself. If you are familiar, with the old Pennsylvania churches (possibly, just through pictures), you might remember seeing the stove operating at one end and exhausted out of the other end. A great deal of stovepipe had to be used and it radiated the maximum amount of heat. This idea can be used, in moderation, in your home.

A stovepipe must be installed to help create a good draft (which will carry the hot gases away quickly and safely). A flue is the same thing as a stovepipe. It is attached to the chimney. Think of the flue or stovepipe as being the interior passageway of the chimney. In it the smoke will rise, in a funnel-like manner, into the exterior passageway of the chimney. This passageway must be able to accommodate this motion.

The draft in a chimney is created by variance in pressure of the outside air, in contrast to the air that is contained in the chimney. The difference of the temperatures, and the height of the chimney, produce the type of draft that will result in your chimney.

## SAFELY INSTALLING STOVEPIPE

Stovepipe turns and bends (as is done with elbows) should be kept to a minimum. The use of only one elbow would be more up to safety standards. When exhausting stovepipe, both horizontally positioned and vertically positioned, the horizontal stovepipe should never be more than 75 percent of the vertical portion of the stovepipe that is used. It is best to attempt a constant vertical rise of the stovepipe, from the stove to the chimney, and especially for a distance of over 5 feet. Stovepipe that is directly connected to a chimney, horizontally, must rise at least ¼ inch per foot. This will induce the rise of an upward movement of hot gases.

The pipe connector needed for each of the models in this book is listed in the general information section of each particular design. Make sure that you purchase the proper stovepipe size to match the connector. If the chimney flue is built with an inside diameter that is much too large for the solid fuel unit, the temperature of the gases can be cooled off too quickly. Where the heat would be compacted longer, in a narrower chimney flue, would be ideal. You will want the stovepipe pieces to be fitted together tightly. Then it can be permanently joined with just a couple of screws to prevent the stovepipe from being shaken apart by high heat temperatures.

Stovepipes are sold in many different gauges (thicknesses) and diameters. A thick pipe gauge is a good investment because it will last longer. A pipe gauge of 24 is recommended (or even thicker if possible). The thicker gauges are indicated by the lower gauge numbers. You can expect to replace the stovepipe on occasion. Do not expect it to last much longer than two or three years. When burning coal, fly ash can build up and weaken your stovepipe. Weak spots are sometimes easily revealed by discoloration. If you are unsure whether the fly ash has built up, try tapping the pipe. A dull thud will probably indicate that the stovepipe should be replaced.

If you follow the instructions and build your solid fuel unit as precisely as possible, you should have an airtight unit. It is not necessary to provide a damper in the stovepipe. It is only the non-airtight units that would benefit from such a damper. By the reduction of air flow, through the common damper, the chances of a chimney fire can be significantly reduced. The only damper that need be provided in an airtight unit are the air controls provided in the inlet air feed, and—for the use of coalburning—the secondary air control system. In the case of a chimney fire, the inlet air-feed controls can be shut down. This will prevent the supply of additional oxygen.

It is not advisable to pass stovepipe through a wall, unless special precautions are taken. You must use an insulated wall thimble or a ventilated thimble that has been specifically made for the use of radiant, solid-fuel units. The thimble must be made of sheet metal or asbestos millboard. It should be at least three times larger in diameter than the stovepipe.

*Never* run stovepipe through concealed places such as a closet or an attic. Stovepipe must have a clearance from any combustible surface or material. The proper clearance would be approximately triple the diameter of the stovepipe. The average 8-inch stovepipe would require a clearance of 24 inches. This is only a general rule of thumb. Requirements vary according to area building codes.

Always take care when attaching the stovepipe to a chimney. If you are using a masonry chimney, a special connector thimble will have to be installed. Once the stovepipe is fitted into this thimble, the connection should be permanently cemented in place. This thimble should not be extended into the flue.

## DO NOT USE SHORTCUTS

If you take shortcuts in installation procedures or if you use inferior quality materials, you will be cheating yourself and your family out of the comfort derived from the use of complete safety measures.

Do not skimp. By building your own solid-fuel unit, you might have saved enough to purchase the proper installation materials. If you have installed your solid-fuel unit, using complete safety standards, you will be able to comfortably sleep nights. You will also derive maximum efficiency from your solid-fuel unit.

## FLUE CAPACITIES

If you are hooking up an add-on boiler, you probably have thought about whether or not you can use a flue that is already being used by your existing heating system. Many ordinances forbid such use. The theory is that operating a solid-fuel unit (when an existing heating system is in use) would have a tendency to hinder the exhaust of the fuel oil fumes because wood smoke is lighter than fuel oil fumes.

My opinion is that a proper installation would create a continual draw, by the solid-fuel burner, and this would aid in the emission of any fuel-oil fumes. Having both heating systems in operation at the same time would only result from an abnormal demand upon the heating systems or the fire not being properly tended. If you are not defying any local codes, there are *some* situations that would allow for a safe installation into an existing flue.

Many experts will advise against such an installation. Use common sense and safety standards to install your unit. Do not violate safety codes. If it is necessary, install a new flue.

A fireplace and a furnace should never be operated on the same flue. The amount of draft that is required for a fireplace to function is an interference with the proper operation of a furnace. If a fireplace is totally closed off and not in operation, then the flue is not affected in any way, by the draft that would be associated with it. You also have to take into consideration that many furnaces are operated with the use of a barometric damper. Refer to the section in Chapter 4 dealing with options and the barometric damper.

The barometric damper can be referred to as the secondary air system of fuel oil or natural gas furnaces. It supplies the extra air to the chimney to help vent exhaust fumes in oil and gas furnaces. The draw of the chimney is regulated by this device. This allows an excess into the chimney. The problem is that these devices (also a vent or hood used with a gas-type furnace) will continue to operate when the solid-fuel unit is operating. This results in the same amount of excess air flow to the chimney. It is my opinion that a solid-fuel unit, burning continuously, would cause a continuous draw on the chimney and that barometric damper would always be open. If you consider the principles behind a chimney draw, it would make the starting of a wood fire extremely difficult and the starting of a coal fire even more so. If the chimney can draw it's air from an alternate source, it would cease to draw air from the firebox. This would probably cause a coal fire to go out within a short period of time. It only stands to reason that if no air is drawin through the coal to feed it, the combustion process cannot continue to take place.

With a device that creates an excess of air, the stack can be easily cooled. This creates a great deal more creosote buildup than normal. In the case of a chimney fire, the device could provide so much oxygen to the fire that it could burn beyond control.

If more than one appliance is connected to the same flue, backdrafts of carbon monoxide can occur. Smoke, ashes, and sparks might backflow between the two heating units. This will *not* happen if you have a top-notch chimney that has been, inspected and maintained. The recommended hookups provide that the connection to be at least 12 to 14 inches below where the existing exhaust pipe to the heating furnace is located. This is one of the installations as mentioned in Chapter 22 that requires checking pipes for creosote on no less than a monthly basis. If the creosote has built up to approximately ¼", clean it.

If you are in doubt about whether or not to use the existing flue as a connection for your add-on boiler unit, or possibly even your radiant stove, follow this basic rule. If your flue checks out legally and is up to the safety standards, consider that the combined area of all the stovepipes that are being exhausted into the existing flue should be less than the area of the flue itself.

In other words, a standard flue, being a foot squared, could accept as many as six to seven 6-inch flue pipes even if all of the heating units were in operation at the same time. *Carefully* check your installation, step by step, to ensure a safe and efficient installation.

## BOILER HOOKUPS

Before you even start to read this section, check with your local building inspector. He will be able to advise you on any state or local building codes that apply to the hook-up of an add-on, solid-fuel burner to your existing heating system. There are probably more ordinances dealing with this type of hook-up than any other installation. There are any number of ways an add-on unit can be hooked into your heating system. Some ways are better than others. Much depends on the layout of your cellar and heating system. Normally you would think that placing the unit next to your existing furnace would be the best location. That might very well hold true, but you might run into the problem of space. Do you have enough room to place the unit next to the existing furnace? If you don't, it doesn't matter because the add-on unit can be placed anywhere in the house and piped to your existing furnace. You might have to put up another chimney if your building codes demand it.

The placement of an add-on is quite flexible. One of my customers hooked up his unit to an existing chimney, hooked it up to his fireplace, and piped it to his furnace. Another customer, having trouble with cold air seeping into his house from his connecting unheated garage, placed the unit in his garage and ran the pipes through a connecting wall, and back to his furnace. By doing this, he killed two birds with one stone. The radiant heat, that was emitted from the unit and exhaust pipe, took the chill out of the garage and, at the same time, the hot water that was produced by the unit kept the house totally heated.

Because add-ons are water jacketed, they can be placed within 6 inches of a noncombustible wall. The location of the unit should be of little problem to the homeowner and the versatility of it's use goes unquestioned.

Assuming that you have now positioned your add-on unit, a number of plumbing materials and small hand tools will be needed to hook up the unit. You will now have to decide whether you are going to use threaded pipe or copper tubing to hook up the unit. Copper tubing is lighter and easier to work with and you don't have to be quite as accurate with your measurements. If you decide to use threaded pipe, find someone who is knowledgeable with pipe layout. With threaded pipe, you really have to be much more accurate in all of your measurements.

To figure out the amount of materials you will measure the path your pipes will take to reach the add-on unit. Take into consideration the elbows that will be needed. Also take into account that you will be installing a union valve and a shut-off valve into each of these lines. A *union valve* is a threaded connection placed in a pipe line so that the line can be disconnected without cutting the pipe. The valve (I prefer a gate valve) will be used to shut off the water to your add-on unit during the summer months or when the unit is not in use. If the unit is not being used for some time, the water must be shut off to your add-on unit because the existing furnace will continue to heat the water in the add-on unit.

The following are materials you will need to hook up your unit.

### Using Copper

Two T's used to tap the add-on unit into existing inlet and outlet lines.

Two 1″ gate valves.

Eight ¾″ thread-to-sweat adaptors (two for each valve, two for your minicirculator, two for connection to the add-on unit).

A number of 1″ elbows.

Two 1″ unions (one for each line; for disconnection if needed).

An amount of 1″ copper tubing.

One roll of Teflon tape (used to seal threaded connections).

One roll of solder.

One small can of soldering paste.

Some steel wool (used for cleaning copper before soldering).

One tubing cutter (for cutting copper tubing).

One butane torch and a striker to ignite the torch.

### Domestic Coil Hookup

An amount of ½″ copper tubing (this depends on the path of your lines).

Two ½″ T's (used to tie into your existing lines).

Two ½″ shut-off valves.

A number of ½″ elbows.

Two ½″ thread-to-sweat adaptors (used to tie lines into coil).

### Threaded Pipe Hookup

An amount of 1″ pipe (this depends on the path of the pipe).

A number of threaded elbows and couplings.

Two 1″ unions (one for each line).

Two 1″ shut-off valves (one for each line).

Two 1″ T's (used for tapping into the existing lines).

One roll of Teflon tape or one can of pipe dope. This is used to seal the threaded joints.

Two or more pipe wrenches.

A pipe threader (this tool should be rented not bought) or the pipe could possibly be precut and threaded. If you do get the pipe precut and threaded, all measurements must be exact.

One pipe cutter (this can be and should be rented).

After comparing the preceding lists, you will probably agree that hooking up an add-on unit using copper is much less expensive and easier than trying to do it with threaded pipe.

Perhaps you're saying to yourself, "but I don't know how to sweat pipe!" Well it's a lot easier than threading. All you have to do is the following.

☐ Measure the tubing to size and cut it.

☐ Once the tubing is cut, clean it with steel wool until it shines.

☐ With steel wool, clean the inside of the fitting, until it shines.

☐ Apply soldering paste to both the fitting and tube, and connect them.

☐ Light the torch with the striker (*not* with a match or lighter). Heat the connection until the solder runs like water.

When melted, the solder will be sucked into the connection. When the solder starts to drip from the bottom of the connection, you are finished. Do not move the connection until the solder has cooled. If you follow these directions, you will have absolutely no problem. Sweating tubing is very simple to do as long as it is done with care.

### The Preferred Hookup Method

To hook up your unit, first shut off and drain the furnace. You should find shut-off valves where fresh water is fed into the furnace and where hot water leaves and returns to the boiler. The feed line to the radiators can usually be found coming out of the top of the furnace. The return line can be found toward the bottom of the furnace. That is the line with the circulator or circulators on it.

By shutting the system down at these points of entry and exit, you eliminate having to drain the whole heating system. Whether you will find shut-off valves at these points depends upon the workmanship of the plumber who installed your furnace.

If shut-off valves are absent, the entire system must be drained. Most furnaces have a drain valve on them. Use this to drain the system. If a drain valve cannot be found, then a drain plug or cutting a pipe open will do. If you do have to drain your system in this manner, be prepared for a mess. Assuming that you have now drained the furnace or heating system, you can begin to install the add-on unit.

Using a tubing cutter or pipe cutter, cut the return line open. This should be between your circulator, or circulators, and furnace. If the cut cannot be made at this point, then anywhere close to the furnace will do.

Allowing for the length of your T's sweat or thread the T into the return line and rehook the line to the furnace.

Once the return line is again hooked up, take the last opening left (on the T you've just installed) and connect one of the shut-off valves to it. Use a short section of tubing (or a nipple if you are using threaded pipe) to make the connection. Before installing each valve, be sure to check the direction of flow of each valve. This can be done by looking on the side of the valve. There you should see an arrow that shows you the direction of the flow as it passes through the valve. If no arrow is shown, then, the valve can be installed either way. See Fig. 24-1.

Next, repeat the instructions, given in the preceding paragraph, only this time on the house feed line as close to the point of exit from the furnace as possible. See Fig. 24-2.

If you will be using a domestic coil, shut off the feed water to the domestic coil on the existing furnace. Look for two ½″ water lines that enter the furnace through an access cover. To determine which one of the two is the feed, just feel them. The cold one is the feed; the hot one is the supply. To make sure you have found the right line, turn on a hot water tap. If nothing comes out, you've found the right line!

Cut the cold water feed line open, and install two T's and a shut-off valve as shown in Figs. 24-3 and 24-4. Once all the T's and valves are installed, make sure all of the newly, installed valves are closed because you cannot turn back on the domestic water lines and reactivate your heating system until this part of the installation is complete. The rest of the installation can now be done without further interruption of your heating and water systems. After filling your systems, don't forget to drain the air out of your lines. This is called purging the system.

Now that the systems are reactivated, begin to run the line from the return line to the add-on unit using tubing (or pipe) and elbows. This will be the feed line to the add-on unit. Fig. 24-2. When the (add-on) feed line is within about 2 feet of the add-on unit, install (using the thread-to-sweat adapters) the minicirculator. Pay attention to the direction of flow. After the circulator is installed, continue the line and connect it to the add-on unit.

Once the feed line is hooked up, start to run the house feed line. This is the line that you run from your existing house feed line to the outlet connection located at the top center of your add-on unit. Other than the union you will place in this line, this should be a straight run of tube (or pipe). See Fig.

24-2. For those of you with domestic coils, use tubing (or pipe) and elbows to connect the domestic coil to the cold-water feed line of your existing domestic coil. See Fig. 24-3.

Once all the lines have been run, the next thing you should do is attach all of the accessories and safety equipment to your add-on unit. Make sure that all threaded fittings are sealed.

Hook up the aquastate to the minicirculator. The packing boxes that hold the aquastate and minicirculator contain directions. If you are not accustomed to working with electricity or if you cannot understand the instructions provided, call in a licensed electrician and let him hook it up for you. This will complete the plumbing part of the installation.

The next thing you'll want to do is the chimney installation. Contact your local building inspector or your local fire department. They will be more than happy to advise you on how to hook up your unit.

### Connecting A Solid-Fuel Unit To A Flue

Do not hook into the same exhaust that a gas furnace is hooked into because exhaust chimneys usually are made out of single-wall stove pipe. Single-wall stove pipe cannot be used because a great deal of heat is radiated from it. If too much heat is radiated it could ignite a fire.

Fuel-oil exhaust chimneys are usually made of either brick or block and they will be tile lined. Refer to the state and local building codes. If your chimney is checked out and in good condition, you might be able to exhaust into the same chimney. Some local codes prohibit this type of hookup.

To hook into an existing flue (this procedure is predominately used for a water-jacketed boiler unit), you would start out by breaking a hole approximately 12″ to 14″ from where the existing exhaust pipe of the furnace is located. This will help exhaust fuel oil fumes and any other fumes that the furnace might have. If this is impossible, break a hole above the existing connection. Try this process before tying into the existing exhaust pipe. This connection looks just like a Y. It cannot be a T. If you try to

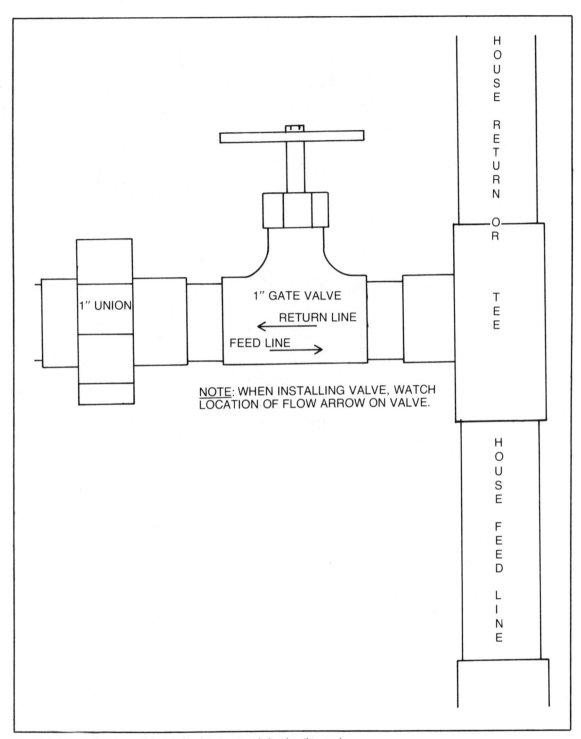

Fig. 24-1. Typical example of a pipe hookup to an existing heating system.

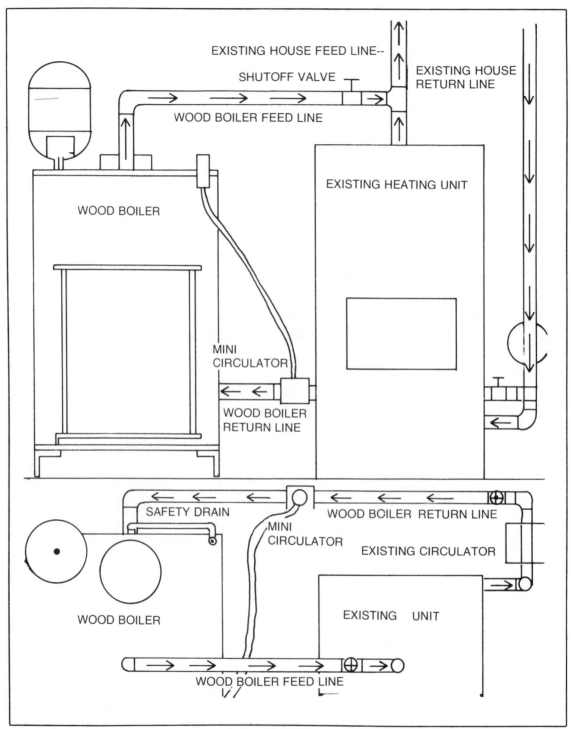

Fig. 24-2. Recommended hookup to an existing heating system.

ののたんHL

| Neighborhood | Address | Phone |
|---|---|---|
| Faneuil | 419 Faneuil S | 617-782 |
| Honan–Allston | 300 North Harv | 617-78 |
| Hyde Park | 35 Harva | 617-36 |
| Jamaica Plain | 12 Sedg | 617-524 |
| Mattapan | 10 Haze | 617-298 |
| Roslindale | 4238 Wash | 617-32 |
| South End | 685 Tre | 617-53 |
| West End | 151 Camb | 617-52 |
| West Roxbury | 1961 Ce | 617-32 |

For further information regarding ESL conve

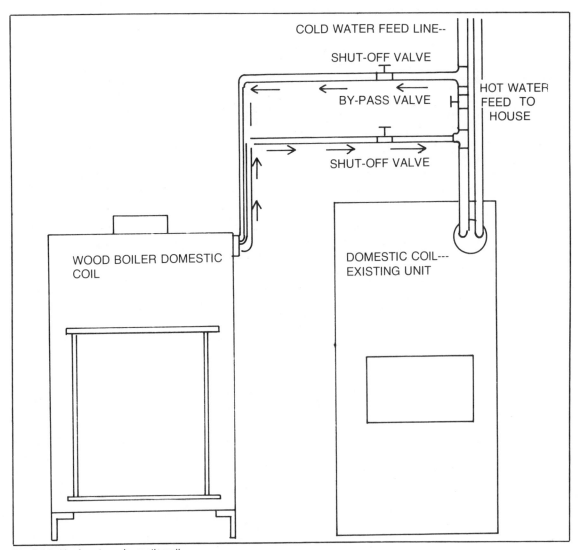

COLD WATER FEED LINE--

SHUT-OFF VALVE

BY-PASS VALVE

HOT WATER FEED TO HOUSE

SHUT-OFF VALVE

WOOD BOILER DOMESTIC COIL

DOMESTIC COIL--- EXISTING UNIT

Fig. 24-3. Hookup to a domestic coil.

use a T, the exhaust fumes from the boiler will be interrupted when the furnace comes on and you will, most likely, get backpuffing and backdrafting from the stove for a second or so. By using a Y, you will be flowing the exhaust together into the chimney. This procedure works very well.

### Boiler Operation

The add-on unit continuously makes hot water. When the water temperature reaches the temperature set on the aquastate, the aquastate turns on the minicirculator. The minicirculator begins to pull water from the furnace. This water is constantly cooling because, when your house is not calling for heat, the furnace is not running. At this point the circulator pushes the cooler water (from the furnace) into the add-on unit. At the same time, it also begins to pull the hot water (from the add-on unit) over to the furnace.

This provides two positive results. The first is that you will keep the furnace off (by keeping hot water in your furnace). Second, you are now storing hot water for future use. Very simply, you are circulating the water between the furnace and the add-on unit.

When your house begins to call for heat, hot water is pulled equally from the furnace and the add-on unit. This gives you all the hot water you'll need. In the event that you forget to load your add-on unit and it begins to go out, the existing furnace will automatically, kick on and provide the heat required by your house. This is why you should never turn off your furnace. It acts as a back up system for human failure.

The domestic coil (if you decide to use one) acts as a preheater. It heats the water even before it gets to your existing domestic coil (or hot water heater). All you have to do is close off the bypass. This detours the water through the coil. The water is heated as it goes to the existing furnace for storage in the domestic coil. While in storage the domestic water will be kept hot by the heating system water that is also stored there. Out of the three installations described in this book, this is probably the most efficient.

### Alternate Hookups

For this system, the extra hot water produced will be stored in a separate storage tank or dumped into the heating system of your house. This might cause your home to be warmer than you want. The benefit, of installing this type of system is that it is an easier system to install and you do not need a minicirculator. You will use the existing circulator.

In the following installations, the hookup of the domestic coil is the same as the last installation. Contact your local building inspector or fire department when it comes time to install the chimney. The only difference in the following installations is that the pipe you decide to tie into (the inlet or outlet pipe on your existing furnace). Refer to Figs. 24-5 and 24-6 and the following instructions.

☐ Cut the return line open somewhere between the existing circulator and where it goes through your cellar. In other words, somewhere before your circulator (preferably as close to the circulator as possible). *Or* cut your feed line open,

preferably, as close to the furnace as possible. See Figs. 24-5 and 24-6.

☐ Install two T's and three gate valves as shown in Fig. 24-4. Once the T's and valves are in place, close the two valves on the T's and open the valve between the two T's. Once this is done you can refill the heating system.

☐ Run the pipes to the add-on unit. The top T and valve will become the feed line to the add-on unit. The bottom T and valve will become the outlet line for the add-on unit. Do not mix up their location. They must be placed in order. Refer to Fig. 24-5 for verification of the location of each pipe.

☐ After the inlet and outlet pipes have been connected to the unit, the only thing left to do is hook up the aquastate. The aquastate will act as part of the safety system by hooking it up to the existing circulator. If you're not an electrician, call one and have him hook it up for you.

### How A Return Line Hookup Works

To bring the add-on unit into the system open the valves on the inlet and outlet lines and close the valve between the two T's. This detours the water (coming back to the furnace) to the add-on unit. There it is reheated and pumped back to the existing heater. If in the event you build up too much hot water, the aquastate turns on the house circulator and the hot water is dumped or pumped through the heating system.

### How A Feed Line Hookup Works

To bring the add-on unit into the system, open the valves on the inlet and outlet lines and close the valve located between the two T's. This detours the water to the add-on unit before it goes to the heating system. In the event of too much hot water being made, the aquastate turns on the existing house circulator and the hot water is dumped (or run) through the house system.

For this installation to work properly, the existing furnace aquastate must be turned down to a low setting to transfer the work load over to the add-on unit. If you forget to tend the fire, the furnace will come on. But by the time it does, the

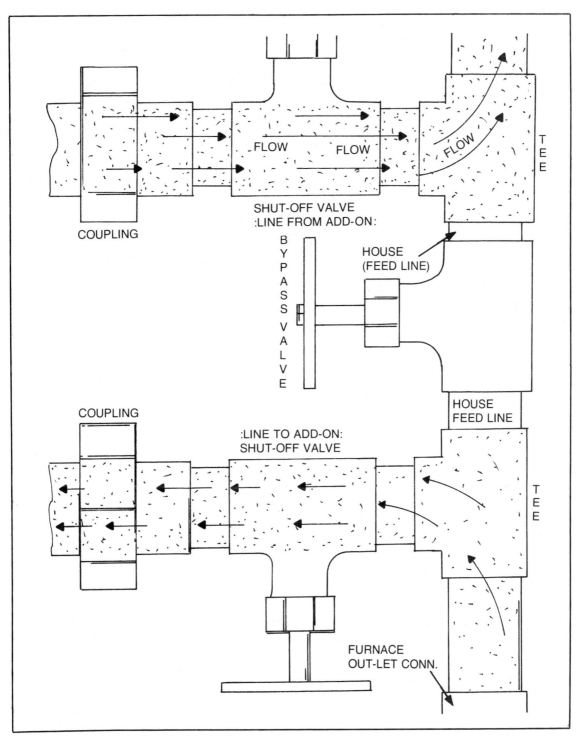

Fig. 24-4. Pipe hookup with the use of a bypass valve.

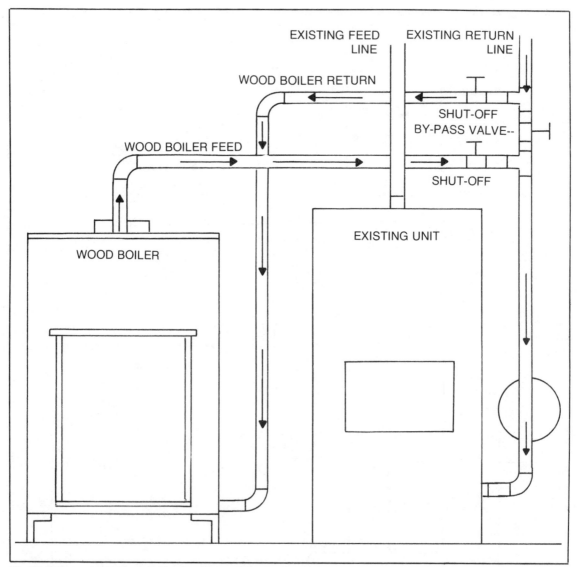

Fig. 24-5. Second recommended hookup to an existing heating system.

house will already be chilly and the furnace will have to work twice as hard to catch up and reheat your house.

## FIREPLACE INSTALLATIONS

This section is for those of you who want a radiant stove and already have a fireplace in your home. You will probably not have to erect a chimney for your stove. You should be able to easily adapt your existing fireplace chimney to accept your stove exhaust. Other than provide a pleasant view, the only thing that a fireplace does is to burn a lot of wood. A fireplace (in most cases) will rob the house of heat rather than supply it. Your fireplace is probably raising your heating costs more than the petroleum companies. A fireplace is a tremendous heat loss factor when compared to an airtight radiant stove.

There are two ways to install your stove. The first way is to build a fireplace cover to seal up your fireplace opening and exhaust your stove through it. The second way is to fabricate a cover that fits in place of your damper, and you can run your exhaust pipe through that.

Covering the opening is a better installation. For one thing, working at the fireplace opening is a lot easier than working inside the fireplace. A better airtight seal can be made at the opening rather than at the top of the fireplace.

## How To Build A Fireplace Cover

Take a piece of paper and draw a square on it. This will represent your fireplace opening. Using a measuring tape, measure across the bottom of the fireplace opening. Likewise, measure across the top of your opening, marking down the measurements as you go, on your piece of paper. After this is done, measure up each side and mark these measurements on your piece of paper. You measure the opening in this manner to assure a snug fitting

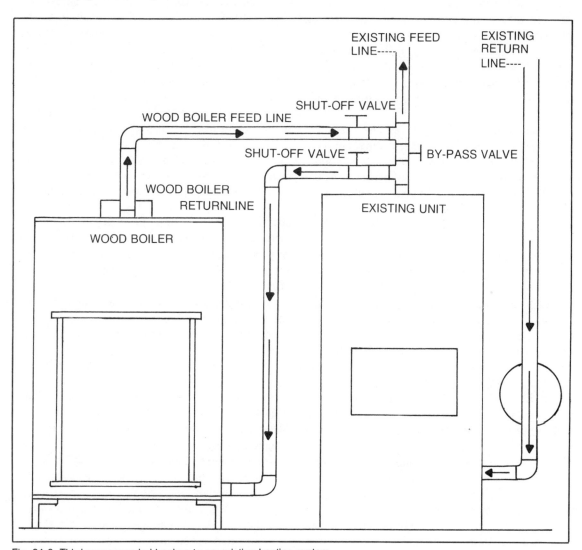

Fig. 24-6. Third recommended hookup to an existing heating system.

371

cover. Few fireplace openings will measure equally on any two sides. See Fig. 24-7.

If you have an arched fireplace opening, you will have to take the following procedure for measuring your opening. Draw a sketch resembling the Fig. 24-13. You can mark your measurements on it. Measure across the bottom of the fireplace opening and record the measurement. Next, measure up each side to the point where the side begins to arch. Record these measurements and place a mark, at this point, on each side of the fireplace opening. Next, go to the center of the opening and measure the height of the opening. Record it on your sketch. Now, go back to the sides. At the point where each side begins to arch, using the tape as a straight edge, measure to the top of the arch. What you are doing is changing your arch into a triangle (see Fig. 24-13). This is how you will build your frame.

Once you have recorded all the measurements, deduct 1/8" from all measurements. This is to assure a tight fit. Later, when installing your frame, these spaces will be filled with fiberglass insulation. Before starting to build your frame, measure the height of the exhaust opening on your stove. Take into account the height of the hearth. See Fig. 24-12 or Fig. 24-18.

Once you know where the exhaust will go through the cover, draw a sketch of the cover and fill in all of the measurements. Pay particular attention to the exhaust hole location. Take this drawing to a sheet metal shop and have them make it for you. By doing this, you will save time because you can be making the frame at the same time that they are making the cover. This way everything will be ready at the same time. See Fig. 24-10 and Fig. 24-15. Using 1"-×-1"-×-1/8" angle iron, cut the pieces to size as shown in Fig. 24-8 and 24-14. Make sure that all the cuts are 45° angles (facing in).

Using a flat surface, assemble angle iron sides. Make sure that all of the corners are on a 90° angle; a 2-foot carpenters' square will be an aid. C-clamp the angles to your work bench.

After checking the frame to be sure that the length and width are correct, tack weld the four corners of the frame together and fit it into your fireplace opening to make sure that it is going to fit properly. See Fig. 24-11 and Fig. 24-17. After this last check, you can proceed to weld the four joints—on the inside only. Do *not* weld the side that you are going to fit your cover to.

After the frame is welded, turn it over, face up, and fit the cover plate on it. Make sure that you match the bottom of the frame to the exhaust hole. Once the plate is in place, use C-clamps to clamp the plate to the frame (clamping at least two sides).

Using a pencil and a tape, mark the center of the angle on the cover plate (on all four sides). See Fig. 24-10 and Fig. 24-15. This is going to be the center of the holes. By doing this, you are assured that the hole will be in the center of the angle iron.

Next, measure each side of your cover. Take each measurement and divide it into four or five equal spaces. This will be the location of each hole. See Fig. 24-10 and Fig. 24-15. Mark each location on the center line. When all of the holes have been marked, centerpunch the holes and drill them. Leave the cover C-clamped to the frame and drill through both the frame and cover. This will keep your holes lined up when you mount the cover. Note: drill 1/4" holes and use quarter-inch bolts to attach the cover to the frame. You can drill a hole that could be tapped out for 1/4" bolts, and thread the holes with a tape. This makes it easier to bolt the cover to the frame after it was in place in the fireplace opening.

Once all of the holes have been drilled, bolt the cover to the frame. Use a high-heat spray paint to paint both the cover and the frame. Give the paint time to dry.

Make sure that the paint is thoroughly dry before you remove the cover from the frame. Using masonry rivets or lag bolts, bolt the cover to the fireplace opening. Two bolts should be sufficient. Make sure that you are installing the frame right side up in comparison to your cover. Don't put it in upside down. See Fig. 24-11 and 24-17.

Now that the cover frame is in place, take fiberglass insulation—make sure that you are wearing your safety glasses to protect your eyes—and pack any spaces between the frame and fireplace.

Now that the frame is in place, wire open, or better yet, take out the fireplace damper plate. This

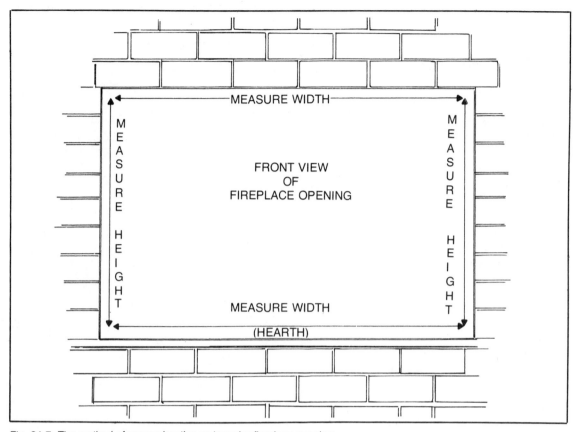

Fig. 24-7. The method of measuring the rectangular fireplace opening.

will prevent your damper from accidently, closing when your stove is in use. If this were to occur, your house would fill up with smoke and you would have no way to reopen it once the cover is in place.

Bolt the cover to the frame and, using a short section of single wall pipe, install the stove. Make sure that the stovepipe does not extend more than about 2 or 3 inches into your fireplace cover. This is important because the less stovepipe that is used the less chance there is of creosote building up. *Never* put an elbow on the end of the pipe that is in the fireplace. This will serve as nothing more than, a creosote builder and it could eventually block off the exhaust. See Fig. 24-12 and Fig. 24-18.

Now that your stove is hooked up to your fireplace, and operating, you might wonder how you can clean the chimney. Refer to the section regarding the cleaning of your chimney in Chapter 22.

Using your cleaning equipment, knock the creosote down the chimney. Slide the stove out of the way, reach in through the opening, and vacuum the residue. Your fireplace might have a shelf that would catch the creosote. In that case, the cover will have to be unbolted and the shelf will have to be cleaned from the inside. When you have finished, just replace the cover and the stove so that it will be ready for use.

### An Alternative Cover System

You might have reason not to want to close off your fireplace opening. If so there is another way to go about installing your unit. You will have to break into your chimney just above where your damper is located and install a pipe there. You will still have to close off your chimney at the point where your fireplace connects to the chimney. This must be an

373

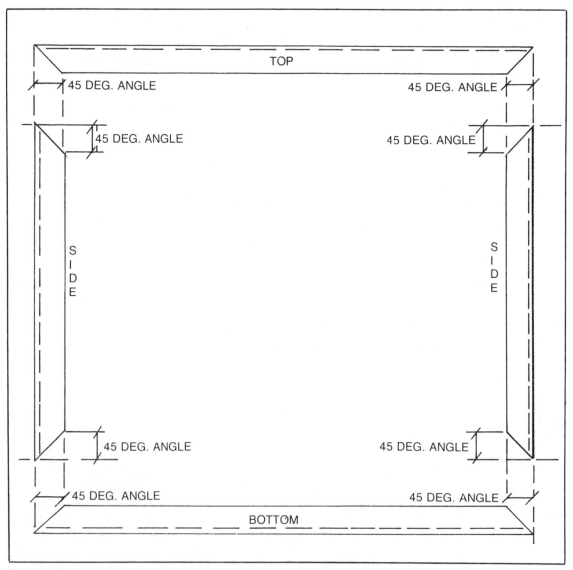

Fig. 24-8. Fabrication of the rectangular fireplace frame.

airtight closure to prevent air from being sucked into your chimney from another source other than your stove.

If the closure fits too loosely you can make a cover plate as shown in Fig. 24-19. After the cover has been made out of steel or sheet metal, it can be bolted to the walls of the chimney with lag bolts. Fiberglass insulation can be used to seal the sides. The only problem with this type of installation is that, in most cases, your damper must be taken out and a plate must be fitted. When cleaning the chimney, you must remove the cover plate in order to get the creosote out of the chimney.

A more acceptable way to install the stove is to tie the exhaust pipe into the cover plate that will be mounted in place of the damper. See Fig. 24-23; you will notice that, instead of using an elbow to make the turn up, a T with a cap has been used. This will later be an aid cleaning the chimney. See Figs. 24-20 through 24-23 for more details.

Any one of the preceding methods will serve as an adequate installation as long as you remember that chimney airtightness is maintained in the installation.

## HOOKING UP AN AIR FURNACE

You will need a few materials and tools for this project. They will include a ¼" drill, a number of drill bits, a small pair of tin snips, a number of sheet metal screws, (if desired) an 8" induct fan and heat senser switch, a number of lengths of 8" (single-wall) stovepipe, a number of 8" adjustable elbows and an 8" finishing collar. If you have a jig saw, with a hacksaw blade, it will come in handy. Hook up your unit in the following manner.

Locate the air plenum at the top of the existing furnace. The air plenum is the area where all the hot air from the furnace collects before going up the

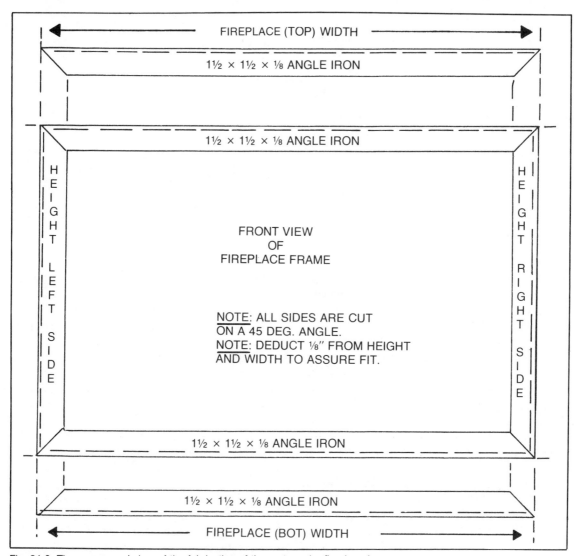

Fig. 24-9. The progressed view of the fabrication of the rectangular fireplace frame.

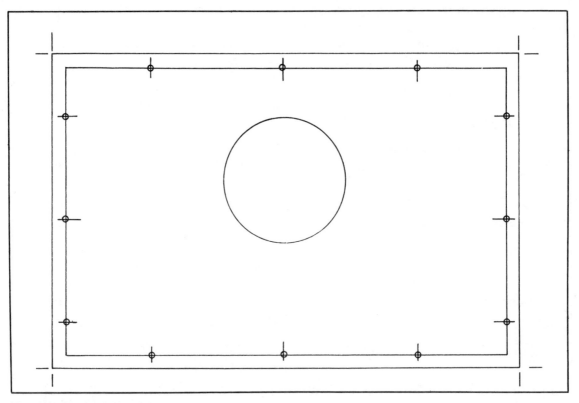

Fig. 24-10. The front view of the fireplace cover.

ducts. Draw a circle, with a pencil or marker, on the side of the plenum (toward the top of the plenum).

Drill a series of holes around the circle (this will make a start cut). Once the cut is large enough, insert shears and cut out the circle. Or you could insert a jig saw blade and cut out the circle.

Once the hole has been cut out, start at the back of your solid-fuel furnace and connect the air exhaust outlet to the plenum. Use the 8″ stovepipe and adjustable elbows.

When you are close to making the connection to the plenum, insert the 8″ induct fan to the run of 8″ stovepipe. Once the fan has been installed (to blow air toward the plenum), slip the 8″ finishing collar over the last section of 8″ stovepipe and insert the stovepipe (first) into the plenum hole and then, sliding it back, into the 8″ stovepipe line. Once the 8″ stovepipe line is complete (connecting the solid-fuel furnace to the existing furnace), slide the finishing collar up to the side of the plenum.

Using the drill and six or eight sheet-metal screws, attach the finishing collar to the side of the plenum. Using the drill and sheet-metal screws, permanently connect the stovepipe connections.

Once the connections are screwed together, insert the heat senser switch in the 8″ stovepipe. Insert the senser near the solid-fuel furnace. When it is installed, connect the wires to the fan and connect the wires of the fan to the electrical outlet. Obtain the aid of an electrician to do the wiring.

Once the senser is hooked up, set it so that when it reaches a certain temperature the fan will come on and when the temperature of the air cools the fan turns off.

You have now completed the installation of your unit. Insulate your furnace and 8″ pipe with fiberglass insulation to help keep the heat in your furnace and ducts. Just make sure it's the type of insulation that is fireproof. Also insulate the entire duct system using the same type of insulation.

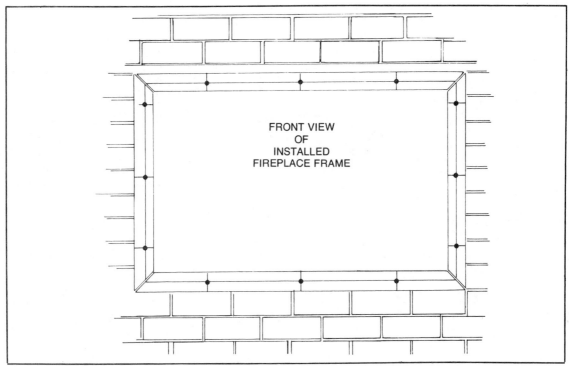

Fig. 24-11. Front view of the installed fireplace frame.

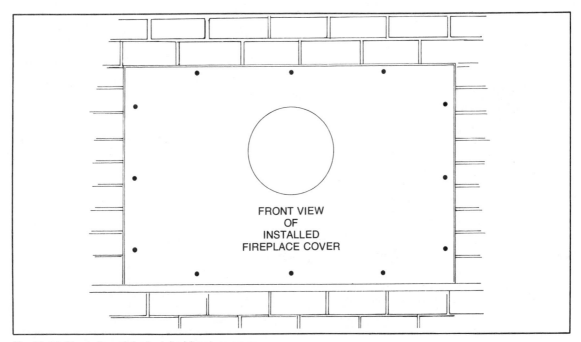

Fig. 24-12. Front view of the installed fireplace cover.

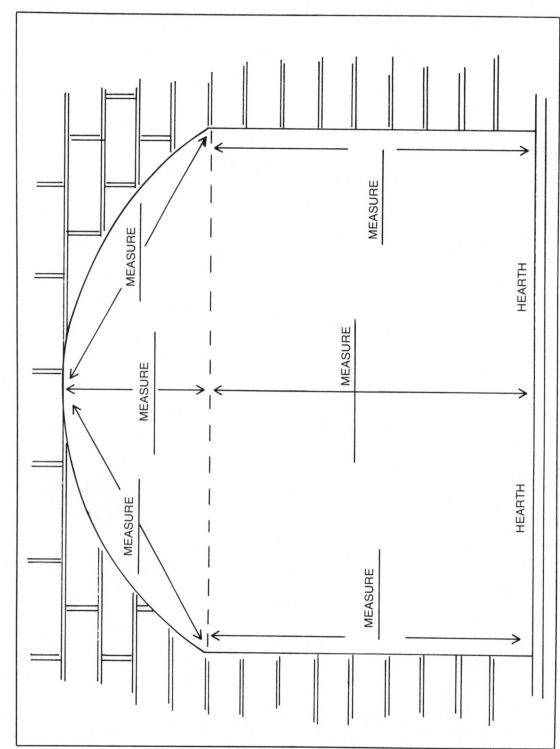

Fig. 24-13. The method of measuring the arched fireplace opening.

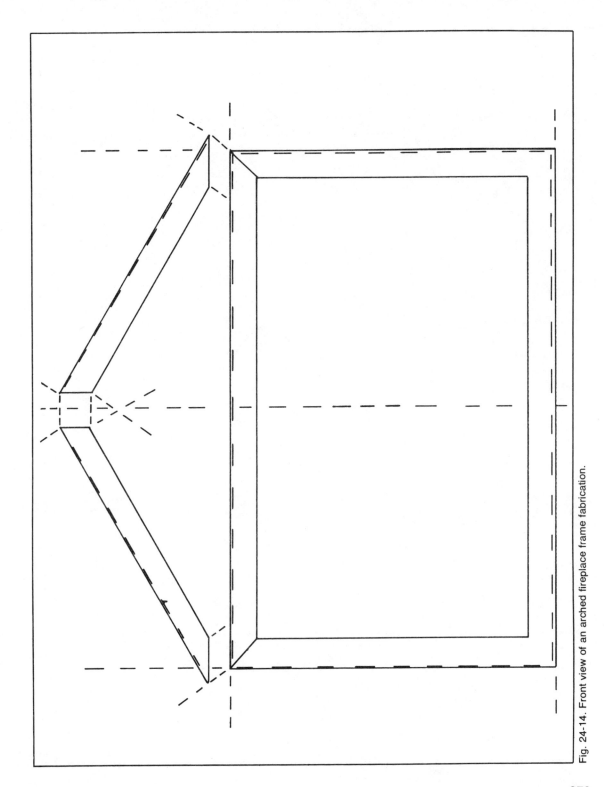

Fig. 24-14. Front view of an arched fireplace frame fabrication.

379

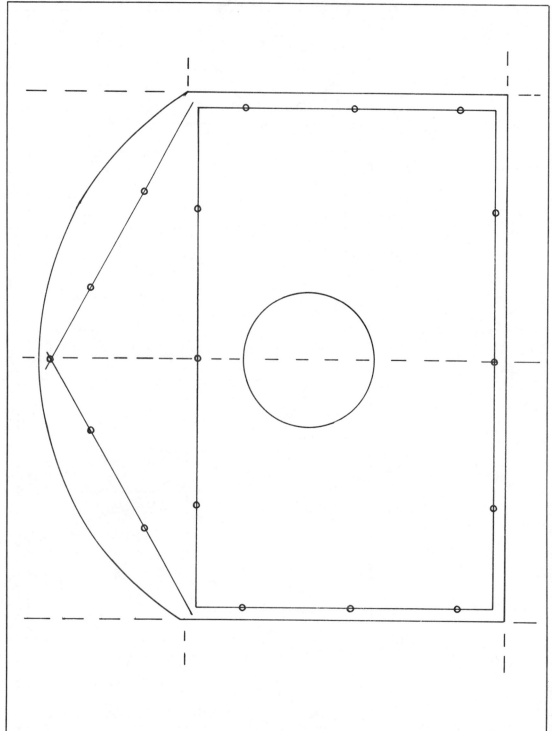

Fig. 24-15. Front view of an arched fireplace cover.

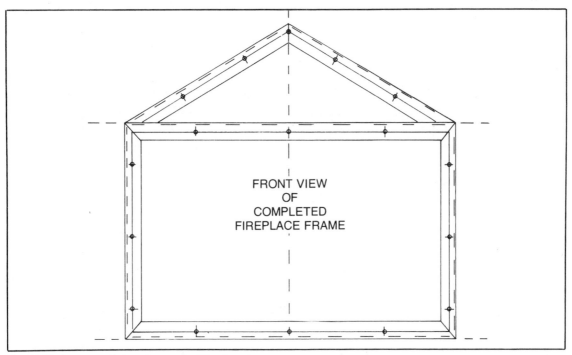

Fig. 24-16. Progressed view of an arched fireplace frame.

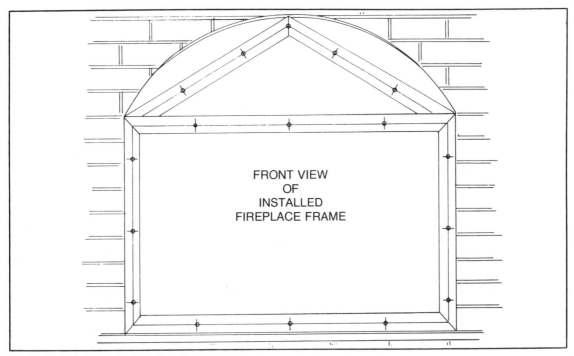

Fig. 24-17. Installed arched fireplace frame.

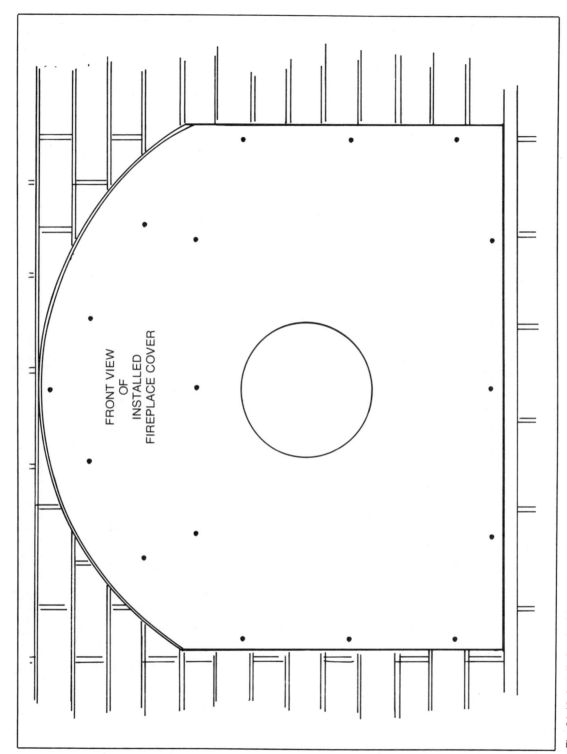

FRONT VIEW
OF
INSTALLED
FIREPLACE COVER

Fig. 24-18. Installed arched fireplace cover.

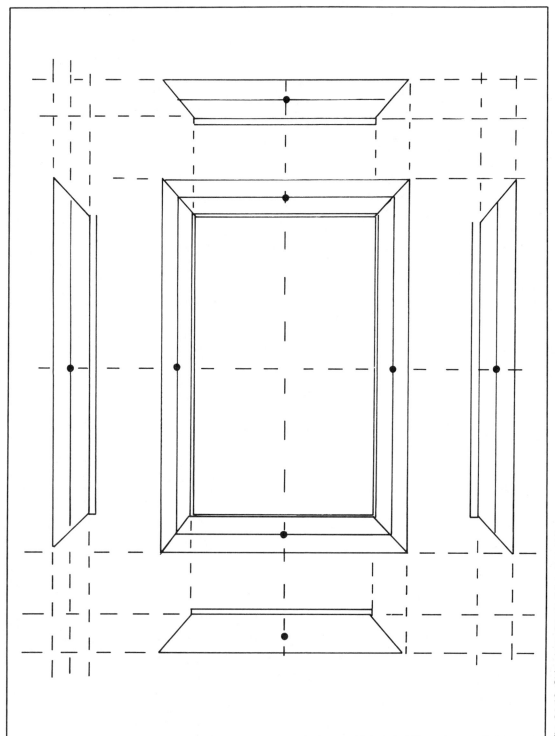

Fig. 24-19. Side view of typical fireplace chimney cover.

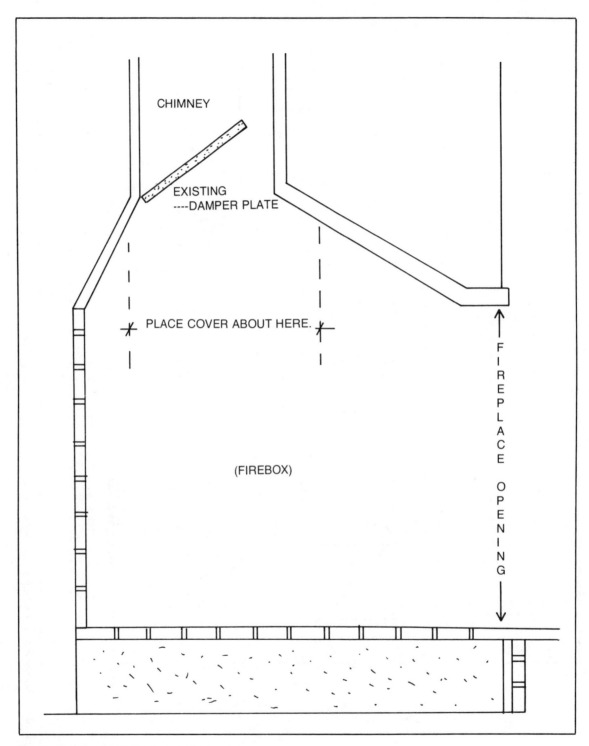

CHIMNEY

EXISTING
----DAMPER PLATE

PLACE COVER ABOUT HERE.

(FIREBOX)

FIREPLACE OPENING

Fig. 24-20. Side view of a typical fireplace.

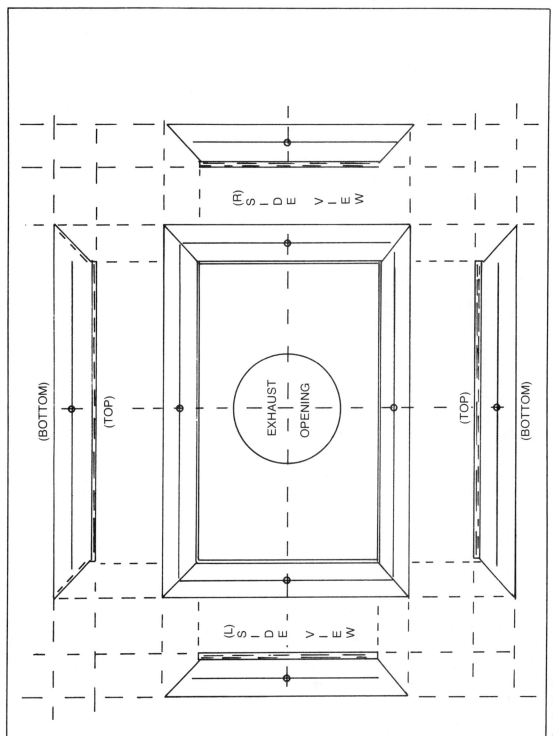

Fig. 24-21. View of a stove installation chimney cover.

385

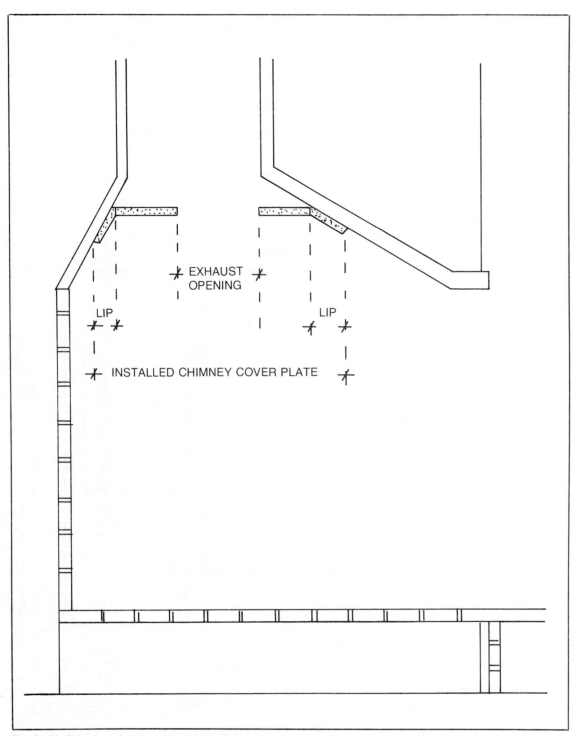

LIP          LIP

EXHAUST
OPENING

INSTALLED CHIMNEY COVER PLATE

Fig. 24-22. Side view of the installed stove installation cover.

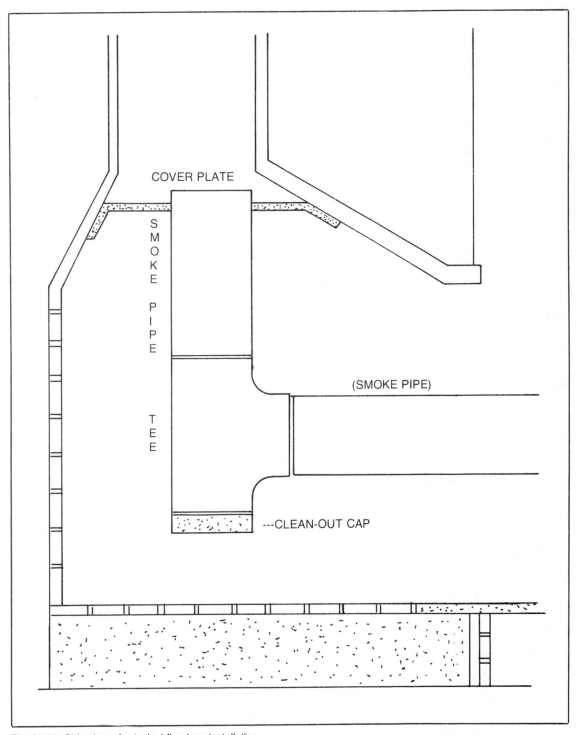

COVER PLATE

SMOKE PIPE

TEE

(SMOKE PIPE)

---CLEAN-OUT CAP

Fig. 24-23. Side view of a typical fireplace installation.

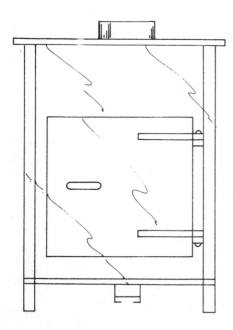

# Glossary

**acetylene**—A gas that is used in welding. It produces extremely hot flames used in cutting the steel plate.

**air control system**—The system that allows air into a solid-fuel unit to create a draft.

**air inlet**—Primary air feed from the air control system. Also referred to as the *draft control* or dampers. In the units described in this book, the controls have been designed to feed the air at a direct level from the bottom of the unit.

**airtight**—Too tight for oxygen or gas to either enter or escape.

**amp service**—The bulk amount of electricity that is brought into your house. Once there it is broken down in your fuse or breaker box panels.

**angle**—A two-sided piece of steel that is formed like an L.

**arc**—A flash of electricity. In welding, it is the electrical connection of the welding rod to the material being welded.

**ash fusion temperature**—The temperature at which the ash, being a by-product of coal, is fused and can form into clinkers.

**backdraft**—A gust of air that is thrust down through the chimney. This usually occurs in relation to a strong wind.

**backpuff**—The explosive sound and smoking that is usually caused by a sudden draft of air on a smoldering fire and the ignition of gases.

**baffle**—A deflecting plate used in a solid-fuel burner.

**boiler (add-on)**—A container in which water is transferred through. It is heated by the burning of either a solid or a liquid fuel.

**bow saw**—A saw with a curved handle. It is used in felling a tree or bucking wood.

**buck**—To chop large logs into firewood.

**bucksaw**—A saw set in a frame and worked with both hands.

**butt joint**—The joint made by placing steel plates end to end.

**cast iron**—A hard, unmalleable iron that is made through the process of casting. It contains a high proportion of carbon and silicon. Cast iron has the properties of a low tensile strength (capable of being stretched) and is very fluid and fusible when molten (melted or liquified by heat).

**C-clamp**—A tool that is used to clamp and draw plates together.

**channel**—A rolled metal bar shaped as a topless rectangle.

**charcoal**—A shapeless form of carbon that is produced during the final stages of the combustion process by the partial burning of solid fuel such as wood or other organic matter that has been burned in large kilns from which air has been excluded.

**chimney**—The structure that acts as a passageway through which the smoke, hot air, and gases, produced from a fire escape.

**chimney fire**—A fire that takes place in a chimney usually due to the ignition of creosote or sparks that have been able to escape the chimney through leaks, cracks, or the pipes not fitting as tightly as they should.

**chipping hammer**—A tool that is used for cleaning welds.

**clinkers**—A hard mass of fused stony matter that is formed, during the process of burning coal, from the impurities within the coal.

**coal gas**—The gases (many of which are noxious) produced during the coal-burning process.

**coil**—As in a heat exchange coil, a spiral of wire or other type of conducting element that is used as a heating element for the transfer of heat.

**combination square**—A measuring device that will aid you in drawing long or short lines on your steel.

**combustible material**—That which catches fire and burns easily.

**combustion**—The process of burning where oxygen is emitted to solid fuel to produce rapid oxidation, accompanied by heat or slow oxidation that is accompanied by very little heat.

**combustion chamber**—An enclosed area where the combustion process is allowed to take place through the burning of solid fuel.

**conduct**—To transmit or carry such as in radiant heat or referring to electricity.

**cord**—A 4′ × 4′ × 8′ stack of firewood.

**creosote**—A black tar-like liquid that is created by burning wood. A highly combustible material and the main cause of many chimney fires.

**damper**—Primary air feed from the air control system. Also referred to as the *draft* control or air inlets. For units described in this book, controls have been designed to feed the air at a direct level from the bottom of the unit.

**disc grinder**—A piece of machinery that is used to grind down welds that are used to cover seams (such as in the fabrication of the Lowboy model's roof).

**domestic coil**—The coil into which the water that, for household use, is preheated and sent through the tap.

**draft**—Air that is either pushed through or pulled through the solid-fuel unit or chimney.

**draft control**—Primary air feed from the air control system. Also referred to as the *air inlet* or *dampers*. In the units described in this book, the controls have been designed to feed the air at a direct level from the bottom of the unit.

**draw**—The means by which the air (usually referred to as a draft) is pulled (such as hot air being drawn to cold air).

**duct system**—The channel for heat to be dispersed throughout the house.

**efficiency**—The evaluation of how much heat a solid-fuel unit is transferring, by means of the burning of solid fuel, to the area that is to be heated and the amount of burnable substance that is used in the form of heating value.

**exhaust**—To draw out or to provide a path to draw out the smoke, gases, hot air, etc., that are produced in, for example, the burning of a solid fuel.

**fabricate**—To construct or build.

**face cord**—A stack of firewood that is 8′ long, 4′ high, but less than 4′ wide (having no absolute standard of measurement).

**fell**—To cut down a tree.

**fixed carbons**—Determinent of firepower of coal and its ignition temperature.

**flash**—The burning of the liquid coating of the eye by the flashing light produced by welding.

**flashburn**—A term used by welders in reference to injury or destruction of body tissue caused by exposure to welding. Similar to a sunburn.

**flue**—A tube in the form of a pipe that passes smoke, hot air, and gases, produced from a fire, to the chimney.

**fly ash**—Unburnable pieces of ash that accumulate in the flue pipe or chimney when coal is burned. Associated with air pollution.

**gasket**—The material that is used for the doors of the stove to make it airtight by preventing leaks of oxygen in or out of the solid-fuel unit (asbestos belt or spun-glass wicking).

**gauge**—Dialed indicator. Standard of measurement.

**grate**—A frame of metal bars that is used for the burning of solid fuel, such as coal, in a solid-fuel unit. Allows the unburnable substances (ash in coal) to fall through or be shaken down into an ash pan.

**hacksaw**—A saw used for cutting metal. It is set in a frame and it is narrow and close-toothed.

**handsaw**—A saw that could be used with one hand.

**hearth**—The stone or brick floor of a fireplace that often extends into a room. The piece of plate that protrudes out from the floor of the solid-fuel burner to catch any ash, hot coals or wood that might fall out of the door.

**heat exchanger**—A unit that exchanges heat to a designated place or area.

**hot-air furnace**—A furnace (enclosed chamber that is used to provide heat) that heats air by burning solid fuel, liquid fuel, or natural gas. It pushes air through a duct system that is used in heating the house.

**insulate**—To cover with a nonconductive material in order to prevent the leakage of heat or emittence of cold air.

**insulated stovepipe**—Stovepipe that has been insulated to keep its temperature from dropping too low when the outdoor temperatures are cold so as not to allow the formation of creosote.

**Jet rod**—A high-production, fast welding rod that is used in the flat welding position.

**joint**—The corner where two pieces of plate come together.

**kickback**—A violent reaction associated with the use of a chain saw.

**limb**—To cut the limbs from a tree after felling it and before bucking.

**noxious gases**—Gases harmful to your health.

**purge**—Removing by cleansing.

**pyrolysis**—Chemical decomposition of a substance by heat.

**radiant**—As used in the form of an energy source, it is the heat that is transferred to an area.

**repoint**—The process where old or broken concrete between the bricks or blocks of a chimney is removed and replaced with new concrete.

**sawbuck**—A support to prevent firewood from slipping while it is being sawed.

**secondary air system**—That which is induced at a high level to the firebox, when burning coal, to create a larger draw on the chimney and to aid in venting.

**shear**—A machine that is used for the cutting of steel for an accurate straight, clean edge.

**slag**—The outer coating of the weld.

**sliding baffle**—A baffle that is designed to slide into position, when burning wood, and out of the way, when you are burning coal, so as not to impede the speedy exit of the gases.

**splitting maul**—A large hammer used to split wood.

**solid fuel**—Combustible material that provides efficient heat.

**solid-fuel burner**—A container that holds solid fuel, burns it safely, and emits heat.

**solid-fuel unit**—A container that emits heat by burning solid fuel or by heat transfer via a heat-exchange method.

**solid weld**—To weld something completely, all the way around, or to weld something from one end to the other.

**square footage**—The area that is measured by multiplying its length by its width.

**stand**—A growth of crops such as trees.

**steel plate**—Iron that has been alloyed with a small percentage of carbon and sometimes with other hard metals such as nickel, chromium, manganese to produce hardness and a resistance to rusting.

**stovepipe**—The metal pipe that is used to carry off smoke or fumes from a stove into the chimney. Referred to in this book as the *flue*, which will most probably be single-wall stovepipe, used for inside of the house.

**tack weld**—A weld that holds something together (no longer than about ⅛″) until a permanent weld can be applied.

**torch**—A cutting torch. Also referred to as a burning torch. Used in the cutting of steel. A device in welding for the production of a very hot flame.

**trivet**—A metal stand used to hold a pot for cooking with the heat of a fire.

**turbulence**—The circular movement of air.

**carpenters' square**—A tool that is an aid in drawing long lines such as for door openings. Also used for checking corners to make sure that they are square.

**ultraviolet**—Pertaining to or producing light rays having wave lengths shorter than approximately 4000 angstroms (one-hundred-millionth of a centimeter).

**volatile**—Components that contain gases that vaporize during the combustion process are volatile. Some of them are noxious gases from the burning of coal. Some are safely used for heating value as in burning wood.

**warpage**—A distortion that is caused by expansion and overheating.

**wedge**—A piece of hard material, such as wood or steel, with a tapered shape from a thick base to a thin edge. Used as a tool to be driven or forced into a narrow opening as in splitting wood.

**weld**—To make as one (such as pieces of metal, etc.) by the heating of metal until it is pliable enough to be able to be hammered or pressed together. To unite by heating until molten (melted or liquified by heat) and fused.

**welding lense**—A tinted glass that is used to deflect, ultraviolet and bright light that is produced in welding. Used as eye protection by welders.

# Index

# How to design, build, install, and operate wood and coal heating units . . . including plans and material lists!

## Build Your Own Solid-Fuel Burning Stove

### by Robert C. and Lenore Roser

Here's your chance to really *do* something about soaring home heating costs . . . by converting to economical wood or coal heat *without investing hundreds of dollars* in a commercially made stove or boiler unit! This unique, illustrated guidebook gives you all the step-by-step instructions you need to *build your own* modern, air-tight, solid-fuel burning stove that's safe, efficient, economical, *and* attractive. It shows how to design and build a wood, coal, or combination wood/coal stove or boiler, how to install it, how to operate it for maximum efficiency, how to maintain it, and even how to build your own accessories to go with it (screens, grates, and ash pans).

This volume covers everything from reading and preparing blueprints and information on materials to stove design principles, selecting a style that suits your specific needs and decorative preferences, and actually putting an original design together. For those less sure of their do-it-yourself skills, it gives valuable tips on selecting and obtaining tools and materials; it provides a thorough explanation of basic stove parts and their functions (air controls, doors, baffling systems, and more); it introduces you to the principles of cutting and welding steel; and it gives detailed plans and instructions for building several stoves designed and tested by the author—including to-scale plans, material lists, and show-how illustrations that make it easy to grasp each procedure. And that's not all! This is also a comprehensive installation, operation, and maintenance guide that makes worthwhile reading for anyone who's thinking of adding a solid-fuel stove as an auxiliary or primary heating source—self-built or commercially made.

The ultimate do-it-yourself volume on fabricating wood and coal stoves, it's a book you can't afford to miss if you're looking for a practical way to cut back on rising home heating costs!

Robert C. Roser is a skilled welder and metal fabricator whose efforts led him to start a company that manufactured and retailed solid-fuel heating equipment. He and his wife, Lenore, believe that anyone with average do-it-yourself skills can build a solid-fuel stove that rivals commercially made units for looks *and* efficiency . . . at a fraction of the ready-made cost!